The History of the University of Cambridge: Texts and Studies

Volume 4

TEACHING AND LEARNING IN NINETEENTH-CENTURY CAMBRIDGE

It was in the nineteenth and twentieth centuries that Cambridge underwent the changes which led to its present institutional structure. The dominance of mathematics was gradually offset by the creation of courses in classics in the 1820s, and moral sciences, natural sciences and history from the early 1850s, in a period when the university was taking back some of the control of teaching and learning it had previously lost to the colleges. During this process, college teaching and examinations both developed to take account of university procedures, and to a degree reacted against them. During the second half of the century, the admission of women and dissenters irrevocably transformed what had been an Anglican male bachelor enclave – an educational wing of the Church of England – into a recognisably modern, secular university. In all these areas, however, as the contributions to this book demonstrate, changes were complicated, negotiated and full of the local nuances expected of a collegiate university.

JONATHAN SMITH works in the library at Trinity College, Cambridge; Dr CHRISTOPHER STRAY teaches at the Department of Classics, University of Wales at Swansea.

The History of the University of Cambridge:
Texts and Studies

ISSN 0960-2887

General Editor
P. N. R. Zutshi
Keeper of Manuscripts and University Archives
Cambridge University Library

1. *The University of Cambridge and the English Revolution, 1623–1688*, John Twigg
2. *Medieval Cambridge: Essays on the Pre-Reformation University*, edited by Patrick Zutshi
3. *Gentlemen, Scientists and Doctors: Medicine at Cambridge 1800–1940*, Mark Weatherall

TEACHING AND LEARNING IN NINETEENTH-CENTURY CAMBRIDGE

EDITED BY

Jonathan Smith and Christopher Stray

THE BOYDELL PRESS
CAMBRIDGE UNIVERSITY LIBRARY

© Editors and Contributors 2001

All Rights Reserved. Except as permitted under current legislation no part of this work may be photocopied, stored in a retrieval system, published, performed in public, adapted, broadcast, transmitted, recorded or reproduced in any form or by any means, without the prior permission of the copyright owner

First published 2001
The Boydell Press, Woodbridge
in association with
Cambridge University Library

ISBN 978-0-85115-783-2

The Boydell Press is an imprint of Boydell & Brewer Ltd
PO Box 9, Woodbridge, Suffolk IP12 3DF, UK
and of Boydell & Brewer Inc.
668 Mt Hope Avenue, Rochester, NY 14620, USA
website: www.boydellandbrewer.com

A catalogue record for this book is available
from the British Library

This publication is printed on acid-free paper

CONTENTS

Introduction	1
The Analytical Revolution from Below: Private Teaching and Mathematical Reform in Georgian Cambridge ANDREW WARWICK	5
A Parochial Anomaly: The Classical Tripos 1822–1900 CHRISTOPHER STRAY	31
'A mist of prejudice': The Reluctant Acceptance of Modern History at Cambridge, 1845–1873 JOHN WILKES	45
Constructing Knowledge in mid-Victorian Cambridge: The Moral Sciences Tripos 1850–70 JOHN R. GIBBINS	61
Learning to Pick the Easy Plums: The Invention of Ancient History in Nineteenth-Century Classics MARY BEARD	89
The Revolution in College Teaching: St John's College, 1850–1926 MALCOLM UNDERWOOD	107
Trinity College Annual Examinations in the Nineteenth Century JONATHAN SMITH	122
'Girton for ladies, Newnham for governesses' GILLIAN SUTHERLAND	139
Models of Learning? The 'logical, philosophical and scientific woman' in late Nineteenth-Century Cambridge PAULA GOULD	150
Where Did Undergraduates Get Their Books? DAVID MCKITTERICK	165
'The advantage of proceeding from an author of some scientific reputation': Isaac Todhunter and his Mathematics Textbooks JUNE BARROW-GREEN	177

Afterword 204
ELISABETH LEEDHAM-GREEN

Bibliography 211

Index 223

INTRODUCTION

The papers collected in this volume derive from a conference with the same title, held at Trinity College, Cambridge, in May 1999. Both the editors had come into contact with scholars working on a wide range of topics in the history of the University. The conference was planned as a forum in which they could meet, present their work and discuss common themes and problems. It was also conceived as a way of complementing the existing published work on the history of the University. The official history of Oxford University is a massive enterprise, now complete in eight multi-authored volumes. The two volumes on the nineteenth century (vols 6 and 7, edited by Michael Brock and Mark Curthoys) contain chapters on a wide range of disciplines, as well as on religion, finance, careers and a host of other topics. The equivalent Cambridge series, in contrast, will when completed consist of four single-authored volumes. A history which is hardly shorter than Oxford's, and surely no less complex, constitutes an almost impossible challenge when tackled in such terms. The volumes which deal with nineteenth-century Cambridge (vol. 3, by Peter Searby, and vol. 4, by Christopher Brooke) have inevitably left many areas lightly sketched or even unstudied. We hope that the papers in the present volume will throw light on some of these areas.

It was in the nineteenth and early twentieth centuries that both Oxford and Cambridge underwent the changes which produced the institutional structures which persist today. Eighteenth-century Cambridge is often characterised as a place of indolence and complacency, where methods of teaching and assessment proceeded along lines little changed from medieval times. It was a place, we are told, where professorial teaching had all but disappeared, leaving colleges as the only institutions which prepared students for essentially oral university examinations, with no structured means of assessing their progress on the way. As a generalisation, this is not wildly exaggerated, but reforms did take place that pointed the way for the later university. In 1702 Richard Bentley introduced a form of written scholarship examination at Trinity College and in mid-century William Powell, Master of St John's, developed a system of college examinations designed to assess the development of the students of that college. John Jebb battled vainly to improve the University examinations and ten Trinity fellows took a stand against privilege in their college.

If the seeds of nineteenth-century Cambridge were sown in the previous century, foremost amongst them must have been the rise of mathematics as the dominant subject within the University. By 1800, in contrast with Oxford and the public schools, where classics dominated, mathematics was the subject in which a student could win himself the greatest honour bestowed by the university on a student, that of Senior Wrangler, the man placed highest in the mathematical tripos. With the introduction of increasingly complex areas of mathematics, the generalist college tutor, who had existed in some form in the university for centuries, became further and further divorced from the areas of knowledge required by students wishing to perform well in the tripos. Consequently, eager students were forced to rely on private coaches to train them to a peak to sit examinations that required rapid problem-solving. Mathematics retained its prominence in the university for much of the century, its position bolstered by the assertion of men such as William Whewell that it was the ideal subject to test the powers of reasoning within a Cambridge 'liberal education', designed to prepare students not for narrow areas of expertise, but to take all the world might throw at them. Challenges to the position of mathematics came in the form of the development of curricula for honours examinations in other subjects. In 1824 the Classical Tripos was introduced. It was to a great extent the brainchild of Christopher Wordsworth, Master of Trinity, who early in his incumbency set about trying to improve the study of classics in the university. As with many of the curricular reforms that came later in the century, many opposing views had to be reconciled and Wordsworth was forced to compromise on a number of matters. Not least of these was the requirement of anyone wishing to take the Classical Tripos to first take honours in mathematics. Curricular development continued with the introduction of the Moral and Natural Sciences Triposes in 1851 until by the end of the century there was a choice of ten subjects that students could take honours in, and some, like Fenton Hort, succeeded in more than one.

In terms of longevity of influence, the written competitive examination was the great success of nineteenth-century education, replacing a system that relied on privilege and patronage with a meritocratic form of advancement, however narrowly defined. At their height, the Cambridge honours examinations are defined by the attempt to discover minute differences in the performance of students and rank them accordingly. They were seen by students and tutors alike as akin to athletic contests, in which more than one promising student had failed through lack of stamina, and Trinity tried to prepare its own students for the university ordeals by working its students hard in college examinations. A culture of competition and emulation pervaded the Cambridge class known as reading men, who intended studying seriously for a degree. Their counter-class, the rowing men (pronounced to rhyme with ploughing), found their metier in other sports.

Throughout the first half of the century the ancient universities were continually criticised on the grounds that they were socially and religiously exclusive, narrowly restricted in curriculum and inefficient in teaching. This pressure culminated in the Royal Commissions of 1850, set up by Lord John

Russell's Liberal government. The resulting revisions of statutes finally brought the colleges out of the middle ages and strengthened the position of the university. The Commissions initiated a period of state intervention in which both universities came to be seen, and even to see themselves, as national institutions rather than as independent bodies owing duties only to themselves. The 1850 Commissions were followed in the 1870s and 1920s by further Commissions which established patterns of funding and set up the now familiar pattern of faculty organisation. The major changes in social exclusion came with the admission of women and dissenters in the 1860s and 1870s. (For the women, however, admission did not mean membership, only granted after the Second World War.) Religious restrictions were lifted by the repeal of the Tests Acts in 1871; by which time the brightest and best graduates were already heading for destinations other than the Church. The changes initiated by the 1850 Commission led to debates on teaching methods and structures as well as on what should be taught. The academic liberals of the 1860s, largely based in Trinity College, laid the foundations of a system designed to supersede both the inadequate pedagogic provision of the smaller colleges and the uncontrolled informal system of private tutoring. The new system of lectures and supervisions grew in a period when the university curriculum was becoming both broader in scope and more specialised in organisation. The steep rise in student numbers from the 1860s also created pressure for new modes of organisation.

The appearance of women from the 1870s constituted a major challenge to what had been (and would continue to be, but in a different way) a male-dominated enclave. The women's colleges of Girton and Newnham, founded in 1869 and 1871 respectively, were at first quite peripheral to the university. Initially, their students were not allowed to use the university laboratories or the University Library and women who took honours were not classed with the men.

Taken as a whole, the papers cover a wide range of topics, but they also converge on a number of areas which may prove to become salient features in future work: college-university relationships, the role of examinations, the politics of curriculum. Their subject is 'local knowledge', on which they also draw in some cases. Yet for several reasons they are of much more than 'local interest', whatever the meaning of that phrase may be. First of all, nineteenth-century Cambridge provided an influential exemplar for other universities, both in Britain and abroad. Secondly, the topics discussed in this book raise general questions. How does teaching and learning take place? Who and what should be taught, and how? How are curriculum and pedagogy shaped and changed by local institutional structures, debates and interests? Such questions need to be investigated, as here, at a local level; but their interest, and their implications, extend to larger contexts. We hope to pursue these questions in dialogue with others who share our interest in them.

Jonathan Smith
Christopher Stray

Acknowledgments

The editors would like to thank all those participants who helped to make the TLC conference a success, and especially David Coleman, David McKitterick, Albert Neilson and Alison Sproston, and the Master and Fellows of Trinity College, Cambridge. We are also grateful to Gordon Johnson for timely advice, and to John and Rita Wilkes for the hospitality they extended to participants.

ANDREW WARWICK

The Analytical Revolution from Below: Private Teaching and Mathematical Reform in Georgian Cambridge

The private tutor and Cambridge mathematics

In his classic study of academic life in Victorian Cambridge *The Revolution of the Dons*, Sheldon Rothblatt made the novel suggestion that the system of private teaching which emerged to dominate undergraduate training from the late eighteenth century should be seen as a *positive* development which 'made a major contribution to the reform of teaching in the second half of the nineteenth century'.[1] Rothblatt's remark is striking because it challenges a widely held view that private teaching was an illicit and iniquitous trade which undermined liberal-educational values and the authority of officially-appointed teachers, fostering instead the worst excesses of competitive examination and mindless cram.[2] But, as Rothblatt pointed out, it was the leading private tutors, rather than donnish college lecturers or distant university professors, who provided the prototypical model of the professional academic who would emerge in the latter decades of the nineteenth century. In this essay I argue that both the rise to eminence of private tutors during the late eighteenth and early nineteenth centuries, as well as their subsequent half century of pedagogical rule, were of deeper and more far-reaching historical significance than even Rothblatt supposed.

The emergence of private teaching has rightly been linked, albeit implicitly, to the combined effect of the introduction of written examinations in mathematics and the unwillingness on the part of the public and college teachers in the University adequately to prepare the most ambitious students to compete in such examinations.[3] W. W. Rouse Ball, for example, the first and very influential

---

[1] S. Rothblatt, *The Revolution of the Dons* (London, 1968), p. 208.
[2] For an influential assessment of private teaching in Victorian Cambridge by one of the reformers who eventually brought about its demise, see A. R. Forsyth, 'Old Tripos Days At Cambridge', *Mathematical Gazette*, 19 (1935), pp. 162–79.
[3] The term 'public teacher' refers to a paid teacher (usually a professor) of the University whose lectures were open free of charge to all members of the University. Each college also

historian of the Cambridge school of mathematics, saw private teaching as the natural companion of written examination to such an extent that he felt any further explanation of the marginalisation of other forms of teaching to be superfluous.[4] On Rouse Ball's showing, attempts by the University to restrict the practice around 1780 were entirely futile, a view he believed to be substantiated by the systematic repeal of such restrictions during the first three decades of the nineteenth century. But a more detailed study of the historical evidence suggests a quite different course of events. I do not deny that written examinations provided a prime motivation for able undergraduates to employ private tutors, but I shall claim that the displacement of public and college teachers by private tutors was a much more managed, protracted and controversial process than Rouse Ball allowed. If we are to grasp both the significance of the pedagogical revolution initiated by these tutors and the historical events that made the revolution possible, it is necessary to separate their rise to prominence into several distinct periods and to look carefully at what, how and who they actually taught.

I shall argue that private teaching *was* strictly controlled within the University until at least the second decade of the nineteenth century, and that the gradual relaxation of the rules thereafter was a controlled process, calculated both to curtail the influence of private teachers beyond Cambridge and to bolster the technical competence of the most able students. Once this point is established, moreover, it reveals a new and previously unexplored relationship between private teaching and the so-called 'analytical revolution' of the 1810s and 1820s. The introduction of continental analysis to Cambridge has been widely studied by historians of mathematics, but very little attention has been paid to the mechanisms by which the new techniques were actually popularised and propagated within the University. The translation of analysis from Paris to Cambridge was not effected simply by overcoming local prejudice and getting a few appropriate questions onto the examination papers; it required, rather, new textbooks, new teaching methods and years of hard work on the part of tutors and students. A careful study of the people, techniques and strategies by which the revolution was practically accomplished highlights two very significant points: first, that it was private tutors who actually mastered and taught the 'd-notation' calculus and other analytical methods in Cambridge; and second, that it was only during this transitional period (and not before) that private tutors displaced the officially appointed teachers of the University to become the guardians of the intellectual elite. The tough, progressive training methods developed by private tutors were much better suited to teaching advanced analysis and its application to the solution of difficult problems than were those of the college lecturer, and it seems very likely that the final relaxation of the

---

had a staff of lecturers and tutors (paid by the college) whose teaching was restricted to members of the college.
[4] W. W. Rouse Ball, *A History of the Study of Mathematics at Cambridge* (Cambridge, 1889), pp. 160–3.

rules governing private tuition in the mid-1820s was intended to encourage the rapid uptake of analytical methods. The remarkable change in undergraduate studies through the 1820s and 1830s was as much a revolution in pedagogy and personnel as it was in mathematical content.[5]

The rise of private teaching in Georgian Cambridge

One reason why the rise of private teaching initiated a major transition in mathematical pedagogy is that although it was originally employed to supplement traditional teaching methods in Cambridge, it actually represented a new approach to university education and imparted new kinds of knowledge and skill. The majority of university teaching in the eighteenth century continued to be based on reading and oral discourse, making very little use of writing or technical problem-solving on paper. In order to clarify this point let us consider for a moment the various ways in which students learned in Cambridge in the later eighteenth century. The main form of undergraduate teaching was large thrice-weekly college lectures in which students were taught the basics required for a pass or mediocre Honours degree. Each lecture lasted an hour, the lecturer generally being a young college fellow preparing to take holy orders or waiting to assume a higher college, clerical or other professional appointment. The main job of the mathematics lecturer was to go through required sections of such important texts as Euclid's *Elements*, ensuring that the majority of students had a least a minimal grasp of geometry, arithmetic, algebra, mechanics, hydrostatics, optics and astronomy. Lectures were run at the pace of the average student and appear to have consisted mainly of the lecturer asking students in turn to state proofs and theorems or to solve simple problems orally.

For the more ambitious students there were several other ways to acquire knowledge in preparation for the degree examinations. First, the college lecturer could provide manuscripts or recommend books to supplement his lectures. Second, students were given varying amounts of help individually by their personal college tutors. In the case of the most able students, the tutor might discuss conceptually difficult problems, recommend further reading and supply privately circulated manuscripts designed to explain opaque passages in advanced books such as the *Principia*.[6] Third, students could pay a member of the University to tutor them privately, a form of teaching that was especially common among the tiny handful of students in each year who wished to learn the mathematical sciences at an advanced level. Beyond its more elementary operations and applications, mathematics was a difficult and highly specialised

---

[5] The development of a new pedagogic tradition of mathematical physics in Georgian and Victorian Cambridge is discussed more broadly in my forthcoming study *Masters of Theory* (Chicago, 2001).

[6] Each student was assigned a personal college tutor who looked after his moral, spiritual and domestic welfare, and kept an eye on his academic progress. See P. Searby, *A History of the University of Cambridge, Vol. III, 1750–1870* (Cambridge, 1997), pp. 120–9.

discipline that few college or university teachers had the inclination or ability to teach.[7] Fourth, students could simultaneously acquire additional knowledge and gain familiarity with the process of oral examination by attending the public disputations of their peers and elders. This was a very important form of learning for students in the eighteenth century, as it showed them precisely how their knowledge would be tested and how to conduct themselves in a public disputation. Fifth, students were entitled to attend the public lectures given by the university professors.[8] This was a relatively unimportant form of teaching since many mathematical professors of this period chose not to lecture at all, and even those who did lecture seldom chose a topic or level of delivery suitable for undergraduates.[9]

The main point to take from this brief survey of Cambridge pedagogy is that professorial and college lectures, tutorial sessions, public disputations and private study were all forms of learning based in the first instance on reading or oral debate. With the gradual introduction of written examinations, however, the preferred form of teaching began to change to suit the new form of assessment. Success in the Senate House Examination depended on the ability to write out proofs and theorems and to solve difficult problems on paper. Ambitious students accordingly turned increasingly to private tutors, usually young college fellows seeking to supplement their meagre stipends. These tutors taught students individually or in small groups and concentrated on imparting technical proficiency on paper. College fellows sometimes filled more than one of the above teaching roles, and in every case would have been a senior or very high wrangler a few years previously. In the following sections I trace the development of private teaching from the late eighteenth century until the early 1830s, paying special attention to the efficacy of the legislation intended to control the practice and to the changing division of labour between private tutors and college lecturers. Since there is virtually no official documentation concerning the contemporary development of undergraduate teaching in Georgian Cambridge, I have pieced together my account mainly from the diaries, correspondence and autobiographical reminiscences of those students and more senior members of the University who experienced the events in question. This approach has the disadvantage of requiring the presentation and assessment of a good deal of detailed and occasionally contradictory evidence, but brings with it rich insights into the undergraduate's experience of changing pedagogical practice.

[7] This form of private instruction in the mathematical sciences had been common since the seventeenth century. See M. Feingold, 'The Mathematical Sciences and New Philosophies', in N. Tyacke (ed.), *England's Long Reformation* (London, 1997), pp. 368–89.
[8] There were three professorships in mathematical subjects in Cambridge in the eighteenth century: the Lucasian Professorship of Mathematics, the Plumian Professorship of Astronomy and Experimental Philosophy, and the Lowndean Professorship of Astronomy and Geometry. For a list of the incumbents of these chairs see W. W. R. Ball, 'The Cambridge School of Machematics', *Mathematical Gazette* vi (1912), pp. 311–23. Rouse Ball (1912), pp. 322–3.
[9] Rouse Ball, *History*, pp. 107, 158.

Although sources on the emergence of private teaching in the later eighteenth century are sparse, there is little doubt that it was the rise of the competitive Senate House Examination in the mid-eighteenth century that prompted the proliferation of the practice. The first direct references to private teaching occur in the 1760s just at the time when the technical content of the Senate House Examination was beginning to increase, and by the 1780s, following the introduction of written examination, the use of private tutors was commonplace. Senior members of the University evidently disapproved of students engaging private tutors as it undermined the notion that the order of merit provided a reliable index of intellectual ability.[10] Students who could not afford a private tutor were clearly placed at a comparative disadvantage, while poor but able undergraduates sometimes compromised their chances in the Senate House by taking students themselves to provide an income. Most troubling of all were cases in which tutors (private or college) were also moderators or examiners, a conflict of interest that laid them open to accusations of partiality and threatened to undermine the integrity of the whole examination process.[11]

In 1777 the University Senate passed graces[12] barring tutors from the office of moderator and forbidding questionists to take private pupils. A further grace in 1781 forbade all undergraduates from studying with private tutors in the two years prior to their sitting the Senate House Examination.[13] It is difficult to assess how effectively these regulations were enforced, but there is very little evidence to support Rouse Ball's influential assertion that 'all such legislation broke down in practice'.[14] Rouse Ball cites Whewell as an authority on this matter, but Whewell actually makes no such claim, and in fact acknowledges that the legislation was 'for a time effectual'. The latter claim is also substantiated by Christopher Wordsworth, a contemporary of Rouse Ball's, who argued that the legislation was effective circa 1800, and that private teaching only became more prevalent during the early nineteenth century when the legislation was in any case relaxed.[15] Strangely, both Rouse Ball and more recent studies following his

---

[10] According to Rouse Ball the first documented case of a private tutor being engaged explicitly to prepare a pupil for a high wranglership occurred in 1763; see Rouse Ball, *History*, p. 162. On the suppression of private teaching in the late 1770s, see S. Atkinson, 'Struggles of a Poor Student Through Cambridge', *The London Magazine* (April 1825), pp. 491–510, at p. 502; W. Whewell, *Of a Liberal Education in General, and with Particular References to the Leading Studies of the University of Cambridge*, 2nd edn (Cambridge, 1850), p. 220; C. Wordsworth, *Scholae Academicae: Some Account of the Studies at the English Universities in the Eighteenth Century* (Cambridge, 1877), p. 260; Rouse Ball, *History*, p. 162; J. Gascoigne, 'Mathematics and Meritocracy: The Emergence of the Cambridge Mathematical Tripos', *Social Studies of Science*, 14 (1984), pp. 547–84, at p. 555; Searby, *History*, p. 130.

[11] H. Gunning, *Reminiscences* (London, 1854), p. xx; 'Mathematics and Meritocracy', p. 555; Searby, *History*, p. 130.

[12] The term used in Cambridge for formal decisions of the Senate.

[13] D. A. Winstanley, *Unreformed Cambridge* (Cambridge, 1935), p. 389. The 'Senate' was the University legislature. It was made up (with one or two minor restrictions) of all resident and non-resident Doctors and Masters of Arts of the University. See Searby, *History*, pp. 52–54.

[14] Rouse Ball, *History*, p. 162. Rouse Ball's assertion is followed, for example, by Winstanley, *Unreformed Cambridge*, pp. 332–3; Gascoigne, *Mathematics*, p. 555; and Searby, *History*, p. 130.

[15] Whewell, *Liberal Education*, p. 220; C. Wordsworth, *Social Life at the English Universities in the*

lead cite the case of John Dawson in support of the claim that private tuition was common in Cambridge beyond the fourth term despite the legislation banning it.[16] Dawson was a retired medical practitioner and largely self-taught mathematician living in the Lake District who offered his services as a mathematics teacher to students, both before they went to the University and during vacations throughout their undergraduate careers.[17] Although without any Cambridge connection, Dawson was responsible for training at least eleven senior wranglers[18] between 1781 and 1800, the period when the legislation against private tuition was most severe.[19] This evidence surely suggests, if anything, that private tuition was indeed an effective method of preparing students for competitive examinations in mathematics, but that such tuition beyond the fourth term was not readily available in Cambridge.[20] Whilst, then, there is no reason to doubt the word of a contemporary such as William Frend who claimed, in 1787, that private tutors were 'universally sought after' and that they were 'absolutely necessary to everyone who wished to make a tolerable figure in the Senate', there is equally little reason to doubt that such private tuition generally took place either during the first four terms (as prescribed by the Graces) or else outside Cambridge during vacations.[21]

These conclusions are further supported by evidence from the first decade of the nineteenth century. One of Dawson's latter successes, George Pryme (6th Wrangler, 1803), provides a rare contemporary account of undergraduate teaching practice in this period, and he claimed explicitly that private tuition was not common in the University in his day.[22] Pryme studied regularly with Dawson both before coming into residence at Cambridge and during the long vacations while preparing for his degree. Lodging in Dawson's house, Pryme was taught six hours a day, the tutor working at the appropriate pace for his pupil, pausing to explain difficulties as they arose.[23] But despite the success of

---

Eighteenth Century (Cambridge, 1874), pp. 114–15. Elsewhere, Whewell (*On the Principles of English University Education* [Cambridge, 1837], pp. 74–5) does actually suggest, vaguely and indirectly, that private tuition was hard to suppress, but he seems to be referring to the 1820s.

[16] Rouse Ball, *History*, p. 162; Gascoigne, *Mathematics*, p. 555.
[17] For Dawson's life and career see *DNB*.
[18] The student at the top of the first class in the degree examination.
[19] Dawson attracted pupils from all over England, but a connection between Sedbergh grammar school and St John's College made him especially popular with Cambridge men.
[20] Had private tuition been freely available in Cambridge it seems unlikely that Dawson would have dominated the training of senior wranglers so thoroughly. See Rouse Ball, *History*, p. 162.
[21] W. Frend, *Considerations on the Oathes Required at the Time of Taking Degrees* (London, 1787), p. 15.
[22] G. Pryme, *Autobiographical Recollections*, ed. A. Bayne (Cambridge, 1870), p. 29. Rouse Ball concludes that Pryme must have been an exception to the general rule that 'nearly every mathematical student read with a private tutor'. It is more likely, however, that Pryme was drawing a contrast with the later period when all students read with private tutors throughout their undergraduate careers. See Rouse Ball, *History*, p. 163.
[23] Dawson charged three shillings and sixpence a week for lodgings and five shillings a week for tuition. See Pryme, *Recollections*, p. 29 and Dawson's entry in *DNB*.

Dawson's pupils, it is clear that even in the 1800s the services of a private tutor were not a prerequisite to Tripos success. Frederick Pollock (Senior Wrangler 1806), for example, made no explicit reference to working with a private tutor in an account of his undergraduate studies.[24] Having read basic geometry and algebra (up to quadratic equations) before arriving in Cambridge – perhaps more than the average freshman would have known – he made excellent use of college lectures, supplementing his knowledge through private study using manuscripts in general circulation.[25] Pollock ascribed his subsequent examination success to an excellent memory – he claimed to know Book I of Euclid's *Elements* 'word by word, letter by letter' – and 'great rapidity and perfect accuracy' of writing.[26] As we shall see in the next section, it remained possible to become Senior Wrangler without the services of a private tutor until at least the early 1820s.

The assertion by Rouse Ball and others that attempts to limit private tuition were ineffectual appears to be based on two dubious assumptions: first, that the complete domination of undergraduate teaching exercised by private tutors from the 1840s – and thus familiar to a wrangler of the 1870s such as Rouse Ball – was the natural and inevitable accompaniment of competitive written examinations and must, therefore, always have coexisted with such examinations; and, second, that the gradual repeal of the rules governing private tuition between 1807 and 1824 was simply an acknowledgement of the futility of such legislation.[27] There is however little reason to doubt that attempts to control private teaching within the University from the late 1770s *were* successful, at least until the first decade of the nineteenth century, and that the gradual repeal of the rules governing the period which had to elapse between working with a private tutor and sitting the Senate House Examination (the period was reduced to eighteen months, twelve months, and six months in 1807, 1815 and 1824 respectively) occurred for other reasons.

The incentive for all prospective Honours students to engage private tutors beyond the fourth term would certainly have increased after the turn of the century as the emphasis on mathematics in the examination continued to grow. In 1799, for example, the enormous importance of mixed mathematics in the Senate House Examination was finally acknowledged by the University. The senior moderator that year took the unusual step of commenting publicly on the

---

[24] Pollock recounted his undergraduate years in response to a letter from De Morgan in 1869 requesting a 'trustworthy account' of the mathematical reading habits of Cambridge men in the early nineteenth century. See Rouse Ball, *History*, pp. 111–14.

[25] Rouse Ball claims that William Dealtry (2nd Wrangler, 1896) was Pollock's 'coach', but Pollock states only that 'there were certain [manuscripts] floating about which I copied – which belonged to Dealtry'. See Rouse Ball, *History*, p. 111.

[26] *Ibid.*, 112. Students could build up a large number of marks in the early stages of the examination by reproducing standard proofs and theorems rapidly and accurately.

[27] Rouse Ball did not assess the relative prevalence of private teaching at different points in the century, and might well have been using his history to undermine attempts to curtail private teaching in the 1880s. See Rouse Ball, *History*, pp. 162–3.

mathematical 'insufficiency' of the questionists[28] from some colleges and, even more significantly, took the unprecedented step of announcing that henceforth no student would receive a degree unless he displayed a 'competent knowledge of the *first* book of *Euclid, Arithmetic, Vulgar and Decimal Fractions, Simple* and *Quadratic Equations,* and Locke and Paley'.[29] This important announcement marked the first step in the emergence of a formal university-wide undergraduate syllabus, each college being thereafter responsible for ensuring that its students met these minimum requirements. By the end of the eighteenth century, therefore, the prestige and emergent syllabus of the competitive Senate House Examination provided a common standard for college teaching throughout the University, and the largest and wealthiest colleges – especially Trinity and St John's – fought fiercely to dominate the order of merit.[30] At exactly the same time that the rules on private tuition were being relaxed, moreover, the structure of the Senate House Examination was being formally altered by the Senate to confine questions on logic to a new fifth day of examination. The original three days would now be devoted entirely to mathematical examination which, in practice, would dictate a student's place in the order or merit.[31] The relative performances of the most able students during these three days were also being judged increasingly on written answers to problems rather than on oral disputations. Indeed, when the parliamentary Commissioners reported in the early 1850s on the development of undergraduate studies in Cambridge, they identified the first decade of the nineteenth century as the period when mathematics, which had become 'more and more difficult to express orally by reason of its symbolic form', had caused 'paper Examination' to overtake the disputation as the prime means of assessing student ability.[32]

This emphasis on the skilled reproduction of mathematical knowledge on paper doubtless encouraged students to engage private tutors, and keen intercollegiate competition meant that they would have done so with the blessing of their colleges. The evidence nevertheless suggests that private teaching *was* practised in accordance with the regulations, and that some students continued to achieve high placing in the Senate House without the benefit of any private tuition at all. This being the case, the relaxation of the rules in 1807, which enabled students to work with a private tutor until the end of their sixth term, quite possibly occurred to enable, or even to encourage, ambitious students to exploit the resources of the private tutor while discouraging the use of non-Cambridge tutors such as Dawson. It might have been a minor embarrassment to the University that parents who had already paid substantial college and university fees were then expected to pay a college

---

[28] Candidates for the degree examination.
[29] Wordsworth, *Scholae*, p. 56.
[30] Gascoigne, 'Mathematics and Meritocracy', pp. 556–7.
[31] Rouse Ball, *History*, p. 209.
[32] *Commissioners' Report* (London, 1852–53), p. 109.

fellow privately to help prepare their sons for the Senate House; but once it was clear that mathematics had become the primary discipline through which the minds of the Cambridge elite were developed and tested, it would have been unacceptable for teaching to have lain substantially in the hands of non-Cambridge tutors.[33] With the proviso that it was sufficiently controlled to suppress accusations of rank unfairness, therefore, private teaching had become a stable and important component of undergraduate instruction: it provided an efficient mechanism for organising the first two years of undergraduate study, thereby raising the level of elite performance in what was emerging as Cambridge's primary discipline, mathematics; it prevented undergraduates from turning to outsiders for tuition; it provided an income for young fellows; and it spared college lecturers and tutors the grind of either drilling students in basic mathematical technique or making special provision for the most able pupils. In a primarily undergraduate institution, the first concern of most fellows was, as we have seen, to further their own careers which, in most cases, lay neither in Cambridge nor in mathematics. But it was not merely the methods of teaching and examining undergraduates that were changing in Cambridge during the first two decades of the nineteenth century. This was also the period when new mathematical methods from continental Europe were gradually entering the University. The introduction of this new mathematics not only accelerated several of the trends discussed above but also had a profound effect on the role of the private tutor in training the undergraduate elite.

The analytical revolution from below

During the eighteenth century, Cambridge tutors had taken little interest in continental developments in mathematics. The acrimonious priority dispute between Newton, Leibniz and their respective followers over the invention of the calculus had soured relations, and from the late 1780s, the dramatic political events in France and the subsequent Napoleonic wars produced a serious obstacle to intellectual exchange between England and France. Continental methods would in any case have seemed irrelevant to many Cambridge tutors, as the study of mathematics in the University was intended not to produce professional mathematicians, but to educate the student's mind through mastery of Newton's mathematical methods and natural philosophy. During the eighteenth century, however, such mathematicians as Euler, D'Alembert, Clairaut, and Daniel Bernoulli had developed a major new field of mathematical study, 'analysis', by the systematic application of the Leibnizian calculus to a wide range of problems in algebra, mechanics and algebraic

---

[33] Whewell claimed that private teaching encouraged students to study harder in the summer vacation rather than in the formal terms and that this was unacceptable to the University. See Whewell, *Principles*, p. 76; *Liberal Education*, p. 218.

geometry.[34] With Newton's laws expressed in differential form – an approach first published by Euler in 1736 – dynamical problems could be tackled systematically using the power of the calculus. By the end of the eighteenth century, Lagrange had recast mechanics and dynamics in fully analytical form using the principle of virtual work and the calculus of variations, while in his monumental *Traité de mécanique celeste*, Laplace had brought Newton's laws of motion and theory of gravitation to a new level of mathematical sophistication.[35] This was surely a book with which Newton's Cambridge followers ought to have been familiar but, as a sympathetic British reviewer of Lacroix's great French textbook on the calculus observed in 1800, the average English mathematician would be 'stopped at the first pages of Euler or D'Alembert . . . from want of knowing the principles and the methods which they take for granted as known to every mathematical reader'.[36]

There was nevertheless some interest in continental mathematics in Britain, and around the turn of the century there were calls both within and outside the University for a reform of undergraduate teaching that would take some account of analytical methods.[37] In 1803, Robert Woodhouse (Senior Wrangler, 1795) attempted to introduce the d-notation calculus and other analytical methods into Cambridge by publishing *The Principles of Analytical Calculation*, but the book had very little immediate effect on undergraduate studies. As we have seen, both the ideology and structure of teaching in Cambridge were extremely conservative and would not be easy to change. The lecturers, college and private tutors, university professors, textbook writers and examiners had all been high wranglers in their day, and many played several of these roles. Most would have been hostile to learning difficult new mathematical methods which would be of no use in furthering their careers and which, for many, carried unwelcome associations with the atheism and radical politics of revolutionary Paris.[38] Abandoning Newton's methods would have appeared to many as a move calculated to undermine both the authority of the Anglican Church and the reputation of England's greatest natural philosopher. Furthermore, with teaching taking place in the colleges and no formal University body to dictate what

[34] On the development of analysis in the eighteenth and early nineteenth centuries see I. Grattan-Guinness, *The Development of the Foundations of Analysis from Euler to Riemann* (Cambridge, MA, 1970); *Convolutions in French Mathematics, 1800–1840*, 3 Vols (Basel, 1990).

[35] J. L. Lagrange, *Méchanique analytique* (Paris, 1788); P. S. Laplace, *Traité de mécanique celeste*, 3 Vols (Paris, 1798–1827).

[36] Quoted in H. Becher, 'William Whewell and Cambridge Mathematics', *Historical Studies in Physical Sciences*, 11 (1980), pp. 1–48, at p. 8.

[37] Becher, 'Whewell', pp. 8–14; H. Becher, 'Woodhouse, Babbage, Peacock, and Modern Algebra', *Historia Mathematica*, 7 (1980), pp. 389–400; P. C. Enros, 'The Analytical Society (1812–1813): Precursor of the Renewal of Cambridge Mathematics', *Historia Mathematica*, 10 (1983), pp. 24–47, at pp. 25–6; N. Guicciardini, *The Development of the Newtonian Calculus in Britain 1700–1800* (Cambridge, 1989), pp. 126–31.

[38] The politics of the analytical revolution is discussed in H. Becher, 'Radicals, Whigs and Conservatives: The Middle and Lower Classes in the Analytical Revolution at Cambridge in the Age of Aristocracy', *British Journal for the History of Science*, 28 (1995), pp. 405–26.

was taught, it would be very difficult to reform the system by edict without major parliamentary intervention. Official changes to university procedure or policy could only be passed by a majority vote of the Senate, and it is extremely unlikely that any proposal formally to replace Newton's methods on the examination papers with those of French mathematicians would have been carried.

As Becher and Enros have shown, the movement that eventually accomplished the so-called 'analytical revolution' in Cambridge began with undergraduates working inside the system.[39] The most famous manifestation of the growing undergraduate enthusiasm for French analytical mathematics was the formation of the short-lived Analytical Society in 1812. The aim of the Society was to invigorate the professional study of mathematics in England by introducing the techniques of French analysis into the potential power centres of the discipline. The Society did not survive long enough to fulfil these ambitious goals, but some of its more prominent members did go on to achieve partial success. Charles Babbage, John Herschel (Senior Wrangler, 1813) and George Peacock (2nd Wrangler, 1813), for example, realised that in order to bring about change it would be important both to produce textbooks from which analysis could be learned and to have analytical questions set in the Senate House so that such studies would pay off in the examination.[40] In 1816 they accordingly completed a translation of Lacroix's introductory textbook on differential and integral calculus, and in 1820 published a further volume containing practical examples.[41] In 1817, one of their number, George Peacock, was appointed a moderator for the Senate House Examination, and he infuriated many of his more conservative colleagues by setting problems in analytical mathematics using the continental d-notation.[42] Two years later both of the moderators – Peacock and Richard Gwatkin (Senior Wrangler, 1814) – were ex-members of the Analytical Society, and both made free use of analytical techniques and notation. Over the next decade more, and more advanced, continental mathematics found its way into the Senate House examination so that, by the end of the 1820s, ambitious undergraduates had to be familiar with the new methods if they hoped to become high wranglers.

---

[39] On early attempts to reform Cambridge mathematics see Becher, *Whewell*; Enros, 'Analytical Society'; M. Panteki, 'William Wallace and the Introduction of Continental Calculus to Britain: A Letter to George Peacock', *Historia Mathematica*, 14 (1987), pp. 119–32; Guicciardini, *Development*, Ch. 9.
[40] On the move by men such as Peacock to a more pragmatic approach towards the introduction of analysis see Becher, 'Radicals, Whigs and conservatives'.
[41] In translating Lacroix's textbook, Babbage and Herschel altered and supplemented the mathematical content to suit their own purposes. See J. Richards, 'Rigor and Clarity: Foundations of Mathematics in France and England, 1800–1840', *Science in Context*, IV (1991), p. 299.
[42] Questions in d-notation calculus had already been set in examinations at St John's College by John Herschel. See Becher, *Radicals, Whigs, and Conservatives*, p. 414.

This familiar chronology of the introduction of analytical methods into Cambridge rightly points to the importance of new textbooks and the infiltration of the Senate House examination in establishing the new mathematics. It reveals nothing, however, of the process by which the analytical revolution was practically accomplished at the level of undergraduate teaching. As one of the founders of the Analytical Society, Charles Babbage, later recalled, even after the translation of Lacroix's textbook and the introduction of questions in the d-notation calculus in the Senate House Examination, the 'progress of the notation of Leibnitz at Cambridge was slow' and taught only by young enthusiasts such as Peacock at Trinity and Gwatkin at St John's.[43] At what point and through which teachers, then, did the new mathematics become commonplace in undergraduate studies throughout the University? These are important questions because, as we shall shortly see, it was private tutors who were primarily responsible for spreading the new mathematics, and in so doing, they not only altered the content, purpose and structure of undergraduate studies, but also assumed a control over the training of the mathematical elite which would remain unchallenged until the last quarter of the nineteenth century.

We know very little about undergraduate teaching methods in Cambridge in the late eighteenth and early nineteenth centuries, but for the period during which the analytical revolution took place – roughly 1815–25 – we have three fairly detailed accounts of undergraduate experience. The earliest and most detailed account is that of J. M. F. Wright, an able student from King's Lynn Grammar School who arrived in Cambridge in October 1815.[44] Having learned the basics of arithmetic, algebra, geometry and trigonometry before arriving at the University, Wright consolidated his knowledge of these and the other required mathematical topics in his first year through college lectures given by John Brown (2nd Wrangler 1799).[45] At the beginning of his second year Wright was able, apparently unexpectedly, to engage the services of a private tutor when a 'friend from the country' sent some money expressly for the purpose.[46] Private teaching – or 'pupilising' as it was commonly known – was certainly commonplace at this time as Wright notes that most high wranglers who obtained fellowships were now prepared to 'receive' private pupils both during term time and the long summer vacation. Wright also claimed that the University had 'fixed' the fees payable for these periods but that 'Fellows of colleges, and others, who are in more request' were able to

---

[43] C. Babbage, *Passages from the Life of a Philosopher* (London, 1864), p. 39.
[44] Wright registered at the University in 1814 but began his studies in 1815. See Searby, *History*, p. 118.
[45] J. M. F. Wright, *Alma Mater; or Seven Years at the University of Cambridge*, 2 Vols (London, 1827), Vol. I, p. 5. Brown was also one of two Trinity tutors, the other being James Hustler (3rd Wrangler, 1802).
[46] Wright, *Alma Mater*, Vol. I, p. 171. Wright claimed that the majority of students were unable to afford the services of a private tutor: *ibid.*, p. 76.

charge substantially more.[47] Apart from revealing the very substantial income a young fellow could now derive from pupilising, these remarks also point to an emerging distinction between those whose only recommendation as a private tutor was their own success in the Senate House, and those who had an established reputation as an experienced and effective teacher. This was an important distinction which became more pronounced over the next two decades, culminating in the emergence of the mathematical 'coach' who made his living by taking pupils.[48]

Wright engaged John Brass (6th Wrangler, 1811), a private tutor of great reputation who, since his normal hours of pupilising were already full, agreed to see Wright for an hour before morning chapel. Wright describes how, arriving freezing cold at six o'clock at Brass's rooms in Trinity Great Court, the latter would jump out of bed and begin teaching in his night clothes. Wright would be set writing out an 'elegant demonstration of some important proposition in algebra, such as Newton's Binomial Theorem', and having made sure his student understood what he was copying, Brass would retire to the bedroom to dress, occasionally peering round the door to check his pupil was not 'stuck'.[49] Wright's account of his studies with Brass provides the earliest written confirmation of the special benefits conferred by a private tutor. The most notable of these were the provision of teaching manuscripts which developed difficult topics in a way designed to facilitate student understanding, and the opportunity for the student to study at exactly his own pace. Working 'together at the table' Brass would push Wright along at what the latter described as '"the speed of thought" – that is as fast as my understanding would carry me', a process which contrasted sharply with the plodding progress of a college lecture delivered to up to a hundred students at a pace that met the needs of the most mediocre.[50] The close personal interaction between tutor and pupil was extremely important in imparting the subtle skills of problem solving. Wright's private tuition, we should also note, was carried out well within the limits prescribed by the regulations which, in 1815, had been altered again to enable students to work with a private tutor until the end of their seventh term.[51]

One aspect of Wright's undergraduate aspirations that separates him sharply from students of a decade earlier such as Pryme and Pollock is his eagerness to learn the new continental mathematics, especially analytical mechanics. By the

---

[47] The rates for a term and the summer vacation were £14 and £30 respectively (those in greater demand charged £20 and £50 respectively). These rates were probably 'fixed' only in an informal sense, as is suggested by the variable rates. See Wright *ibid.*, Vol. I, p. 171.
[48] The term 'coach' was first applied to private teachers in the mid-1830s. The origin and meaning of this term is discussed in A. Warwick, *Masters of Theory* (Chicago, 2001), ch. 2.
[49] Wright, *Alma Mater*, Vol. I, p. 172.
[50] *Ibid.*, pp. 172–173. For a strikingly similar first-hand account of private teaching in the late 1820s see A. Pritchard, *Charles Pritchard: Memoirs of his Life* (London, 1897), pp. 38–9.
[51] Searby, *History*, p. 130.

end of his second year (the early summer of 1817), Wright was keen to begin studying not just Newton's *Principia*, a required book in the third year, but also Monge's *Géometrie descriptive*, Lagrange's *Mécanique analytique* and Laplace's *Traité de mécanique celeste*.[52] The first Senate House Examination containing questions on continental mathematics had taken place just six months earlier, and it is clear that Peacock had succeeded in generating considerable enthusiasm for the new mathematics even among students who were not directly under his tutorial control.[53] What also emerges from Wright's account of his first two years of undergraduate study is that although the most ambitious students studied the advanced parts of traditional subjects from privately-circulated manuscripts or with private tutors, the latter did not, circa 1817, teach the analytical methods which now provided an alternative to traditional geometrical and fluxional techniques. Over the summer of 1817, Wright began to study the above books and although he gradually made progress with the *Principia* – the mathematical methods of which he had been taught in his earlier studies – he found himself unable to follow the French works.[54] He managed only the first seven pages of Laplace's *Mécanique celeste*, for example, before being stumped by 'the doctrine of Partial Differentials, which had not yet found its way into any work on the subject of Fluxions, in the English language'.[55] The 'uncommon fame' of Laplace's work in Cambridge at this time was nevertheless so great that Wright was determined to master it somehow. For the time being he returned to further study of Newton's *Principia*, 'as far as the Eighth section', and then made further study of the fluxional calculus in which he already had a good grounding.[56] Wright at last made some progress when, possibly at Peacock's suggestion, he began to study the latter's recently-completed English translation of Lacroix's introductory textbook on the calculus. But even after working through this text he still found Laplace in the original 'too much' for him.[57]

At the start of his third year, Wright began again to attend Brown's lectures, the whole of the seventh term being devoted to the first book of Newton's *Principia*. Brown, who was also Wright's personal tutor, was well aware that his lectures would not be sufficient for the most able men, and he provided manuscripts to get them through the more advanced parts of Newton's work. According to Wright, it was impossible for even the best student to 'make his way through the Principia' without such manuscripts, the majority of which

---

[52] Wright, *Alma Mater*, Vol. II, p. 2.
[53] Peacock was at this point an assistant tutor working under James Hustler.
[54] Wright did not appear to have difficulty reading French, but he gives no indication as to where he learned the language.
[55] Wright, *Alma Mater*, Vol. II, p. 2. Methods equivalent to partial differentiation were employed in the English fluxional calculus, but they were neither identified by a special notation nor subject to systematic development. See N. Guicciardini, *The Development of the Newtonian Calculus in Britain 1700–1800* (Cambridge, 1989), p. 140.
[56] Wright learned fluxional calculus from Dealtry (1810).
[57] Wright, *Alma Mater*, Vol. II, p. 3.

were 'in the hands' of private tutors.[58] The relaxation of the regulations on pupilising in 1815 had made it permissible to work with a private tutor until the end of the first term of the third year and, Wright reveals, the significance of this concession was that it enabled the top men to get a solid foundation in this most important of texts.[59] Unable to afford a tutor in this crucial term, Wright began to skip Brown's lectures in order to push ahead with the first, second and parts of the third book of the *Principia* using manuscripts he had 'scraped together' over the summer. He also continued his study of fluxions, making such rapid progress on all fronts that, towards the end of the term, he found himself so far ahead of his peers that, with Brown's collusion, he ceased to attend lectures altogether.[60]

It was in the latter part of this term and over the Christmas vacation that Wright finally began to make substantial progress with the French works. He made a systematic study of Lagrange's *Mécanique analytique* and several other minor French works and, during the second term of his third year, worked with great difficulty through Lacroix's three-volume treatise on the calculus. In the last term of the third year the lectures were on optics and astronomy, and, feeling he had little to learn from Brown, Wright at last worked his way through much of Laplace's *Mécanique celeste* and studied Jean-Baptiste Biot's recently published *Traité de physique*.[61] It was also the custom this term to start working through problems from past examination papers in preparation for the Senate House, and Wright felt it advantageous to learn the physical topics using analytical methods because of their 'more ready and convenient application in the resolution of problems'.[62] Wright would at this point have been able to draw on Peacock's examination papers of the previous year which included problems in continental mathematics, and with Peacock and Gwatkin the moderators for 1819, he would have anticipated more of the same in his examination.[63]

---

[58] Several of these manuscripts later formed the basis of introductory textbooks on the *Principia*. See the prefatory comments in J. Carr, *The First Three Sections of Newton's Principia; with Copious Notes and Illustrations* (London, 1821), J. M. F. Wright, *The First Three Sections of Newton's Principia; with Copious Notes and Illustrations* (London, 1828); and J. H. Evans, *The First Three Sections of Newton's Principia* (Cambridge, 1834).

[59] Wright, *Alma Mater*, Vol. II, p. 24.

[60] *Ibid.*, pp. 24–25. It is also worth noting that although Wright discussed several lecture courses he attended by professors of the University, including Samuel Vince's lectures on experimental natural philosophy, he made no mention of attending any lectures on mathematics: *ibid.*, pp. 27–35.

[61] On the British reception of Biot's work see M. Crosland and C. Smith, 'The Transmission of Physics from France to Britain: 1800–1840', *Annals of Science*, 33 (1976), pp. 1–61, at pp. 7–8, 36–41.

[62] Wright, *Alma Mater*, Vol. II, p. 46.

[63] Wright ought to have been a high wrangler but achieved only a pass degree. Due to a bizarre series of oversights and accidents, Wright failed to keep a required Act in his ninth term and could not compete fairly in the Senate House examination. See Wright *Alma Mater*, vol. II, pp. 35–60. For further biographical details of Wright's subsequent career see Searby, *History*, p. 120.

Wright's undergraduate experience reveals the extent to which even the most enthusiastic student had to struggle by himself to master the new mathematics in the years immediately after 1815. The majority of college lecturers and private tutors would have been unable or unwilling to help their pupils in this respect. As Babbage's comments above imply, we must assume that, apart from rare cases such as Wright, the few students who obtained a good grounding in the new mathematics circa 1820 did so because they had the good fortune to have an enthusiast – such as Gwatkin at St John's or Peacock at Trinity – as a lecturer and personal tutor.[64] An excellent example of the latter case is that of George Airy, who arrived at Trinity in 1819, and whose undergraduate experiences make an interesting contrast with Wright's. Unlike Wright, Airy was extremely well-prepared in mathematics by the time he arrived at the University. Having received a very sound grounding in arithmetic and algebra by the age of twelve, he went on to grammar school in Colchester where he studied geometry and fluxional calculus.[65] Commencing in the spring of 1817, he also went twice a week to be tutored by an ex-Cambridge mathematician, Mr Rogers, who had come as a mathematical master to the school.[66] Acting as a private tutor, Rogers taught Airy geometry, algebra, mechanics, hydrostatics, optics, trigonometry, fluxional calculus and Newton's *Principia* to the end of the ninth section – the standard topics required for an Honours degree at the University. In a little over a year Airy had outstripped his teacher – who thereafter declined to teach him – and although Airy was somewhat disparaging of Rogers' powers as a mathematician he did not underestimate the benefit he received 'for its training [him] both in Cambridge subjects and in the accurate Cambridge methods of treating them'.[67] In the summer of 1819 Airy was examined in mathematics by a fellow of Trinity College, who was so impressed with his knowledge and ability that he sent Airy's problem solutions to Trinity to be seen by other fellows including his future tutor, Hustler, and Hustler's assistant tutor, George Peacock.

Airy was admitted to Trinity on the strength of his mathematical ability and Peacock, who was working to consolidate the place of the new mathematics in undergraduate studies, quickly took him under his wing. Despite his head start in mathematics, Airy attended college lectures to make sure that he could reproduce elementary mathematics in exactly the form required in college examinations and the Senate House. Realising that this would hardly tax Airy's ability, Peacock gave him a copy of the translation of Lacroix's *Differential Calculus* as well as a copy of the recently completed *Examples* in differential and

---

[64] Peacock stated in 1817 that he intended to use his position as a mathematics lecturer at Trinity to further the analytical revolution. See Rouse Ball, *History*, p. 121.
[65] G. B. Airy, ed., *Autobiography of Sir George Biddell Airy* (Cambridge, 1896), p. 19. Airy, like Wright, learned the fluxional calculus from Dealtry (1810).
[66] If the biographical fragments given by Airy are correct, 'Mr Rogers' must have been Thomas Rogers (10th Senior Optime, i.e. 10th in 2nd class, 1811).
[67] Airy, *Autobiography*, p. 20.

integral calculus.[68] Airy 'betook' himself to these with 'great industry' together with William Whewell's new d-notation treatise on mechanics and, quickly perceiving that he would need to read French in order to 'read modern mathematics', he began the study of the language with the help of his sister during the Christmas vacation. By the long vacation at the end of his first year Airy was reading Poisson in the original, 'struggling with French words'. As he followed College lectures and studied advanced French mathematics in his own time, Airy recalled that Peacock 'always had some private problems of a higher class for me, and saw me I believe every day'.[69] Airy makes no reference to having worked with a private tutor as an undergraduate, and it is not difficult to see why he would have had no need of one. The majority of such tutors would not have been able to teach him the analytical mathematics he desired to learn and he had already mastered most of the traditional mathematical topics required in the Senate House. It is in any case clear that Peacock willingly played the part of an unpaid private tutor, setting Airy problems, helping him with difficulties and giving Airy free access to his own library of mathematical books when absent from Cambridge during the vacations.[70] Airy's sound mathematical training and confidence also enabled him to make substantial progress on his own, even to the extent of making original contributions to mathematical physics. When he had great difficulty following the standard physical explanation of precession in Samuel Vince's (Senior Wrangler, 1775) *Astronomy*, Airy wrote out an explanation of his own in analytical form which later became part of his extremely influential *Mathematical Tracts*. Likewise in trying to work through Robert Woodhouse's (Senior Wrangler, 1795) *Physical Astronomy*, Airy was compelled to master the technique of 'changing the independent variable', a learning experience that required him to 'examine severely the logic of the Differential Calculus'.[71] Through his second year, Airy attended Peacock's college lectures while, in his own time, obtaining a thorough mastery of the differential and integral calculus together with its physical applications, and solving problems set privately by Peacock.

At the beginning of his third year, Airy was told by Hustler, who gave the third-year lectures, that there was no point in him attending formal classes any further. It was arranged instead that Airy and his two most able peers would join the questionists of the year above in their final term's examination preparation.

---

[68] Comparison with Wright's undergraduate accomplishments suggests that Airy's knowledge was roughly that of a good second-year man when he entered Trinity.

[69] Airy, *Autobiography*, pp. 24–26, 29; W. Whewell, *An Elementary Treatise on Mechanics* (Cambridge, 1819). It is not clear which of Poisson's works Airy was reading but it was probably the *Traité de mécanique* of 1811.

[70] Airy, *Autobiography*, pp. 28, 30. Airy moved in his second term to rooms on Peacock's staircase in Nevile's Court.

[71] Ibid., pp. 29–30; S. Vince, *A Complete System of Astronomy*, 3 Vols (Cambridge, 1797–1808); R. Woodhouse, *An Elementary Treatise on Astronomy, Vol. II, Containing Physical Astronomy* (Cambridge, 1818); G. B. Airy, *Mathematical Tracts on Physical Astronomy, the Figure of the Earth, Precession and Mutation, and the Calculus of Variations* (Cambridge, 1826, 1831).

Unfortunately the questionists appear to have been offended by the presence of the precocious younger men – referring to them scoffingly as 'the impudent year' and the 'annus mirabilis' – and, to avoid further bad feeling, Airy and his contemporaries went instead three times a week to Peacock's rooms where he set them questions. Airy completed his third year in the summer of 1822 with further studies of advanced mathematics, privately tutoring less able undergraduates, designing a calculating machine, undertaking simple experiments in optics and mechanics, and completing his first original mathematical manuscripts. In October 1822 he became a questionist himself, attending thrice-weekly problem classes, and, in the Tripos of 1823, he was senior wrangler and first Smith's prizeman.[72] Airy was clearly as well-prepared in French mathematics, and especially French mathematical physics, as any Cambridge undergraduate could have been in the early 1820s. After his examinations, he began taking private pupils to generate some income, was elected to a fellowship and mathematical lectureship at Trinity, and continued his original investigations into mathematical physics. In the mid-1820s, he also helped to consolidate the position of the new mathematics in the University by writing his *Mathematical Tracts* (which provided an introduction to lunar theory, the figure of the earth, precession and nutation, and the calculus of variations) and, as Lucasian professor, by giving well-attended lectures in 1827 and 1828 on mechanics, optics, pneumatics and hydrostatics.[73]

Private teaching and analytical revolution

The reminiscences of Wright and Airy tell us a good deal about the undergraduate training system around the time of the analytical revolution and about the means by which the new mathematics was first introduced. Wright learned most of his mathematics as an undergraduate, but even in the years 1815–19 was taught continental calculus neither by his college lecturer nor by his private tutor.[74] Even in mastering advanced English mathematics he relied heavily on privately circulated manuscripts and the training offered by his private tutor. That Airy's experience a few years later was very different was not due to any major reform in the content or style of undergraduate teaching, but to his exceptional knowledge of mathematics before entering the University and to his good fortune in having Peacock as a lecturer and tutor. Peacock must have realised that the analytical revolution would be accomplished only if he and his fellow enthusiasts produced a generation of students who could answer the analytical questions set in the Senate House and then go on themselves to teach

---

[72] Two Smith's prizes for mathematics were awarded each year, usually gained by the highest wranglers. See Airy, *Autobiography*, pp. 33–40.
[73] *Ibid.*, pp. 49–66; Crosland and Smith, 'Transmission and Physics', p. 14.
[74] Both Brown and Brass graduated before the formation of the Analytical Society in 1812, and neither became a member of the Society. On the formation of the Society and its members see Enros, 'The Analytical Society'.

the new methods to other undergraduates. In the case of Airy, Peacock's efforts were well rewarded.

But despite the accomplishments of students such as Wright and Airy, it remained a mark of the uphill struggle faced by reformers in the early 1820s that, even in 1822, it was still possible to become senior wrangler with little or no knowledge of the new mathematics. Here the case of Solomon Atkinson is informative. The son of an impoverished Cumbrian farmer, this extremely ambitious and largely self-taught student – who as an undergraduate had 'much discussion' about mathematics with Airy – was unable to afford the services of a private tutor. Used to working on his own, Atkinson cleverly used college lectures and standard treatises to guide his own private study. As with Pollock before him, it seems that hard work, an excellent memory and a thorough grasp of the relatively elementary mathematics which still dominated the examination papers enabled Atkinson to surpass his more affluent and knowledgeable peers in the Senate House.[75] Atkinson recalled with satisfaction that he had beaten Gwatkin's 'little coterie' of St John's men who had enjoyed 'all the best advantage that could be derived from the ablest instructions', a comment which suggests that Gwatkin's enthusiasm for the new mathematics might actually have prejudiced his students' chances in the examination.[76] It is almost certainly the case, however, that Atkinson was one of the last undergraduates to win the coveted senior wranglership both without a substantial knowledge of advanced analytical methods and without the help of a private tutor. According to Babbage, it was only 'a very few years' after the publication of the book of examples in Leibnizian calculus in 1820 that the 'd' notation was widely adopted within the University, and this adoption was a prelude to the systematic introduction of more advanced analytical methods to undergraduate studies.[77] In order to see how and why this occurred, we must look more closely at several changes in student life taking place in the 1820s and early 1830s.

First, during the early 1820s both the place of mathematics in undergraduate studies and the apparatus of mathematical examination were further formalised. In 1823 the system of appointing just two moderators and two examiners to take complete responsibility for the examination was instituted. It was also confirmed that, in order to preserve continuity, the moderators of one year would become the examiners the next year, a system which further entrenched the power of a small number of moderators and examiners to control the content of the

---

[75] Atkinson, 'Struggles'. Atkinson published his article anonymously and concealed his identity by implying that he had been an undergraduate circa 1805. He was actually the senior wrangler of 1822 as is confirmed by Venn's *Alumni Cantabrigienses*. On his interaction with Airy, see Airy, *Autobiography*, p. 30.
[76] *Ibid.*, p. 510. It should also be noted that although Atkinson was very critical of the practice of private tuition, claiming that, by the early 1820s, a private tutor was a virtual necessity for Honours students, he made no suggestion that the regulations were being abused.
[77] Babbage, *Passages*, p. 40.

examination.[78] In 1822 a new Classical Tripos was founded in order to satisfy the complaints of those who felt that the dramatic growth in mathematical studies was marginalizing classical studies to an unacceptable degree.[79] From this point, the Senate House Examination was often referred to as the 'Mathematical Tripos' in order to differentiate it from the new 'Classical Tripos'. Second, the appearance during the 1820s of new books giving accounts of various physical topics in the Continental d-notation calculus made it easier for enthusiastic college lecturers and private tutors to teach the new methods; and once such methods were being widely taught they could be used to set more, and more advanced, problems in the Tripos examination. In addition to the translation of Lacroix's textbook and the book of examples produced by Peacock, Babbage and Herschel, Whewell published textbooks giving analytical treatments of mechanics and dynamics in 1819 and 1823 respectively; Henry Coddington (Senior Wrangler, 1820) and Woodhouse published accounts of optics and astronomy respectively in 1823; and in 1826 Henry Parr Hamilton (9th Wrangler, 1816) published an analytical geometry and Airy published his *Mathematical Tracts*.[80] To accommodate the new topics, the number of days of mathematical examination in the Mathematical Tripos was extended to four in 1828.[81] The new regulations also made the examination more progressive: the first two days, sat by all candidates, were devoted to easy questions (solvable without the aid of the calculus) while, on the last two days, the candidates were given questions on the 'higher and more difficult parts of mathematics' according to a pre-classification into four groups by oral disputations. It was also decided that all the examination questions would henceforth be given in printed form – rather than given out orally – so that future candidates could study the papers to see what kinds of topic and problems they were likely to be set.[82] Finally, the number of students obtaining Honours in the Senate House Examination increased dramatically throughout the period in question. Between 1813 and 1827, for example, the numbers almost doubled, an increase that further swelled the numbers attending college lectures and heightened the pervasive atmosphere of competition.[83]

All of the above developments served, either directly or indirectly, to enhance the role of the private tutor as an undergraduate teacher. Atkinson's account of

---

[78] J. M. L Glaisher, 'The Mathematical Tripos', *Proceedings of the London Mathematical Society*, xviii (1886/7), pp. 4–38. Prior to 1823 the number of examiners assisting the moderators had varied from year to year.

[79] Until 1850 students wishing to sit the Classical Tripos had first to obtain Honours in the Mathematical Tripos. See Searby, *History*, pp. 166–7.

[80] Whewell, *Elementary Treatise*; H. Coddington, *An Elementary Treatise on Optics* (Cambridge, 1823); R. Woodhouse, *A Treatise on Astronomy Theoretical and Practical* (Cambridge, 1821–1823); H.P. Hamilton, *Principles of Analytical Geometry* (Cambridge, 1826); Airy, *Mathematical Tracts*.

[81] W. Hopkins' evidence, *Commissioners' Report* (London, 1852–1853), Evidence p. 239.

[82] Glaisher, *Mathematical Tripos*, p. 14.

[83] Cambridge admissions more than trebled from around 120 to over 400 between 1800 and the early 1820s. See Searby, *History*, p. 61.

his undergraduate studies makes it clear that, despite the peculiarity of his own case, by the early 1820s the majority of ambitious students found the services of a private tutor extremely valuable. And as the most able wranglers trained by tutors such as Peacock and Gwatkin began themselves to become moderators and set Tripos questions in the new mathematics, so their peers, in the role of private tutors, began to prepare the most able students to answer such questions.[84] Since there were no official regulations prescribing which mathematical topics (beyond the most elementary) might or might not be examined in the examination, young moderators and examiners were free to set whatever problems they thought the best students might reasonably be able to tackle.[85] Through this mechanism, both the range of subjects making up the unofficial mathematical syllabus as well as the level of technical performance expected of a high wrangler came to be defined and continually inflated by the best private tutors and their most able pupils. The effect of this inflation was to make the private tutor a useful aid to any aspiring Honours student and a virtual necessity to those seeking one of the fiercely contested places among the top ten wranglers.

The very content of analytical mathematics also lent itself to this system of tough competitive learning and examining. As Becher has noted, the teaching of analysis, especially to an advanced level, required 'specialised and cumulative learning over a period of years'. This was a process ideally suited to an educational regime intended to push students to their intellectual limits and then to differentiate minutely between their relative performances in written examinations.[86] Such cumulative, competitive learning was also accomplished more effectively by private tutors using individual tuition, specially prepared manuscripts and graded examples and problems, than it was by college lecturers teaching large classes to the pace of the mediocre student. Even George Peacock, a college lecturer who did not as a rule take private pupils, found it expedient to train Airy in the new mathematics using the methods of the private tutor. During the 1820s, as success in the Senate House Examination came to depend upon the ability to solve difficult problems using advanced analysis, it was young college fellows who had just sat the Tripos examination and who wished to derive an income by pupilising, who were best able to drill ambitious undergraduates in the required techniques. It is noteworthy in this context that, by the

[84] Whewell claimed that the rapid rise of competitive examinations had been aided by the fact that 'Examiners, for the most part, alternate the employment of examining with that of private tuition'. See *Commissioners' Report* (1852–53), p. 74.
[85] Glaisher, *Mathematical Tripos*, p. 19; W. Hopkins, 'Presidential Address', *British Association Report* (London, 1853), pp. xli–lvii, 7. The Mathematical Tripos lists in J. R. Tanner's *A Historical Register of the University of Cambridge* (Cambridge, 1917) show that during the period 1820–1840 more than 75 percent of the examiners were between just four and eight years from graduation. A considerable majority of those setting the examination papers would therefore have been under thirty years of age.
[86] Becher, *Whewell*, p. 2. Cambridge private tutors seem to have been more successful in teaching analytical methods to large numbers of students than were their contemporaries, including Lacroix, in Paris. See J. L. Richards, *Mathematical Visions: The Pursuit of Geometry in Victorian England* (Boston, 1888), pp. 302–3.

mid-1820s, even the established college lecturer and reformer, Richard Gwatkin, was reputed to be the finest private tutor (rather than lecturer) in the University, a reputation that bespoke Gwatkin's realisation that pupilising had become the most effective (and most financially rewarding) means of furthering the analytical revolution.[87]

I suggested above that the gradual relaxation of the regulations on pupilising should not be understood, as Rouse Ball suggested, as a straightforward acknowledgement that the practice was impossible to suppress. As we have seen, the relaxation in 1807 served a range of purposes, while that of 1815 enabled the elite students to advance their knowledge of the *Principia* beyond the level reached in college lectures. The final relaxation of the rules in 1824, which enabled undergraduates to work with a private tutor until the end of their ninth term, should also be understood in the above context. Even circa 1820, college lectures were of little value to ambitious students like Wright and Airy beyond the seventh term, and, following the adoption of the d-notation calculus and the rapid proliferation of analytical topics during the early 1820s, it would have been clear that, without major reform, the traditional structures of college and University teaching could offer little to aspiring wranglers in their final year. It seems likely that, by the mid-1820s, many members of the University realised that a further influx of analytical methods was inevitable, perhaps even desirable, and that it was neither practicable nor in their own interests to leave the intense preparation required in these subjects to college lecturers or university professors. Faced with the invidious choice of either completely reforming undergraduate teaching — which would have been very difficult to get through the Senate — or relaxing the rules on private teaching, the University adopted the easier, and in the short term probably more effective, latter option.[88] A further advantage to legalising the use of private tutors throughout the nine undergraduate terms was that it made the most effective teaching in Cambridge accessible to students from all colleges (assuming they could afford the fees).[89] The rise of competitive examinations as the measure of the intellectual elite had created severe problems for the smaller and poorer colleges in the University who could not afford to keep a large staff of able mathematical lecturers. The rapid increase in the content and standard of the Mathematical Tripos during the 1820s would have exacerbated this problem and given further advantage to the large and wealthy colleges.[90] By offering their services to any able student

---

[87] Atkinson, 'Struggles', p. 505.
[88] It would not have been necessary to lift the restrictions on private tuition entirely, as the last summer vacation and tenth term were traditionally used for revision and practice at problem solving. Private tutors soon came to oversee this work and there is no doubt that, in this sense, the rule came to be flagrantly ignored.
[89] Private tutors employed a discretionary scale of fees. Pupils from aristocratic or wealthy families were expected to pay above the normal rates while bright but poor students paid 'about one half' the normal rates. See C. A. Bristed, *Five Years in an English University*, 2 Vols (New York, 1852), Vol. I, p. 150.
[90] *Commissioners' Report*, p. 79.

who could pay, the best private tutors eased this problem and provided an important model for a university-wide teaching staff.

A useful contemporary account of the rise of the private tutor during the mid-1820s is provided by William Hopkins (7th Wrangler, 1827), who was not only an undergraduate during this period but went on to become the first private tutor to make a life-long career of pupilising. It was in 1822, following an unsuccessful career in agriculture and the death of his first wife, that Hopkins, already thirty years old, enrolled himself as a student at Peterhouse. Being ineligible for a normal college fellowship – having remarried while an undergraduate – Hopkins settled in Cambridge and made his living as a private tutor.[91] Drawing upon his first-hand experience of undergraduate life in the mid-1820s, Hopkins recalled that the training of a rapidly expanding number of ambitious students and the introduction of continental mathematics had not been accomplished by college lecturers (who, he noted, had singularly failed to rise to the challenge) but by private tutors.[92] Hopkins believed, moreover, that it was precisely the rapid and simultaneous expansion in both student numbers and the content and difficulty of analytical mathematics in undergraduate studies (led by young private tutors and examiners) that had virtually forced the University to increase the number of written papers in the Senate House Examination, and dramatically enhanced the status of private tutors.[93] By the end of the 1820s, he estimated three decades later, 'the effective mathematical teaching of the University was almost as completely, though not perhaps so systematically, in the hands of Private Tutors, as [in 1854]'.[94]

The enormously increased importance of the private tutor by the end of the 1820s is also made visible in a different way by the work of J. M. F. Wright. Having failed to obtain an Honours degree and a fellowship, Wright earned his living as a mathematics teacher in Cambridge, and by producing a series of self-help aids for undergraduate mathematicians. In 1829 he published books on 'self-instruction' in pure arithmetic and 'self-examination' in Euclid's geometry, and, in 1830, he published an edition of Newton's *Principia* which included 'notes, examples, and deductions' covering required aspects of this difficult text.[95] Lastly, and most remarkably, in 1830 he began a weekly journal, *The Private Tutor and Cambridge Mathematical Repository*, which was intended to make

[91] Hopkins also held various University posts for which he was eligible. For biographical details see *DNB*.
[92] Hopkins also recalled that Airy's professorial lectures of 1827–1828 had been useful to those learning the new mathematics.
[93] Charles Pritchard (4th Wrangler, 1830) recalled that his college, St John's, not only encouraged him to work with a private tutor but was prepared, if necessary, to help cover the expense. See Pritchard, *Memoirs*, p. 39.
[94] Hopkins, 'Presidential Address', pp. 6–7. Charles Pritchard (4th Wrangler, 1830) also claimed that by the late 1820s 'the most important parts of the tuition were carried on by private tutors'. See Pritchard, *Memoirs*, p. 38.
[95] J. M. F. Wright, *Self-Instructions in Pure Arithmetic* (London, 1829); *Self-Examination in Euclid* (Cambridge, 1829); *The Private Tutor and Cambridge Mathematical Repository*, 2 vols (Cambridge, 1830).

'the usual aids' of the eponymous private tutor directly available to all undergraduates, especially those unable to afford the fees of an actual tutor. Appearing every Saturday, Wright's journal contained expository essays on the new mathematics, problems for the reader to solve (solutions being given the following week), and detailed accounts of how examinations, both written and oral, were conducted.[96] Students were informed what they might usefully 'write out' to gain speed and accuracy, which mathematical formulae ought to be committed to memory, which treatises contained serious errors (corrections being given), and the questions most commonly sent in by readers were answered in catechetical style. Each issue of the journal was divided into 'four principal compartments', one for each year of undergraduate study, the first three compartments 'comprising every branch of mathematics in order of lectures at Trinity College'. After two years the *Private Tutor* had grown into a complete self-tutor for the undergraduate mathematician circa 1830, and Wright announced he could now bring his 'labours to a satisfactory conclusion'.[97]

That Wright never updated these notes, despite the continued growth of analysis in undergraduate studies, suggests that the majority of students chose to work with a real private tutor, but the two volumes do highlight the importance of private tuition by 1830 and provide some insight into the relationship between private and college teaching circa 1830. The sectional divisions of the *Private Tutor* indicate that college lectures continued to provide a basic framework for ordinary undergraduate study and now included the new analytical subjects. In the second year both the 'd' notation calculus and analytical geometry were major topics of study while, in the third year, students were expected to acquire some knowledge of the calculus of variations, finite differences and celestial mechanics according to Laplace. By this time, however, the training of the most ambitious students was firmly in the hands of tutors who made a substantial living from private teaching, and, Hopkins reveals, by the mid-1830s even students who aspired only to a pass degree had begun to supplement college lectures with private tuition.[98]

Conclusion: Reform and Pedagogical Innovation

The pedagogical focus adopted in this essay casts new light on the analytical revolution which occurred in Cambridge during the second and third decades of the nineteenth century. By focusing both on the individuals who actually taught the new mathematical methods and the teaching techniques that they employed, we can begin to understand how the tacitly accepted syllabus of a

[96] Wright, *Private Tutor*, Vol. I, pp. 145–50.
[97] *Ibid.*, Vol. I, p. 1; Vol. II, p. 406. A typical example of a reader's question is (Vol. I, p. 156) 'What is an imaginary angle, and is its cosine imaginary?' The fourth 'department' was concerned with the solution of problems.
[98] Hopkins reveals that prospective non-Honours students continued to rely on college lectures until the mid-1830s. See Hopkins, 'Presidential Address', p. 7.

conservative institution was able to change so thoroughly over a relatively short period of time. The strongest and most vociferous advocates of reform were, in the main, relatively junior members of the University, and the success of their enterprise relied on the fact that it was they who acted as private tutors and examiners. This is not to say that the reforms could have been accomplished without the tacit agreement of more senior members of the University, and it is in this context that we should understand the gradual relaxation of the rules governing private tutoring. As we have seen, the changes in 1807 and 1815 were almost certainly intended to increase the technical competence in mixed mathematics of the most able undergraduates, while that of 1824 effectively accelerated the university-wide introduction of continental analysis.

A pedagogical approach to mathematical studies in Cambridge also reveals a deeper relationship between rising levels of technical competence in the University circa 1800 and the changing techniques by which mathematics was taught and examined. The analytical revolution was, as we have seen, but one stage, albeit an important one, in developments in undergraduate studies that had been underway since the last quarter of the eighteenth century. During this period, mixed mathematics had slowly marginalised more traditional subjects, to become the most important determinant of an undergraduate's career. Moreover, this relentless rise in technical skill was intimately related to the competitive ethos and the desire to discriminate between the performances of highly trained students. In order to accommodate these goals, the University turned increasingly to written examinations while the students resorted to private tutors.[99] Taken together, these two developments mark an important break with the traditional economy of university education, an economy which had for centuries been based on reading, oral debate and oral disputation.

These observations also suggest a broader historiographical reappraisal of the significance of mathematical study in Cambridge in the decades around 1800. The pursuit of mathematics and the mathematical sciences in the University in the eighteenth century has generally been compared very unfavourably by historians with the contemporary accomplishments of continental mathematicians. The remarkable advances in analysis and mechanics made by men such as Euler, D'Alembert, Lagrange and Laplace do not appear to have been matched by mathematicians in Newton's own university, something which has led some historians of mathematics to conclude that intellectual life in eighteenth-century Cambridge was moribund. Recent studies of British mathematics after Newton have shown that this assessment is incorrect: it was only in the second half of the eighteenth century that British mathematicians, including those in Cambridge, began to fall behind their continental peers, and that, even then, the former made more effort to keep in

[99] The profound importance of the switch from oral to written examination is discussed in A. Warwick, 'A Mathematical World on Paper: Written Examinations in Early 19th-Century Cambridge', in P. Galison and A. Warwick, eds., *Cultures of Theory*, special issue of *Studies in the History and Philosophy of Modern Physics*, Vol. 29b, 3 (1998), pp. 295–319.

touch with continental developments than has generally been supposed.[100] When considered from a pedagogical perspective, both the introduction of technical subjects and the new methods of teaching and assessing them make Cambridge appear more rather than less educationally innovative than the majority of continental universities. It is clear with the benefit of hindsight that tutors in Cambridge were actually leading the way, albeit unwittingly, in developing techniques of technical education which would become commonplace over the next two centuries.

---

[100] Guicciardini, *Development*, pp. 257–60.

CHRISTOPHER STRAY

A Parochial Anomaly: The Classical Tripos 1822–1900

In 1913 a friend of Henry Jackson, then Regius Professor of Greek at Cambridge, wrote to him praising the 'attractive personality' of Gilbert Murray, Jackson's opposite number at Oxford. In his reply, Jackson suggested that:

> Oxford is very successful in breeding 'attractive' scholars: more than Cambridge. And this is not surprising. For we dare not talk our shop in a mixed company, and even in a scholars' party we are very conscious of our limitations as specialists.[1]

Here perhaps, self-confessed, is the parochialism of my title. It seems, indeed, to be a double parochialism, operating at two distinct levels. First, there is the parochialism of specialists, confined to their separate corners. As another Cambridge man, J. C. Stobart, had recently described them, they were 'like miners working underground each in his own shaft, buried far away from sight or earshot of the public, so that they even begin to lose touch with each other'.[2] Stobart was referring to the advanced division of labour in which specialisation operated within, as well as between, academic fields. What made the mutual isolation of the scholarly miners he described so striking, and to him so alarming, was the fact that they were all classicists, excavating in the same field. Second, there is the parochialism of a system that promoted specialisation, in comparison with another – the Oxford system – where classical scholars seemed to be able to join in a more general cultured discourse. Here, then, we have two contrasted institutional styles, of which one is different in a way that disadvantages it in relation to the social and cultural life of the wider society.[3]

---

[1] Henry Jackson to J. A. Platt, 15 August 1913: R. St J. Parry, *Henry Jackson OM: A Memoir* (Cambridge, 1925), pp. 184–5. Jackson was a central figure in the curricular politics of late-Victorian and Edwardian Cambridge. A pioneering reassessment of his work is provided in Robert B. Todd's chapter in Christopher Stray, ed., *The Owl of Minerva* (*Proceedings of the Cambridge Philological Society*, supplementary volume 28), 2002.
[2] *The Glory that was Greece* (London, 1911), p. v.
[3] For an extended discussion, see C. A. Stray, 'Curriculum and Style in the Collegiate University: Classics in Victorian and Edwardian Oxbridge', *History of Universities*, 16: 2, pp. 183–218.

So much for 'parochial': is 'anomaly' then redundant? Perhaps not, for the Cambridge system was historically based not just on specialisation, but on the predominance of some subjects over others. Since the early eighteenth century, mathematics had been the dominant subject in the University, and classics had long lived in its shadow. The ritual and symbolic focus of Cambridge mathematics, the annual crowning of the Senior Wrangler and his bathetic counterpart the Wooden Spoon, had been done away with in 1909, only a few years before Jackson wrote those comments about Oxford and Cambridge.[4] We might say, then, that Cambridge classics was not only parochial in being Cantabrigian and specialist, but also anomalous in being Cantabrigian but not mathematics. Yet by the time the post of Senior Wrangler was abolished, mathematics was no longer dominant in Cambridge in numerical terms.[5] Its recruitment had been overtaken by that of the Natural Sciences Tripos, and a growing number of other courses had become firmly established. To find evidence for the parochial or anomalous status of the Classical Tripos, we need to go back to the previous century.

Before we do so, I should make explicit the analytic perspective employed here. My overall interest is in seeing how fields of knowledge are shaped by the social, political and institutional contexts within which they are constructed, maintained and changed. My introductory remarks have already hinted at some of the relevant contexts. Within Cambridge, the relationship between classics and mathematics is crucial. In a wider context, the comparison with Oxford is important, for three reasons. First, because comparison is always useful in identifying presences and absences. Second, because Oxford constituted Cambridge's significant other – and vice versa. Together they provided a pair of contrasting exemplars for the new university curricula established in Britain and its colonies in the nineteenth century. Oxford was more central to and held a higher profile in English high culture than did Cambridge. Hence my description of Cambridge classics as 'parochial', rather than just different from the Oxonian model. Finally, the comparison is important because it was invoked in Cambridge in debates on curricular change, especially in the 1850s and 1860s. Several aspects of the relationship deserve further investigation. For example: to what extent did each place look to the other in considering change; to what extent was this specific to situations and subjects; and just what were the mechanisms of information and comparison? In Henry Jackson's case, his knowledge of Oxford came largely from membership of the joint dining club called the Ad Eundem, a title taken from the formula with which the two

---

[4] Senior Wrangler: top of the first class in the Mathematical Tripos. Wooden Spoon: bottom of the third class (junior optimes), hence the lowest-ranking student to gain Honours. The title seems to have appeared around 1800; the earliest printed reference I know is in [W. Paley], *Gradus ad Cantabrigiam* (London, 1803), p. 137.

[5] Which do not of course translate directly into prestige ratings. Thus in Oxford the final classical course, Literae Humaniores (Greats), was overtaken in recruitment terms by Modern History in 1898, but continued to be referred to as the University's premier course in the University handbook until the First World War.

universities recognised the validity of each other's degrees.[6] He had been going to its dinners since 1869 and thus had more than forty years' experience of discussions which must often have included a comparison of notes — especially on the two great issues which hung over both places from the 1870s to the early 1920s, the admission of women and the status of compulsory Greek.

Foundation and early years, 1822–57

The Classical Tripos was established in 1822, the first examination taking place two years later. Its foundation seems to have resulted from a confluence of several forces. In the text accompanying his pioneering chart of Oxford and Cambridge matriculations, J. A. Venn wrote that by the eighteenth century

> Oxford had definitely become the home of the humanist, Cambridge already specialised in mathematics. But the mathematical tripos, while conferring a lasting prestige on Cambridge, was no doubt answerable to a considerable extent for the falling off in the number of students entering the University, for non-mathematicians were not only discouraged from presenting themselves, but when in residence often formed a neglected and discontented body.[7]

Venn does not tell us who he was thinking of, nor what evidence he had. But it is clear that a concern to bring classics into some kind of parity with mathematics was among the concerns of John Jebb, who in the early 1770s mounted a campaign to have a new university examination established. Jebb had powerful allies, and several times almost carried his proposals. In the end, however, he fell foul of his own rebarbative personality, the hostility of some members of the then ruling body of the University, the Caput, and the emerging revelation that he was a unitarian.[8] The timing of his campaign might be explained by the fact that a few years previously, in 1765, William Powell, the new master of St John's, had instituted a rigorous system of college examinations. St John's was then the largest college in the University, and known especially for its production of mathematicians; Jebb's campaign may therefore represent a reaction against the dominance of both college and subject (he was himself a fellow of one of the smallest colleges, Peterhouse).[9]

---

[6] The club was founded in the winter of 1864–1865 by the Sidgwick brothers Henry (Cambridge) and William (Oxford). Its first meeting took place in February 1865; it was wound up in 1921. See the correspondence in the Jackson papers, Trinity College Library, Cambridge: Add Mss c 47 10–11,13–14.

[7] J. A. Venn, *Oxford and Cambridge Matriculations 1544–1906 . . . with a chart* (Cambridge, 1908), p. 14.

[8] The Caput, which was abolished in the 1850s, was a group of five senior members of the University who had a power of veto over proposals submitted for discussion in the Senate. On Jebb's campaigns see most recently Peter Searby, *History of the University of Cambridge: Vol. 3, 1750–1870* (Cambridge, 1997), pp. 163–6.

[9] Jebb's campaigns also belonged to a set of theological and ecclesiastical debates made possible by Cambridge's relatively low-church orientation compared to that of Oxford. See

Soon after Jebb's proposals finally failed, Trinity overtook St John's, and by the early nineteenth century was firmly established as the largest college in the University. It drew its students, on average, from higher in the social scale, and had fewer sizars – poor students who had once worked their way to a degree by waiting on their social superiors, but were now in effect given inferior scholarships. Trinity was also noted especially for its classicists, as St John's was for mathematicians. Its increased recruitment can plausibly be related to the expansion of the reformed public schools which began in the 1780s and 1790s with such schools as Rugby and Shrewsbury. The wave of urban middle-class prosperity in this period, on the back of the Industrial Revolution, supported the learning of knowledge which made one – or one's son – a gentleman.[10]

This wave was supported by the cultural reaction to the French revolution, which promoted safe learning at the expense of whatever knowledge might be seen as radical or subversive.[11] Here – to prolong the metaphor – we are swept into difficult waters, for both mathematics and classics were ambiguous. Mathematics might be seen as safely asocial, or as dangerously detached from safe social and religious sentiments. Charles Kelsall, writing in 1814, published a 'barometer' of curricular subjects in which the topmost place was held by arithmetic, which he praised for its utility. At the bottom was what he called 'speculative algebra' – that is, the French analytical mathematics then filtering into Cambridge.[12] Classics, similarly, could be regarded either as safely traditional, or as filled with a range of social and doctrinal utterances, some of which might promote radicalism. The crucial questions, for reformer and reactionary alike, were: what kind of mathematics, or classics? And how were they conveyed to young men?

Such questions must have loomed large in the thinking of Cambridge dons in the years after the defeat of Napoleon. The level of matriculations rose in both universities, especially in Cambridge, which pulled ahead of Oxford around 1819. Numbers continued to rise until the mid-1820s.[13] On the continent, similar increases had given rise to alarms about the 'excess of educated men' – in other words, about the danger of having too many well-educated young men around whose energies were not absorbed in paid employment.[14] Cambridge

---

J. Gascoigne, *Cambridge in the Age of the Enlightenment* (Cambridge, 1987); A. M. C. Waterman, 'A Cambridge "via media" in late Georgian Anglicanism', *Journal of Ecclesiastical History*, 42.3 (1991), pp. 419–36.

[10] C. A. Stray, *Classics Transformed: Schools, Universities, and Society in England, 1830–1960* (Oxford, 1998), pp. 34–8.

[11] See W. R. Ward, *Victorian Oxford* (London, 1965), pp. 13–14.

[12] C. Kelsall, *Phantasm of a University* (London, 1814), pp. 120–1 For French mathematics in Cambridge, see 'The Analytical Society (1812–1813): Precursor of the Renewal of Cambridge Mathematics', *Historia Mathematica*, 10 (1983), pp. 24–47.

[13] This poses a problem for Venn's interpretation of the matriculation figures (see note 4 above).

[14] L. O'Boyle, 'The Problem of an Excess of Educated Men in Western Europe, 1800–1850', *Journal of Modern History*, 42 (1970), pp. 471–91.

was surely not untouched by such alarms. Curiously enough, it was in this same post-Napoleonic period that Cambridge mathematics was invaded by the French analytic mathematical techniques decried by Kelsall. These were introduced by a group of young Trinity fellows, among them Peacock, Airy and Whewell, who included analytic questions in the Tripos when they served as examiners.[15]

In 1820, Christopher Wordsworth was appointed Master of Trinity; he became Vice-Chancellor later the same year. Wordsworth, the brother of the poet, was a conservative high Anglican and a keen classicist. He soon set about planning the introduction of a classical examination, but met with suspicion from other colleges, notably Trinity's great rival St John's. The time was in some ways ripe. Oxford had set up its Honours examinations in 1800, subsequently divided into separate examinations in classics and science in 1807. Trinity was riding high, its numbers growing on the back of the expansion of the public schools. The high rate of matriculations may have dulled the resentment of mathematical dons – there were enough students for everybody. Nevertheless, the shape taken by the new Tripos reflected a series of compromises that reflected resistance from the mathematicians. Wordworth's original plan had been for an examination that would be compulsory for all except the top ten Wranglers. He also hoped that it would include composition in Latin and Greek: the splendidly useless exercise, little practised on the continent, which was the mark of an educated English gentleman. In the event, what emerged was a voluntary examination, excluding Latin and Greek composition, taken after the Mathematical Tripos, and only by men who had obtained Honours in that examination. Ironically, the relevant measure was passed after Wordsworth had served his term as Vice-Chancellor, and probably only succeeded because he deliberately took a back seat in the proceedings. He also received crucial support from James Monk and Charles Kaye. Monk, fellow of Trinity and Regius Professor of Greek, had been campaigning for a classical examination before Wordsworth's arrival. Over twenty years later, Wordsworth remembered that

> Advice . . . from . . . Professor Monk . . . was given very usefully and very generously, and very encouragingly. Indeed my obligation to him during all that period (you know probably he had been looked upon as the person most likely to succeed to the Mastership) I can never forget . . .[16]

Kaye, then Master of Christ's, took over Wordsworth's proposal and by watering it down managed to get it through the Senate. He himself had selflessly refused to apply for the Greek chair once Monk had announced his candidacy.[17]

---

[15] On the introduction of French analytic mathematics to Cambridge, see Enros, 'Analytical Society'.
[16] C. Wordsworth to W. Whewell, 16 July 1845; Trinity College Library, Add MS a 78/34. Quoted by permission of the Master and Fellows of Trinity College.
[17] Kaye and Monk had earlier worked together on the Porsonian journal *Museum Criticum, or Cambridge Classical Researches*, which first appeared in 1813.

The urbane Winstanley reports that some mean-minded dons thought Wordsworth was conducting a Trinity campaign in founding the Tripos.[18] One would not need to be very mean-minded to suspect that. What Wordsworth thought was good for the University was certainly especially good for the leading classical college. In his letter to Whewell, Wordsworth wrote that 'The cry from some was that a fatal blow was aimed at the peculiar honour and glory of the University, Mathematics. Others there were, who saw clearly it was a scheme intended, or if not intended, most certainly calculated, to add frightfully to the number of Honours which already fell abundantly to the share of Trinity College.'[19] As so often, curricular issues were entangled with college rivalries. Writing to his brother William at the time, Wordsworth had reported that his proposal had been

> voted on in the Senate and met with a powerful and highly respectable support but principally by the opposition of the Johnians (Wood was not in the University) it was thrown out by a considerable majority.[20]

A more complicated question, which has not to my knowledge been considered, is whether the promotion of French analytic mathematics within Trinity played any part in all this; in other words, whether Wordsworth may have been reacting against a particular style of mathematics – algebraic, involving unknown quantities – rather than against the domination of mathematics as such.[21]

The new Tripos began life with small numbers. Seventeen men obtained Honours in the first examination, of the sixty-six who had just come through the Mathematical Tripos. In the next twenty-five years the numbers of successful candidates increased rather slowly, settling at around thirty a year (by contrast the mathematics numbers were often in excess of 150). The subject matter of the examination was as constricted as the numbers. After the continental blockade was lifted in 1816, the expanding published output of German classical scholarship poured into Britain. The new comparative philology of the 1820s and 1830s laid foundations for a study of language in which Latin and Greek could be illuminated by comparison with Sanskrit. The Classical Tripos, however, showed little evidence of these advances. In the 1820s two young fellows of Trinity, Julius Hare and Connop Thirlwall, who had both mastered German, were keen to spread the gospel of *Altertumswissenschaft*, and in the early 1830s they founded a journal, the *Philological Museum*, to propagate it. It sold

---

[18] D. A. Winstanley, *Early Victorian Cambridge* (Cambridge, 1955), p. 67. Winstanley was a fellow of Trinity 1903–47 and Vice-Master 1935–1947. His four books on the history of the University in the eighteenth and nineteenth centuries are still important sources.
[19] Letter cited in note 15 above.
[20] Letter to William Wordsworth, 5th August 1821. William Wordsworth papers, Dove Cottage. James Wood was then Master of St John's.
[21] That this question has not been raised reflects the lack of work on the interaction of disciplines with institutional contexts, as opposed to studies of their separate development.

poorly, and collapsed when they left Cambridge – Hare to a rich family living, Thirlwall when Wordsworth expelled him for criticising the institution of compulsory chapel.[22]

The mathematics bar must have taken a considerable toll on those classical students who could not cram their way to a place in the Junior Optimes (the lowest class of mathematical Honours). In 1814 Kelsall had identified this nexus of minimal mathematical attainment with literary talent in his reference to 'that splendid badge of literary distinction, the wooden spoon'.[23] The encounters of classicists with the mathematics bar can be illustrated by the experiences of three Trinity undergraduates. Richard Shilleto, one of the best-known Cambridge scholars in the narrowly linguistic Porsonian style, was Wooden Spoon in 1832. In the Latin disputations which preceded the written examination, he discomfited a Johnian opponent by stating the well-worn theme 'Is suicide justifiable?' 'Quid est suicidium' he asked, 'nisi suum caesio?' (What is suicide but the slaughter of pigs?) Shilleto was at Trinity College and his opponent belonged to St John's, whose members were commonly nicknamed 'hogs'. The Johnian's Latin was poor, so he opposed Shilleto's argument only with difficulty, and without seeing the joke. The moderator, however, did understand, and shared it.[24] A younger Trinity undergraduate, Thomas Evans, who went on to teach at Shrewsbury, and later became professor of Greek at Durham, failed completely at mathematics. Evans was agreed to be one of the half-dozen best composers of Greek and Latin in Victorian England. While still at Cambridge in the late 1830s, he took his revenge on the mathematicians by publishing a poem in Greek called *Mathematogonia, or the Mythological Birth of the Nymph Mathesis*, in which he poured elegant scorn on the curriculum that had blocked his path. His poem, loosely based on Hesiod's *Theogony*, tells of the fashioning of Mathematics from the triangle and other figures by Hephaestus at Zeus's command. It is borne by the Furies first to the Nile delta ('a country which is triangular') and eventually to the banks of the Cam. Here it is set down 'to generate disputes and sharp provocations to madden [the inhabitants'] minds . . . a Death destroying everything, a second Sphinx, one born to compose inscrutable riddles and generate havoc among mortal kin'.[25] Montagu Butler entered Trinity, whose Master he later became, in 1852. On 6 March 1853 he reported to his father 'I am reading Maths pretty hard with my "coach"'. On 17 December the following year, however, he confessed his error 'in not taking maths seriously at the start. It was intellectual (and therefore moral) cowardice'. On the night of 4–5 January 1855, just before his final examination, he had 'a

---

[22] Winstanley, *Early Victorian Cambridge*, pp. 75–8.
[23] Kelsall, *Phantasm*, p. 31. On the Wooden Spoon, see note 3 above. Kelsall himself had left Cambridge in 1803 without taking a degree: see D. Watkin 'Charles Kelsall', in C. S. Nicholls, ed., *Dictionary of National Biography: Missing persons* (Oxford, 1993), pp. 371–2.
[24] W. W. Rouse Ball, *History of the Study of Mathematics at Cambridge*, pp. 173–81.
[25] *Mathematogonia, or, the Mythological Birth of the Nymph Mathesis* (Cambridge: W. P. Grant, 1839). (Translation kindly provided by Christopher Collard.)

ghastly dream . . . of real geometrical figures . . . . . . the shattered bodies of Trinity classicists among the Junior Optimes'.[26]

Autonomy and Competition: The Tripos 1857–79

The next phase in the history of the Tripos began in 1854 when the mathematical restrictions on entry were dropped; the change took effect in 1857. At the same time new triposes were founded in moral and in natural sciences.[27] Although the new courses attracted few students for some time, the pattern of the curriculum had been changed. In the next twenty-five years, numbers rose into the sixties—about half those of the Mathematical Tripos. The content of the exam, however, was very little changed. In 1849 an ancient history paper had been added, but seems not to have been taken very seriously by candidates.[28] A vigorous debate on reform began only with the death of William Whewell early in 1866. Whewell, who had become increasingly conservative in his curricular opinions, was succeeded as master of Trinity by William Hepworth Thompson, a classicist who was prepared to countenance change. Only a few weeks after Whewell's death, William Clark and Robert Burn, two fellows of Trinity, circulated proposals for the inclusion of substantial history and philosophy papers in the Tripos. Their plan prompted a flurry of flysheets that between them give a useful picture of contemporary Cambridge opinion.[29] Several authors pointed to the example of Oxford, either as a model to follow, or as a foreign body to be avoided. For the conservatives, the incorporation of history and philosophy meant degrading the curriculum by including the learning of facts, rather than training in linguistic analysis. Ancient history, averred one author, was alien to classics as practised in Cambridge. A friend of Clark's, Alfred Barry, then headmaster of Cheltenham College, wrote to him to warn of the distorting effect of Latin and Greek composition, which now bulked large in the examination. Barry, who was an experienced and thoughtful teacher, was not happy with the equation of excellence with compositional skill, having known boys who excelled in other areas of classics.[30] The problem was that great emphasis was placed on composition papers, and it was generally assumed that a first class could not be gained if one did not do well in them. This complaint was to grow louder over the next twenty years; in the next year, 1867, it was uttered with his usual rhetorical overkill by Frederic Farrar in his chapter in *Essays on a Liberal Education*.[31]

It was certainly true that a Cambridge style existed: to conflate contemporary descriptions, it was masculine, narrow and hardheaded. Its focus was on the

---

[26] J. R. M. Butler papers, Trinity College Library, M/3/1/235, 281, 285.
[27] On the Moral Sciences Tripos, see Gibbins' chapter.
[28] See Beard's chapter for the development of ancient history.
[29] A set of these flysheets is preserved in the papers of Robert Burn in Trinity College Library.
[30] A. Barry to W. G. Clark, 9 May 1866, Trinity College Library Add. MS c. 176/1.
[31] F. W Farrar, ed., *Essays on a Liberal Education* (London, 1867).

mastery of intricate details of language; questions of historical context, and even of literary worth, took second place in what was commonly known as 'pure scholarship'. As Henry Jackson said in decrying it in 1877, 'What . . . "pure scholarship" meant was this. [Undergraduates] read Thucydides, but not Grote; they studied the construction of the speeches, but did not confuse themselves with trying to study their drift. They read the Phaedrus, but had no Theory of Ideas. . . .'[32] This was a kind of scholarship that scorned the Oxford practice of studying set books. It was nicely summarised in an article on Cambridge in an American journal in 1860: 'knowledge, not of books, but of the language which includes all the books'.[33] The Cantabrigian classicist should be able to translate any text placed before him, rather than getting off a few specified texts by heart. He should be able to 'translate through a brick wall', to use the phrase of Percy Gardner, a classicist who had experience of both places:

> The system of Shillito [sic] and other noted teachers of classics was to lay all the stress on words, and to neglect the subject matter of the ancient writers. Exact scholarship was the one thing they aimed at. They liked to see a man, as they put it, translate through a brick wall, turn classical phrases into elegant English, and English prose into readable Greek and Latin, without troubling oneself what was the full bearing of the passage.[34]

I suggest that in this high-risk, problem-oriented ideology of knowledge we can see the influence of Cambridge mathematics. Certainly the mindset promoted by the Mathematics Tripos was visible in the writing of Cambridge men. In 1847, the Eton master William Johnson (later Cory) recalled a recent visit he had had from his friend Henry Maine: 'He and I went through several hard subjects in the old Cambridge way, in that method of minute comparison of opinions without argument which I believe to be peculiar to the small intellectual aristocracy of Cambridge.'[35] This is an interesting passage, and not just because it contains the earliest use of the phrase 'intellectual aristocracy'. Johnson was referring in particular to the discussions of the Apostles, but one can see in it a characterisation of a Cambridge style, which in its marginalising of 'argument', contrasts sharply with the logic-chopping of Oxford.

In the early days of the new multi-Tripos curriculum, several bold spirits attempted several of them. Henry Gwatkin of St John's gained four first classes. It was said that he would have secured a fifth first, had the science and theology examinations not been held at the same time.[36] Such feats became more difficult

---

[32] Quoted by Winstanley, *Later Victorian Cambridge* (Cambridge, 1947), p. 211. For the context, see C. A. Stray, '"Thucydides or Grote?" Classical Disputes and Disputed Classics in Nineteenth-Century Cambridge', *Transactions of the American Philological Association*, 127 (1997), pp. 363–71.
[33] *The Undergraduate* 1.1, p. 56.
[34] Percy Gardner, *Autobiographica* (Oxford, 1933), p. 13. Gardner went up to Cambridge in 1865.
[35] F. W. Cornish, ed., *Extracts from the Letters and Journals of William Cory* (Oxford, 1897), p. 46.
[36] A similar feat was performed by Fenton Hort of Trinity.

as new material was added to examinations. In the 1870s, a radical solution was found: the division of triposes into two parts. This was established practice in the Mathematical Tripos. Its extension throughout the curriculum was proposed in response to a memorial from the Headmasters' Conference, whose members argued that the increasing weight of material in mathematics and classics meant that men could not realistically read both. To avoid excessive specialisation, the headmasters proposed making divided triposes universal, so that one could read Part I of one subject, then change to another for Part II. The reform was agreed in 1879 and came into effect in the early 1880s.

With this reform the Tripos expanded its range and changed its shape. The history and philosophy which had already been incorporated in a small way now had their own sections in Part II. So did comparative philology, which could call on the services of the Professor of Sanskrit (the chair had been established in 1867). Traditional scholarship was represented in the Literature section – so called, though some claimed it was simply text criticism. More surprising was the inclusion of a section on classical archaeology, though this included a hefty dose of art. The new section was taught by Charles Waldstein, a German-American Jew and the first teacher for the Tripos not to be a Cambridge man.

The third leg: The Tripos after 1879

This new structure was dictated in outline by the University-wide change to divided triposes. But much of the detail must have been hammered out in committee meetings, and to these we have no access. All we can do is to read back from the results to what went on in smoke-filled rooms. Several conclusions can be drawn.[37] First, the two-part structure made possible a compromise between traditional liberal education, conceived in classics as a linguistic soaking in ancient texts, sharpened by composition, and the newer research-oriented ideology which favoured the specialised study of subject matter. Second, the basis of the compromise was that the new Part I course, which enshrined the traditional style, gave access to a degree. Here lay the Achilles' heel of the reform: for in the next twenty-five years, while overall numbers climbed to around 150, almost all of those students sat Part I, and then left Cambridge or changed to another Tripos. Soon after the reformed Tripos got under way, James Headlam of Kings College, himself an undergraduate reading classics, commented on it as follows:

> The Classical Tripos more than any other is marred by a difficulty which is the great hindrance to really satisfactory educational work. It has to meet the requirements of two quite different classes of students[.] On the one hand there are those undergraduates who are of sufficient intelligence and ambition not to remain satisfied with the ordinary

[37] Compare Beard's discussion in her chapter.

degree, but have no great love for learning or turn to any particular branch of it. These are the men who are referred to by those who tell us that the Universities exist for the purpose of giving a good Education such as to train men to be 'English Gentlemen'. . . . On the other hand, we find a considerable number of men every year who really merit the name of Scholar . . .

He goes on to emphasise that he does not 'undervalue the use of the carefulness and accuracy of verbal criticism and composition; for those who can bear it is good. But it is food not for babes but for strong men, and . . . the majority of the candidates for the Classical Tripos are not strong men.'[38]

To make sense of these comments, we have to remember that the verbal criticism and composition Headlam identifies as food only for strong men was dominant in Part I: which was exactly what the babes would focus on, as they headed for a degree after two years' study. These babes would become 'English gentlemen', and they came largely from the public schools. In the great surge of state intervention in education between 1850 and 1870, these schools had been investigated by Royal Commissions, just as the ancient universities had been: but they had been let off more lightly. The Clarendon Commission, which dealt with the nine leading public schools in the early 1860s, had ended by proposing that their curriculum should incorporate new subjects; but the proposed new pattern allowed classics three-fifths of the total time. In fact, the Commission was more concerned with financial management, especially in Eton, than with the curriculum; and the schools largely carried on as before. Each year they sent up dozens of young men to Cambridge, trained in translation from and composition in Latin and Greek, who went through Part I – more of the same – then took their degree and left. This was, then, a classic case of university reforms being subverted at the level of secondary education.[39]

As for Part II, it plodded on with small numbers – perhaps ten percent of the Part I totals – some sections having no candidates at all in some years.[40] Here too the scars of political compromise can be seen. The Literature section, which represented the toehold of traditional Cambridge scholarship in the new specialised Part II, was unlike the other four sections in that it was compulsory. This was presumably one reason why some students did not go on to Part II. Not until 1895 was this restriction lifted. By that time, the resident classical teachers had been sent a questionnaire by the Special Board for Classics on the state of the Tripos, and the overwhelming consensus was that Part II was a

[38] J. W. Headlam, MS in author's possession, nd but c. 1885.
[39] On the Clarendon Commission, see C. Shrosbree, *Public Schools and Private Education: the Clarendon Commission, 1861–4, and the Public School Acts* (Manchester, 1988); on classics in the schools, see Stray, *Classics Transformed*, pp. 167–201.
[40] For a more detailed account, see C. A. Stray, 'Renegotiating Classics: The Politics of Curricular Reform in Later Victorian Cambridge', *Echos du Monde Classique/Classical Views*, 42, ns 17 (1998), pp. 449–70.

failure. This gloomy conclusion provoked a round of reform attempts, including a proposal to split the Tripos into three parts, all of which failed. Effective reform came only after the First World War, when the aged Henry Jackson secured the removal of degree status from Part I.

The war constituted a sharp dividing line in several areas: but not in the campaign to give women full membership of the University, for which they had to wait till after another world war. Yet in the last quarter of the nineteenth century, the entry of women students to the picture had added a whole new dimension to the history of the Classical Tripos. It challenged preconceptions, threw assumptions into relief and provoked debates that offer the historian a glimpse of shadowy areas. In the 1870s, small numbers of women students had their college teaching supplemented by a group of liberal dons, who later examined them at degree level. The reforms that divided the Tripos also provided for the publication of women's degree results: not integrated with the men's results, but alongside them. It was easy enough to conflate the two lists and make comparisons, and the inevitable triumph came in 1887, when Agnata Ramsay's name stood alone in the first division of the first class in the women's list, and the corresponding part of the men's list was blank. The triumph was all the more striking since this was the Part I list: in other words, it recorded performance in the traditional linguistic stronghold of male scholarship. For the most part, women students struggled through Part I, before going on to Part II and raising their marks in the non-literary sections. Their absolute numbers were very small; but in relative terms it is noticeable how much more likely they were to go on to Part II. In the 1880s and 1890s, the percentage of men doing so declined, from 15 to 7.5 percent, while the percentage of women doubled, from 10 to 20 percent.[41] Given the paucity of Part II candidates, their presence in the lists will have been noticeable: in 1900, for example, eight male and three female candidates secured Honours.

The vain attempts of the 1890s to secure effective reform of the Tripos were witnessed by a young Trinity undergraduate who was elected to a fellowship in his college in 1899. This was Francis Cornford, a pupil of Henry Jackson who in 1931 became the first holder of the chair of ancient philosophy. As an undergraduate editor of the *Cambridge Review* and then as a young fellow, Cornford became familiar with the intricacies of academic politics. In 1903 he published a pamphlet on the Tripos, pointedly subtitled 'an essay in anticipation of further reform'.[42] What brought him lasting fame outside classical circles, though, was the little book which appeared five years later: *Microcosmographia Academica, being a Guide to the Young Academic Politician*.[43]

---

[41] For detailed figures see C. Breay, 'Women and the Classical Tripos 1869–1914', in Stray, *Classics in Cambridge*, pp. 49–70.
[42] F. M. Cornford, *The Cambridge Classical Course: an Essay in Anticipation of Further Reform* (Cambridge, 1903).
[43] This is best read in Gordon Johnson's book, *University Politics. F. M. Cornford's Cambridge and his Advice to the Young Academic Politician* (Cambridge, 1994), which reprints Cornford's text and sets it in its historical context.

Some of Cornford's coinages – the principles of the Wedge and of Unripe Time, for example – are now well known, and often quoted. What I want to stress here is that the dismal record of failed reform attempts in classics must have formed a central part of the experience on which he drew to write *Microcosmographia*. And this is germane to the topic I mentioned above: the shaping of knowledge fields by institutional politics. In the second half of the nineteenth century, we can see academic subjects gradually taking shape in a recognisably modern way. They acquired their boards of studies; the beginnings of a hierarchy of posts, with the lecturerships and readerships established from 1883;[44] scholarly journals; and so on. The intercollegiate teaching pioneered in Trinity from the late 1860s began the shift of emphasis from college to university in lecturing provision. Yet the process was slow and uneven. It was hampered in the later decades of the century by shortage of money. Two Royal Commissions had diverted college funds to the University, but the rural rents on which the colleges largely relied fell during the agricultural depression of the 1870s and 1880s.[45] Doubtless also there were college rivalries that delayed the growth of intercollegiate teaching – one of the subjects of Cornford's 1903 essay. We should remember, too, just how late some things appeared whose existence we now take for granted. Cambridge had no chair of Latin till 1869; of ancient history till 1898; of ancient philosophy or comparative philology till 1931. The Faculty of Classics itself dates only from the mid-1920s; its secretary's filing system in the early 1950s consisted of little more than a shoebox full of cards.

The point I am making is a simple one: at any historical moment, the state of an institutional formation like Cambridge classics resembles a geological site, containing a wide range of strata. Unlike such a site, however, it is a dynamic system. Its dynamics are inherently political: they involve debate on the allocation of scarce resources, debate in which vested interests and opinions collide. Furthermore, earlier strata are consciously invoked as competing ideal images of the institution and its parts are brought into play. Throughout the period I have been considering, such debates were tied into the University's system of decision-making in such a way that reform initiatives advanced within the body of classical teachers were often defeated at the university level. This prompts the question: To what extent do particular subject fields act as symbolic identifiers of institutions? In Cambridge, mathematics was for much of the nineteenth century not just something studied in Cambridge, but the subject that defined what Cambridge was about. In Oxford, on the other hand, it was classics, in the form especially of Greats, which played this role. And that

---

[44] In classics, for example, J. S. Reid was made Lecturer in Ancient History; in 1899 he was elected to the newly-founded chair in the subject.
[45] In addition, while some small colleges grew in the second half of the century, St John's suffered a decline in numbers which left it short of money. See Underwood's chapter for a discussion of the St John's case.

is the basis for seeing Cambridge classics, in both local and wider contexts, as a parochial anomaly.[46]

On the other hand, if we compare the two versions of classics in relation to the process of academic specialisation which has been going on for over a century now, we might come to a different conclusion. The new Part II set up here in 1879 enshrined two principles: specialisation and choice. The second principle was being hailed at much the same time in the USA, where the elective system was spreading rapidly. By 1900 even conservative strongholds such as Princeton had succumbed. Neither principle, however, was applied in a pure form. The case of the Literature section (compulsory from 1882 to 1894) has already been mentioned; and the number of sections one could choose was progressively limited. Nevertheless the principles were there. The onward march of the division of labour spread from Cambridge to the new civic universities, where separate degrees in Latin and Greek became common. In Oxford, on the other hand, this movement was resisted. The Greats pattern was one of integration rather than specialisation: no wonder Greats has been described (by a Cambridge classicist) as a white elephant.[47]

I have argued that Cambridge classics in the nineteenth century was a strange beast. It was reared in the shadow of a powerful institutional tradition of mathematics, and after shaking off its influence, staggered from one political compromise to another in its development as a modern academic formation. It was hampered by being part of a larger institution. The classics course led to a degree awarded by the University, and both the content and organisation of the course were subject to debate and decision at university level. It also suffered from the nature of its intake – the cohorts of public schoolboys who came up armed with skills in translation and composition and looked for more of the same. Here, as was emphasised above, the degree-giving status of Part I played a crucial part. I have called it an Achilles heel; taking the influx of students into account, one might think of it rather as a Trojan Horse. To understand Cambridge classics, one needs to understand its relation to other subjects, especially mathematics; to the context of decision-making in the University; to the schools that supplied candidates; and finally, to Oxford, which provided not only an alternative destination for students, but also an alternative model of what classics might be.

---

[46] For comparisons of Oxford and Cambridge classics, see O. Murray's review of Stray, *Classics Transformed*, *Classical Review* ns 50.1 (2000), pp. 256–9; Stray, 'Curriculum and style . . .'.

[47] For Oxford classics, see the chapters by R. Jenkyns and O. Murray in vols 6 and 7 of the *History of the University of Oxford*, eds. M. Brock and M. Curthoys, 1998–2000. The white elephant was identified by Mary Beard in her 'The Invention (and Reinvention) of "Group D": An Archaeology of the Classical Tripos, 1879–1984', in Stray, *Classics in Cambridge*, pp. 95–134, at p. 133.

JOHN WILKES

'A mist of prejudice': The Reluctant Acceptance of Modern History at Cambridge, 1845–1873

The teaching of modern history at Cambridge dates from 1724,[1] when Bishop Edmund Gibson persuaded George I to endow Regius professorships there and at Oxford, in order to train men for the Diplomatic Service. Although the scheme itself rapidly withered away, successive sovereigns continued to appoint professors, on the 'advice' of the prime minister of the day. Some incumbents made a serious attempt to provide a worthwhile course of lectures during the three months in which they were required to reside: others were less conscientious. By the 1840s, when the University reform movement was under way, both professorships were seen as minor items of prime ministerial patronage rather than seats of scholarship. Furthermore, the Cambridge chair was vacant in all but name. The aged William Smyth had ceased to lecture in about 1840, after thirty-three years in office. Once a considerable scholar, his failure to update his lectures in later years (not to mention a style of dress some sixty years out of date) had made him almost a laughing stock among later generations of undergraduates.[2]

It was not their fault that the unreformed Regius professors, taken as a group, contributed so little to education at both universities. They were 'outsiders', expected to reside only during the term in which they lectured and not particularly welcome if they stayed on. They had neither an ex-officio attachment to a college nor any opportunity to influence university decision-making. Most important of all, they were obliged to conduct their business in the face of a deeply-held feeling within the University that they were superfluous, since modern history was not a fit subject for the education of undergraduates. Many residents considered that the subject lacked the necessary characteristics to be an effective vehicle for liberal education; that it could not be examined fairly or at an appropriate level for university studies, and that its inextricable links with

---

[1] Fulke Greville Lord Brooke established 'A Publique Lecture of Historie' in 1627. It did not survive the English Civil War. See J. P. C. Roach, *A History of the County of Cambridge and the Isle of Ely*, Vol. 3 (1959) (Victoria County Histories series, 1959), p. 207.
[2] Smyth (1765–1849) had been appointed in 1807: see *DNB*. Peter Searby, *A History of the University of Cambridge, Vol. 3, 1750–1870* (Cambridge, 1997), pp. 236–42.

contemporary politics and religion would give rise to endless discord. This paper examines some of the changes in intellectual climate and material practices at Cambridge that permitted modern history to emerge as a single-subject degree course during the 1870s.

The collection of convenient prejudices called the 'theory of a liberal education' that had come to dominate Cambridge thinking during the first half of the nineteenth century held that an undergraduate course of studies should cultivate a high, disinterested moral tone (both for its own sake and as a worthy counterbalance in itself to the materialistic tendencies of the age) and at the same time develop the student's intellect through the solving of difficult abstract problems. The 'theory' rested on the taken-for-granted psychological assertion that mental exercise trains the mind as physical exercise improves the body. The trained mind would become, as it were, a sort of mental steam engine, capable of powering its way through any kind of problem. Just as Mr Brunel's locomotives could whisk any cargo from London to Bristol with effortless ease, so the First-Class man could address himself to moral theology, prison reform or the government of India with equal facility. C. A. Bristed, a close observer, noted that Cambridge 'does not propose to itself as its primary objective *the giving of information*, but rather the developing and training of the mind, so that it may receive, arrange, retain and use to the best advantage, such information as may be afterwards desirable or necessary'.[3]

Residents were equally convinced that the University already possessed the most effective means of converting theory to practice in the long-established subjects of mathematics and classics, the latter considered primarily as philology rather than literature. Abstract, disinterested, demanding (and thereby morally improving), they were the best available exercise machines for the intellectual gym. There was no need for anything more. *The Fourth School*, an anonymous Oxford flysheet of 1849, enquired rhetorically whether the study of modern history was 'as good an exercise of the mind, with a view to the cultivation and improvement of its powers, as the existing and usual studies of this place?'[4] The implied answer was clear. *Fraser's Magazine* (1845), attempting to support history, did precisely the opposite, so far as the dons were concerned, when it asked why should not 'the gentle constraint of authority . . . conduct the student into a path which requires only to be trodden to be enjoyed?'[5] Subjects were not

---

[3] C. A. Bristed, *Five Years in an English University* (London, 3rd edn., 1874), p. 386. Author's italics. Bristed's account of Cambridge in the 1840s, written from the standpoint of a cultivated New Yorker, is full of fascinating detail. Thorold Rogers made the same point, albeit with a sting in the tail, when he said that a liberal education, '. . . does not so much aim at getting the mind right on particular points, as on getting the mind into the way of being right. It does not deal with matter, but the method. . . . Hence, were it perfect, it would cultivate the intelligence so largely as to render easy the acquisition of any knowledge.' *Education in Oxford* (London, 1861), p. 2.
[4] Anonymous, *The Fourth School* (1849), Oxford University Archives G A Oxon c65 (179).
[5] Anonymous, 'Cambridge Studies', *Fraser's Magazine* (December, 1845), p. 673.

there to be enjoyed. The aim was to endure and subdue, preferably after taxing bouts of manly mental combat.[6]

History was also exposed to a different line of attack. William Whewell was the most thorough expositor of conventional educational thinking at Cambridge. In successive versions of his *Of a Liberal Education* (1837–1852), Whewell distinguished between 'permanent' and 'progressive' studies. Permanent studies were 'those portions of knowledge which have long taken their permanent shape; – ancient languages with their literature, and long-established demonstrated sciences'. Progressive studies were 'the results of the mental activity of our own times; the literature of our own age, and the sciences in which men are making progress from day to day'.[7] Progressive studies were necessarily in flux, and therefore objectionable. Whewell considered that university teaching could appeal to either 'a spirit of respect', or a 'spirit of criticism'. The former required students to familiarise themselves with 'undoubted truths' and 'works of unquestioned excellence'. The spirit of criticism required the student to enquire for himself. As the 1837 edition made clear

> . . . the respectful system appears to me to be the proper line of education. . . . the student ought to have placed before him, something which is of a stable and permanent kind; – in which it is a good mental exercise to struggle with the apparent objections because it is certain that by effort and practice they may be overcome; – and in which it has been ascertained that admiration is not the result of novelty, or of some transient bearing upon the feelings of the the age. . . . The critical system seems to me to be properly addressed, not to students who are undergoing education but to philosophers who have already been completely educated.[8]

The critical system accustomed men to deliver superficial and hasty judgements, which had no place in English education and might even be subversive. Such students were educated to become judges of philosophical systems. Whewell observed – with his usual bleak irony – that this was 'an office which few Englishmen will ever have to fill'. Controversy was both inconvenient and inimical to the aims of education as Whewell saw them. Undergraduate education ought to consist only of 'right' answers. Unfortunately, modern history was full of controversy.

[6] The psychological foundations for these assertions do not appear to have been challenged at the time, partly because no countervailing body of psychological theory existed, still more because the idea of intellectual development through mental exercise accorded well with the social psychology of the time: particularly the concept of 'manliness' as successful struggle against temptation. It followed that teaching materials should be selected primarily as suitable for mental exercise, grist for the mill, as it were. Bristed observed that 'the University has decided . . . that classical and mathematical studies are the best means, and it undertakes to teach them thoroughly.' See Bristed, *Five Years*, p. 386.
[7] William Whewell, *Of a Liberal Education in General; and with Particular Reference to the Leading Studies of the University of Cambridge* (Cambridge, 1845), pp. 5, 5–6.
[8] William Whewell, *On the Principles of English University Education* (Cambridge, 1837), pp. 50–51.

The notion of 'right answers' was also crucial in quite a different way. Examination candidates in maths and classics were assessed according to closely defined criteria that all the players; students, colleges and private coaches understood. Unpredictability of any kind was the last thing anyone wanted when an entire career might hang on the result of a single examination. As the memorialist of the mathematics coach Edward John Routh pointed out, independence on the part of a student 'was not encouraged; for independence would rarely, if ever, be justified by the event'.[9] The problem was that no one could devise a standardised marking scheme for any topic in modern history worth discussing. While a low-level factual error in history could be marked down rather like an arithmetical error or a faulty Greek accent, how could anyone judge historical opinions? If no question could go much beyond factual recall, the standard of learning must remain below that which any university could tolerate.

For many centuries the University had based its examination on set texts, specified by statute. Since no such texts existed for Modern History, how could students be coached or examinations conducted fairly? As a contributor to the parallel Oxford debate pointed out: 'Is it, in fact, easy or even practicable to test fairly in it the proficiency of the Candidate? Where is the standard-author, like Thucydides?'[10] The debate often crossed the border between educational theory and politics. The Rev. H. M. Wilkins, commenting on the Oxford University Commission Report in *Blackwood's Edinburgh Magazine* (1853), accused the Commissioners of setting aside '. . . the cardinal principle which distinguishes the English from foreign universities – the principle that instruction should be conveyed by lecturing on standard authorities, instead of abandoning students to the ambitious novelties of theorists'.[11] An anonymous contribution to *The Times* in 1849 asked whether a school of modern history at Oxford was desirable 'without any provision being made for the particular books to be read, or against a superficial and inaccurate mode of study to which this subject is so peculiarly open?'[12]

The lawyer Charles Marriott combined two objections in one during the debate on the Oxford School of Law and History in 1850 when he 'feared the introduction of party spirit, and wished for better textbooks'.[13] Commentators worried that appointments to history teaching posts would be made on a partisan basis and that tutors so appointed would attempt to brainwash the students or even penalise those whose political or religious views differed from their own. It is a commonplace that a candidate's religious and political views

---

[9] A. R. Forsyth, 'Edward John Routh', *Proc. London Mathematical Society* ser. 2 v (July 5, 1907), p. xvi qu. Sheldon Rothblatt, *The Revolution of the Dons* (London, 1964), p. 203.
[10] Anonymous, *The Fourth School* (1849), Oxford University Archives G A Oxon c65 (179).
[11] H. M. Wilkins, 'The Oxford University Commission Report', *Blackwood's Edinburgh Magazine* LXXIII (1853), p. 226.
[12] Anonymous, *Hints to Members of Congregation III* (Oxford, 1849).
[13] *The Times*, 8 December 1849, p. 5.

counted for more than his professional skills in the appointment to chairs and other posts at Cambridge and Oxford. In appointments to such subjects as modern history it was thought that politics would be all. Any professor so elected was bound to use his position for political indoctrination. It is significant that vice-chancellor Philip Wynter's letter to the Duke of Wellington, on the merits of John Ormerod of Brasenose College as candidate for the Oxford Regius chair, focused on something other than Ormerod's considerable historical and linguistic skills:

> In many respects I should consider his [Ormerod's] appointment as good a one perhaps as could be made. But . . . his political opinions are understood to be Whig . . . the late Dr Arnold's appointment was a good one and his lectures showed vast powers of mind and immense knowledge. But I confess I always had some anxiety as to the effect which they might ultimately produce among the young men. Whenever he had an opportunity he availed himself of it to extenuate . . . the acts of those who are recorded in History as adverse to what I venture to believe your Grace would consider sound constitutional principles both in Church and State.[14]

The fear of ecclesiastical subversion was equally real. Oxford's sectarian factions were more virulent and powerful than at Cambridge. E. B. Pusey, admittedly an extremist even in his own time, nevertheless represented the views of devout churchmen at both universities in his contribution to the Hebdomadal Board's critical commentary on the Oxford University Commissioners Report. He alleged that the Commissioners 'hope to allure the students off from controversy by the presence of scientific men and by brilliant lectures in Modern History or Physical Science, (as if modern history were not especially fraught with controversy, so that it can scarcely escape it except by ignoring religion)'.[15]

Adam Sedgwick, the Cambridge geologist, was an enthusiastic private reader of modern history. 'History is to our knowledge of man in his social capacity, what physical experiments are to our knowledge of the laws of nature.' Nevertheless, he advocated that ancient rather than modern history should be in the undergraduate curriculum, as being 'undistorted by that mist of prejudice with which every modern political question is surrounded'.[16] Whewell himself

---

[14] Philip Wynter to the first Duke of Wellington (1842) British Library, Add. MS 40459 f. 251 qu. E. G. W. Bill, *University Reform in Nineteenth-Century Oxford: a Study of Henry Halford Vaughan* (Oxford, 1973), p. 61.

[15] Oxford University Hebdomadal Board, *Report and Evidence upon the Recommendations of H. M. Commissioners for Inquiry into the State of the University of Oxford* (Oxford, 1853), *Evidence* pp. 307–8.

[16] Adam Sedgwick, *A Discourse on the Studies of the University* (1833), eds. E. Ashby and M. Anderson (London, 1969), *Preface*, p. 7. Sedgwick read von Ranke's *History of the German Reformation* in translation. 'What a glorious history! How full! How rich! How wise, how honest! I shall never again endure the rounded periods and syllabub of Robertson. I seemed to be in a new world of mind and matter as I went along, and I hardly allowed myself time for sleep till I had finished the three volumes.' J. W. Clark and T. M. Hughes, *Life and Letters of the Rev. Adam Sedgwick*, Vol. ii (London, 1890), p. 113.

saw a clear link between undisciplined education and political unrest, noting darkly that in Germany and France '. . . we are told that there prevails among the young men of the Universities a vehement and general hostility to the existing institutions of their country . . . such a consequence may naturally flow from an education which invokes the critical spirit, and invites it to employ itself on the comparison between the realities of society and the dreams of system makers'.[17] He no doubt looked on the revolutions of 1848 as a natural consequence of defective education.

Last (and in those politically incorrect days, least) came the undergraduates. They did not want modern history any more than their masters. The reading men knew that historical knowledge would not raise one's place in the mathematical or classical class lists, or carry any weight in a fellowship competition. The great majority of 'poll men' (those reading for a pass degree only) apparently did only as much work as they had to. When they turned out in large numbers for celebrated incumbents such as Charles Kingsley at Cambridge and Thomas Arnold at Oxford, it was as much to hear a good storyteller as to learn history. All the more fun if the story annoyed the powers that be.[18]

History and Moral Sciences 1851–1860

How did history contrive to join the Cambridge curriculum in the face of such obstacles? If it were the whole story, one might perhaps rest on Mark Pattison's characteristically mordant observation of 1855, about the introduction of modern studies generally. 'At the time we adopted them we scarcely knew the full meaning of what we were doing. We felt we could not be without them, yet we did not know why we wanted them . . .'[19]

The mood at Cambridge was pragmatic rather than wistful. Although one can cite a handful of internal proposals for reform during the first forty years or so of the nineteenth century, residents generally wanted as little change as possible. Benjamin Dann Walsh of Trinity, himself a would-be reformer, lamented that the 'spirit of innovation has always been most loudly deprecated in our Universities, and there is no place where the attachment to old usages is so strong'. However, Walsh's subsequent observation reflected the views of more politically aware individuals that 'these are not times in which it is safe to remain far in the rear of improvement. When the tide of public feeling sets so strongly in

---

[17] Whewell, *Principles* (Cambridge, 1837), p. 51.
[18] The conservative heads of houses were always sensitive to any potentially disturbing novelties. In the cases of two professors who tried to lecture conscientiously, John Symonds in the 1770s and William Smyth, the heads limited the number of undergraduates who could attend, the reason given being that they might be distracted from more important college work. This official discouragement was not unique to history, but the subject may well have been particularly disliked because of its perceived links with politics. See Searby, *History*, p. 235.
[19] Mark Pattison, *Oxford Essays* (Oxford, 1855), p. 281.

favour of reforms, political, civil, and ecclesiastical, the swimmer who attempts to stem it will be overwhelmed in its waves'.[20]

Cambridge therefore set grudgingly to work, via a long series of reforming syndicates. The opening words of the first report (8 April 1848) set the tone. 'The Syndicate, admitting the superiority of the study of Mathematics and Classics over all others as the basis of general education, and acknowledging, therefore, the wisdom of adhering to our present system in its main features. . . .'[21] The Syndicate's minimalist policy could not, however, ignore the politically-charged questions of what to do with the professors, including of course the Regius chairs of history. They therefore attempted to kill two birds with one stone by putting the professors to work with the pollmen, whose low standards of attainment made excellent ammunition for the University's enemies. In addition to their other studies, pollmen were not to graduate unless they had attended the lectures of at least one professor, received his certificate of attendance and taken his examination. The first exams for pollmen under this dispensation would be held in 1851.[22] This part of the Syndicate's report was politically well judged. Outsiders could be persuaded that the University was reforming. The pollmen and the professors were alike given something to do. Reading men and the subjects they read were both unaffected.

The report marked a decisive moment for Modern History, in that for the first time the subject formed part of the regular teaching and examination structures of the University. History was *in*, if only as a result of the triumph of expediency over educational theory. Unfortunately 'in' did not mean 'significant'. The Syndicate proposed the introduction of new Honours Triposes in Natural Sciences and Moral Sciences. The latter was to consist of Moral Philosophy, Political Economy, Modern History, General Jurisprudence and the Laws of England. However, it was suggested as part of the package that the professor of modern history should be an examiner in Jurisprudence. That subject, together with Natural Sciences, would form the basis of an extension of studies.

The originator of this idea was almost certainly Whewell, who had remarked in the course of a letter containing 'a few suggestions' (eight and a half pages) on curriculum reform which he sent to Prince Albert in March 1847, well before the Syndicate reported, that 'The Professor of Modern History may naturally be expected to turn his attention to International Law'.[23] Although there was no reason why the professor might not embrace both subjects, it is not unfair to suggest that Whewell wanted to find the professor something to do that he (Whewell) regarded as worthwhile. The professor himself, Sir James Stephen, told the Commissioners late in 1850 that since his appointment in the previous

---

[20] Benjamin Dann Walsh, *Historical Account of the University of Cambridge* (London, 1837), pp. 105–6.
[21] C. H. Cooper, *Annals of Cambridge*, Vol. 4 (Cambridge, 1908), p. 702.
[22] Cambridge University Commission 1852, *Evidence*, pp. 113, 457–8.
[23] William Whewell to the Prince Consort, 8 March, 1847. Royal Library Windsor, Prince Consort's Papers.

year he knew no more about the state of history at Cambridge beyond the mere fact that a numerous and apparently interested audience had come to his lectures. His scheme for reform proposed a preliminary exam that would divide students into 'proficients' (that is, clever students) and non-proficients. The proficients would take classics and maths only, the others a final examination in at least two sciences, moral or physical. The latter would not be able to take classics or maths again. Professorial classes, including his own, would be recruited 'not perhaps from the ablest men, but still from men of whom it is unjust to despond, and who might thus be rescued from the temptations and penalties of a misspent youth'.[24] This hardly constitutes a ringing endorsement for his subject. Stephen was Whewell's man and his suggestions were close to Whewell's own.[25]

A series of reforming Syndicates culminated in a decisive vote in 1854, when the Senate threw out a recommendation for separate Honours in Moral Sciences. Any student who had passed the Previous Examination might go on to study the subject and be examined, yet it was not to carry a bachelor's degree in its own right, nor to have a Board of Studies: the latter stipulation probably inspired by a fear that some political or religious faction would capture the board and distort the course accordingly. Neither was there any provision made for teaching beyond that of the professors, who already had to cope with the poll men. Reading men were expected to study by themselves for the few months they would need: after all, were they not mental athletes? Consequently, no college saw the need to create lectureships in the subject.

Given such handicaps, it is hardly surprising that Moral Sciences attracted only a handful of candidates. In 1860 there were none at all. Although the course suffered from a lack of incentives to study, the heart of the matter was that it did not command respect in its own right. It had been cobbled together from subjects that had happened to possess an endowed chair and whose subject matter was considered inappropriate in principle for the work it was called on to do.[26] Consequently, the task of regularising so many different preoccupations and material practices proved intensely difficult. Neither students nor their teachers liked the course. J. W. Clark, who was an undergraduate from 1852 to 1856 and went on to become a fellow of Trinity and University Registrary,

[24] Cambridge University Commission 1852, *Evidence*, p. 112.
[25] Peter Searby has summarised Whewell's arguments against poll men being allowed to attempt the Classical Tripos. The best classicists were 'the intellectual aristocracy of the land . . . The characteristic education of the nation is *their* education.' It was therefore essential that they had previously studied maths in depth. Ordinary degree people, 'dull of intellect, or idle or inert in study', were unlikely to amount to much, so that mathematical study was not essential. Searby *History*, p. 517 citing Whewell, *Of a Liberal Education*, 2nd edn (1850), pt. 2, pp. 7–43. The pecking-order of subjects could hardly be clearer.
[26] A resident writing in October 1848 as 'A Member of the Senate' noted that it was necessary in practice to combine several sciences in one Tripos, 'in order to include all of which we have Professors; and the combinations made seem to exhibit very natural alliances between the several branches.' A Member of the Senate 'Letter to a Friend upon the proposed additions to the academical system of education', p. 5.

attended Stephen's lectures on the foreign policy of Louis Quatorze, 'delivered with the solemnity of which he was master, and in language far above the comprehension of the young fellows who sat below him'. The exam was on a set book, Guizot's *History of the English Reformation.* Clark thought it 'a work which may be of great historical value, but is repulsively dull, especially in the English translation which we were expected to use ... I wrote very little – and that little was sad stuff – but I was let through! The truth was that all the Professors hated this system and did their best to evade it'.[27]

The pattern of examination questions in these years reflects these difficulties, showing as it does a strong bias towards constitutional and legal history of a non-technical kind, or simple historical facts, presumably because these could easily be graded on a basis of factual recall. Fenton Hort, always a conscientious student and later an examiner, said that the new Triposes consisted 'for the most part of information, and involve the exercise of few faculties but memory'. Hort's feelings are revealing. Only classics and maths could give 'real mastery over the facts of *any* Science and security against the intellectual snares of popular superficiality' and thus be truly educational.[28] The moral sciences had neither the principled case for their academic worth that had long been granted to mathematics and classics, nor a lobby group of residents in their favour.

Peter Slee, in his excellent *Learning and a Liberal Education,*[29] considers that the chief challenge to the supremacy of classics and (irrelevant) mathematics came from the natural sciences, because they were able to offer an acceptable alternative paradigm of hard study, advanced learning and practical usefulness. Other subjects were able to enter through the breach, as it were. He singles out the Caius medical lecturer W. H. Drosier, who argued more firmly than anyone before him that, in Slee's words, 'mathematics and classics did not have a monopoly of educative technique'. Drosier also pointed out that if the new subjects had proper academic status then more students and teachers

---

[27] A. J. Shipley, '*J*': *A Memoir of John Willis Clark* (London, 1913), pp. 42–3. Fenton Hort, when he was made examiner in 1853 (the year after he had taken the paper as a student), tried to compose a paper that conformed to the original idea of the Tripos: namely, to bind the five sciences together by asking questions which bore on the mutual connection of the sciences, and the joint application of them to practice in actual history. 'This will be an innovation upon the doings ... of my two predecessors.' F. J. Hort to his mother 8 November 1853. A. F. Hort, *Life and Letters of Fenton Anthony John Hort,* Vol. i (London, 1896), pp. 264–5.

[28] Fenton Hort to the Senate. Cambridge University Archives (hereafter CUA), UP 21, pp. 1–4. Hort had a right to an opinion since he had taken first classes in both moral and natural sciences, was Third Classic and would have been highly placed in mathematics if he had not been ill at a crucial time.

[29] Peter R. H. Slee, *Learning and a Liberal Education: The Study of Modern History in the Universities of Oxford, Cambridge and Manchester 1800–1914* (Manchester, 1986). There is much valuable additional detail in Dr Slee's unpublished Ph.D. thesis, 'History as a Discipline at the Universities of Oxford and Cambridge 1848–1914' (Cambridge, 1983). Enthusiasts may also wish to consult the present writer's 'The Development of History as an Academic Subject at the Universities of Oxford and Cambridge c. 1840–c.1873' (unpublished D.Phil. thesis University of Ulster, 1984).

would take them up and could develop their potential as true means of education.[30]

The argument is persuasive, although we need more published work on science at Cambridge and Oxford during this period before the picture becomes clear. There was a general pressure to reform studies that were not attracting students, especially students of the 'right' social class. Furthermore, broader thinkers inside the University were coming to challenge the claims of classics and maths to be uniquely suitable for education. John Grote, the Knightbridge Professor of Moral Philosophy (whose early death has prevented full credit being given for his work as reformer), argued that a properly constituted scheme of study would stimulate candidates and make the course more homogenous, while leaving it wide and – significantly – 'create in the University its own line of reading . . . bringing some men here who would not otherwise have come, and making some who *are* here more instructed men and more useful men in the country'.[31] The anonymous author of the 1862 edition of the *Student's Guide* series even went so far as to offer mild criticism of both maths and classics.[32] Such indications as these suggest a gradual sea change in attitudes to history and the moral sciences, whereby university opinion moved from grudging acceptance of their inevitable presence to modest arguments in their support.

An unhappy marriage: History and Law 1860–1873

The moral sciences were able to offer a Tripos in their own right from February 1860 onwards.[33] It was not long before practical experience justified the apprehensions of earlier critics. The initial problem appears to have lain in the wide range of reading required to cover all the subjects, with Modern History identified as the principal culprit.[34] The results were so unsatisfactory as

---

[30] Slee, *Learning and a Liberal Education*, pp. 31–3, citing W. H. Drosier, *Remarks on the New Regulations Recommended by the Syndicate of October 27th 1859 for the Moral and Natural Sciences Examinations* (Cambridge, 1860).

[31] John Grote, 'To the Members of the Senate', 22 February 1860, pp. 5–6. Italics in original.

[32] '. . . there are manifest dangers arising from an exclusive attention to either classics or mathematics as those studies are usually pursued'. Maths was said to '. . . altogether leave untouched the field of probable reasoning which is most generally useful for the purposes of life'. A classical man . . . has constant practice in probable reasoning . . . but his conceptions are often confused, his knowledge loose and unsystematized, and he is in danger of attributing too much weight to mere authority.' The moral sciences were commended '. . . to the mathematician they afford wider interests and and an exercise in probable reasoning; to the classic they impart clearness, system and independence of thought, *Student's Guide to the University of Cambridge* (1862), p. 101.

[33] The Senate decided the matter on 23 February 1860. Details and regulations were issued on 7 March 1861.

[34] H. M. Gwatkin crammed for Moral Sciences in 1867. His letters show that over a period of about nine months he read Macaulay, Hallam's *Constitutional History* and Guizot, as well as 'a miscellaneous heap of books of every sort' including De Tocqueville, Pearson's *Early and Middle Ages of England*, Mommsen and 'Laing's Norway', Max Müller, Guizot's *Civilisation en France*, the six volumes of Hallam's *Middle Ages* and *Constitutional History*, besides half Genesis and the whole of Joshua in Hebrew, 'and a little more Political Economy: Mill Bk

to promote a rapid debate, to which the most perceptive and revealing contribution was by H. R. Luard, the University's Registrary. He considered it mistaken 'to attempt to examine young men of 21 or 22 on the whole range of historical subjects. Political Economy is an exact science – Moral Philosophy, as it has come into the system, has meant little more than the mastery of certain stated books; but to the historical portion of the examination there has been no limit whatever'.[35] The matter was pressed with what ranked in nineteenth-century Cambridge as exceptional haste. The Board of Moral Sciences, following Luard's lead, reported that Modern History was '. . . the least satisfactory portion of the examination, the subject being too extensive to be properly dealt with as a subordinate branch of the Moral Sciences Tripos'.[36] They recommended that History and Jurisprudence should cease to be part of Moral Sciences.

Jurisprudence was covered under the Law Tripos, but what should be done with History? Luard's suggestion that it should form a Tripos in its own right fell on deaf ears, even though he indicated how standards in the subject could be raised:

> I would on no account name any books, but would encourage the student to master the history of the time by reference to original documents, with of course, the help of any modern or ancient histories he may find founded on them. But I would lay the onus of choice on the student, and I should hope that the examiners would, as far as possible, endeavour to prevent the possibility of cram, by themselves avoiding the stock historical compendiums. . . . A student would thus be led to think and examine by himself . . . we might thus make History a branch of education almost as valuable as any other. . . .[37]

'Almost' gives the game away. While Luard was a highly respected figure and a capable medieval historian in his own right, a separate Tripos was a step too far for most residents. A Syndicate was established on 28 November 1867 to decide on the future of Modern History at Cambridge. One of the proposals was that the subject should be combined with Law. Henry Sidgwick, by this time becoming a leading spirit in curriculum reform, and much else besides, sought advice on that question from James Bryce at Oxford, asking what Bryce's views were as to the union of Law and History in one school. 'There are very few people at Cambridge who have or ought to have any strong opinions on the subject . . .'[38] In any event the syndicate rapidly recommended

---

iii in any case . . .' H. M. Gwatkin to J. B. Mayor 14 March 1867 and to his sister 2 August, 24 August, 9 September, 15 December, 1867. Emmanuel College Archives, Gwatkin Correspondence.

[35] H. R. Luard, *Suggestion*, p. 14.
[36] CUA 28:8, Moral Science Tripos, no. 18.
[37] Luard, *Suggestions*, p. 15.
[38] Sidgwick to Bryce 26 December 1867. Bryce to Sidgwick 4 Jan 1868. Bryce Papers 15/2 no. 104. The latter is Bryce's acknowledgement. A full reply has not survived, or was never written.

that Law should indeed be combined with Modern History to make up a new Tripos.

The 'discussion in the Arts School', which customarily took place between the publication of a syndicate's report and a vote on its recommendations, shows both the persistence of traditional views and signs of a thaw. No speaker advocated history as a subject in its own right. Several sided with Dr Waraker, a lawyer from Sidney Sussex, when he said that Law was a better mental and general training than history, since the former came closer to mathematics and the latter was 'a mere effort of memory'. Most contributors thought that suitably beefed-up history was acceptable or, in W. H. Thompson's formal language, that it was a 'more natural classification to range Modern History with Law than with [Moral] Science . . . if History was properly treated by the Examiners it would prove to be a very valuable adjunct in the course of Legal education'.[39] The Senate accepted the Syndicate's recommendations, the new Tripos was duly created and the first college lecturers designated as teachers of modern history were appointed.[40]

Unfortunately, Law quickly found History just as impossible as Moral Sciences had done. The first two exams, held in 1870 and 1871, both produced unacceptable results. The Board of Legal and Historical Studies reported in February 1872 that '. . . the subjects of Law and Modern History cannot with advantage be treated together in the same examination, and that a class list arranged according to credit obtained in the two subjects is very far from representing the requirements of the candidates. They also find that the subject of History is so large and varied that it requires a separate and distinct examination.'[41] Professor Abdy summarised the problem at a discussion of the Board's Report in April 1872. Very few candidates had made a special study of history and none had more than half marks. Then came the crux. The examiners had been unable to reward merit in the legal branch as they would have wished because the papers in history were too poor. Abdy was reinforced by Henry Latham, tutor and future Master of Trinity Hall, traditionally a lawyers' college, who said that no student took the Tripos because he liked history, and the fact that the history element was 'a troublesome and disturbing element of the Examination to Candidates in Law, discredited the whole study of History . . .'[42]

---

[39] Thompson remarked that 'The scheme did not say that Hallam's History should be got up, but that the student should investigate certain parts and make what he could of it', if that constitutes a defence.
[40] Charles Henry Pearson at Trinity (1869), T. W. Levin in Modern History and Philosophy at St Catherine's, Bryan Walker (of Trinity Hall) in History and Law at Corpus and Edward Aikin (of Trinity) in Modern History at Jesus. Henry Sidgwick taught the subject at Trinity from 1867 as part of his work as Lecturer in Moral Sciences, handing over to Charles Henry Pearson from 1869 to 1871. Sidgwick to F. Myers 10 October 1871. See A. S. Sidgwick and E. M. S. Sidgwick, *Henry Sidgwick: A Memoir* (London, 1906), p. 213.
[41] CUA 28:10, Historical Tripos, 1868–1902.
[42] *Cambridge University Reporter*, 1 May 1872.

It was clear that the lawyers would not long tolerate anything that might disturb their career prospects. History's few supporters remained in difficulty. Henry Sidgwick said that he would not vote for the report separating History and Law because 'it would lead to an interval, probably not very short, when there would be no Examination in History'. He also recalled that when the Law and History Tripos had been devised he was for it, since Law and History were mutually beneficial, but since that time the attitude of the University towards new Triposes had changed and he thought some separation might be effected now, though still holding that some study of Law should be combined with that of History. Sidgwick's ambivalence is revealing, coming as it did from a comparatively open-minded thinker and reformer. While realising that it might be both politically possible and educationally desirable to give history a Tripos of its own, Sidgwick could not bring himself to see the subjects as having enough intellectual weight to justify that honour.[43]

Towards the Modern History Tripos

Law and History having collapsed, Luard and others (presumably including Sidgwick himself) managed to penetrate a fog of indifference and get a Syndicate set up in May 1872 to decide the next course of action. It was fortunate, therefore, that after so many vicissitudes History at Cambridge acquired substantial support in the persons of two real historians: Sir Adolphus William Ward, then Professor of History and English Language and Literature at Owens College, Manchester (the future University of Manchester),[44] and Sir John Seeley. The latter was Charles Kingsley's successor as Regius Professor of History and famous in church circles as the author of the controversial *Ecce Homo*. Both were deeply aware of the revolution in historical studies emanating from von Ranke and others in Germany that had left official Cambridge opinion untouched. They were big guns, albeit firing in different directions.

Seeley and Ward together made a valiant incursion into the citadel. Each was prepared to rest his case for the subject on theoretical grounds, thereby elevating the status of history from the unmanageable catalogue of facts that many residents still considered it to be. Ward's views can be traced from a number of published articles, notably 'The Study of History at Cambridge', which

---

[43] His private thoughts can be found in a letter of October 1871. 'I have to teach history this term: no successor having turned up to Pearson: and Cambridge breeding no historian. We are thinking of taking some healthy young resident and locking him up with a Hume. It is rather a disgrace to us that we all take so small an interest in the human race ...' Sidgwick to F. Myers: 10 October 1871, *Henry Sidgwick*, p. 252.

[44] Ward was born in Germany, the son of a consular official and did not go to an English school until he was sixteen. He then went on to a classical training and a fellowship at Peterhouse. He had seen the work at first hand, having been law and history examiner in 1871. In the words of T. F. Tout, his collaborator and successor, 'He was one of the earliest and best of the interpreters of German scholarship to English readers.' Tout, *Memoir*, in A. T. Bartholomew, *A Bibliography of Sir Adolphus William Ward 1837–1924* (Cambridge, 1926).

appeared in the *Saturday Review* in July 1872, and a pamphlet on the Historical Tripos itself.

Ward stressed what he called 'Historical power': a characteristic embodying both the bundle of skills appropriate to a historian and the ability to use them effectively. The examiners would test whether the student

> has read much and accurately, whether he has mastered the methods of criticising Historical materials and authorities both outwardly and inwardly; i.e. both as to their form and as to their contents; whether he can bring his reading and knowledge concerning one Historical period or subject to bear upon his reading and knowledge concerning others and finally, whether he can communicate his knowledge in the various forms to which Historical composition lends itself.[45]

His scheme specified that at the 'preliminary' stage candidates should demonstrate a command of the rudiments of general history, and a somewhat more advanced knowledge of the history of England, together with historical geography and the leading principles of political economy and constitutional law. They would not be expected to study original authorities. Those who could pass this stage satisfactorily would then be allowed to go forward to a separate examination for Honours. Ward considered that the correct way to study history at the undergraduate level was to combine both periods and subjects, in ancient, mediaeval and modern history. Periods studied alone would be 'deadening' and lead men to become 'annalists'. Attention to subjects only would make students 'doctrinaires'. Therefore candidates for Honours would take 'one of a series of Historical subjects on questions' and 'one of a series of Historical periods', both selected and published in advance by the board of historical studies. Ward gave specimen subjects for 'broad investigation', all of which comprised historical movements rather than chronologically defined topics.

Ward thus recognised history as a discipline in its own right, with various levels of proficiency, each capable of being tested in a practical way. Although the exact relationship he proposed between special and general subjects was not fully worked out, he nevertheless understood that a better criterion had to be found for setting the limits of study in a history course than the arbitrary constraints of set books. In short, Ward believed that history was a means of education in itself: precisely the ground on which traditional Cambridge had always refused to accept it. That it was capable of being recognised at all is good evidence for the opening up of the University and the beginnings of the move towards its becoming the national institution its external critics desired.

Sir John Seeley argued his case in the most forthright and dramatic fashion in his inaugural lecture, given in February 1870. He stated bluntly that any well-ordered subject could provide the means of training the mind: there were no special virtues in classics or mathematics. Then, granted that all subjects were

---

[45] A. W. Ward, *Suggestions Towards the Establishment of a History Tripos* (Cambridge, 1872).

equal, as it were, Seeley asked why a student should choose to read history. He answered that history was the key to understanding and appreciating democracy and the politics of democracy: an education for citizenship. Cambridge should be the centre of a school of political science; that is of history and political economy, two sciences joined together to make a 'school of statesmanship.' The details of subjects and courses should reflect that end.

Seeley's radical lecture caused much dissension in the University, besides inspiring W. H. Thompson's classic remark as he left Seeley's lecture-room: 'I did not think we should have cause to regret poor dear Kingsley so soon.'[46]

It is impossible to say how far residents were persuaded more by Seeley or Ward, than the changing climate of the times and what appeared to be the unstoppable expansion of the University. The 1860s had seen the first stages of a great transformation in both Cambridge and Oxford. The abolition of religious tests, associated with an increasing wish to see the universities staffed by expert 'career tutors', whose ambitions did not lie elsewhere, together with the first stirrings of the 'endowment of research' movement, all helped the cause of internal reform. History gained no more than incidental benefit from these developments, for confidence in the subject remained fragile, yet benefit there was.

The wording of the Syndicate's Report embodies much of the archaeology of curriculum development at Cambridge, together with chunks of nutritious fudge and faint praise:

> The Syndicate consider that History, as the subject of an independent Tripos, requires to be placed on a wider basis than its subordinate position in other Triposes has hitherto allowed; and believe that in this manner its efficacy in education may best be secured. . . .They propose therefore that Ancient and Mediaeval History should have their due place in the Tripos, as well as Modern History, so that History may be placed before the Student as a whole. . . . They propose likewise that the study of History be accompanied with the chief theoretical studies which find their illustration in History . . . In thus recommending the inclusion of certain subjects which have already a place in the Classical Tripos, the Moral Sciences Tripos and the proposed Law Tripos, they are following a principle upon which the University has recently acted. They may anticipate moreover considerable advantage from the treatment of important subjects from different points of view.[47]

The inclusion of 'theoretical studies' gives the game away. The University was still not prepared to accept History's intellectual credentials, so the subject had

---

[46] Quoted without attribution and in a slightly different form by Susan Chitty, *The Beast and the Monk: a Life of Charles Kingsley* (London, 1974), p. 258.
[47] The Report appeared on 3 December 1872. The signatories included W. H. Thompson the Vice-Chancellor, the lawyers Abdy and Latham, the political economist Marshall, Fenton Hort, the Knightbridge Professor, Henry Sidgwick and Basil Hammond of Trinity: the last one of the most important, and most neglected, pioneers of historical studies at Cambridge.

to be 'beefed up' with brainwork. The nine-paper Modern History Tripos was therefore to include only five papers in History proper, plus Principles of Political Philosophy and General Jurisprudence, Constitutional Law and Constitutional History, Political Economy and Economic History, International Law and Treaties. The discussion in the Arts School on the Syndicate's Report did not challenge the Report's conclusions, confining itself to criticising details of the syllabus.[48] No one chose to initiate a debate on issues about the nature and functions of the subject that preoccupied Ward and Seeley, and – in time-honoured academic fashion – the Tripos was designed so as to meet both schools of thought.

Cambridge did, however, at last accept the logic of the situation. If History could not be abolished or combined satisfactorily with some other subject, then it must be granted independence. The Modern History Tripos was accordingly approved in 1873 and held its first examinations two years later. One is left with a firm conviction of the deep reluctance with which those steps were taken. In spite of the work of Sir George Prothero, Basil Hammond and an increasing stream of brilliant teachers and researchers, it would be many years before Modern History in Cambridge could lay aside the chilly welcome that marked its birth and eventually match its counterpart in Oxford as a leading seat of historical scholarship and teaching.

[48] There were several pious wishes. Pearson of Emmanuel College said there should be some instruction and examination in the study of ancient inscriptions and manuscripts. Henry Latham said the syndicate agreed that such study was important and thought the phrase 'original matter' in the regulations would cover it. Dr Campion observed (rather like the bad fairy at a birth) that it was well the Tripos was not simply 'pure History', for it would soon degenerate into mere annals. If he was thinking of Ward's scheme he did not say so. Nor did any speaker question the union of ancient and modern history in the Tripos. The lawyers were not mollified by Sidgwick's view that only departments of Law closely connected with History had been selected. The Board believed that History taken alone would not afford the best course of education, or the best basis for the future study of History. For the historian some knowledge of Political Economy and of Constitutional Law was most desirable. See *Cambridge University Reporter*, 11 February 1873, p. 89.

JOHN R. GIBBINS

Constructing Knowledge in Mid-Victorian Cambridge: The Moral Sciences Tripos 1850–70

Mid-Victorian Cambridge witnessed a remarkable series of events that resulted in a reconstruction of its fabric, its organisation, its statutes, its curriculum, its teaching and learning. The identification of this period by Rothblatt as revolutionary is an exaggeration.[1] At the end of our period most of what existed could be identified as old, and the new had been fashioned to complement and enhance the historical inheritance. Much had been achieved by insiders who had welcomed the attentions of the Royal Commissioners. But the rival characterisation by Stephen and Annan of the period and the key actors in the moral sciences as 'reactionary', challenged only by the 'disproportionate part played by Sidgwick' in curriculum reform, also exaggerates the situation.[2] This second picture overamplifies the 'radical' reformist intentions and achievements of Henry Sidgwick and his colleagues, both before and after the 1870s, and thus underplays the ideals and accomplishments of the second generation of reformers who followed Whewell, Sedgwick and others from the 1830s and 1840s. What I wish to attempt in this chapter is not a replacement representation, but an investigation of primary sources that suggest, and go some way to support, a revisionist picture of our period.

My focus is on several groups of scholars who, between the achievements of Whewell and of Sidgwick, constructed the curriculum in the moral sciences. My raw materials are documents that have been little used in recent work on the history of education: examination papers for fellows and undergraduates, rival flysheets advocating or rebutting reading lists, rival proposals for reform of the syllabus, and documentary evidence of struggles over the appointment of university professors, college tutors and fellows. The established histories of

---

[1] S. Rothblatt, *The Revolution of the Dons* (London, 1968).
[2] N. G. Annan, *Leslie Stephen: His Thought and Character in Relation to his Time* (London, 1951); N. G. Annan, *Leslie Stephen: The Godless Victorian* (London and New York, 1984), pp. 34–47; S. Collini, D. Winch and J. Burrow, *That Noble Science of Politics: A Study in Nineteenth-Century Intellectual History* (Cambridge, 1983), p. 341.

the University and the curriculum of the time are of only partial help on these topics.[3] I look especially at the choice of books and examination questions for the philosophy papers; the election of moral science tutors; the appointment of professors to chairs in philosophy and political economy; and the appointment of examiners for the various subjects in the curriculum. The reason for this is that these posts were considered to be, and carried, proof, not only of scholarly merit, allegiance, and quality, but intellectual and political investment for the future. We must, however, go beyond the warnings on the use of such sources by Collini et al. that it would be 'foolish to infer too neat or coherent a conception of the science of politics from the evidence of syllabuses and reading-lists: the minutes of the various meetings that established and revised these papers tell a story of disagreement and confusion, and we all know how little of the story such records tell'.[4] Primary sources are the best resources we have for reconstructing the past, and the sources we have on my topics are rich, diverse and growing.[5]

Three groups of questions focus my attention below. First and briefly, 'What is the construction of knowledge?' Second, 'Who constructed knowledge, in the fields of the moral sciences, and why did they do so in Cambridge in the period 1850–1870?' Third, 'What were the lines of division between the parties that fought over the construction of knowledge, who won and why, in this period?' My answer to this last question is that we can identify three groups of rival architects who fought over the treasured goal of the University: what it was seen to produce and what the public were expected to consume. The parties to this debate were wide and diverse, but three coteries can be identified very simplistically as reactionaries, radicals and reformers; the reformers emerging triumphant in our period. But the reformers of one period often became the reactionaries of a later one, as with the group around Whewell who by the 1860s were the establishment to be dethroned. While we will concentrate upon disputes internal to Cambridge, it is important to remember that all parties were aware of the competition they had with external bodies to construct and transmit knowledge to elites in Britain. Cambridge was aware that four other geographical spaces were contesting the territory: Oxford, London, Edinburgh and St Andrews. Battles between them had been raging for years, and at the outset of our period Cambridge was still smarting from the broadsides of Mill in his diatribes against Cambridge studies, Sedgwick's *Discourses* and Whewell's *Ethics*; a sensitivity made more profound by the arrival of the Parliamentary

---

[3] M. Garland, *Cambridge Before Darwin: The Ideal of a Liberal Education 1800–1860* (Cambridge, 1980); T. W. Heyck, *The Transformation of Intellectual Life in Victorian England* (London, 1982); Rothblatt, *Revolution*; P. R. H. Slee, *Learning and a Liberal Education: The Study of Modern History in the Universities of Oxford, Cambridge and Manchester 1800–1914* (Manchester, 1986); D. A. Winstanley, *Early Victorian Cambridge* (Cambridge, 1940), *Later Victorian Cambridge* (Cambridge, 1945). A partial exception is Collini et al., *Noble Science*.
[4] Collini et al., *Noble Science*, p. 357.
[5] For example, the Mayor Papers, Sidgwick MSS and Henry Jackson MSS in Trinity College Library.

Commissioners.[6] Cambridge was battling for control of the Victorian intelligentsia and professions, competing especially hard with the non-university elites of the cities, represented here by Mill and the Philosophical Radicals in London.[7] National control and not just local control of the moral science agenda was in dispute in what follows.

Language, metaphor and theory: The construction of knowledge

The favoured metaphor used by William Whewell to describe intellectual pursuits such as research, curriculum design, and teaching was 'discovery'. To prepare and launch students on a voyage of discovery was the ambition shared somewhat with Whewell's successor in the Knightbridge chair of moral philosophy, John Grote, who replaced 'discovery' with 'exploration'.[8] By contrast I propose that a better image of teaching and learning at the time, was 'construction'. By this I mean that the authors of Tripos curricula, booklists, examination papers and teaching topics were actually designing, determining and producing, not discovering, what was worth knowing in each area of knowledge. Those professors and tutors who delivered the curriculum were inculcating and reproducing what was considered worth knowing, not from scratch but from the resources available in tradition, ancient and modern. Students competed in 'cramming', 'sweating', and 'loafing' in order to become the perfect product of the construction process:[9] students who would go out into the world to employ, enact and reproduce this knowledge in their various professions, from the clergy and teaching to diplomacy and banking.[10] Once reconfigured in this way we can revise our picture of intellectual rivalries in the period in terms of market-competitive activities. Mid-century Cambridge, Edinburgh, Oxford and London were offering and selling rival products, rival constructions of what was worth knowing, what was true, right and beautiful, to a market of parents, school headmasters, and employers. The libraries, tutorial and lecture rooms were the factory production lines, designed and valued for their efficiency. The politically charged meetings of Syndicates, Boards of Studies, and committees, in which the selection of books, authors and topics of study were determined, were sites of power in which the construction of knowledge, and later the material structure of the University, were at stake.

[6] J. R. Gibbins, 'John Grote, Cambridge University and the Development of Victorian Ideas', Ph.D. thesis (University of Newcastle upon Tyne, 1989), chs 2–3; J. S. Mill, 'Professor Sedgwick's Discourse on the Studies of the University of Cambridge' (1835) and 'Dr Whewell on Moral Philosophy' (1852) in J. B. Schneewind, ed., *Mill's Ethical Writings* (London, 1965).
[7] J. Roach, 'Liberalism and the Victorian Intelligentsia', *Cambridge Historical Journal* XIII, 1 (1957), pp. 58–81; 'Victorian Universities and the National Intelligentsia', *Victorian Studies*, III (1959), pp. 131–50.
[8] J. Grote, *Exploratio Philosophica* (Cambridge, 1865 and 1900).
[9] L. Stephen, *Sketches from Cambridge by a Don* (London and Cambridge, 1865); J. A. Venn, *Early Collegiate Life* (Cambridge, 1913).
[10] W. C. Lubenow, *The Cambridge Apostles* (Cambridge, 1998), chs 3–7.

In construction theory, knowledge is not objective and to be discovered by individuals but rather social (not subjective) and made or manufactured in human interaction by the efforts of those in a participating community.[11] My choice of construction language and theory is made for two reasons, the first and most decisive being that it describes well the enterprise and achievements of the competing coteries I study. The other taps a current in the modern debate on the best methods of doing revisionist intellectual and cultural history. Broadly, construction theory is a development from the history of science, especially the work of Thomas Kuhn, the sociology of knowledge and cultural studies. It claims that a special purchase on understanding the past comes from 'looking at the social-discursive matrix from which knowledge claims emerge and from which their justification is derived: the values/ideology implicit within knowledge posits; the modes of informal and institutional life sustained and replenished by ontological and epistemological commitments; and the distribution of power and privilege favoured by disciplinary beliefs'.[12] In brief construction theory claims that knowledge is created, transmitted and established within discursive battles for knowledge/power; or, in different terms, it claims that what stands has been honed in a battle over production, reproduction and consumption involving competing parties.[13]

My choice is influenced by the closeness this theoretical position has to the most traditional understanding of historical actors; the idea that actors are agents with free will, who despite their social location, can have a decisive role in shaping events. However my position needs to be distinguished from that of several related figures in the construction family if it is to be useful here. Behaviourist constructionists are those, like Peter Berger, who wish to reject structuralist socialisation theory and yet set the notion of agency within specific social and historical contexts and limits.[14] The idealist form of constructionism, exhibited best in the work of ethnomethodologists like Gadamer, see knowledge as the construction of agents' minds within social discourse. In our field this notion is used in the work of Paradis and Postlewait.[15] Structuralist constructionism, best exhibited in marxism and feminism, brings back moderate determinism by understanding agents as fashioned by the economic or gendered forces of the age.

While closest to the idealist position, exemplified by Kuhn, my claims are influenced by the work of several poststructuralist historians who have argued

[11] M. Crotty, *The Foundations of Social Research* (London, 1999), pp. 42–3.
[12] K. J. Gergen, 'Metaphor and Monophony in the 20th-century Psychology of Emotions', *History of the Human Sciences* VIII, 2 (1995), p. 20; I. Velody and R. Williams, *The Politics of Constructionism* (London, 1999), p. 2; V. Burt, *An Introduction to Social Constructionism* (London, 1995); J. Shotter, *Conversational Realities: Constructing Life Through Language* (London, 1993).
[13] M. Foucault, *Power/Knowledge: Selected Interviews* (Brighton, 1980).
[14] P. Berger and T. Luckmann, *The Social Construction of Reality* (London, 1967).
[15] J. Paradis and T. Postlewait, eds., *Victorian Science and Victorian Values: Literary Perspectives* (New York, 1985).

that agents can choose to act within existing constructions or re-catalogue knowledge for themselves, in battles of knowledge/power. My hypothesis is that the mid-century Moral Sciences Tripos and curriculum, and its attendant teaching and learning strategy, were shaped by and within battles between actors who intended to establish certain positions as true and right and to exclude other positions by the application of categories within discursive practices held to be privileged in their day.

Tripos, syllabus, booklists and examinations

My story tells of some of these battles between professors, fellows, tutors and their allies over what students would consume and take away as truth, knowledge and good practice. Examinations were, in this sense, surveillance, a form of disciplining, and the syllabus, reading lists and lectures a kind of control on knowledge. A Tripos we may understand in this framework as the negotiated agreement in the University as to what constituted knowledge in that field or discipline. Committee, syndicate and flysheet battles were about what was worth knowing and whether it was compatible with the mission of the colleges and university, and society at large as represented by the Parliamentary Commissioners. The syllabus contained the canon of knowledge, problems, questions and answers, as well as setting the system of surveillance to ensure that candidates were meeting the standards of knowledge acquisition and skill disposition approved. Special Boards of Examiners were established to regulate the implementation of the standards; they reproduced the knowledge that the syndicates had produced. Hence the Special Board of the revised Moral Sciences Tripos prior to 1904 had these tasks:

(i) to mark out the areas of study under each examination paper;
(ii) to publish a list of books on which questions would be set;
(iii) to modify the above from time to time;
(iv) to arrange and set schedules of examinations.

Excellence in style and method were prioritised in the regulations for marking the answers.[16]

Examiners can then be seen as the gatekeepers of knowledge and standards, past whom all those seeking to pass into public life must pass. As quality assessors their job was to certify that, to the best of their knowledge, each passing candidate had acquired the standard of knowledge and skills prescribed by the syndicates. To ensure that the gold standard was not open to question, women had to be separated in their entry into this system and passage through it until after the end of the century; and were even examined in separate rooms. Lists of successful candidates were to be published in a manner and order that clearly respected the ownership of knowledge by the University, and which

[16] *Cambridge University Calendar* (Cambridge, 1904), pp. 64–6.

communicated in an unchallengeable manner the hierarchy of excellence in list form. The world was to know what Cambridge classed as knowledge in the publication of pass lists. A man's status, career and fame was seen as hanging on his place in the lists, because his position indicated his capacity for consuming and deploying the knowledge that the University, through its examiners, thought was worth knowing. Payment of examiners was poor, but the posts were highly sort after because, like membership of a disciplinary academy, it indicated one's status as guardian of the knowledge. Appointment was achieved only by invitation from the Special Boards or, in special circumstances, by the existing examiners to ensure the right calibre of men were chosen. It is highly significant that the Calendars for the century always recorded who the examiners were by name for each Tripos; significant because the list provided legitimacy and comparative measures of quality control. From the Calendars we could gather the name, university, college and degrees of all examiners as well as each candidate. Cross referencing to past Tripos results allows the reader to calibrate exactly the standing, value and later performance of each student and examiner (using a notational system allowing identification of examination ranking, medals and scholarships won, fellowships, masterships, tutorships and professorships gained, professional posts such as bishoprics and Bar appointments), and so be able to establish with some accuracy the quality of each output. Once admitted to the University and Tripos, women were given their own separate league tables.

Between them the parties to these constructions established an agenda as to what was knowledge, or the knowledge worth having for two generations of students. Who the students were and where their career destinations lay has not been well documented outside the Calendars and Venn's *Alumni Cantabrigienses*.[17] We know many went into the Church as senior leaders, into the Civil Service at home and abroad, especially the Indian Civil Service. As opportunities in the Church lessened the secular professions drew candidates, especially law, education in the public schools, publishing, and politics, though not especially into banking or any entrepreneurial activities. Being a small and reclusive group the members of the Cambridge Apostles form an unrepresentative, but still a useful and illustrative seismic sample.[18] From 1860 to 1914 the professions attracted 93 percent of the Apostles, of whom only 3 percent went into the clergy, 26 percent into law, 20 percent became schoolmasters and 43 percent (123) university dons. Only 11 percent ever dabbled in business. In these positions, the consumers of the Cambridge education were able to reproduce the knowledge learned with consummate ease and with singularly good effect. Publishers were anxious to reproduce the Cambridge curriculum as advertisements in the Cambridge Calendars reveal.

---

[17] J. and J. A. Venn, *Alumni Cantabrigienses* (Cambridge, 1940–54).
[18] Lubenow, *Apostles*.

Disputes, degrees and the determination of knowledge

In this brief description of three parties to the construction of the Moral Science Tripos between 1855 and 1870, I will identify three major combatants. Other parties existed, namely a group best identified as the Theologians and Divines, self-confessed upholders of Christian dogma, the group later to dog Darwin and the authors of *Essays and Reviews* (1861), and a group we can call the University Administrators, best represented by Romilly, whose self-confessed task was to uphold the standing of the University.[19] Categorising my three parties is a task fraught with problems, some of which reach to the heart of my venture here, but necessity requires the production of terms to convey my meaning. My categories are reactionaries, reformers and radicals (collectively the last two being 'progressives').[20] Most of these groups either shared the social space of the others or would do after the period on which I reflect. So Whewell and his supporters were once reformers but in my period are reactionaries; the reformers in my period are labelled later by Sidgwick as conservatives, and even my radical group around Sidgwick, Stephen and Fawcett are held to represent the past and to be a block on reform by the end of the century. However three groups can be identified as contributing to the debate on what constituted knowledge in morals, philosophy, history, politics, economics and law in our period.

Following two decades of reforming zeal, by the mid-1850s Whewell and his circle had achieved a position of eminence from which they felt able to orchestrate and conduct the construction and reproduction of knowledge. The best identification of this group is the one given by Cannon, who called them the Rationalist node of the *Cambridge Network*.[21] Assisted by Adam Sedgwick, Herschel and others, this group sought to colonise all disciplines and areas of the curriculum with dons fit and able to transmit their version of knowledge.[22] The intellectual structure of this enterprise is cleverly set out by Simon Schaffer; the cultural links in construction and diffusion are set out by Cannon.[23] Dismissive of the 'steam' philosophy of London and the new cities, the rationalists felt able to incorporate some of the more 'geometric' ambitions of the Scottish school and William Rowan Hamilton from Ireland. But the main sources were still the Cambridge staples of Plato, Euclid, Samuel Clarke, Newton and Bacon. So the Moral and Natural Sciences were constructed in Cambridge around these figures, as part of the group's colonial ambitions,

---

[19] J. P. T. Bury, ed., *Romilly's Cambridge Diary, 1823–1842* (Cambridge, 1967); M. E. Bury and J. D. Pickles, *Romilly's Cambridge Diary, 1842–1847* (Cambridge, 1994).
[20] H. Becher, 'From Mathematics to Moral Philosophy', in *William Whewell: A Composite Portrait*, ed. M. Fisch and S. Schaffer (Oxford, 1991), p. 25.
[21] S. F. Cannon, 'Scientists and Broad Churchmen: an Early Victorian Intellectual Network', *Journal of British Studies*, 4 (1964).
[22] Becher, 'Mathematics', pp. 24–9.
[23] Simon Schaffer, 'The History and Geography of the Intellectual World: Whewell's Politics of Language', in *William Whewell: A Composite Portrait*, ed. M. Fisch and S. Schaffer (Oxford, 1991); Cannon, 'Scientists'.

seeking certainties from the world of flux, truth from progressive acts of observation, induction, discovery and reason.

By 1860 they felt that their script was being lost to two groups, the new 'progressive' reformers around John Grote, Joseph Mayor and his brothers, Henry Roby, J. B. Pearson, John Venn, Leonard Courtney, J. B. Lightfoot, F. J. A. Hort and John Seeley, and the emerging young radicals, led in this period by Leslie Stephen but soon to enlist Henry Sidgwick and Alfred Marshall, from within, and Henry Fawcett from without. Venn sat comfortably between them. The reformers were essentially the inheritors of the other node of the Cambridge Network, the romantics and idealists. They sought to bring the French Eclectics, German idealism, critical theology and hermeneutics, and the Scottish idealist James Ferrier into the curriculum. The radicals can best be identified as the disciples of the alien creeds of the steam philosophy, utilitarianism and empiricism and materialism. They sought to introduce the books of John Stuart Mill, Bentham and Alexander Bain into the prescribed reading lists, supported in 1874 by the *Westminster Review*.[24] It is this group that C. M. Ingleby railed against as the 'enemy' in his letter to the Electors in 1872 supported by his epic essay on *Reflections Historical and Critical on the Revival of Philosophy at Cambridge* and letters of 1870.[25] Held at bay by the reformers, and then during a reactionary period identified with the election of Thomas Rawlinson Birks, the radicals came to show their ambition only with the election of Fawcett to the Political Economy chair in 1863 and of Sidgwick to the Knightbridge chair of Moral Philosophy in 1883.

The intervention by Clement Mansfield Ingleby (1823–1886) in the battle over the Moral Sciences Tripos is illuminating. Ingleby entered Trinity College in 1843, graduated senior optime in 1847 and became MA in 1850 and LLD in 1859. He entered his father's legal firm in Edgbaston, but soon redirected his efforts into Shakespearean 'hermeneutic' research and the teaching of logic at a local Institute.[26] His philosophical corpus included *An Introduction to Metaphysics* (1869); *An Outline of Theoretical Logic* (1856), essays on Bacon, De Morgan, and Sir Rowan Hamilton in the *British Controversialist*, and critical commentaries on Bacon, Coleridge and J. S. Mill in his *Essays* of 1888 edited by his son Holcombe. Ingleby first indicated his polemical and political intentions in dedicating his 'Revival' of 1870 to James Hutchinson Stirling, the idealist author of *The Secret of Hegel*.[27] That he had reached his target is illustrated in the letter appended in the Cambridge University Library copy from Ingleby to H. R. Luard who was the Registrary and Chair of the Board of Moral Sciences in 1870.[28] The intention of the essay and letters of 1870 was to ensure that the

[24] Anon, 1874.
[25] C. M. Ingleby, *Reflections Historical and Critical on the Revival of Philosophy at Cambridge* (Cambridge, 1870); letters from Ingleby in Cambridge University Library Cam.c.870.9, CUR 39.9.61.
[26] H. Ingleby, ed., *Essays of C. M. Ingleby* (1888).
[27] J. H. Stirling, *The Secret of Hegel* (1865); Ingleby, *Reflections*.
[28] CUL Cam.c.870.9.

revival of the professional study of philosophy at Cambridge from 1855–70 was not diluted by bringing history, jurisprudence and English law into the Tripos, nor diminished by poor appointments and selection of books and questions. Ingleby wished to see the subject revived but under the tutelage of a Grotian-style reformer and idealist such as Stirling. He wished to argue against the appointment of another 'divine' and against a 'Millian' radical.

Reviewing recent curricular debates, Ingleby repeats the received view that metaphysics and logic have taken second place to mathematics and classics in the University. Whewell is given some credit and John Grote more for the revival of the subject, but the subsequent appointment of Maurice, 'a divine,' is portrayed as 'a humiliating confession' either that the University had no suitably qualified candidates for the Knightbridge chair, or 'that philosophy was at a discount on the Cam'.[29] Replying to a rebuff from the University Registrary, Ingleby did not retreat but added fuel to his claims.[30] In further letters of 1872 he advocates appointing a scholar such as Stirling grounded in the modern traditions of philosophy: such idealism, as well as the past history of philosophy, being encoded in the set books of 1855–60. Ingleby also rails at the Syndics who established the Tripos, for their exclusion of professional philosophers on the Board of Studies; their regulations that excluded many suitable students; and their inculcation of the implication that the Moral Sciences were a 'shady' subject that held no prospect of a fellowship.[31] On electors to philosophy chairs (the Professors of Divinity, Greek and Modern History, the Vice Chancellor and the Master of Peterhouse in 1872) and examiners for Tripos, he argues that appointing non-philosophers was leading to the dilution of specialism.[32] But he saves his hardest punches for chapter IV on the selection of textbooks. Examination questions had to be made on the basis of books set. Ingleby contrasts the approved lists of 1860 and 28 March 28 1867 and rails at the reactionary exclusion in the latter of three key idealist texts: Fichte's *Ethical System* which he sees as replaced by Bentham; and two Kant texts including the *Critique of Pure Reason* which is ejected in favour of Victor Cousin's commentary; similarly with the idealist *Institute of Metaphysics* of James Frederick Ferrier.[33] Kant is pioneered as essential, and Stirling is quoted in support of the claim that Hume must be studied to understand Kant, and Kant as a precursor to Hegel.[34] He quotes approvingly the Hare Prize essay of 1868 by Norman MacColl of Downing, who uses Kant and Hegel alongside several German commentators and British translators.[35] The final chapter examines the questions set and complains of their balance and coherence, especially the questions on Kant. By

---

[29] Ingleby, *Reflections*, p. 25.
[30] Ingleby to Luard, 1870 in CUL Cam.c.870.9
[31] Ingleby, *Reflections*, pp. 26–31.
[32] Ingleby, *Reflections*, p. 36.
[33] Ingleby, *Reflections*, p. 48.
[34] Ingleby, *Reflections*, pp. 53–8.
[35] Ingleby, *Reflections*, p. 60.

1872, when the chair became vacant on the death of Maurice, Ingleby ran a near-successful campaign championing Stirling for the Knightbridge chair, against three Grote Society members (Sidgwick for the radicals, Venn and Pearson for the reformers) and the reactionary Birks. The grounds for failure were unexpected to all parties. Both Stirling and Ingleby had ignored the utterly inadequate income supporting the incumbent to the chair and the assumption that its holder would have access to a College living.[36] Luard and his colleagues responded by appointing Birks (3 votes) to the vacant post of Knightbridge Professor of Moral Philosophy. With an electorate balanced in favour of divinity, Venn, Pearson and Sidgwick managed to split the reformers, obtaining one vote each.[37]

John Grote and reform

My case study covers the period 1855–70, spanning the guardianships of philosophical knowledge of John Grote and Frederick Denison Maurice. I choose this period for several reasons. First, it is often ignored or underplayed in the established literature we have, being sandwiched between two great reforming movements and two personalities – William Whewell and Henry Sidgwick. Second, this period saw the crucial widening and tuning of the Tripos that made it more acceptable to the University if not, as yet, to candidates. Third, this period belies the two contesting constructions of the moral sciences and philosophy in Cambridge at that time, the 'reactionary bastion of classics and mathematics' and the rival contention of 'revolution'.

In 1855 William Whewell the Knightbridge professor resigned, overburdened with his duties as author, editor, Master of Trinity College and periodically vice-chancellor of the University. John Grote was elected in his place and immediately began the dual task of preparing lectures and planning reforms for the Moral Science Tripos. Prior to the reform of the Tripos in 1860, the Moral Sciences had been in fairly serious disrepute both inside and outside the University. The rules allowed only postgraduate students to take the course when they were seeking fellowships, MAs or Doctorates. But the reasons for this disrepute were academic as well as administrative. Under Whewell's direction a Moral Sciences Tripos had been created in October 1848, but it had no homogeneity, the subject matter including general examinations in Moral Philosophy, Political Economy, Modern History, General Jurisprudence and the Laws of England. However, two other issues compounded the problem. Firstly a new Tripos in Law was established and it also included the courses in Jurisprudence and Law. It had begun to attract those students who were considering the law as a profession. Moreover the Classical Tripos had begun to include courses in philosophy. Secondly the Moral Sciences Tripos did not

[36] CUL CUR 39.9.61.
[37] CUL O xiv.53.47

lead to the award of a degree.[38] A student needed a BA before going on to honours in moral sciences and this ruled it out as a course of study for the bulk of undergraduates. The Senate had been petitioned to remove this anomaly in 1854, but had refused on the grounds that the moral sciences did not offer a suitable subject matter for the education of undergraduates, a popular prejudice that recurs in the succeeding arguments about academic reforms.[39]

After considerable pressure, the Senate in 1859 approved a petition for the appointment of a syndicate 'to consider whether any changes should be made in the regulations concerning the Moral Sciences Tripos'. The scheme recommended was that of J. B. Mayor and John Grote. Its major suggestions were (a) to allow an undergraduate with a pass in honours to obtain a BA degree; (b) to set up a Board of Moral Sciences to agree on an examination, syllabus and booklists; and (c) to recommend the replacement of English Law by a study of mental philosophy.[40] The two leading reformers, Mayor and Grote, feared that the Senate would be prejudiced against the recommendations, and submitted flysheets in their support to the Senate.[41] Mayor's appeal is the most comprehensive but Grote's paper reflected his conviction of the value of philosophy in the universities. Grote firstly echoes the complaints of J. S. Mill and others that Cambridge is

> surely almost the only school of higher instruction in the world which takes (may it be said so?) no account of logic or philosophy in any form, and makes no attempt to educate the reasoning powers by any other means than mathematics and grammar or ancient literature.

and recommended correction as soon as possible. He ended by pleading that

> I would like to see the University taking a wide interest in the intellectual movement of the country, in order to be able to influence it for the good.

The recommendations of the committee were fully accepted on 23 February 1860 and the Board of Moral Sciences set to work to discuss the examination scheme and books for the Tripos. The booklists and schemes that were submitted tell us a great deal about the dominant areas of interest in philosophy at the time and Grote's recommendations can be supposed to be indicative of his own preferences.[42] The documents reveal firstly Grote's preference for the

---

[38] Sidgwick, 'Philosophy at Cambridge', *Mind*, I (1876), p. 224.
[39] In a biographical note in the *Exploratio* Grote wrote, 'Myself, not owing much I think to any philosophical teaching . . . I owe almost all such interest as I take in philosophy to what is next best to teaching, if it is not better, to companionship.' Grote, *Exploratio*, p. xxxv.
[40] CUL Cambridge University Papers D.C. 5650.
[41] J. Grote, *Remarks on the Proposals of the Syndicate in Reference to the Moral Science Tripos* (Cambridge, 1860); J. B. Mayor, *Remarks on the Proposal to Grant the Degree of B.A. to Persons who have Obtained Honours in the Moral Science Tripos*. More details can be found in Winstanley, *Later Victorian Cambridge*, pp. 186–90.
[42] J. Grote, *A Draft Scheme of the Examinations in Moral Sciences* (Cambridge, 1860); Trinity College Library Add. MSS a.62/61. H. J. Roby, *Remarks on the Criticism of Whewell and*

philosophers of England and Scotland at the expense of the Continentals, 'Kant's Critique of Pure Reason, is the only book of modern German philosophy which I would have.'[43] H. J. Roby correctly identifies this as a weakness and in particular points out the omission of any reference to Hegel.[44] Second, the 'Draft Scheme' reveals Grote's reservations about the confused metaphysical rambling of Coleridge, as well as the practical position of Comte, Bentham, Austin and Spencer.[45] Finally, it is apparent that Grote, along with others, followed Whewell's preferences for a historical bent to studies, and supported the idea that papers in Modern History include both 'History and Political Philosophy'.[46] In recommending the works of Montesquieu, De Tocqueville and Mill, he hoped to pioneer the introduction of politics as a subject distinct from economics and history, a hope that was finally fulfilled in a reform of 1867.[47] The proposal reflected the Vichian and Liberal Anglican background to Grote's views on historical development.[48]

The reform of the Moral Sciences Tripos was not the limit of Grote's reforming activities, for he was a member of a select group at Trinity who achieved fairly radical reforms of the tuition system, the revision of rules governing the use of religious 'tests', and the award of scholarships and fellowships, and who managed to force through a scheme for limiting the powers of the Master of the College in all matters concerning college finance and access to college rooms. John Grote's role in these vitally-needed reforms is hardly mentioned in the recent literature on the reform of Victorian Cambridge, though at the time he was called a 'revolutionary' and a 'left-wing' reformer by his more conservative enemies.[49] In reality, Grote was a prime mover in that lengthy process which helped bring about the major academic and structural changes needed to bring the University into line with the new society of the times.[50] But once again William Whewell as master resented Grote's reforming activities. He wrote to his prospective wife, Lady Affleck, 'And our friend Mr Grote and others like him have found me employment for Friday.' He describes the opinions of 'the boys' as 'odious' and one proposal concerning the elections amongst fellows as 'hateful'.[51] As before, Grote had been mindful of the challenges to Cambridge and the University world from competing groups

Professor Grote on the List of Books which have been Laid before the Board of Moral Sciences (Cambridge, 1860).
[43] Grote, *Draft Scheme*, p. 10.
[44] Roby, *Remarks*.
[45] Grote, *Draft Scheme*, pp. 5–10.
[46] Grote, *Draft Scheme*, p. 3.
[47] See also Collini et al., *Noble Science*, pp. 339–63.
[48] D. Forbes, *The Liberal Anglican Idea of History* (Cambridge, 1952); Cannon, 'Scientists'.
[49] Winstanley, *Early*, p. 347; *Later*, p. 252.
[50] Robson, R., 'Trinity College in the Age of Peel', in *Ideas and Institutions of Victorian Britain: Essays in Honour of G. S. R. Kitson Clark*, ed. R. Robson (London, 1967); Rothblatt, *Revolution*; Garland, *Before Darwin*; Winstanley, *Early Victorian Cambridge*, *Later Victorian Cambridge*.
[51] TCL Add. MS a.81/395; Add. MS a.81/401.

and bodies from outside. As before, his response is one of careful but liberal reform, not the conservative reaction exhibited by Whewell in his later life. Grote wished to preserve what was good in the old system,[52] but supported the Royal Commission on some democratic reforms.[53]

Teaching and talking politics

In their chapter on the teaching of politics in mid-Victorian Cambridge, Collini, Winch and Burrow take the normal line, stating that 'To say the study of politics hardly figured in the Cambridge curriculum before 1860 is to say very little, so few were the subjects which appeared there in any form'.[54] Their coverage of events up to 1872 is brief and suggests little improvement in the matter. My short case study here suggests we may need to revise this picture and see instead a battle developing to bring new subjects into the field of elite knowledge. Politics, law and history to Grote were an embodiment of the conversation of minds over time:

---

[52] Grote had become a Senior Fellow in 1854 as the result of an unfortunate incident recounted by Winstanley. An existing senior fellow and Regius Professor of Greek, W. H. Thompson, had been removed from his fellowship: Joseph Edleston, a radical liberal, had petitioned the Home Secretary concerning the propriety of his election to and retention of both a Senior Fellowship and a Regius Chair (Winstanley, *Early*, pp. 303–12). Grote himself supported reforms to the rules concerning election of Regius Professors in 1857 and Seniors and fellows in the next few years, becoming, particularly heavily involved in the latter, writing two printed flysheets on reform of the statutes in 1859. In May 1857 Grote was elected onto a Governing Body Committee set up to propose reforms to the whole college statutes, which went on to propose, according to Joseph Romilly, absolutely 'drastic changes' (Winstanley, *Later*, p. 343). Grote was a persistent critic of the College establishment and Romilly once records after a long meeting, that Grote was 'infinitely tiresome' (Romilly 1853–64, *Diaries* MS Cam. 6804–6842).

[53] On this point Grote stayed loyal to Whewell's old dreams. The two had fallen out on most other matters by 1860, as the new, and ever more liberal, professor challenged one after another of the Master's, once liberal but now, old and reactionary looking reforms of three decades earlier. Siding with the Commissioners and Edleston, Charles King and Westlake, Grote engendered the sustained wrath of the aging master. As Winstanley notes, when Grote in 1857 proposed that 'there shall be an annual meeting of the Master and the whole body of the fellows on the Commemoration Day, with power of adjournment, and that any representative, petition or enactment to be made by the colleges of any time for amendment of the existing statutes, proceed from that body', democracy was considered to have overleaped the bounds. Romilly called the proposal hateful and mischievous, Sedgwick claimed that 'Such a measure would put in the hands of every fellow, soon after he was elected a torch, with the invitation to try its efficiency' (Winstanley, *Early*, pp. 343–48). Grote's proposal was carried twelve years later (Winstanley, *Later*, p. 252). On a related issue of the election of seniors and fellows Grote proposed that six of the senior fellows should constitute the appointment board and that they should be able to elect 'without the consent of the Master'. In a virulently worded reply the Master demanded for himself 'Such powers as may enable him to promote the well-being of the Body over which he presides' and adds 'When there is a question of power between sixty persons on one side and one on the other, to refer it to the whole body of sixty one, each person having an equal vote, is a palpably absurd proceeding.' CUL, Cam.c.857,15.

[54] Collini et al., *Noble Science*, p. 344.

Sociality or political life has been the gradual conversion of this state of things into one of mutual understanding and consideration: bare power has become authority by the prevalence of the feeling on the one side of obedience that is duty, and on the other that the exercise of it is not for private benefit, but for the benefit of all.[55]

Analysis of political history was understood as mind meeting minds, not just old documents, practices, institutions and activities. A respect for the minds of many different others was influenced not just by humanism, but by a real belief that by engaging the widest possible past and present sources, we may discern a picture coming out, a picture of growing benefit to all and social inclusion.[56]

In one sense, we should not be surprised by the lack of interest in or even recognition of a social and political theory in Grote's writings. Political and social issues were important not only to Grote but to many other representatives of the two schools of Cambridge philosophy up to 1860. However, the formal structure and compulsory reading for the moral sciences were very narrow up to then and would encourage both insiders and outsiders to place little stress upon political and social issues.[57] Discussions of contemporary political and social issues had to be conducted within the straitjacket of the regulations for the Moral Sciences, Classical and Law Triposes and their attendant list of books agreed for study. Creative tutors could and did run rings around the regulations, but politics entered more genuinely by extrapolating from set texts and classical authorities to their modern equivalents. Discussions of democratic Athens and republican Rome, Pericles, Socrates, Plato, Aristotle and Cicero could be turned into vehicles for the discussion of democracy in contemporary Europe, as could the otherwise tame-looking histories of Guizot and Hallam, Bentham on laws, Kant and Fichte on ethics and Adam Smith, Ricardo, Malthus and J. S. Mill on political economy.

The key philosophers touched on, in the 1837 fellowship examinations Grote sat, were Locke, Brown, Berkeley, Stewart, Butler, Paley, Cicero and Aristotle. Political issues covered only about one third of the questions set, and economic and social issues were hardly represented at all. Between 1848, when the Senate agreed on an honours course in Moral Sciences for students who had already graduated in another Tripos, and 1855, when Grote took the Knightbridge chair, Whewell's personal impact and his books were predominant. There were two separate papers on Whewell's *Elements of Morality* and about one third of the questions covered within them were of a political character. Separate papers in Political Economy, Modern History, General Jurisprudence and the Laws of England were added to Mental and Moral Philosophy in the 1848 reform. Generally the impression gained from these papers between 1855 and 1866 is

---

[55] J. Grote, *A Treatise on the Moral Ideals* (Cambridge, 1876), p. 224.
[56] Grote, *Exploratio*, Vol. 2, pp. 205–9; *Moral Ideals*, pp. 267–74.
[57] Collini et al., *Noble Science*, pp. 341–6.

one of extreme diffusion of disciplines, but over-specialisation within them, so that Moral Philosophy rests on Plato, Aristotle, Grotius, Clarke, Butler, Mackintosh and Stewart with the occasional reference to Kant or Coleridge.

The reformed Tripos of 1860 did allow a deeper and wider study of political and social issues as Sidgwick, Rothblatt and more recently Collini have argued.[58] Being allowed to sit for the Tripos for the first time, undergraduates found themselves faced with examinations in Moral Philosophy, Mental Philosophy and Logic, Modern History, Political Economy and General Jurisprudence. The key modern texts for the former were by Dugald Stewart, Paley, Whewell, Kant and Fichte; and by Descartes, Locke, Reid, Kant, Cousins and Hamilton for mental philosophy. On 'History and Political Philosophy' students had to read Plato, Aristotle, Montesquieu, Guizot, Hallam and 'Brougham's Political Philosophy'; and Adam Smith, Malthus, Ricardo, J. S. Mill, McCulloch, Jones, Carey and Chevallier for 'Political Economy'. Bentham was covered under 'Jurisprudence'. Little change occurred as a result of the modifications of 1867 except the removal of the papers on 'History' and 'Jurisprudence'. In 1870, under the guidance of F. D. Maurice, Fichte's *Ethical Works* were dropped from the approved reading though Kant's *Einklarung in die Metaphysik der Sitten* and his *Tugendlehre* were added to Moral and Political Philosophy; Kant's own *Kritik der Reinen Vernunft* was dropped under Mental Philosophy but Ferrier's *Institutes of Metaphysic* and Cousin's *Philosophie de Kant* were added. By 1880 under Birks' leadership Kant's *Groundwork* remained and Grote's *Examination of Utilitarianism* was added to the former and his *Exploratio Philosophica* to the Mental Philosophy examination syllabus.[59] But from this time onwards the professionalisation of teaching in both philosophy and politics developed rapidly under Sidgwick's guidance and politics especially came out into the open as an independent and respected course of study, though German influence began to wane.[60]

The examination papers in fact provide a better guide to what was actually taught and discussed in the moral sciences at the time than either the formal syllabus or the booklists. These are available in the *Cambridge Calendars* for 1854–5. Both in the areas of politics and of philosophy there are surprises. Questions were regularly set on the political issues of rights, justice, law, obligation, theories of the state, the origins of private property, on the political philosophy papers between 1860 and 1867.[61] On the mental philosophy papers for undergraduates and fellows the questions were even more revealing, as they regularly contained questions on German idealist philosophers before the period when convention agrees these subjects were unpopular. Questions on Kant's ethics appeared three times in the Moral Philosophy papers in the Moral Sciences

---

[58] Rothblatt, *Revolution*; Sidgwick, 'Philosophy at Cambridge', *Mind*, Vol. 1, no 2 (1876); Collini et al., *Noble Sciences*, pp. 344–7.
[59] *Cambridge University Calendar* 1860, 1870, 1880.
[60] Winstanley, *Early, Later*; *Cambridge University Calendar*.
[61] TCL 330 a.1.18–21.

Tripos papers in 1863 and 1864, and nine questions on Kant appeared in the Mental Philosophy papers.[62] In the Trinity fellowship examinations of October 1860 a question appeared on the epistemologies of 'Locke, Hume, Kant, Fichte, Schelling and Hegel', the last three reappearing in the paper for September 1864. In October 1863, when as usual the examiners were Grote and Whewell, question 11 read 'Give an account of the general relation to each other of the successive German Philosophies of Kant, Fichte, Schelling and Hegel' and in September 1862 there was a question on 'the Kantian doctrine' of space and time'.[63] Questions on Fichte's moral philosophy appear three times, in December 1863, November and December 1864 in the Moral Sciences Tripos examinations, set presumably by Grote and his colleagues H. J. Roby and J. B. Mayor.[64] The paper in History and Political Philosophy of November 1864 also had questions on consent theory, divine right, prescriptive and expediency theories of authority, the origins of the feudal system, on checks and balances, two questions on Montesquieu and one on liberty.[65] Kingship, democracy, republicanism, representative government, constitutions and liberty regularly appear in the History and Political Philosophy papers and Adam Smith, Locke, Malthus, Ricardo and Mill on Political Economy.

When put alongside Roby's advocacy of Vico and Hegel for the Tripos in 1860, this evidence suggests an interest in and knowledge of both political philosophy and German idealistic thought by at least Grote, Whewell and the two moral science tutors of the time, a knowledge demanded equally of all fellowship candidates of Trinity and of undergraduates. We should also keep in mind that H. J. Roby was along with Grote, Henry Maine, and Robert Ellis deeply interested in Roman law and was later to produce definitive works in this area; and questions on natural law, the law of nations and international law regularly appeared in fellowship examinations. In many ways the period 1861–6 was the high water mark for the influence of German thought on the Moral Sciences Tripos in mid-Victorian Cambridge, with not only a noticed increase in quantity but in complexity and diversity of questions.

James Ward, fresh from his studies of idealism in Germany in 1873, would have found the Moral Sciences Tripos congenial to his interests.[66] In the paper of 6 February 1861 in Mental Philosophy, five out of the ten questions set dealt with aspects of Kant's work. On 7 February there were questions on the progress of metaphysics from Locke to Kant, Fichte's system and its context and a comparison of Bentham and Coleridge. On 28 November 1861 the Moral Philosophy paper had two questions on Kant, on the source of value and the supreme role, plus a long analysis of a piece on duty by Fichte. Kant appeared again in six questions in the examination of Mental Philosophy of 29 November

[62] St John's College Library (hereafter SJCL) P.6, 2.14, 15.
[63] SJCL P.2.19.
[64] SJCL P.6 2.14–15.
[65] SJCL P.6, 2.15.
[66] J. Ward, *Essays in Philosophy* (Cambridge, 1927), pp. 19–31, 47–53.

1861, one of which also included the systems of Fichte and Schelling.[67] In the various Moral and Mental Philosophy papers of November 1866 there are six questions on Kantian idealism and three on Fichte.

Serious intent is revealed in the following, which may explain that low enrolment for the course was due to restrictive admission rules, its limited postgraduate constituency and belief that it would not lead to a fellowship, its complexity and profundity rather than its backward and reactionary character or its lack of accommodation of positivist and utilitarian ideas. Moral Philosophy papers 27 November 1866, Question 9, 'What does Kant mean by the "principle of the autonomy of the will". Give the process by which he establishes this principle. Give a careful comparison of the meaning given by Kant and Fichte respectively of the terms, "Freedom", "Will", "Categorical Imperative". Explain clearly the meaning Kant gives to Achtung, Maxime, Interesse'. That on 26 November 1866 contains as Question 9, 'Explain Fichte's answer to the question, "What is the criterion of the correctness of our convictions of our duty?" Comment on his analysis of the operation of conscience. Compare it with Butler's and discuss any incompleteness or error you may perceive in either'. Two of the questions under Mental Philosophy leave little room for avoidance of key issues. Question 9 on 27 November reads 'How far are synthetic propositions a priori possible? How far are they possible without intuitions? Give instances'. Question 8 of 29 November reads, 'Explain the words transcendent, transcendental, as used by Kant. Distinguish Transcendental from Empirical Idealism. Explain how the former deals with the question, whether the past duration of the world has been finite or infinite? Explain the connection (according to Kant) between the transcendental use of reason, and the logical.'[68]

While under Maurice's direction German scholarship remained important, the frequency of questions declined, with Ferrier substituting for Fichte by 1870. Still in November and December of that year Kant's *Critique of Pure Reason*, his comparison with utilitarians, with Plato, Aristotle, Descartes, Whewell and Mill are questioned, along with his ideas of the moral agent, pleasure and aesthetics.[69] Coleridge, Schleiermacher, Trendelenburg, Cousin and Ferrier plus the absolute, idealism, and the 'understanding' appeared in 1869; and in 1868 amongst other questions on Kant appeared an essay in the History of Philosophy paper entitled, 'Give some account of German Philosophy since the death of Hegel', and in 1862 a question on Jacobi. Under Birks such questions dwindled and Sidgwick, despite his admiration for Kant, was not the man to restore idealistic studies to the University curriculum. Mozley noted that Sidgwick found reading Kant 'like a difficult mathematical book . . . he did not think Hegel was intelligible at all – I suppose that opinion does not do

[67] CUL L 952 b.1.38.
[68] CUL L 952 b.1.43.
[69] CUL L 952 b.1.47.

justice to Hegel'.[70] We know from Ingleby that Kant was at the heart of questions until the 1870s even if not formulated as he wished.[71]

Teaching itself, we are told by Stephen and others, was not regarded as an important activity for professors, formal tuition being left to the poorly-paid and overworked college tutors of the day and the highly-paid private tutors like Shilleto, who were masters of the arts of cramming.[72] To some extent the moral science students during Grote's tenure of office were lucky. First, he took teaching seriously until his illness in 1864, and as against the practices of several professors, including Charles Kingsley the Regius Professor of Modern History who taught spasmodically, he lectured every week of every term on all days except Wednesdays.[73] Second, Grote was aided by several excellent college moral science tutors, all to have illustrious careers, including Henry Sidgwick at Trinity College, H. J. Roby and J. B. Mayor (followed by Isaac Todhunter) at St John's, Leslie Stephen at Trinity Hall, and John Venn at Caius. Third, teaching was aided at the time by excellent libraries but especially in the colleges supplemented by useful personal collections. Fourth, the teaching groups were small but contained some students to challenge the tutors including F. J. A. Hort, later Professor of Divinity, R. L. Ellis and J. B. Pearson. Fifth, Grote's professional colleagues included challenging and influential teachers such as the Professor of Political Economy Henry Fawcett, Sir James Stephen followed by Charles Kingsley in the Chair of Modern History, and Henry Maine, Regius Professor of Civil Law between 1847 and 1854, a year prior to Grote's election. Unfortunately student recruitment was poor for the Moral Sciences Tripos, with only seventy-eight successful candidates between 1855 and 1866.

Political and social debate could also be expected within the context of Trinity social life where many influential liberals of the day as well as Christian socialists could be relied upon to direct conversation. Cambridge had its intellectual and debating societies, some of which like the Republican Club,[74] the Apostles[75] and the Grote Society regularly turned their attention to politics. The Grote Society was to have a major and long-term impact upon Cambridge intellectual life, since it gave rise to the Moral Sciences Club. Founded by Grote to bring the young moral sciences tutors together, on a suggestion from Joseph Mayor, the Grote Society originally included John Grote, Henry Sidgwick, John Venn, Joseph Mayor, later Professor of Moral Philosophy at Kings College, London, J. B. Pearson, classical and medieval historian, Aldis Wright the Trinity Librarian, and Ralph Benjamin Somerset. Occasional visitors were allowed to converse after a generous dinner, usually at Trumpington, and we certainly

---

[70] TCL Add. MS c.104/66–8.
[71] Ingleby, *Reflections*, pp. 70–81.
[72] Stephen, *Sketches*.
[73] CUL Cambridge Papers E.A.17.
[74] CUL Add. 4251 (B) 713a.
[75] Lubenow, *Apostles*, pp. 226–30.

know of a visit by Sidgwick's future brother-in-law and Archbishop of Canterbury, E. W. Benson.[76] I suspect that selected visitors to Trumpington Rectory, such as George Grote and Alexander Bain, were given visitor status and allowed to attend meetings. Alexandrina Jessie Grote was given membership after being proposed by Henry Sidgwick: she was the first female member.[77] The Grote Club, as it was known after Grote's death, added F. D. Maurice, Alfred Marshall, later Cambridge Professor of Political Economy, John R. Mozley, future Professor of Divinity at Oxford, William K. Clifford, future Professor of Logic in London and J. F. Moulton, and regularly turned its attention to social and political issues.[78] According to Joseph and Jessie Mayor, the term 'Society' was coined by John Grote though it became nicknamed '*Sabia Conversazion*' according to Alexandrina Jessie Mayor after a comic drawing room scene in a play by Giassick.[79]

Participation in politics was rarer but not unknown. Trinity could number J. Westlake and J. Rigby as liberal Parliamentary candidates, while Robert Leslie Ellis, Grote's close friend, was a prospective candidate for Bath. St John's College had H. J. Roby, L. H. Courtney; Trinity Hall had Henry Fawcett and Professor James F. Stephen was a successful candidate at Harwich in 1865.[80] When we add to this the number of fellows who became heavily involved in the legal profession, the upper echelons of the civil service, in journalism, and in doing good deeds amongst the working masses of London, Cambridge and some northern cities, we come up with a picture of a college and a university far more politically and socially aware, informed and active than might have been suspected. This was the cultural ambience in which Grote's political and social theory was conceived.

Reformers and radicals

The premature triumph of the liberal reformers met its first serious challenge in 1862 when a vacancy opened for the chair in Political Economy. The Grotian reformers put forward Grote's close friend Joseph Mayor for the post, fully expecting that the young radicals would give support. The radicals, however, had a different agenda, one that was to lead to the triumph of Sidgwick in 1883. Leslie Stephen recounts the conspiracy that led to the utilitarian Fawcett's narrow victory, which marked the zenith of the power of the mid-century idealist

---

[76] TCL Add. MS c.104/69.
[77] *Ibid.*
[78] Lubenow, *Apostles*; J. R. Gibbins, 'John Grote and Modern Cambridge Philosophy', *Philosophy*, lxxiii (1998), pp. 453–5; J. M. Keynes, *Essays in Biography* (London, 1933), pp. 158–68; Marshall's commonplace book TCL Add. MS c.104/65; J. R. Mozley J. B. Mayor, 1904, TCL Add. MS c.104/66; J. B. Pearson to J. B. Mayor 1867, TCL Mayor Papers; L. Stephen to J. Venn, Gonville and Caius College Library Venn papers C12/14.
[79] TCL Add. MS c.104/7–69.
[80] C. Harvie, *The Lights of Liberalism: University Liberals and the Challenge of Democracy* (London, 1976), pp. 269–71.

movement.[81] Mayor was a product of the romantic wing of the Cambridge movement, a liberal and a Broad Church cleric. Fawcett represented all that Mayor, Grote, Whewell and the now dwindling bunch of Coleridgians distrusted: he was a positivist, a laissez faire political economist and utilitarian, whose key reading was Mill's *Political Economy* and Buckle's *History of Civilization*.[82] Mayor's 'character and abilities were all that could be desired . . .' according to Stephen, but the battle was about a lot more and became even 'a Church and political question'.[83] In the end Fawcett won by ninety votes to eighty through the device of encouraging a third party to stand from Mayor's own college, St John's; Leonard Courtney's candidacy split the Trinity and St John's phalanx.[84] This was ironical as Courtney, as his later books reveal, was an opponent of everything utilitarian and an advocate of Kantian idealism.[85] If Mayor had joined the line of descent of professors teaching for the Moral Sciences Tripos, from Whewell to Grote and F. D. Maurice in philosophy and Charles Kingsley in history, the romantic idealist axis would have been almost complete. As it was, Fawcett would later be joined in 1872 by T. R. Birks and in 1883 by Henry Sidgwick in philosophy and J. R. Seeley in history in 1869, forming a line of a very different character in the 1870s and 1880s.

Yet even this was not unopposed. In 1872 Ingleby took up a political assault to save that tradition and line, building on the foundations he had laid in his historical and critical survey of Cambridge philosophy in 1870.[86] In letters to Luard and others in the University on the advantages of appointing James Hutchinson Stirling to succeed Maurice, he wrote of the need to appoint 'One who is absolute master of Kant and Hegel; who belongs to the Hegelian right (not like Arnold Ruge, who is of the left), who is a thorough German Scholar and modern linguist. . . .'[87] He saw the enemy as clearly as had Whewell, Hare and Maurice in the 1830s:

> there is among you a clique who are half way over to the school of sensualism, with whom Moral and Political Philosophy is an absurdity, and indeed philosophy of any sort is an impossibility. You have men lecturing in your midst whose ill-conceded or half revealed sympathies are with the '*Aufklarung*', whose negative workers are men like Colenso, and whose positive workers are Mill and Bain. Unless the five gentlemen in whom the election to the vacant chair is vested have their eyes fully open these things, we shall see one from the enemy instituted in Maurice's place.[88]

[81] L. Stephen, *Sir William Fawcett: A Biography* (London, 1885); L. Goldman, ed., *The Blind Victorian: Henry Fawcett and British Liberalism* (Cambridge, 1989).
[82] Stephen, *Fawcett*, pp. 97–8.
[83] Stephen, *Fawcett*, p. 121.
[84] Stephen, *Fawcett*, pp. 116–23.
[85] W. L. Courtney, *The Metaphysics of John Stuart Mill* (London, 1879), *Studies in Philosophy* (London, 1882), *Constructive Philosophy* (London, 1886), *Studies New and Old* (London, 1888).
[86] Ingleby, *Reflections*.
[87] CUL, CUR 39.9.61.
[88] CUL, CUR 39.9.61.

In their efforts to resist and avoid this fate, the electors resorted to extreme measures and appointed the reactionary Thomas Rawlinson Birks. Schooled by Whewell in the rationalist and intuitive arts of mathematical and moral geometry, fired by a narrow and devout religious enthusiasm, Birks set about the task of resisting the radicalism and utilitarianism in what can best be described as philosophical tracts – long in polemic but short on philosophy; sharp on attack yet weak on defence; heavy with righteous moralism and short on measured argument. Birks represented the worst, but may have been the last, of the old reactionaries who had dominated the period 1840–50. He managed in four short years to strengthen the radicals and utilitarians, such as Sidgwick and Fawcett, while weakening the rationalists and intuitionists. He turned students away from the moral sciences inside the University and fulfilled the worst characterisations of Cambridge philosophy from outside made by John Stuart Mill. My guess is that Birks' presence and teaching contributed to the severe intellectual, political, religious and personal crisis of Henry Sidgwick from 1868 to 1878, which nearly led to his departure from the University with its imaginable but incalculable loss.[89] Sidgwick's sad essay on the state of philosophy in Cambridge of 1876 is to be read against this background and not as a commentary upon the reformers of the period 1855–70.[90] Even the anonymous author of the article on 'Moral Philosophy & Cambridge' for the utilitarian *Westminster Review* of 1874 expressed a judgement against Birks, not Cambridge philosophy, and advised the appointment at the next opportunity of one of the younger and more qualified moral science tutors, from amongst John Venn, Joseph Mayor or Henry Sidgwick.[91]

In college and university politics Whewell and Sedgwick, great liberal reformers in their youth, reacted against the reformers who took their place, including John Grote, Joseph Bickersteth Mayor, H. J. Roby and Leslie Stephen. In their turn, these figures were soon overshadowed by the group around Sidgwick, but in the late 1850s John Grote's proposals for the democratic reform of Trinity could still be labelled as 'revolutionary', 'hateful' and 'mischievous'.[92] By the 1870s the spread of democratic practices and the new liberalism of Gladstone proved too much for even those good old liberals who had supported John Morley and James Bryce in the *Saturday Review*. The Cambridge liberalism associated with Maine, Grote, Mayor, James Fitzjames Stephen in the 1860s gave way[93] and was replaced by an interesting form of analytic conservatism associated most obviously with the later Maine, Fitzjames Stephen and Seeley.

---

[89] J. B. Schneewind, *Sidgwick's Ethics and Victorian Moral Philosophy* (Oxford, 1977), pp. 14–62; A. Donagan, 'Sidgwick and Whewellian Intuitionism', *Essays on Henry Sidgwick*, ed. B. Schultz, pp. 135–40.
[90] Sidgwick, 'Philosophy at Cambridge'.
[91] Anon, *Westminster Review*, 1874, pp. 430–64.
[92] Winstanley, *Early*, p. 347; *Later*, p. 252.
[93] Harvie, *Lights of Liberalism*.

The above account should have made it clear that the traditional view is in need of modification. What happened in the 1870s was not a 'Revolution' that suddenly transferred sovereignty to the University elite, using new teaching and learning strategies, but an imperceptible shift which tilted the balance from positivism to idealism, from drawing-room and debating society to lecture theatre and tutorial, from college and private club to universities and public institutions.[94] We can anticipate that this process of professionalisation and institutionalisation impacted upon Cambridge, London, Oxford and Scottish networks and institutions and effected competitive tussles between them for students, professional and state recognition and funding. What then of the internal rivalries, controversies and struggles in mid-century Cambridge, and what of John Grote's role and influence?

As the obituaries to Grote testify, his work was known about by only a small circle at Cambridge at the time. This group included, apart from Mayor and Whewell, John Venn, W. K. Clifford, John Llewelyn Davies, Leslie Stephen and his brother James Fitzjames, F. D. Maurice, Thomas Birks, F. J. Hort and above all Henry Sidgwick. None of them did much to popularise or explore Grote's work except Mayor, Hort and Sidgwick. Of them all Sidgwick is the greatest paradox. Grote Society members appeared regularly as candidates for the Knightbridge chair before 1883. Mayor and Venn competed with their friend Hort in 1866; in 1872 three Society members, Venn, Sidgwick and Pearson, split their vote and sealed their own fates and that of Cambridge philosophy that decade by letting in Birks. In 1883 Sidgwick was finally elected after a long wait, as the best candidate to develop professional philosophy in the University. The result was hardly surprising when the electors were long-time compatriots, including John Seeley, Leslie Stephen, Venn, Hort, Todhunter, Caird, Campion and Fowler.[95]

Our debt to Joseph Mayor is however the strongest, and it is only through his efforts that Grote's reputation and influence can be discussed. Without his efforts Grote's youthful question 'whether all that I have read and that I write will ever come out and show itself in such form as to be of any benefit to others which is what I most care about at present', would have been answered in the negative.[96] The thirty-six-year struggle took its toll and almost definitely handicapped a brilliant career. Unfortunately for philosophy, Joseph Mayor produced only lectures and one superb little survey of ancient philosophy for us apart from his editions of Grote. His commonplace book, kept from 1868 to 1881, reveals regular contact with his Grote Society and St John's colleagues and a phenomenal reading and writing schedule in the classics, theology, history and philosophy. With an eclectic blend of Broad Church theology, liberal Anglican historical reading, British and German philosophy, plus the regular

---

[94] T. W. Heyck, *The Transformation of Intellectual Life in Victorian England* (London, 1982), pp. 155–89, 221–4.
[95] CUL University Archives, O xiv 52/53.
[96] TCL, Mayor Papers.

classics, Mayor best exemplified the Grote style and mind. His failure to secure a permanent Cambridge post probably settled Grote's fate in the University.

In some senses Sidgwick is the natural inheritor of Grote's mission and ideas. He too set out to reconcile utilitarianism, Scottish common sense and institutional philosophy. He too insisted that utilitarianism could only be coherent if it accepted a fundamental intuition, which ought to promote the greatest happiness of the greatest number. In his final book, *Philosophy, Its Scope and Relations*, he also expresses and develops several of Grote's epistemological theories, especially the ideas that science, history and philosophy are different but compatible modes of thought, that philosophy must deal with the ideal as well as the actual, that much psychology of mind rests on fundamental confusions, and that sociology has a valuable but discrete role to play, one very different to that of philosophy.[97] In addition, we know that Sidgwick helped Mayor to edit both the *Examination* and the *Exploratio Part II*, and he reviewed two of Grote's central works. Leslie Stephen too implied that Sidgwick may have learnt from Grote in a letter he wrote to John Venn in 1990 eliciting material for his obituary to Sidgwick in *Mind*: 'I have fancied that he, like you, was a friend of John Grote and may have been more or less stimulated by him. If you can tell me anything about that – as anything else – I should be grateful.'[98] In addition, F. Y. Edgeworth notes some similarities between the two.[99]

But why did he insist, against the evidence produced both here and by Cannon and Annan, that there was no intellectual coterie at Cambridge in the first six decades of the nineteenth century? What reasons can be given for Sidgwick's lack of recognition of the Cambridge rationalist tradition from the Platonists to Clarke and down to Whewell? Why did he repeatedly insist that German ideas were cold-shouldered at Cambridge, when in Coleridge, Hare, Maurice, Whewell and the Moral Sciences Tripos we have contrary evidence? Why did Sidgwick, and Stephen, not recognise the romantic and idealist turn in John Grote's thought, when both circumstantial evidence of his respect for Ferrier and his explicit affiliation to idealism in the *Exploratio* supported this?[100] Why did they both – Sidgwick and Stephen – ignore the consistent idealist thread from Coleridge to Whewell and on to Grote and Maurice, which was broken only by the appointment of Birks and later Sidgwick to the Knightbridge Chair? To answer is hazardous.

One hypothesis is simply that they were right and that the fertile minds of

---

[97] H. Sidgwick, *Philosophy: Its Scope and Relations* (London, 1902).
[98] Gonville and Caius College Library, Venn Papers, C 12/3.
[99] F. Y. Edgeworth, *New and Old Methods in Ethics* (Oxford and London, 1877), p. 39; also pp. 25, 33, 50–1.
[100] Gibbins, Ph.D. thesis; Gibbins, 'Liberalism'; Gibbins, 'Grote and Modern Cambridge Philosophy', pp. 456–7, 462–6; R. O. Preyer, 'The Romantic Tide Reaches Trinity: Notes on the Transmission and Diffusion of New Approaches to Traditional Studies in Cambridge, 1820–1840' in Paradis and Postlethwait, eds, *Victorian Science*; R. Paulin, 'Julius Hare's German Library in Trinity College Library, Cambridge', *Transactions of the Cambridge Bibliographical Society*, 9, 2 (1987), pp. 174–93.

Annan, Cannon, Sanders, Forbes and myself have spun a web too fragile to sustain their claims. A second hypothesis is that they both lacked the insight to see the Cambridge of their day as anything more than the home of rationalism and reaction. A third hypothesis is that Sidgwick's 1876 essay was a disguised attack on Thomas Rawlinson Birks, under whose chairmanship philosophy in the Cambridge of the 1870s languished. A final hypothesis is more complicated and contentious as it suggests that neither of them wished to advertise the idealism of Cambridge. This hypothesis has five elements, all worthy of further research.

Firstly, neither Sidgwick nor Stephen, for whom we owe thanks for the conventional inside picture of Victorian Cambridge, had any native youthful attachment to the subjective approach to philosophy. We should remember here that it is to Leslie Stephen that we owe the castigation of Coleridge's idealist philosophy as a 'heap of fragments' and 'random dissuasive hints', 'simply appropriated from Schelling'.[101] While Grote stressed that his earliest feelings indicated mind, personality and thought to be the key to philosophy, Sidgwick and Stephen were attracted by Mill, positivism, Comte and utilitarianism. Neither was impressed by the anti-positivist and metaphysical tone of Cambridge philosophy, which they thought was out of touch, uninspired and even reactionary. Secondly, both were antipathetic towards idealism and German thought though Sidgwick read German, and would probably have considered that associating it with Cambridge would put their university in even worse repute than it was already. It was better for Cambridge to be painted as scientific, mathematical and intuitional in philosophy than to be cast as metaphysical and idealist. Sidgwick's general antipathy to idealism is nicely illustrated in a passage from Lewis Nettleship's 'Recollections'. Nettleship confirms Sidgwick's own recollection of a trip to Germany in 1862 in which T. H. Green and he renewed an old schoolboy friendship. Also in the party were Dakyns, Dicey, and Bryce. The entire group were fully devoted to absorbing German thought, with the 'exception of Sidgwick who was studying Arabic'.[102]

Thirdly Sidgwick saw himself as the future saviour of Cambridge philosophy and the likely architect of a new school or movement in the University. In his picture of the past, present and future there was no place for alternative men of genius or novel philosophical movements. In particular, Sidgwick had no interest in promoting the work and reputation of Whewell and John Grote; his interest lay in playing down their contributions, especially to external audiences and in particular to his friends at Oxford, including Thomas Hill Green. This last point provides a fourth strand to this argument. Sidgwick felt embarrassed by Cambridge philosophy prior to 1870 but thereafter he wished to

---

[101] L. Stephen, *The English Utilitarians*, II (London, 1900), pp. 373–4, 380.
[102] Balliol College Library, Oxford, Nettleship MSS, 23–65; R. L. Nettleship, *Works of Thomas Hill Green*, Vol. 3 (London, 1885–88).

see it steered in a direction set by himself and in competition to that of the Oxford of Jowett, Caird, Green and Bradley. It would have been of no help to Sidgwick in his effort to revive Cambridge philosophy in opposition to Oxford idealism to have idealist fellow travellers in his own university. A neutral label rather than a negative one would avoid hostages to fortune, and a picture of Cambridge as a university steeped in classical, mathematical and scientific studies would suffice.

Finally, close textual and biographical study reveals that Sidgwick learnt more from both Whewell and Grote than he was willing to admit, especially in the fields of ethics and the criticism of utilitarianism. To have praised Whewell and Grote too demonstratively would have deflected attention from his task and his own originality. The novelty of the *Methods of Ethics* of 1874 lies, as Sidgwick argues, in the rigorous analysis 'of the different methods of obtaining reasoned convictions as to what ought to be done'.[103] In the more constructive context, however, we find Sidgwick developing, like Grote, an eclectic system, taking the best elements of common sense, intuitionist and utilitarian systems, and blending them into what is later called 'Ideal Utilitarianism'. Sidgwick, like Grote, asserts that utilitarianism can show that all men do seek pleasure, but it needs the intuition that we 'ought to so seek it' before we can have a complete theory.[104] Jerome Schneewind argued in an early review along lines similar to those of J. R. Mozley and Edward Caird at the time:

> Their ethical views show striking similarities on important issues, and even Sidgwick's epistemology, as revealed fairly clearly if not in detail in his posthumously published works, can be seen as showing Grote's influence. If one adds Whewell to the line of succession, an interesting continuity seems to become visible.[105]

Mozley remembered of Grote:

> I have his *Treatise on the Moral Ideals* (which you edited, and were so kind as to send me), before me, and it seems to me that, though the word 'ideal' has real metaphysical attributes, yet that these are not pressed by him in the way of building up an abstract system. There seems to me a likeness between Grote and Sidgwick in this, and I believe they were more on the same plane than any other two of us five.[106]

Another Grote Society member and moral science tutor, J. B. Pearson commented on the association as follows:

---

[103] H. Sidgwick, *The Methods of Ethics*, 7th edn (London, 1907), p. v.
[104] Sidgwick, *Methods*, p. 98.
[105] Schneewind, Review of L. D. MacDonald, *John Grote: A Critical Estimation of his Writings*, *Philosophical Quarterly*, p. 172; E. Caird, Review of J. Grote, *A Treatise on the Moral Ideals*, *The Academy*, XL, 3 (1877), pp. 140–1.
[106] Mozley to J. B. Mayor, TCL Add. MS 104/66.

I for one, do miss him very much; he was always so thoroughly kind and understanding, and I think such men as Sidgwick were more likely to think his opinion worth having than his successors.[107]

Mayor himself confided to Mrs Sidgwick in 1904 that

I think there is no doubt that S. was the one with whom he most enjoyed discussing philosophical questions.[108]

Personally I feel a moderate version of the final hypothesis is correct. Sidgwick had genuine philosophical doubts about the idealism of Grote, Green and Bradley.[109] But whether consciously or unconsciously, Sidgwick played down his association with his mentor and of their common concerns. He remained largely silent about his mentor's interests, ideas, originality and significance, and by successfully attaching the label he did to mid-Victorian Cambridge he has hindered a true appreciation of Cambridge and of Grote's significance for over a century.

It must be remembered that Sidgwick was more disenchanted in 1876 than he was at any time. Birks had obtained the Knightbridge chair in 1872 and Sidgwick had to wait in anguish until 1883 to obtain satisfaction. The incumbent Birks had in his youth been lauded at Trinity, but after failure to get the chair in 1865, had pursued a profession in the church. His evangelical fervour, his moralistic style and his almost total lack of originality nearly put the seal of death on the Moral Sciences Tripos during his stewardship; it was only revived in 1883. Birks himself paid lip service to Grote in several works but never noticed his true originality. For himself, his significance is in restoring the Whewellian imprint on Cambridge philosophy for another decade, most especially in regard to religious rationalism. This conciliating attitude to science was most apparent in his 1858 lecture on *Natural Science, The Handmaid of Revelation*.[110] According to Birks, scientific discovery reveals the 'wonder' of God's creation, which will help ripen religious faith'.[111] Philosophy, like science, if studied in this spirit 'becomes truly the handmaid of Christian faith'.[112] Life under Birks must have been an anguish for Sidgwick as well as for his students.

While not in any way an idealist, John Venn is another Grote Society member who benefited from John Grote's company. From 1864 he examined in the Moral Sciences and lectured three times a week on political economy and logic. Testimony to the influence of Grote is made by Venn in his letter to Mayor of 1866 and is recorded in his obituary in *The Caian*.[113] In addition to regular

---

[107] TCL Mayor Papers.
[108] TCL Add. MS c.104/68.
[109] Schneewind, *Sidgwick's Ethics*, pp. 392–411.
[110] T. R. Birks, 'Natural Science: The Handmaid of Revelation', *Things that Accompany Salvation* (London and Edinburgh, 1858).
[111] *Ibid.*, pp. 43–4.
[112] *Ibid.*, p. 45.
[113] TCL Mayor papers; H. T. Francis, 'John Venn: In Memoriam', *The Caian*, 1923, pp. 120, 127.

meetings Grote had also read over and advised on the first draft of *The Logic of Chance* published in 1866, which J. S. Mill respected.[114] Like Grote, Venn exhibited clarity in thinking, a care for language, an eclectic vision and above all a determination to seek out the truth. Venn, Pearson, and Mayor were all candidates for the Knightbridge chair and all offered a form of Cambridge philosophy in the Grotian and not Whewellian and Birkian mould. On Sidgwick's death, it was to Venn that Leslie Stephen turned for confirmation that Sidgwick owed a larger debt to Grote and the Society than had ever been paid by Sidgwick in his lifetime.[115]

However, it was from within the idealist movement itself that the most interesting developments took place. At Cambridge James Ward, an idealist who quoted Grote on the interdependence of subject and object, immediate and mediate thought, knowledge of acquaintance and judgement, developed a scathing series of attacks, firstly on positivist psychology of mind and secondly on naturalism in all its forms. Ward was versed both in science and in German idealist philosophy.[116] Ward had read Grote and had committed his private views on him to Charles Whitmore in an untraced letter. William R. Sorley (1855–1935), another original idealist with a Trinity College background, obtained the Knightbridge chair in 1900. He was the only Cambridge contributor to *Essays in Philosophical Criticism* (1883), dedicated to T. H. Green, and he had a profound influence in transmitting the Cambridge idealist tradition to Michael Oakeshott.[117] Somewhat closer to Ward, and in the idealist tradition at Cambridge, was George Frederick Stout (1860–1944). Stout's thought covered the fields of epistemology and ontology, where he argued for the unity of thought and being. He wrote several texts on psychology that were distinctly anti-positivist and anti-phenomenalist and in later life he produced two texts of great interest to idealists, the Gifford lectures on Mind and Matter and God and Nature.[118]

We may conclude that in these developments we can identify a battle to construct and embed what the protagonists believed to be the knowledge worth knowing in the widest field of the moral sciences. That, in the end, we can see more continuity than change over the century, in teaching and learning, is down to the weight that history and prescription put upon all agents of change, and not to any lack of polemical intent or witnessed vitriol. We can conclude, however, that there was not a clean sweep for the radicals in the form of 'Sidgwick's Cambridge', nor a 'Revolution of the Dons'; more a triumph of gradualism and moderate reform, in which incorporation, rather than conquest,

[114] Gonville and Caius College Library (hereafter GCCL) Venn Papers C52/1–46.
[115] GCCL Venn Papers C12/14.
[116] C. D. Broad, 'The Local Historical Background of Contemporary Cambridge Philosophy', in *British Philosophy in Mid Century*, ed. C. A. Mace (London, 1957), p. 35.
[117] Gibbins, 'Grote and Modern Cambridge Philosophy', pp. 473–7.
[118] G. F. Stout, *Mind and Matter: The First Two Volumes Based on the Gifford Lectures Delivered in the University of Edinburgh in 1919 and 1921* (Cambridge, 1931); G. F. Stout, *God and Nature*, ed. A. K. Stout (Cambridge, 1952).

best summarises historical events. Nor should we subscribe to the jaundiced picture of 'Philosophy at Cambridge' of 1876 given by the *Westminister Review* of 1874 and Henry Sidgwick in 1876. Much had been achieved by Whewell, Grote and the new Moral Sciences college tutors before Sidgwick's accession to the Knightbridge chair in 1883. In the context of political rivalries over the Tripos, this essay can be seen as a post-election exhortation that 'being so bad observers should not expect too much too soon',[119] as Sidgwick's reforms turned out to be more in the mould of moderate reform rather than radical revolution in terms of teaching and learning. In his reaction against continental philosophy, especially German idealism, he was out of tune with modernising currents of the day. What had changed for all parties were the demands of the outside world for the preparation of men for professional life rather than for the clergy or the life of a literary gentleman. In this, the reformers of our mid-Victorian period were as relevant or more relevant than any other party.

[119] Sidgwick, 'Philosophy at Cambridge'.

MARY BEARD

Learning to Pick the Easy Plums: The Invention of Ancient History in Nineteenth-Century Classics[1]

The Cambridge Classical Tripos, as we know it, was invented in 1879. That is to say, the structure of its courses, its disciplinary boundaries and – in modern jargon – its general principles of student progression were originally defined in a series of proposals approved by the University in that year.[2] These had been masterminded by B. H. Kennedy (Regius Professor of Greek and ex-headmaster of Shrewsbury), with the backing of his heroic (and much abler) lieutenant, Henry Jackson – ancient philosopher, Regius Professor of Greek between 1906 and 1921, and the power behind many of the reforms that from the 1860s on, rather belatedly, brought Cambridge out of the eighteenth century.[3] Their

---

[1] Many thanks are due to the patient editors and conference organisers, Jon Smith and Chris Stray; likewise to Paul Cartledge, whose 1999 Cambridge seminar on Greek historiography gave (a version of) the paper the chance of another outing. University documents cited by date only can be found in two guard books in the Cambridge University Library (University Archives), CUR 28.7 and 28.7.1.

[2] It was first set for examination in 1882. For full details of the reforms, see M. Beard, 'The invention (and re-invention) of "Group D": An Archaeology of the Classical Tripos, 1879–1984', *Classics in 19th- and 20th-Century Cambridge: Curriculum, Culture and Community*, Cambridge Philological Society, Supplementary Volume 24, ed. C. Stray (Cambridge, 1999), pp. 95–134. The general background to this, and to all the other classical reforms and controversies covered in this paper, is best found in C. Stray, *Classics Transformed: Schools, Universities, and Society in England, 1830–1960* (Oxford, 1998).

[3] Those who can stomach hagiography will find a useful account of Jackson buried in R. St J. Parry, *Henry Jackson O. M.: A Memoir* (Cambridge, 1926); and of Kennedy in the even more absurdly adulatory chapter in F. D. How, *Six Great Schoolmasters* (London, 1904), pp. 89–137 (largely on his, increasingly mythologized, years at Shrewsbury; also terrifyingly evoked by an ex-pupil, J. E. B. Mayor, in an obituary in *Classical Review* 3 [1889], pp. 278–81). For Jackson's impact on Cambridge reform, see E. S. Leedham-Green, *A Concise History of the University of Cambridge* (Cambridge, 1996), pp. 175–6 (the admission of Roman Catholics and women); C. N. L. Brooke, *A History of the University of Cambridge*, Vol. 4 (Cambridge, 1993), pp. 71–2 (the invention of the supervision system); 117–18 (the abolition of compulsory chapel). And compare this to the contemporary student view in 'Those in Authority', *The Granta*, 28 January 1893, pp. 160–1; this is a mixture of the usual style of patronizing undergraduate wit ('Dr Henry Jackson . . . is among the most valuable of the products of Sheffield, which include a great variety of interesting objects, from a cloud of smoke almost unequalled in richness and volume to a knife with as many blades as there are

89

scheme divided the Tripos into two Parts, drawing the sting of (or some would say watering down) an examination that had been a mammoth test of not much more than translation into, and out of, Latin and Greek.[4] Part I now emphasized language and translation skills; Part II (which remained optional until 1918) offered students the chance to work in one or more of the specialized subdisciplines that make up *Classics*. The strikingly unimaginative series of letters they used to identify the different branches of the subject in Part II are those which are still used in the Tripos today: *A* for literature; *B* for philosophy; *C* for history; *D* for archaeology, *E* for philology and linguistics.[5] And these, indeed, are the subdisciplines that would now generally be regarded as the key components of classical learning as a whole, in Cambridge and elsewhere.[6] So completely have we internalized Kennedy and Jackson's vision of the subject – a vision that was at the time, as we shall discover, hotly contested and highly controversial.

This paper is about ancient history in the new Classical Tripos of 1879 and in the so-called 'Old' and 'Intermediate' Triposes which it replaced.[7] It traces the shifting story of ancient history within a Tripos which was itself undergoing a slow and complex revolution, as it responded to (at the same time as it was instrumental in affecting) the changing intellectual map of late-nineteenth-century Cambridge; as it repositioned itself in the face of the challenge, or threat, of a range of entirely new Triposes and subjects of study. Many of these were, inevitably, the brainchildren of leading classical scholars; for within the humanities, it was almost impossible to reach power and prominence in mid-Victorian Cambridge without having come up through Classics. But I am also concerned with the wide-ranging debates on the aims and methods of teaching, learning and examining which were prompted by the attempts to establish a specific place for historical study within Classics. These raised a number of

---

years in the Christian Era') and touching tributes ('Dr Jackson's method of giving advice is characteristic. He never tells you what to do, but helps you to make up your own mind on the subject; and somehow with his assistance you contrive to make it up the right way').

[4] The general move towards Triposes in two Parts had been encouraged (though not initiated) by the University's 'Double Honours Syndicate' (1877–78).

[5] Subject definitions may, of course, shift slightly (until 1903, *A* signalled translation rather than literary studies in our sense); but only very occasionally has another letter been added to the scheme: X for 'interdisciplinary studies' arrived in the 1980s; *F* for Roman Law came on the scene in 1967 and was abolished in 1983. *O* is the *lettre de convenance* currently used to refer to papers from *O*ther Triposes available to classical undergraduates.

[6] It was, in other words, the Cambridge model of Classics (rather than Oxford Greats) that was exported to the new provincial universities in the late nineteenth and early twentieth centuries; it is now enshrined in the official 'benchmarking' statement demanded by the government's Quality Assurance Agency to establish a frame of reference for degrees in Classics nationally.

[7] The Classical Tripos was established in 1822, and first examined in 1824 – but the 'Old Tripos' (as I and others use the term) often refers to the period after it was 'split' from the Mathematical Tripos, i.e., after the requirement was removed that a student should take Mathematics before proceeding to Classics. The process of splitting started in 1849 and was complete by 1854. The 'Intermediate Tripos' is the name given to a reformed version of the 'Old', first examined in 1872.

questions — about the possibility of fair assessment, how distinction was to be judged, and what the examination system was *for* — that did their nineteenth-century protagonists credit; questions that our own generation has shelved, rather than answered — and to which we might do well to return.

My main focus is not the internal debates within ancient history itself: which periods should be taught, and why;[8] how far the undergraduate syllabus should reflect developments in continental (and particularly German) scholarship; what a teacher was looking for in a student's analysis of (say) the reforms of Solon or the fall of the Roman Republic. All these were no doubt of crucial importance to the leading characters in my story, at which the examination questions sometimes hint. It must have been, for example, a strong intellectual and educational agenda that led an examiner in 1860 to devise a question which ran: '"The tribes in the state of antiquity were constituted in two ways, either according to the house which composed the tribes or to the ground they occupied." Explain and illustrate this statement of Niebuhr's both as regards the history of Athens and Rome.' (The explicit mention of Niebuhr is the signal: do not, so the implied message for future candidates ran, ignore what the modern German historians have to say.[9]) But the documentation that we have in abundance and on which I am principally drawing — the University debates on Tripos definition and structure, the speeches recorded word for word in the *Cambridge University Reporter*, the flysheets[10] of outrage, posturing and, sometimes, extremely acute argument — only occasionally touches on these aspects, and it would require a completely different type of investigation to bring them to light. It would also inevitably involve a careful look at the (slightly) different configuration of ancient history as it was taught from the 1870s in the Historical Tripos. This would not, I am confident, change the main thrust of this paper — but it would be bound to alter its nuances; if for no other reason, because the intellectual implications of studying the ancient world as part of a historical continuum stretching up to the modern world would shape the problem rather differently. That is for another occasion. My subject here is ancient history as part of classics.

Equally, I shall not be exploring in any detail what lay behind the different forms of intellectual specialisation within classics, nor behind the gradual development of a cadre of dons who would have seen themselves as 'ancient historians' (rather than 'classicists'[11]). It is worth emphasising at this point,

---

[8] Although whether the examination should focus on special periods at all (rather than just ancient history in general, start to finish) will be one of the aspects I consider; see below, pp. 102–4.
[9] For the crucial importance of Niebuhr and other intellectual debates within Ancient History at Oxford, see O. Murray, 'Ancient History', *The History of the University of Oxford*, Vol. 7, ed. M. Brock and M. Curthoys (Oxford, 1997), pp. 520–42.
[10] The *Reporter*, which began to appear in 1870, is the official printed record of university events. Flysheets are circulated printed statements contributing to or provoking debate in the Senate.
[11] Although, in fact, they are not likely to have used the word 'classicist' either; which is a much more recent term of art. The documents of the period do not make it entirely clear what title would have seemed to them the most 'natural' to express their group identity —

however, that the subject was defined as a discipline long before its practitioners would have defined themselves as anything else but 'classical scholars'. True, there was a symbolic moment in 1898 when the chair of Ancient History was established (to be filled in 1899 by a man best-known for his editions of Cicero[12]), and there had been lectureships in Ancient History since 1883; but for all the period with which I am concerned, and a good deal later too, those who taught and wrote ancient history in Cambridge did so within the context of the technical and literary study of ancient texts.[13] Put at its simplest, *ancient history* was not taught by self-styled *ancient historians*.

Reforming Classics, inventing Ancient History

The reform of the Tripos in 1879 was hugely contested; and the victory of Kennedy and Jackson was by no means a foregone conclusion. 'That I have lived to see the Classical Tripos remodelled . . . and that I have been allowed to take part in that work is very gratifying', wrote Kennedy, pompously, in a triumphalist flysheet[14] – but not without reason; we could easily have ended up with a very different style of Tripos (and very different in its intellectual definition) from the one we have come to take for granted. There was partly opposition from the maverick fringe, who were busy working away at their own schemes for a New Tripos – inspirational or inane, depending on your point of view. One serious suggestion, just a few years earlier, had been to test ancient and modern languages together by asking men to translate not from English into Latin and Greek, but from French and German – so killing two birds with one stone.[15] Others, self-styled traditionalists (of whom the insufferable Charterhouse schoolmaster, T. E. Page was the worst – or best), wanted to keep the Tripos as (they thought[16]) it always had been, viz., a test of translation and

but 'scholar' would probably have done as well as any. For revealing remarks on specialisation in classics, see *Reporter*, 1 April 1879, pp. 496–7.
[12] J. S. Reid.
[13] A classic late-nineteenth-century case would be J. E. Sandys, a mainstay of history teaching in both the Classical and Historical Triposes, who was, at the same time, the busy editor of Demosthenes, Aristotle's *Rhetoric*, Euripides' *Bacchae* and Cicero's *Orator*; or J. W. Headlam, whose prize-winning dissertation on election by lot at Athens was preceded by an unsuccessful dissertation on Greek philosophy. It was not until the mid-twentieth century that ancient historians generally rejected the title of 'classicist' – or, if they kept it, risked seeming irremediably old-fashioned and unprofessional. As classics once more sees virtue in its own interdisciplinarity, radical ancient historians of the twenty-first century are likely to find 'classicist' an increasingly congenial label again.
[14] 18 March 1879.
[15] W. G. Clark, 23 March 1868. A maverick suggestion perhaps, but not a maverick man: as we shall discover (below, p. 100), Clark was one of the initiators of discussion about reform of the Tripos that was to lead to the 1879 revolution. This particular proposal was, in fact, accompanied by another much more to our taste – that the Tripos should include a compulsory dissertation.
[16] In fact, as we shall see below (pp. 96–7), there had been a history paper in the Tripos since 1849. For an unconvincingly favourable assessment of Page, see W. J. N. Rudd, *T. E. Page, Schoolmaster Extraordinary* (Bristol, 1981).

composition skills: the 1879 proposals were an appalling experiment, he railed in a letter to *The Times*, 'a pure freak of inventive genius'; and, to make it worse, 'the *corpus vile* of this experiment is to be composed of the picked classical students of half of England'.[17] But on every side the protagonists were looking over their shoulder at the development of new Triposes. For some, like A. A. Vansittart, these could act as a dumping ground for the bits of classical learning that they did not want to pollute the pure form of the Classical Tripos. His idea of a reformed classics course in the 1860s had been an extraordinary philological fantasy, consisting in just Greek and Latin language, philology and (compulsory) Sanskrit. As for philosophy, that 'belongs more properly in the Moral Sciences Tripos'; while history, he argued, could be mopped up by a new Ancient and Modern History Tripos.[18] Meanwhile those who thought of themselves as reformers were torn, on the one hand, between taking advantage of the pickings (the problem with the Moral Sciences Tripos, for example, which had been established in 1851, was that it attracted very few students – conscripting ancient philosophy could have been an advantage); and, on the other, deploring these narrow definitions of Classics. J. R. Seeley (joint Senior Classic in the Tripos of 1857, Professor of Modern History from 1869 to 1895) might normally have been ready to cannibalize any bit of classics he could in the interests of building up a new Historical Tripos, but even he spluttered at the lunacy, for classics, of Vansittart's proposals; 'the introduction of Sanskrit into the examination,' he wrote, 'in place of History, would, in my opinion, ruin the Examination finally'.[19]

These debates are usually seen in terms of a clash between the upholders of 'Pure Scholarship' (essentially enormous quantities of translation and prose and verse composition – though its exponents glossed it more mystically) and the up-to-the-minute modernisers, who wanted to define classical learning in a much wider sense. And the victory of Kennedy and Jackson is seen to depend on the neat compromise between the two camps, which kept Part I more or less to the path of Pure Scholarship, while allowing many more radical flowers to bloom in the optional Part II. In part this is clearly true; and the protagonists certainly chose to package themselves in those starkly opposing terms, sometimes, as in the case of T. E. Page, almost to the point of self-parody. But many more issues – of teaching, learning, examining and grading – were at stake, issues that we have tended to sideline by concentrating on (what must seem to us) the heroic campaign to broaden the classical curriculum.

Consider, for example, the intense series of debates throughout the run-up to the 1879 reform, on whether the examination candidates in the Classical Tripos should be ranked in a strict order of merit (Senior Classic, Second Classic, Third

---

[17] 10 March 1879.
[18] Flysheet, 16 May 1866. Vansittart was a Trinity man and fanatical philologist, whose main academic work was a collation of various readings in the New Testament and who built himself a very grand pile, Pinehurst, on Grange Road.
[19] Letter (n.d.) 1867.

Classic, etc); or whether, as was eventually decided, they should be ranked alphabetically in more or less broad classes (First Class, Second Class, Third Class – themselves to be split into a number of (sub-)divisions, of which only the division of the Second Class into II.1 and II.2 still remains). Interminable pages of the *Reporter* chew over this long-running controversy, which we now tend to dismiss as a quaint, but impenetrable, obsession of these mid-Victorians, driven as they were by order and rank (even the deceptively modern Jackson, who was in favour of broad classing, could confidently assert, apparently without irony, 'The men can always be divided into three classes'[20]). But obsession or not (and worries we don't share can always be dismissed as obsessions), the emotional and intellectual investment in the problem ought to signal to us its importance. In fact, this issue of precise ranking versus the system of broad classification we are used to hits right to the heart of the examining process: what it is for, what kind of judgement on a candidate we can expect it to deliver, what kind of result (framed in what terms) represents the fairest type of judgement on the candidates or their abilities. They were absolutely right, in other words, to get hot under the collar about it.[21]

There was also, inevitably, a good deal of debate about the particular line-up of subjects that were to be given star billing in Part II. Just imagine, huffed Page (of course), in an attempt to discredit the idea of an archaeological component, 'an examination in which high distinction may be obtained for a knowledge of chorography and topography, of Italian dialects, and the *Corpus Inscriptionum*'.[22] For the most part though (granted that rampant philological ideologues, such as Vansittart, wanted to be rid of history – and almost everything else – on principle), there were few strong objections to the presence of ancient history *per se* in the reformed Tripos – even if (as we shall see) a question mark hung here too over the nature of the examination, and how you should test it. What

---

[20] *Reporter*, 1 April 1879, p. 495, recording a discussion in the Arts School on 27 March. This discussion provides the best entry point into the different arguments on either side: that broad classing was fairer, because it did not attempt to rank men (sic) more precisely than any examination system could; that the order of merit was fairer, because it did not group together – as if equal – men of very different achievements ('The alphabetical method had been adopted for the third class in the years 1851–1858, and had been given up probably because it was found to be grossly unfair, some of the men being worth nothing and some having just failed of a second class', p. 494); that the order of merit adversely affected students' working habits, driving them simply to obtain as many marks as possible; that the order of merit could always recognize equal talent by a liberal use of the *bracket*; and so on.

[21] Cultures inevitably internalise their own methods of assessment and ranking; for all that we recognize the arbitrariness of our present classification system (or lament, much as our nineteenth-century predecessors did, the unfairness of ranking as an 'equal' II.1 the clever student who just misses a first and the idle boaty who just scrapes out of the II.2s), examiners of the Classical Tripos continue to police (and to some extent believe in) the class boundaries. And those boundaries have life-changing implications for the students concerned, the difference of a few marks effectively excluding some candidates from research funding (just as the order of merit determined academic careers in the late nineteenth century – for it was regularly used as the basis for fellowship elections).

[22] Letter, *Times*, 10 March 1879; Page was later to turn his wrath to the prospect of classical archaeology within the school curriculum (see Stray, *Classics Transformed*, pp. 207–10).

emerged from the reforms was a small foothold for history in the remodelled Part I,[23] and a main section (*C*) devoted to the subject in Part II.

The structure of Section *C* seems at first sight a relatively familiar one, in fact an unremarkably 'modern' way of dividing an undergraduate course in ancient history. There was to be a general paper of questions on 'Greek and Roman History, political, constitutional, social, and literary', an essay paper with general historical topics (one question to be answered in three hours), as well as two papers on special periods — one of Greek and one of Roman history. In 1883, the first year in which these papers were actually set (there had been no candidates for the Section in 1882), the special period of 'Grecian History' covered 514–429 BC, matched by a Roman period of 133–44 BC ('The Fall of the Republic' as it might have been entitled). Both these examinations demanded answers to what have become our old chestnuts: 'Discuss the circumstances and date of the transfer of the confederate treasury from Delos to Athens. Give some account of the documents from which we derive our knowledge of the Athenian tribute-revenue'; 'What was the real basis of the traditional hegemony of Sparta? To what extent did this tradition survive during the period of Athenian Empire?'; 'Explain the immediate cause of the rupture between Caesar and the Senate in 49 BC. On what grounds does Caesar defend himself?'

Not that it is quite so familar on closer inspection. As always in the history of pedagogy, the deeper you look the stranger things become. First of all, the full lineup of Section *C* papers also included a paper on Greek and Roman Law (which was, like the others, a compulsory element in the Section). Although the history of law has recently been successfully reclaimed for mainstream ancient history,[24] a *compulsory* paper on law in an ancient history course would be inconceivable in modern terms. Here then we have a hint of the radically different disciplinary boundaries of the late nineteenth century, which regularly classified the study of law and legal history within history in general: in fact, the first version of what was to become the Historical Tripos started life in the early 1870s (rather unsuccessfully, it must be admitted) as the 'Law and History Tripos'. But the questions too, for all their ostensible overlap with our own, imply a version of the subject and educational priorities that are strikingly unfamiliar. Except on the general essay paper, there was no choice of questions, apart from an occasional either/or: candidates were asked to answer as many as twelve questions in three hours. No doubt the canny ones would have been able to make up a few minutes by a speedy handling of the regular 'map question' ('Draw a map illustrating the campaigns of Alexander in Asia'; 'Draw a rough

---

[23] In the new Part I, there were two 'half papers' (one and a half hours each) on 'Greek History (including Literature), and Greek Antiquities' and 'Roman History (including Literature), and Roman Antiquities'.

[24] See, for example, P. Cartledge, P. Millett and S. Todd, eds., *Nomos: Essays in Athenian Law, Politics and Society* (Cambridge, 1990); though, as usual, the new wave does not recognize its nineteenth-century avatars.

map of Attica and the Boeotian borderland. Mark the chief mountains and the following sites: Athens, Eleusis, Marathon, etc'); but even so the time constraints must have meant that a question like 'Enumerate our authorities for Caesar's career, estimating the relative value of the more important among them' got exactly the answer it appeared to ask for: in other words, a list. Facts, not argument, were the order of the day. Nonetheless, for all these differences, this clearly is an examination in ancient history broadly as we understand the term.

But 1879 was not the first introduction of ancient history into the Classical Tripos. Despite all the myths of an unsullied era of Pure Scholarship, there had, in fact, been an ancient history paper in the Old Tripos since 1849 (hence in part, no doubt, the general lack of opposition to history's inclusion in the new course). It had been introduced during the reforms that first started to remove the 'mathematical restriction'; the only paper that was then required apart from translations and compositions, it comprised twelve questions to be answered in three hours, no choice of questions (though occasionally an either/or) and no set periods – knowledge was to be shown over the whole range of ancient history (or at least their definition of it[25]), from archaic Greece to the Flavian emperors. Again, sitting this paper must have been a breathless race: 'Describe the effect produced on Greece by the death of Alexander the Great, and trace the subsequent course of events to the close of the Lamian War', quickly followed in the 1865 paper by 'Name the chief authors who flourished at Rome during the reign of the four immediate successors of Augustus: and examine briefly the influence of the age upon their writings'. *Briefly* was the word, at just fifteen minutes a question (and with a rubric to the paper which ran, threateningly, 'N.B. In all instances dates are required'). It seems hardly surprising then that the paper was modified in 1867, divided into four sections, two broadly Greek, two Roman, with one question to be answered from each – and soon after reduced further to just three sections and three questions.[26] This paper survived the introduction of the 'Intermediate' Tripos, first examined in 1872 (which added a few more non-translation papers) and was not replaced until the revolution of 1879. Some of the subjects now set (but by no means all; many of the questions are strikingly similar before and after the change) expanded to fill the new lavish time allowance of forty-five minutes or an hour per question: 'Give your estimate of the probable results to Greece and to the world if Alexander had lived to consolidate his Asiatic conquests' (1867); 'What shapes did satire assume in Greek literature, and in Roman writers other than satirists? Define the term in its strictly Roman sense; and give an account of Lucilius,

---

[25] It was 'history' largely defined by the great ancient historical texts, as R. Burn emphasized in *The Student's Guide to the University of Cambridge* (Cambridge, 1862) (see below, p. 99). Although not entirely: by the usual fudge Alexander the Great was allowed in, despite being the subject of no 'major' ancient historical writing.
[26] The reduction to three questions in 1872–1875 was followed by a return to four questions in 1876.

comparing his manner and range of subjects with those of Horace and of Juvenal' (1873). As this last question sharply reminds us, it was a hallmark of the history papers right through this period that the history of literature (and of philosophy) counts as *history*. It is a significantly less familiar model of the subject, then, in its definition and style of testing; but still an obvious relation of ancient history as we know it.

Told in this way, the history of ancient history in the Classical Tripos from 1849 on looks secure and relatively uneventful. In fact, the flysheets, reports and discussions through the 1850s, 1860s and 1870s tell quite a different story. Up until the Kennedy-Jackson reforms, everyone who had a stake in Cambridge Classics seems to have found the history paper deeply unsatisfactory. Whatever else they disagreed about, they were united in the view that this paper (for all its longevity) was *no good*. Criticism came to the surface on three particular occasions – which I shall explore in turn, as each of them raises wider issues of teaching and learning.

1855: The limits of 'complete knowledge'

The first trace of dissatisfaction comes only six years after the introduction of history into the 'Old' Tripos, and just one year after the Board of Classical Studies (the precursor of today's Faculty Board) was established. In fact the very first initiative of the Board was a report which – alongside some (as they would become) perennial complaints about the overloading of the Tripos examiners – dealt with the sorry state of the history paper.[27] Their crucial piece of evidence was presented in the form of a table of marks averaged over the three years 1853–55, showing what percentage had been achieved in each paper of the Tripos by undergraduates in each of the final class divisions:

Class of candidate	Latin Verse Comp.	Latin Prose Comp.	Greek Verse Comp.	Greek Prose Comp.	Latin Verse Trans.	Latin Prose Trans.	Greek Verse Trans.	Greek Prose Trans.	History
1sts	59	66	62	66	70	72	75	$73\frac{1}{2}$	35
2nds	37	52	34	$43\frac{1}{2}$	63	56	54	$52\frac{1}{2}$	21
3rds	24	37	14	27	47	41	43	39	10
1 failure	14	24	7	13	35	29	$25\frac{1}{2}$	$25\frac{1}{5}$	10

You could hardly fail to spot that history was the rogue element in the mark spread, with even the first-class candidates only managing to scrape an average of 35 percent in the paper (the thirds an abysmal 10 percent – though not, it must be admitted, all that much worse than their 14 percent in Greek Verse Composition). The Board certainly spotted it, observing:

[27] 10 December 1855.

... with regret, that a large proportion of the Candidates fail to obtain any high number of marks for the examination in History. It is possible that this result may have arisen from other causes than the want of attention to the subject on the part of the Candidates. The nature and extent of the subject render it difficult for even the best Candidates to exhibit anything like a complete knowledge. Some of the questions proposed occasionally require much of the whole time allowed for the paper in order to their receiving a satisfactory and complete answer; and the attention of the best prepared persons may have been so much engaged by one portion of the paper, as to leave too little time to answer the remainder even when the requisite information was at hand.

This is a remarkable document for several reasons. Immediately striking is the fact that the Board could regard the examination results as data to be collated, reflected upon and politicised; that they took their job to include analysis of student achievement, and of the University's success in teaching and testing. For perhaps even more striking is that they did not instantly reach for the standard teachers' alibi for student failure and suggest, as usual, that it directly correlated with student idleness (in fact, they explicitly sidelined that argument). Instead they floated the idea that it was the fault of the examination, or rather of the mismatch between the subject and the structure of the paper. Specifically, they were concerned that you could not write a 'complete' answer to questions in the time available. Given the kind of questions I have already quoted, it is not hard to imagine how their Board's discussions must have gone: could anyone, gentlemen, 'Narrate the events which led to the elevation of the Flavian family to the throne' *and* give 'the characteristics of the laws passed during their tenure of it' in a quarter of an hour – as they had been asked to do in February 1853.

The underlying problem is easier for us to make out than it was, apparently, for them. In managing the first examination paper in the Tripos that was not an exercise in translation or composition (where, for all the vagaries of stylistic judgment, there were some agreed criteria for assessing the work – not to mention whether a candidate had answered 'completely' or incompletely), they were faced with the crucial question of how you judged a quite different type of test. From their concerns, and their tentative suggestions for the future, it is clear that they saw a satisfactory answer not in terms of a good *selection* of material, or of a powerful argument deploying (and this is our shibboleth) *relevant* information, but – impossibly, of course – as a display of total knowledge; they were treating the examination in history more or less on the model of an unseen translation. Get it all and get it right.[28] Hence they ponder on 'whether

---

[28] One suspects underlying this, the widespread use of what we would call 'negative' marking – that is, deducting marks from a notional total for what appears to be incorrect or missing, rather than (positively) giving credit for the material presented by the candidate. Our own experience in marking unseen translations shows, unsurprisingly, that positive marking produces much 'better' marks than negative.

Candidates should not, in their answers, be limited to a selection, at their own discretion, of a fixed number of questions, *complete answers* to which should receive the whole number of marks assigned to that paper' (my emphasis). A *choice* of questions in a Classical Tripos examination was a radical idea; and they got no further than pondering it. For the time being, they contented themselves with making sure that the candidates knew the score – that they were aware that the history paper was 'a disturbing cause in the assignment of places in the Tripos' and (back to the old alibi, I am afraid) that they should work hard at it; they wished, as they put it, to prevent 'the subject of History from being regarded with indifference by any of the candidates'. This certainly was the message of Robert Burn when he wrote the chapter on the Classical Tripos for the *Student's Guide to the University of Cambridge* in 1862. He started by explaining the 'aims and objectives' (in our terms) of the paper: 'The object of the paper of questions in Ancient History, which completes the schedule of Examination, and to which an eleventh part of marks is assigned, is to test the student's acquaintance with the subject-matter of the principal Greek and Latin historians, Herodotus, Thucydides, Livy and Tacitus.'[29] And he went on to paraphrase for the undergraduates the Board's advice: 'The History paper should by no means be regarded with indifference, although it may seem to have but a small proportion of weight assigned to it. The Classical Board in their Report of 1854 stated distinctly that this Paper acts with considerable force as a disturbing cause in the assignment of places, and this statement has been fully borne out by the subsequent Examinations'. For all the good intentions, then, nothing had obviously changed by 1862.[30]

So who, finally, were these men on the first Board of Classical Studies, who took the brave step of examining their own examining? The predictable answer is that they are the usual mixed bag that made up most nineteenth-century boards and syndicates: the ultra-conservative E. H. Perowne (who went on to be Master of Corpus); the committed reformer W. H. Thompson (the philosopher and teacher of the young Henry Jackson, later to be Master of Trinity); other future big-shots of University politics (W. H. Bateson, who was to become Master of St John's); the ferocious W. M. Gunson (who reputedly turned round Classics at Christs by getting the undergraduates to work harder – and whose bark was far worse than his bite); a small collection of future schoolteachers and parsons (W. H. Brown, who was to be head of Charterhouse; Arthur Wolfe, best known as the author of *Three-hundred Original Hymn Tunes*; and Thomas Field, classicist, Baltic explorer, expert skater and future Rector of Madingley); and 'H. Vansittart' (who can only be a misprint, I have concluded, for our friend

---

[29] Although, as I noted above (n. 25), they conveniently turned a blind eye to the fact that the 'principal historians' had nothing to say about one of their favourite subjects: Alexander the Great.
[30] A further report (26 May 1858) had returned to the problem, to recommend that 'questions should be framed so as to discourage the use of compendiums and to promote the study of the original authorities.'

'A. A')[31] – a good cross-section of Cambridge University personalities. What is significant is that (Vansittart, and to a lesser extent Gunson, apart) most of them were not leading players in the later, decisive, reforms of Classics; many of them, in fact, would usually be counted as the crusty old predecessors of Jackson, Sidgwick, Seeley and company. They serve as a reminder that the reforming generation of the late nineteenth century had probably learned more from those predecessors than they usually acknowledged.

1866: Showy and superficial thinkers

The second occasion on which the problem of history and the history paper prompted widespread university debate was in 1866. It was in the context of what quickly became known as 'Clark and Burn's Memorial' – a proposal addressed to the Classical Board for root and branch reform of the Tripos; its authors, two fellows of Trinity, W. G. Clark and Robert Burn. Their idea was to limit the amount of Pure Scholarship in the Tripos and widen the range of other subjects covered. The scheme was never adopted; but one of the proposals – that there should be not one but two history papers (a paper of 'Questions' on History and Antiquity requiring relatively short factual answers; plus a paper in which the candidates wrote a more substantial single historical Essay in three hours[32]) – caused intense reaction.

The *most* intense was a head-on attack by Vansittart on the presence of any history at all in the examination. He outlined two routes to success: the tougher and more honourable, which was to embark on the 'toilsome struggle after scholarship: daily blunders where we thought ourselves soundest: constant humiliation as our blunders are detected...'; and that apparently advocated by Clark and Burn, which was 'to sit and swallow plums of science – plums which we need not pick for ourselves, for will there not be plenty of tutors to put them in our mouths? and to think what wise boys we are growing'. He went on (archly) to predict that, if the proposals were adopted, 'the one increase on which we might safely count is an astounding increase in bumptiousness.'[33] But more moderate responses turned on the nature of a (long) essay both as a method of teaching and as a means of testing. You could like it (or pretend to like it, or at least accept it) as a teaching tool, without thinking that it was suitable as part of an examination. This, at least, was the broad position put

---

[31] For fuller details of their careers, see the entries in the relevant volumes of J. and J. A. Venn, *Alumni Cantabrigienses: A Biographical List of all Known Students, Graduates and Holders of Office at the University of Cambridge* (Cambridge, 1922–54). There is no sign, as suspicious readers might have wondered, that this report was all part of the (later) plot by Vansittart – if it is he – to remove history from the Tripos entirely (as documented in the next section); though, of course, the internal dynamics of the fledgling Board are lost to us.

[32] The distinction between 'question' and 'essay' is crucial in the terminology of this debate: an essay required the kind of extended treatment that a question did not, and was allotted considerably more time.

[33] Flysheet, 16 May 1866.

eloquently by E. M. Cope (who the very next year was to be pipped to the post for the Regius Chair of Greek and to die – it was said of thwarted ambition – n 1873):[34]

> It seems to me that an Essay to be worth much as a test of knowledge and intellectual power requires both time and thought in a far greater degree than anything else that can enter into an examination, and also than the limited duration of any examination can allow. All questions have at least two sides, most have a great many more. A man of words and of rhetorical habits and powers, δημηγορικός as Plato calls him, an empty, showy and superficial thinker, can often make a display . . . which will outshine the imperfect work – imperfect only by reason of the want of time – of a man of real knowledge and ability. It is true that this quickness and ready dexterity, this power of making much of a little, does often gain the same kind of advantage in social and public life; but I think at any rate it should be *our* object to keep if possible this mischievous influence out of our University Examinations.

This was a quite different issue from that of 'complete knowledge' that had preoccupied the Board ten years earlier. Cope was raising the question of how you could judge a piece of considered argument (i.e. an essay), completed under time constraints that made proper consideration impossible. How far were the examiners bound to end up rewarding qualities they would not wish to reward and had not set out to test: speed of thinking (rather than depth), rhetorical (rather than intellectual) skills? Responses to Cope's objection ranged from hearty agreement[35] to rather more subtle reflections on the nature of the examining process. You could agree with 'the *spirit* of Mr Cope's able remarks on essays' ran one flysheet, but it was the business of examiners to ensure that they did not set topics which could privilege the showy ('but rather such as should bring out deeper and more exact knowledge, and encourage a more than superficial study of the parts of history from original authorities in preference to what is now in vogue, a light skimming of the cream from historical cram-books.'[36]) Henry Sidgwick, in fact, turned the whole argument on its head by arguing that good, clear, rhetorically-honed expression was one of the very things that the examining process should be testing and rewarding:[37]

---

[34] Flysheet, 18 May 1866. Chris Stray points out that Cope himself went way over time in his own praelection for the Greek Chair in 1867 – presumably not much good at (essay) planning himself.

[35] For example, Arthur Holmes (another failed candidate for the Regius Chair the following year) confessed to having changed his mind – against the long essay: 'Although the substitution of "Historical Essay" . . . for "Answers to Questions in History" was lately considered at my own suggestion by the Classical Board, facts which have since come to my knowledge lead me to believe that Essay writing as a test would often be far from satisfactory' (19 May 1866).

[36] W. C. Green (Second Classic in 1856, who ended up as Rector of Hepworth, via teaching at Rugby), Flysheet, 9 October 1866.

[37] Flysheet, 1866.

I cannot think that the faculty, when knowledge has been carefully acquired, of expressing it with lucid arrangement in polished and correct English, is one to be despised and neglected. I am aware that the most thoughtful men have often great natural difficulty in producing their ideas; but surely this difficulty is just what educators ought to endeavour to overcome.

An essay, in other words, could only count as worthy of a high mark if it was lucidly argued; rhetoric was, after all, part of a classical education.

Underlying the discussions at this point was also the question of how far the nature and scheme of the examination could influence the way candidates worked. Did a good examination, with a well-chosen syllabus, have the effect of improving the students' regime of work through the year? How, in particular, could students sensibly prepare for an examination in which questions could, in principle, be drawn from any period of ancient history? On all sides of the debate, two words recur again and again. The first is 'cramming'. For if almost anything could come up on the paper, the students would be bound to take refuge in some cheap compendium and mug up all of their history second-hand, without even thinking about the great historians – whether ancient or modern. So, as J. E. B. Mayor put it, 'the reign of some English Florus has succeeded to that of Livy, who even in ruins has become a bugbear to many a student'.[38] (Only Sidgwick, again, stood out, in hinting that there was a degree of hysteria in this fear of cramming: for after all, 'abridgements, however useless when taken alone, may be read with some advantage at the close of such a course as ours: they give some order and connexion to the fragments of more detailed and vivid knowledge which the student has already picked up'[39] – a good revision aid, in other words.) The second word is 'tip-fancying' (Victorian jargon for what we call 'question-spotting'). This again was seen to be connected with the open-endedness of the syllabus. For if the examination was a lottery, then the student's best bet was to scour past papers and see what looked most likely to come up this year. As Vansittart wondered (though he obviously had other axes to grind): 'Do they [sc. the undergraduates] select those parts of history which will illustrate the authors they are studying, or those which have not been set of late years?'[40] The introduction of some kind of 'set period' was clearly hovering on the agenda; and that, in fact, was to become the main focus of the next round of debates.[41]

1873: A Disturbing element again?

Nothing came of Clark and Burn's Memorial – or not directly at least. Indirectly, it had served to light the touch paper of Tripos reform; while, at

---

[38] Flysheet, 25 May 1866.
[39] Flysheet, 1866.
[40] Flysheet, 30 January 1867.
[41] J. E. B. Mayor had already strongly promoted the idea in his flysheet of 25 May 1866.

the same time, prompting the reduction in the following year, 1867, of the number of questions to be answered on the history paper.[42] The problems of that paper remained, however; and in 1873 there was a direct attempt to introduce set historical periods and/or set authors into its syllabus. This was endorsed in a report by the Classical Board[43] (one cannot help but suspect the hand of Henry Jackson behind it – though there is no direct evidence for it) and widely debated in flysheets and in a memorable discussion in the Arts School.

Kennedy, for example, in a spirited paper which probably preceded the Board's report, returned to the old 1850s argument that the history paper was a disturbing element in the marking scheme.[44] His view was not so much that set periods were necessary but that the paper should be made easier ('its constitution implies too high an idea of the powers and acquirements of the candidates generally'). He echoed Sidgwick in his general distrust of the scaremongering about 'cramming' and 'tip-fancying': there was, he argued, 'an excessive dread of *cram, tips* and the like, which are supposed to give the lucky speculator and cleverly tutored sciolist an undue advantage against the sounder and abler scholar. As an old Examiner I do not believe in the importance of this danger, where Examiners are fit for their work, as we trust that ours always are ... All knowledge ... deserves *some* credit. The mere crammer and tip-fancier, be his speculation ever so lucky, will, as a poor scholar, break down upon the whole and stand low in the total marks.' He turned, for an example of difficulty, to the recent history paper of 1873: out of the twelve questions, of which the candidates had to choose three, there was 'only one (4 of Division B) which the best scholars of the year, supposed to be fair historians, would be likely to select with the prospect of even half the maximum mark'. (It ran straightforwardly, 'Describe the foreign policy of Philip of Macedon, confirming the description by a historical outline of his most important military success, and a particular account of his diplomatic triumphs over Athens.' – and was, not surprisingly, felt to be easier than the monster about the history of satire that I quoted above.[45]) The maximum mark presumably went to those candidates with the maximum information: a significant indication for us that – even with just three questions in three hours, the scheme of marking must still have emphasised the goal of *complete knowledge*. There is no sign of a more argumentative or discursive approach being required.

Kennedy's was not the only voice. Gunson, who had been one of the authors of the 1855 report, repeated their old trick and produced another tabulation of marks in the Tripos, averaged for 1872 and 1873 – which demonstrates (see below) fairly convincingly that the history paper was not the disturbing element that Kennedy and the Board claimed; that, if they were to

---

[42] See above, p. 96.
[43] 26 May 1873.
[44] Flysheet, 1873.
[45] See pp. 96–7.

turn their attention anywhere, it should have been to the philology paper (which had been introduced when the 'Intermediate' Tripos was first examined in 1872).

	Latin Prose Comp.	Latin Verse Comp.	Greek Prose Comp.	Greek Verse Comp.	Latin Prose Trans.	Latin Verse Trans.	Greek Prose Trans.	Greek Verse Trans.	Philosophy	Philology	History
Senior Classic	76	82	81	73	$84\frac{1}{2}$	84	84	81	62	49	69
First Class	$63\frac{1}{2}$	63	65	$62\frac{1}{2}$	76	$70\frac{1}{2}$	75	73	52	$41\frac{1}{2}$	$56\frac{1}{2}$
Second Class	44	43	46	42	63	58	60	$58\frac{1}{2}$	33	$20\frac{1}{2}$	34
Third Class	34	34	$32\frac{1}{2}$	28	53	46	46	$43\frac{1}{2}$	$23\frac{1}{2}$	11	$18\frac{1}{2}$
Fail	$21\frac{1}{2}$	$15\frac{1}{2}$	$20\frac{1}{2}$	$9\frac{1}{2}$	$44\frac{1}{2}$	$36\frac{1}{2}$	$30\frac{1}{2}$	$28\frac{1}{2}$	15	5	12

'No change was necessary,' concluded Gunson.[46] And he was backed by Arthur Holmes, who claimed that he had been remarkably impressed by the work done for the history paper in general; just as he hit right to the heart of one central objection to set periods: that is, by what criteria should you choose the periods? 'History only entered in an incidental manner into the Tripos examination, and there seemed no reason why one special period should be prepared rather than another.' The idea of basing the paper explicitly around set authors was, he suggested, even worse: for how would you ever manage to set anything on Alexander the Great?[47] Henry Jackson, however, took Gunson's argument and (at an entirely different level of sophistication) turned it emphatically upside down. It was no good, he pointed out, claiming that the history paper was functioning well simply because the undergraduate marks obtained were in line with those of other papers – because history was a different discipline from those tested in the other papers and the marks *ought* to be out of line: '. . . History ought to be a disturbing element, for if not, no special knowledge had been elicited. From this point of view, the agreement of the marks obtained in other parts of the examination proved nothing in favour of the existing paper.'[48] If the main focus of my paper were the growing specialisation of historical study, as a discipline in its own right within classics, this would be one crucial, originary moment.

The 1873 debate also broached explicitly the question of lecturing and its relationship to the examination and the syllabus. This had its bathetic – and no doubt memorable – side, coming as it did in the speech given during the discussion in the Arts School by Professor J. E. B. Mayor (Latin professor,

---

[46] *Reporter*, 4 November 1873, pp. 69–71.
[47] *Ibid.*, p. 70.
[48] *Ibid.*

vegetarian, well-known eccentric and a firm supporter of set periods).[49] Mayor argued that the quality of lecturing would be much improved by a change to set periods – and then with daunting prolixity (or in a brilliant filibuster) which faced down even the Arts School stenographers, he treated the assembled company to some samples of the kind of lectures you would be able to deliver under the new dispensation. The stenographers must have laid down their pens – and what appeared in the *Reporter* was just this: 'Professor Mayor gave illustrations of the kind of lecture which would be encouraged by such a limitation'.

Mayor had made a fool of himself, again; but he was a clever fool. And Robert Burn (of Clarke and Burn) who spoke last in the debate in the Arts School – and in favour of set periods – opened by implicitly welcoming Mayor's contribution and underlining the importance of seeing things from the lecturer's side; he was, he said, 'glad to see the discussion removed from the point of view of the Examiner to that of the Lecturer'. What Mayor and Burn had brought into the University eye was the simple fact that decisions about examining affect not only what students learn, but also what their teachers (then or now) decide to teach – and how.

Them and Us

How far to treat the past as if it were familiar territory, how far to celebrate its sheer foreignness, is every historian's dilemma. To explore the history of one's own institution (university, faculty, subject . . .) raises that problem in a particularly acute form – with a treacherous line to be drawn between, on the one hand, conscripting Jackson and Mayor into our own debates, enlisting them as colleagues *avant la lettre*, and on the other consigning them to a strangely alien world that can count as 'ours' only by virtue of the (deceptive) continuity of name and place ('Faculty of Classics, University of Cambridge'). In this case, we could do well to attend carefully to the debates of our nineteenth-century predecessors, however quaintly we find them expressed. For in discussing the very nature of examining, the methods of fair ranking, the question of what is being judged in the classing of an essay, they were facing head-on problems that we have not solved, but have, by and large, conspired to shelve. *Our* communal myth (and it is one that eventually emerged from the debates I have been reviewing) is that essays *can* fairly be judged, that as examiners we *do* see through showy rhetoric to the emptiness underneath, and that we *will* always be prepared to award high marks to good arguments – even if we do not agree with them. And so every year we manage to believe sincerely that we are being even-handed in marking undergraduates' efforts in ancient history (and so much else); though I very much doubt that we could *show* that to be the case.

---

[49] *Ibid.* For a perceptively wry appreciation of Mayor, see J. Henderson, *Juvenal's Mayor: The Professor Who Lived on 2d a Day*, Cambridge Philological Society, Supplementary Volume 20 (Cambridge 1998).

Even more recently we have come to shelter behind the illusion of *transparency*, and to believe that the principles on which we mark and grade scripts can be succinctly stated and (helpfully?) shared with the students. From the late 1990s 'Criteria used in assessing Classical Tripos Questions, Essay papers' have appeared annually in the Faculty's handbook for students (*Cambridge Classical Courses*). Here a II.1 essay is broadly defined as follows:

> Wide reading, interpreted intelligently with some independent thought. Well organised and presented with little or no irrelevance and referencing generally correct.

And within this overall rubric four possible subdivisions of the II.1 are envisaged, ranging from 'a very good II.1' which itself comes in two forms:

> Two alternatives: (i) uneven performance with independence of thought earning A marks but not consistently sufficient knowledge or good enough presentation to pass the first-class boundary; (ii) a thoroughly well-informed, well organised performance without sufficient sign of originality to pass the first class boundary.

right down to a low II.1 – 'just enough knowledge and ability to organise and present it to merit a II.1' – which is still to be clearly distinguished from the II.2, defined as:

> A moderate level of reading and analysis with adequate presentation, usually well within the confines of a course, with little or no independent thought. Regurgitation of received information, some irrelevance and mistakes, and/or short measure.

Predictably these definitions took the Faculty Board of the 1990s many weeks to hammer out; there was an intense debate on how exactly we might be able to pin down the difference between (say) a 'mid' and a 'moderate' II.1. We were, in the end, pleasantly satisfied with the result. What Jackson and Kennedy, let alone Mayor and Vansittart, would make of it all we can, of course, only guess. But my hunch is that it would be (for all of them) a nightmare scenario come true: a figleaf of precision and examining-technique acting as an alibi for our unwillingness to face what *they* were prepared openly to discuss. How *do* you mark an essay?

MALCOLM UNDERWOOD

The Revolution in College Teaching: St John's College, 1850–1926

The period between the first and third University Commissions saw the complete reconstruction of the relationship between the colleges and Cambridge University, and partial reconstruction within the colleges themselves. In 1850 there existed an association of colleges, nearly independent in means of instruction, and united as the University chiefly in its privilege of granting degrees. By 1926 this had become, for educational purposes, a framework of interdependent bodies linked to each other and to the University by faculties and departments. The process can be viewed in constitutional terms as the rise of the University at the colleges' expense – literally, since after 1882 they were forced to make regular financial contributions to it. Early reformers who thought that the first Commission had not demanded enough change in the colleges' corporate share of money and power would have been pleased at the outcome.

Constitutional struggle reflected deeper themes. The demand for change, and the mechanics of it, were really concerned with the way teaching should be organised and with what subjects should be taught: this was the issue that in the end united the colleges in a new university framework. This chapter seeks to illustrate from the history of St John's the changes in teaching methods that took place during the period, and to identify some of the pressures that brought them about.

If a passer-by had been stopped in the street of a large town in 1800 and asked to name one famous thing he knew about Cambridge, he would probably reply 'the Tripos'. What had begun as the three-legged stool from which in the middle ages a senior graduate posed questions to those seeking the degree of BA, had become by the end of the eighteenth century the name of a written examination held in the Senate House comprising questions chiefly on mathematics – including, by the early nineteenth century, applied mathematics in the shape of hydrostatics and mechanics – with additional questions on natural and moral philosophy. Its huge mathematical bias was due to the dominance of the school of Newton and his successors in the Lucasian chair in the late-seventeenth and eighteenth centuries. Its most important practical feature was the strict ordering of successful candidates within an honours list of three classes, the name of the highest – the wranglers – being drawn from the world of disputation, vulgariter 'wrangling', in which the exam had its origins. Yet the medieval student sought to shine in debate and to satisfy his masters with his skill, not to gain a precisely defined place in a published list of honours. It was competition for these places and the rewards that they entailed, which gave the later examination its cutting edge and its prestige.[1]

High performance in the Cambridge Tripos in the early nineteenth century led often, though not inevitably, was coveted for its local prestige and the reward of a college fellowship. The Tripos and its counterpart, the Oxford Honours Schools, had a large influence on the introduction of competitive examinations in the civil service and as a measure of ability in schools after 1850.[2] Of the undergraduates reading for degrees the majority would be satisfied with the Ordinary degree, which required a far lower standard in the mathematical Tripos than did Honours, but, after 1822, included Greek and Latin. The core of college instruction in the first half of the century consisted of lectures in the same subjects as those required by the Tripos, and the mid-course Previous established in 1822. These lectures, however, were delivered by a handful of tutors and their assistants to classes undifferentiated in ability, so although they were exam-oriented, they did not always provide sufficient individual tuition.[3] A tutor of the standing of James Wood, of St John's, who wrote a standard university text book on algebra (*The Elements of Algebra*, 1795), regularly recommended private tutors in classics as well as mathematics for his pupils.

In the earlier nineteenth century, the strongly mathematical emphasis of the qualification for honours was acceptable. The restricted subjects of the exams did not disturb a society whose public administration was small, and in which the need for qualifications in particular branches of natural science, and in languages, law, geography and history, was only beginning to be articulated. Some of these subjects were dealt with in lectures given by the University's professors, but these lectures remained tangential, especially for honours students. William Quekett came up to St John's in 1821. He considered that his decision not to read for honours allowed him time to cover subjects which reading for honours would have precluded. The courses of lectures he recalled, however, those on fen drainage by the Jacksonian Professor of Experimental Philosophy, and on the Greek New Testament, would have had some relevance for the final university exam, as bearing on hydrostatical problems and on

---

[1] W. W. Rouse Ball, 'The Mathematical Tripos', *Cambridge Notes* (Cambridge, 1921), passim.
[2] J. P. C. Roach, *History of Public Examinations in England, 1851–1900* (Cambridge, 1971), pp. 13–14.
[3] Those taking Honours at Cambridge did not outnumber those taking Ordinary degrees until 1885. See S. Rothblatt, *The Revolution of the Dons: Cambridge and Society in Victorian England* (Cambridge, 1981), p. 81.

Scripture.[4] The establishment of the Previous actually led to fewer undergraduates attending certain professorial lectures than before, because another, more elementary, exam now had to be worked for. In 1822 a separate classics Tripos was established, but open until 1850 only to those who had taken mathematical honours.

The very success of the University exams, as they became more complex, gradually caused problems in the relationship between the University and the colleges, which handled the admission and instruction of undergraduates. In 1837 hydrostatics, mechanics and divinity were added to the subjects to be taken for the Ordinary degree, and this further complicated the position for some college tutorial classes, which could not cover all the required subjects with their available staff. This situation resulted in an extension of the network of private coaches. William Whewell of Trinity College deplored both the lack of attendance of undergraduates at the lectures of mathematics and classics professors, and the system of private tuition whose supplementary labour added substantially to the expense of a Cambridge education.[5] In 1843 he sought to involve the professors in the design of the University examinations; this, he hoped, would make their lectures part of undergraduate instruction. He attributed the defeat of his scheme to the reluctance of the colleges, particularly St John's, with its large share of honours, to change the system.

St John's had in fact a very strong internal system for assessing knowledge in its twice-yearly exams that *did* reflect the range of knowledge likely to be demanded of undergraduates by the University. The exams were established in 1765 by the efforts of William Powell, Master of the College, and tested, at the end of the Michaelmas and Easter Terms, the grasp of each year of undergraduates on the required authors. Despite this, Powell was not a suppporter of the extension of exams into an annual test administered by the University: his view was that every college should sharpen its own discipline, confirming the respective roles of tutor and college classes. What he opposed was the element of anonymity implied in a bigger university test. The examiners appointed annually would be 'wholly strangers to most of the students, to their abilities, their previous education, and the professions or stations for which they were designed'. Some of the St John's exam reports, written into the exam books year by year, convey, despite their brevity, an underlying familiarity with the college life of those examined.[6]

Powell's view was sustainable while a manageable body of required

---

[4] The decision was a purely technical matter caused by the date of his admission: he had not been entered before July 1821 so could not fulfil the residence requirements for honours by keeping that October term. He decided not to wait another twelve months 'on my father's hands', but to start in the Lent Term. See William Quekett, 'Life at St John's in 1821', *The Eagle*, Vol. 15 (1889), pp. 149–54.
[5] D. A. Winstanley, *Early Victorian Cambridge* (Cambridge, 1940), p. 158.
[6] T. Baker, *History of St John's College*, ed. J. E. B. Mayor (Cambridge, 1869), Vol. 2, p. 1059; Examination Book, St John's College archive (henceforth SJCA), C15.6.

knowledge – mostly theoretical and grounded in Euclid, Locke and Paley – was preserved under the umbrella of the single Senate house exam.[7] The spheres of college and university could overlap although they might not exactly meet. The ground was restricted to relatively few authors, though the drill of expertise in handling them was severe and familiarity with particular kinds of mathematical problems, or with the principles discussed in the texts of Paley and Locke, had to be practised. What was tested, in the main, was a sureness in handling arguments, whether philosophical or mathematical. The middle years of the nineteenth century, however, from c. 1850–1870, saw a slow broadening of the stream of knowledge, as organised and tested by the University in the form of examinations, into more and more clearly distinguished rivulets. Separate Triposes in natural and moral sciences, which included questions on history and law, botany and geology – material hitherto officially treated only in the professors' lectures – had been set up in 1848, and more were to follow.

This broadening was a response to the need felt both within and without the University to train a wider section of its members for careers in an expanding industrial society, and a growing empire. Managers and administrators should be equipped with definite knowledge in mechanical science and engineering, various branches of natural science, economics ('political economy') and history, to help them to assess and act upon propositions put before them. The movement was encouraged by pressure from the Government, as part of its reform programme for the University, for a wider range of subjects to be made available as Triposes to students who had passed the Previous, without having to pass a second examination for the B.A. consisting largely of maths and classics.[8]

At an early stage of this process of diversification, in 1849–50, twenty-two fellows of St John's, headed by Francis Bashforth, later a ballistics expert and inventor of a chronograph, petitioned the College Seniors for an increase in the teaching staff of the college.[9] In 1848 the college had revised its statutes, dating from 1580, giving some formal recognition to changes in teaching practice, but these had said little beyond replacing prescriptions of Aristotle and Plato no longer observed with general references to arithmetic, geometry, Greek and Latin, and, as more advanced subjects, logic, mathematics, natural and moral philosophy and theology. The tutors and assistants lectured to large classes of men on the two tutorial 'sides' into which members were grouped for the administration of their fees and college accounts. T. G. Bonney, the geologist, recalling college instruction in 1852, said that the maths lecturers would dictate questions and then perambulate the class giving help or criticism. In Classics men would be called on to construe and then a commentary given to the whole

---

[7] While the Senate House exam papers were written after 1828, some questions on Euclid in SJC college exams continued to be viva voce until 1870 (Education Board Minutes of 8 October 1870, SJCA CC1.1).
[8] Royal Commission Report, Cambridge, 1852, pp. 27–8.
[9] Petition, SJCA D103.52.

class. This was a schoolroom situation in which instructors covered between them all the required subjects. Not surprisingly they recommended to individual pupils that they hire private tuition. The lecturers of this generation had of course been brought up in a system that fostered what could really be called a general education. George Liveing, the chemist, recalled that he had lectured in college for two years on Paley's Evidences.[10]

The criticisms by Bashforth and his colleagues of the prevalence of private tuition and its costliness suggest that although the college's examination system was rigorous, its requirements were met in great part from the pockets of individuals, not by college instruction to match them. They recommended that more fellows be engaged to lecture, financed by an increase in tuition fees, that the 'sides' be ignored and the classes made smaller and determined by ability, and that the lecturers specialise in fewer subjects. It is to be noted that these criticisms were aimed at reducing the *cost* of education as it reflected a weakness in the college as a vehicle of instruction. There was no suggestion that the *standard* was low, although it was pointed out that greater specialisation by lecturers would outweigh the advantages even of being individually coached by a private tutor.

In 1853 the seniors responded to such criticisms by redistributing revenue and cautiously reforming the lecturing staff to cope with the courses of studies 'now demanded by the University' as far as possible within the college. Traditional fees for ancient posts were diverted to fund a third additional lecturer on each tutorial side. George Liveing was appointed to lecture in Chemistry and Joseph B. Mayor in Moral Philosophy. Another promising development was the establishment of the college chemistry laboratory in 1853, with Liveing appointed as its salaried superintendent in 1860, when he also became university professor of Chemistry. The College had thus given the two new Triposes of moral and natural science specific attention.[11]

Henry John Roby, a fellow who was fully behind the extension of lecturing, observed in 1858 that the provision of more college instruction, as against ever-expanding private tuition, was not merely a matter of cutting the costs of education. He saw the danger of coaches training in technique for exam passing rather than really stimulating original thought, encouraging 'the disposition to evade difficulties with *apparent success*, rather than grapple with them and confess their reality' (my italics). On this view it was not merely a matter of the teaching ratio, but of the freeing of instruction from Tripos mania. Roby thought this was more likely to take place in a college framework in which the teachers were not

---

[10] T. G. Bonney, 'A Septuagenarian's Recollections of St John's', *The Eagle*, Vol. 30 (1909), p. 301. T. R. Glover, *Cambridge Retrospect* (Cambridge, 1943), p. 89.
[11] This and the following on the reforms of 1860 are drawn from a Report on the Education Fund, 1909 (copies in SJCA SBF77); see also on tutors and lecturers, J. B. Mullinger, *History of St John's College* (London, 1901), pp. 299–302. I have not found any other authority for the titles of Liveing and Mayor 1853–60, but they both figure in the list of examiners, who also had lecturing duties, in the College rentals at that date.

immediately dependent for a livelihood on the private fees and exam triumphs of their pupils.[12]

In 1860 the staff of lecturers was increased to ten, two-thirds of tuition payments going direct to the tuition fund rather than to the tutors. Teaching appointments were placed in the hands of the governing council of the college – the master and seniors – rather than being left with an even more select club of the master and the tutors. Under the new statutes approved by the University commissioners, both tutorships and lecturerships were made statutable offices.

The real impact of reform, however, began with the new university regulations for examinations in 1865. These involved the putting back of the Previous Examination to the fourth term, and the General to the end of the second year, leaving augmented 'specials' to be taken at the end of the third year. The specials were now to include 'law, mechanism and practical science'. On 13 June 1866 the Education Board of the college discussed 'the changes that would be necessary in the College lectures and examinations in consequence of the scheme adopted by the Senate as a substitute for the present method of obtaining the B.A. degree'. On 16 October it recommended that certain elements in the maths papers for the first year be made more suitable for freshmen, and classical subjects were re-ordered to concur with the new order of university examinations. The second years' Christmas exam was dispensed with, and college poll men were separated from the honours men by not being required to take any college exam in their second year, at the end of which they could now sit the General.

Gradually additional lecturing staff were taken on. In 1867–68 the college educational staff supported out of corporate funds included the lecturer in Hebrew (P. H. Mason, appointed in 1854), superintendent of the laboratory (1860), a lecturer in moral sciences (J. B. Pearson, 1864), chemistry (Liveing, 1853), a lecturer in law and modern history (Bryan Walker of Corpus, appointed temporarily by the board, 3 November 1868), and the Linacre lecturer in medicine. Other lecturers in mathematics, classics, of moral philosophy and scripture, still the basic subjects, were supported from the tuition fees: W. H. Besant (1853), C. E. Graves (1866), F. C. Wace (1864), J. E. Sandys (1867). Additional lecture rooms were first built in 1869.[13] The revenue from endowments was thus being used to support the newer Triposes and special subjects, while the members paid through their fees for the teaching in subjects most of them would be taking for the General. In 1871, at a period of high growth in student numbers, there were six corporately-supported lecturers and eleven in maths and classics supported from tuition fees.[14]

[12] H. J. Roby, *Remarks on College Reform* (Cambridge, 1858), p. 19.
[13] Education fund accounts, SJCA CC1.5, biographical sheet for Besant, attached obituary from royal astronomical society, SJCA C3.6 p. 148. An additional collegiate motive for the appointment of a law lecturer was the establishment of the McMahon Law studentship in 1864.
[14] *Report of the Commissioners into the Property and Income of the Universities*, Vol. 1 (London, 1874), p. 179.

More lecture courses and special papers were organised within the college. A paper in philology, to have 'three fourths of the weight assigned to each of the present papers in prepared subjects' was added to the annual classical examination; William Heitland was engaged to deliver a new course of classical lectures each term, being paid out of the existing salary of the principal classical lecturer; Henry Gwatkin was authorised to give a course of lectures on Ancient History. In 1873 the question of 'relieving the classical lecturers of non-classical subjects' was discussed: an additional moral science lecturer was recommended and others in theology, and an annual law exam was established to be set at the same time as that in natural science. The process continued as subjects diversified. On 14 July 1884 the Education Committee agreed, after discussing the proposal for a lecturer in mathematical physics, to secure the services of Joseph Larmor. He was appointed fifth lecturer in mathematics in place of F. C. Wace. It was recognised that there was no demand for a sixth lecturer in 'ordinary mathematics'.[15]

To assess progress in the special subjects being added to the general diet of mathematics, moral philosophy, scripture and classics, the May college examination for all years was eventually, in 1875, replaced by an exam restricted to second-year men preparing for the general university exam, and a series of special examinations. College teaching and assessment would now cover all the options open to both poll and honours men. The new Triposes founded in the 1870s did not require the previous gaining of honours in maths, and although the University General Examination for poll men remained, the stage was set for increased specialisation in the BA throughout the University career. A College Order of 4 June 1874 stated that in Easter Term 1875, and until further notice, there should be 'several special examinations in theology, mathematics, classics, natural science, moral science, law and history'. Undergraduates should be classed separately within their years, and in maths and classics by order of merit. Preliminary exams would be held for freshmen in subjects of the Previous, and exams for second-year men in the subjects of the general. All second-year undergraduates were required to pass either one of the special examinations set for that year or the college exam in the subjects of the General. Third-year men who were honours candidates were required to pass the exam in their special subject, and those not candidates for honours, who had not yet passed the General, were required to attend the college exam in subjects for the General.[16]

The principle of the integration of college teaching with the course of university exams had now been reaffirmed, but the cost of supporting it, as the range of Triposes increased, and specialisation within them deepened, remained a problem. In 1882 it was recognised that the proportion of stipends

---

[15] Education Board Minutes, 8 October 1870, 13 February 1872, 28 February 1873. An exhibition for proficiency in natural science had been awarded since 1868, as part of the minor scholarship awards, Conclusion Book, Order 13 June 1867. Education Committee Minutes, 1884, SJCA CC1.2.
[16] SJCA Conclusion Book, 1873–95, pp. 17–18.

of college lecturers drawn from corporate funds must be increased in the case of natural science, moral science and medicine because, unlike mathematics, classics and theology, the small number of students in them did not bring in sufficient tuition fees.

The college's corporate income, however, declined in the period between 1882 and the first world war, and from the 1890s there was also a decline in student numbers, and hence in tuition fees, a fall in both elements of college funding. One result was the decline in the income of tutors in uneven proportions, according to the size of their tutorial sides.[17]

At the same time, changes in both finances and organisation in the University tended to break down college isolationism. Intercollegiate lectures began in the late 1860s, and in 1875 a meeting of tutors at Trinity College agreed that these lectures should carry a separate capitation fee, charged to students going outside their own college, to be paid into the tuition fund of the college in which the lectures were held.[18] After 1882 the colleges were compelled to support the University by an annual contribution, which went to support more university lectureships, and in the 1890s the lectures arranged by the new university boards of studies began to rival those given in the colleges. In 1894, the year the University Engineering laboratory was founded and just previous to the admission of research students to the Cavendish Laboratory, the college physics laboratory incorporated in the Penrose building was closed, although the chemistry laboratory survived until 1914, where was taught, among other things, organic chemistry for medical students taking the first MB.[19]

To William Heitland, writing to the master in 1893 against a proposed additional classics lectureship, the day of the self-contained college was clearly past. To avoid straining the corporate funds, he advocated the transfer of lecturing in New Testament Greek to the theology lecturers, 'a steady refusal to ignore the intercollegiate system', and the careful selection of suitable men in small number.[20] The last two proposals he applied to disciplines besides classics.

Lectures remained the means of college instruction, aided by private tuition, until the first decade of the twentieth century. Supervision, the scheme of personal teaching to small groups which has gained prevalence at Cambridge,

---

[17] Sir H. Howard, *Finances of St John's College Cambridge, 1511–1926* (Cambridge, 1935), pp. 329–33; A. C. Crook, *The Foundation to Gilbert Scott* (Cambridge, 1980), pp. 145–6. The two theology lecturers were appointed in 1872 as a result of the ending of the Anglican monopoly of university posts, when it was anticipated that special instruction would henceforth be needed in this subject.

[18] SJCA D104.114–17. W. H. Bateson told the University Commissioners in 1878 that there had been no college order approving intercollegiate lectures D104.129 8; Admission of outsiders, and the fees, was before 1883 left to the lecturers. The St John's payment scheme for lectures and tuition in 1883 laid down a subsidy of £3 from the Education fund (which received all tuition fees not retained by the tutors) to pay the fees of students of St John's attending only outside lectures; £2 for those attending one course of college lectures; nil for those attending two or more courses of college lectures, or less than £7 per term tuition fee (1883, SJCA SBF77).

[19] E. Miller, *Portrait of a College* (Cambridge, 1961), p. 103.

[20] SJCA D103.211.

was recalled by Harold Jeffreys as having only just come in when he came up in 1910, but its seeds were sown earlier. The returns by lecturers to the University Commissioners in 1878 allow us to see something of how the lectures functioned as a teaching medium. Numbers of students varied with branches of the subject, between six and thirty, so that there might have been the atmosphere of a supervision in some subjects. In making their returns, the colleges were asked to state whether *intercollegiate* lectures were 'catechetical' or 'delivered in the manner of a professorial lecture'. The replies show how the lecturers carried out the process of instruction.

In classics the classes for non-honours pupils and outside students were large, but Johnian honours men were taken in 'select honour classes'. These were small groups 'seldom exceeding seven' on a subject prearranged with the lecturer. There was dialogue on the subject, and the men were dealt with 'in much the same manner as private pupils'. J. E. Sandys was fully aware that the small classes were intended to correct the disadvantage of the absence of a 'catechetical element' in the large professorial classes, so they were already seen as a model for intensive instruction. The lectures in law were said to be 'professorial', with very little catechising; theology was a mixture of the two methods, with some set papers, depending on the numbers involved. P. T. Main's lectures on Chemistry used a similar mixture, though the numbers were below a dozen. For practical demonstration sessions, however, Chemistry drew much larger numbers, between fifteen and twenty-eight, and the fees were all expended on laboratory expenses. Marshall and Foxwell – between them covering the political economy and moral philosophy for moral science – reported that the lectures were not 'strictly catechetical'. They were much more like a modern large university class, consisting of a 'consecutive exposition, but . . . liable to be interrupted by interpellations on the part of students, and questions and repetitions on the part of the lecturer'. The answers to papers set for the course were 'separately criticised' with each student. The great object of the lecturers was said to be 'to put themselves in sympathy with their hearers', and the tenor of Foxwell's report shows a lecturer energetically commending his discipline. Bonney described his geology lectures as 'professorial, but with opportunity of conversation after'.[21] These surviving returns suggest that in the late 1870s lectures were being used to some effect to provide a mixed form of instruction including an element of personal supervision. Foxwell's 'not strictly catechetical' and Bonney's 'professorial but with opportunity for conversation' perhaps indicate an uneasiness with the distinction made by the Commissioners. Both these lecturers emphasised dialogue as much as one-sided instruction.

Between 1893 and 1900 several proposals were made to lighten the financial responsibilities of tutors, and share out their income equally, by handling the tuition fees centrally. They eventually resulted in the creation of the office of

[21] SJCA D104.129.

tutorial bursar in 1900, which also freed the tutors to concentrate more on their responsibilities as educators.[22] Alongside this, a report was submitted in 1901 on the conduct of college teaching and supervision, the personal system employed in some other colleges for intensive instruction. These developments were precipitated by the retirement of John E. Sandys as tutor and the increasing workload of Donald Macalister, who was finding it impossible to deal with all the teaching required in medical subjects. It was Macalister who moved that the committee on teaching and supervision, consisting of Larmor, Tanner, Shore and Sikes, be set up.

Supervision developed from the conscientious methods apparent in some of the returns. In history Joseph Tanner as lecturer was recalled by Benians as having given weekly supervision in 1899. A special lecturer in Church history was appointed in 1896, part of whose duties was to supervise the other voluntary historical work for the theological Tripos.[23]

A committee on College teaching was concerned in 1901 whether mathematics teaching, in which the college had hitherto covered the whole ground, should become more like classics teaching as envisaged by Sandys in 1894, by relying more on intercollegiate lectures and adopting 'the methods of the private tutor'. Its large staff of five lecturers, some of whom also were dedicated coaches, in the event proved able to distribute the required subjects for the honours and ordinary courses, with Larmor now handling applied mathematics. Harold Jeffreys later stressed the self-sufficiency of the college in 1910, when he came up.[24]

Natural science was a Tripos in which fewer lecturers were stretched over a range of courses. A letter written to the bursar in 1896 by P. T. Main, the superintendent of the Chemistry Laboratory, complains that one lecturer cannot cope with the Chemistry needed for the first MB course and part one of the Natural Sciences Tripos. In addition there was practical work in the laboratory drawing about fifty students who needed supervision.[25]

At the suggestion of Donald Macalister, who was finding his workload in medical subjects overwhelming, the committee on teaching and supervision was set up in 1900. By then in the case of medicine there was some urgency. Students of the college had actually complained that they were less well prepared than those of other colleges: eight of these had already organised courses of supervision, in groups of two or three.[26] The report recommended the appointment of a supervisor in physics, as well as in chemistry for the MB and in physiology, and stressed that the mechanical sciences would need similar

[22] Report on a College Office and Liability of Tutors, 1898 (printed reports etc., SJCA C5.20). Vacant Rooms in College, May 1898, SJCA SBF 52. Orders made for the management of tutorial business, SJCA CM592/7.
[23] *Eagle*, Vol. LV (1952), 12, Miller, *Portrait*, p. 104; Educational Committee Minutes, SJCA CC1.3, 3 December 1896.
[24] 'Johnian Maths, 1910–14', *Eagle*, Vol. LX (1964), pp. 154–7.
[25] Letters of the Superintendent, SJCA D82.1.
[26] Report on Teaching, SJCA D100.52.

arrangements in the near future, as numbers increased. The Council took up the report to the extent of deciding that 'general supervision' (such as had belonged to the duties of the old principal lecturers) should be given by three fellows over the range of physiology, botany, zoology and comparative anatomy, at a termly capitation fee to be met from the education fund. In medical studies, however, Dr Macalister was asked to make special arrrangements, and these were the employment of two supervisors from outside the college, for an hour a week to each student in the chemistry and physics for the M. B. Macalister was himself to be appointed Director of Medical Studies, in place of the general lectureship in medical studies.[27]

These measures were aimed at plugging obvious gaps in teaching as they arose, but more were needed. The concern for the future of the mechanical sciences expressed in 1901 soon had to be addressed. The very next year Tanner corresponded with a man named Parker who wished to lecture at the college in engineering, combining it in a sandwich with his engineering practice. He had noticed that other colleges had appointed lecturers in mechanical sciences, and compared English practice hitherto unfavourably with that in France and Australia where the lecturers were 'in touch with actual work'. Tanner replied that the college did not want a lecturer in engineering but suggested that he apply to the engineering laboratory. Parker's response was that he had hoped for a college base from which to give morning lectures, and to which he could return in the evenings for 'let us say coffee and engineering conversation'.[28] Parker's proposal may sound a trifle eccentric, but it voiced a yearning for practical education which, whether misguided or not, had been expressed at intervals since the 1850s. In 1905 Gerard Williams, a mining engineer in South Africa, wrote to Tanner advocating the substitution of modern languages for Greek in the Little-Go and a greater emphasis on technical education for commercial uses. Once again the lack of time for specialisation was highlighted: Williams recalled how 'dear old Professor Liveing dismissed the metallurgy of gold in ten minutes', whereas German and American universities incorporated the latest work in their lectures.[29]

While remaining unenthusiastic with his correspondents, Tanner had to respond to the problems of teaching the mechanical sciences when appointed to review it with Edward Sikes in 1903. St John's suffered in the case of engineering from a bad reputation. It was treated as a sub-branch of mathematics, which ignored the 'strong specialist vocation' felt by many engineers. Caius, King's, Trinity and Emmanuel had taken the lead in encouraging it as a separate subject for which they had appointed directors of studies. A somewhat later and perhaps frivolous instance of the élite spirit was the reunion of engineering Tripos candidates at the Red Lion Hotel in 1922. The notice for it stated that 'at

[27] SJCA CM625/7, 626/12, 642/9. Macalister's title was not, however, changed in the education fund ledger until 1906–7.
[28] Tanner, tutorial and general correspondence (1902), SJCA TU12. 4.77–8.
[29] SJCA, TU12. 7.187.

9 pm in the vicinity of the Red Lion all engineering lecturers, demonstrators and *especially* the examiners will be warmly received. To ensure the *safety of the latter* a guard of honour of firsts under the sergeant major will parade with T Squares and Slide Rules. Refreshments obtainable from within.'[30]

A critique of teaching methods, centring on the use of directors of studies, was the nub of the 1903 report. The Tripos demanded a combination of lectures, given in the Engineering Laboratory, with corrected course work. The laboratory set the examples for this, but left the students to get them corrected. The report recognised that the 'old ideal' of the University lecturer setting and correcting examples had broken down through 'too great a lack of mutual interest', and that where colleges failed to provide for this the student was driven to find a coach. The coaches, however, never tailored their teaching to the specific content of the Laboratory lectures, so a great deal of excess 'cramming' went on. Some colleges had accordingly appointed directors of studies, taking two or three pupils at a time, setting examples and resolving problems more closely related to the laboratory lectures. The College Council was sufficiently moved by the report to appoint a supervisor of Engineering, G. B. Matthews, during the year 1904–5, but this was to be overtaken by developments across the range of studies.

The immediate occasion for these was the resignation of Donald Macalister from his tutorship, leaving Joseph Tanner and Edward Sikes, neither of them a scientist, to guide the college careers of 220 undergraduates.[31] The committee appointed to consider the situation reported on 17 and 20 March 1905.[32] It blamed a decline in overall numbers, which had resulted in the impoverishment of the Education Fund. The overall decline in intake in the college, from 121 in 1881 to permanently below 100 after 1890, fell to 71 in 1904. The committee suggested employing a third tutor, from a good school, specially devoted to the natural sciences, who would attract students, but this was ruled out by cost: the proposed natural science tutor could not be secured below an estimated £800.[33] Declining college entry meant declining fee income, in addition to the improving but still reduced level of corporate revenues.

So the college decided on a different solution. This was to offer better-organised instruction, using existing personnel at lower cost. Bushe-Fox, a lawyer admitted fellow in 1903, was appointed as third tutor, but with him a Director of Natural Science Studies, Lewis E. Shore, and Directors of Studies in

---

[30] SJCA CM674/10, 679/11, and Report in SBF54. It was E. E. Sikes who had suggested that it be considered. For the reunion see Tanner Papers, TU12.26.45.

[31] Macalister asked to be relieved of the tutorship on 9 December 1904, SJCA CM706/10. In 1906–7 fifty men were receiving college instruction in natural sciences, as against thirty in maths and thirty-five in classics. Report of a committee to consider instruction in science, 1911, in SJCA SBF54.

[32] Report, in SJCA SBF54.

[33] The lack of men from these schools was thought to put parents off sending their sons, since they were 'well aware that a college so composed fails to provide some of the most important advantages for a university career'. Unfortunately these 'advantages' are not spelled out.

many other subjects, among them Bushe-Fox himself in law, and Henry F. Baker in Mathematics and Mechanical Science.[34] The directorships were placed on a fixed stipend of £50, or in some cases were funded by capitation fees of their students.

It was in some cases a far from perfect solution. Baker conceded to Tanner in 1907 that he would like to be let off supervising the Mechanical Science men: 'I do not find I have any real authority with them, and I hate farce.' The last part of his letter sums up the problem presented by this area of applied maths: '. . . last term we [the College] provided a lecture – the lecturer was a student of Engineering before the Mechanical Labs began – but the men were told at the Laboratory not to go, and they were allowed to give it up after a few attendances. You will remember I took on this supervision of the Mechanical men at the last minute after I had accepted the supervision of the Maths men – just as a stopgap.'[35] Such difficulties, however, compelled more adventurous recruitment. Baker's unease led to the appointment of H. B. Jenkins as Director in Mechanical Sciences; he also became a demonstrator in the Laboratory, thus solving the problem of liaison with it. He was succeeded on the same basis by Peel of Magdalene College.[36] Extending facilities for supervision was one way of keeping up with competition from other colleges, but by the outbreak of the First World War it was still organised as a voluntary supplement to lectures and demonstrations, for which separate fees were paid.[37] Pupils were set written work and supervised in classes that could exceed six, and sometimes had the disadvantages of the old tutorial lectures, the weakest not airing their problems, or not attending the supervisions.

By 1913 most of the much-needed supervision and lecturing in biology, anatomy, chemistry and mechanical sciences was done by non-fellows, but geology and physiology, physics and botany had fellows combining posts as lecturers and directors or supervisors. The same applied to history which had no less than three fellow-lecturers, with Tanner as overall Director. Extremes of the in- and out-college lecturer in the pre-war period were provided by Robert Webb and Joseph Tanner. Webb taught mathematics as coach and lecturer. In addition to a fixed stipend of £200, £49 was drawn from the fees of students of St John's coming to his lectures, nothing from attendance from other colleges. By contrast Tanner was almost a public lecturer, adding £331 15s to his fixed stipend of £125 from the fees of outside students. The latter tendency increased with the growth of special subjects. Guillebaud anticipated a class of 100 in the college for his lectures on the Economics Special.[38]

[34] SJCA CM718/7, 12 May, CM721/4, 9 June 1905.
[35] SJCA TU12. 9. 9, 11 January 1907.
[36] SJCA CM776/6.
[37] Early supervision lists are preserved in SJCA CC1.21. On the inadequate level of instruction for undergraduates preparing for examinations in history, see P. A. Linehan, 'Group III Managers' (SJCA ARCH 3.11, p. 9).
[38] SJCA SB6.6 (dividend sheets), CC1.4 (Education fund accounts) 1912–13, pp. 121–6; stipends of college lecturers 1910–11, in SBF54; Tanner Papers TU12.26.18 (1922).

According to Ebenezer Cunningham, the war hastened the pressure for more systematic intercollegiate arrangements.[39] H. F. Baker, indeed, in recommendations for the post-war period drafted in 1916, advised centralising the administration of the colleges for all but social purposes, just as the two tutorial sides of St John's had been subordinated to the college office and tutorial bursar. Others wished to organise teaching better within the college. In 1918, in a college report on natural science teaching and the tutorial system, Marr advocated appointing a Director of Studies or assistant tutor in each branch of natural science. In the event a breakthrough was made with the appointment of a praelector of natural sciences, William H. R. Rivers, in 1919. His duties were to chair a natural sciences committee that would nominate supervisors, carry out research, and coordinate lectures and supervision with the needs of science students — in effect a chief director for natural sciences.[40] In 1921 a praelectorship was also established in the college's main traditional strength, mathematics.[41]

The problem about the relationship between lectures and supervisions, and how these were to be paid for, was only properly tackled with the University reforms of 1926. Before the Great War members of the college were charged a tuition fee of £7 a term, which went to maintain the college staff of tutors, lecturers, directors of studies and supervisors, with additional fees for supervision. The Education Fund subsidised those attending lectures outside college. In 1922 this system, college centred, was replaced by one in three parts. There was firstly an education fee of 4 guineas per term payable by everyone; secondly fees for lectures paid according to a general university scale; thirdly fees for college supervision on a fixed scale determined by the amount of supervision usual in each subject. The main change in 1926 was that all formal lecturing was undertaken in the faculties, college contributions to the University having been substantially increased. Supervisions, on the other hand, continued to be organised among the colleges, the rates not varying with different subjects, but being graduated according to the amount of supervision received; and a network of college supervisors grew up, teaching small groups of students regularly for a set number of hours per week.

The Gordian knot of college independence vis-à-vis university provision had been cut by a redistribution of functions, but not without some causes for alarm. William E. Heitland had written to the Senior Bursar in March 1919 expressing concern at the consequences of a move by the General Board of Studies to support a body of college lecturers by a percentage college contribution from tuition funds. He saw the risk as that of progressively impoverishing the smaller colleges, and added some prophetic comments:

---

[39] Ebenezer Cunningham, Typescript Memoirs, SJCA ARCH2.12, p. 58.
[40] Baker, 1916 SJCA SBF 54; Report on Natural Science teaching, 2 December 1918, ibid. and CM1041/5, 1042/2.
[41] Thomas J. 'I'Anson Bromwich was appointed, SJCA CM1102/4.

> That a considerable share of college revenues should be transferred to the University is a demand which seems to me imminent. For the Natural Science departments are already claiming much, and will surely claim more. Inquiry (another commission?) must follow, and the question whence the money is to be got is not likely to be answered by a large state grant.
>
> Now, so long as it is the University that directly and really despoils Colleges I see no honest objection to that result. If the Colleges must suffer, that is the best way.
>
> But the so-called 'voluntary' plan of pooling resources seems to me ruinous to the poorer colleges, particularly if carried out on the plausible lines of a percentage.[42]

In the event the state did contribute towards the research and teaching needs of the University, supported by a variety of fund-raising initiatives, but the colleges also contributed directly, by a percentage grant increasing with income, to the University's needs.

Yet this redistribution of wealth was only part of the answer to a question that was to overshadow the history of the University in the twentieth century. The provision of endowment by the State is turning out to have been a short episode in its history. Whatever the nature of future provision, it is important to keep a balance of aims in university education, as did the Duke of Devonshire, Chancellor 1892–1908. He declared in the course of a letter that aimed a mild blow at compulsory ancient languages:

> In the long run the old universities must respond to national wants or they will dwindle and become insignificant. Hence the opinions of great capitalists and commercial men are of importance, however remote may be their relationship *to that pure knowledge which it is the function of a university to foster* (my italics).[43]

His double insight should give us pause to reflect.

---

[42] Original Letter, 17 March, in SJCA SBF54.
[43] Cyclostyled copy of a letter to the Vice-Chancellor, n.d., but after the South African War, i.e. between 1901 and 1908; SJCA D103.225. Probably the letter forwarded by the Vice-Chancellor in 1901–2, Ward of Peterhouse, to the Master, and by him to the Senior Bursar, on 2 August 1902 (D92.32.35,36).

JONATHAN SMITH

Trinity College Annual Examinations in the Nineteenth Century

The rise of the competitive written examination was one of the major developments in nineteenth-century education. From its germ in Trinity College at the beginning of the eighteenth century, it grew in the nineteenth, until by the second half of the century it pervaded the Universities, professions and the civil service, forming a series of rites of passage for ambitious young men. Within the University of Cambridge, the establishment of the primacy of the Senate House Examination in the mid-eighteenth century was one of the crucial steps in the development of the modern university; the greater emphasis on written rather than oral work being a defining factor in its development. This examination, together with other examples of the great nineteenth-century examinations, has received the attention of historians of education and society.[1] Of less interest has been the nature and purpose of those examinations that the Cambridge colleges annually set their pupils.[2] This is not entirely surprising. By the mid-nineteenth century, the examinations that led to University Honours had, to a great extent, replaced patronage as the door to careers and social status. They have been seen variously as a means of codifying acceptable non-radical knowledge and passing it on to future generations; as a means for some to reach heights that were previously denied to them without sponsorship; or as pedagogical engines, producing an end-product assessed and graded like coal, to be put to use at various levels in society.

The annual college examinations were more humble. These examinations offered no ticket to a successful career, nor were they the means of showing that a man was imbued in the accepted knowledge, but by 1830 they were universally accepted as an essential part of a Cambridge education. From that

[1] For example J. Gascoigne, *Cambridge in the Age of Enlightenment* (Cambridge, 1989), S. Rothblatt, 'The Student Sub-culture and the Examination System in Early 19th Century Oxbridge', in L. Stone, ed., *The University in Society*, Vol. 1 (Princeton, 1974), pp. 247–303; Warwick, *Masters of Theory* (Chicago, 2001); C. A. Stray 'The Shift from Oral to Written Examinations: Cambridge and Oxford 1700–1914', in *Assessment in Education* viii.1 (2001).

[2] But see Gascoigne, 'Mathematics and Meritocracy: the emergence of the Cambridge Mathematical Tripos', *Social Studies of Science*, xiv (1984), pp. 554–7, and *Cambridge in the Age of the Enlightenment*, pp. 224–8.

year the Cambridge University Calendar, published each year by authority, reported that as part of the method of proceeding in Arts

> the Undergraduates are examined in their respective colleges yearly, or half-yearly, in those subjects which have engaged their studies. By this course the students are prepared for those *public* Examinations which the University requires candidates for the degree to pass.

From this point of view, the essential purpose of the college examinations was one of preparing students for the greater task ahead, those University examinations that they would be required to take in order to proceed to a degree. Beyond this, however, they allowed the examiners and the college tutors responsible for their students' work to assess the progress of their men and to take whatever action was deemed necessary when they fell below the standard required. In this dual role of preparation and assessment they form part of a pedagogical system which we can trace back to the foundation of the college itself.

Prehistory of the Annual College Examination

To understand better the role played by the college examinations, we need to look at the means by which the college prepared and assessed its students in the sixteenth to eighteenth centuries. Since before the introduction of the great Elizabethan statutes of 1560, which still in many ways pertained for much of the nineteenth century,[3] Trinity had a number of pedagogical tools that allowed it to do this. Before college men could perform the acts in the public examinations that would lead to their degree, they were required to prove themselves in the subjects of the trivium before the Master or Vice-Master, the Head Lecturer and the Seniors – the eight most senior Fellows who, together with the Master, formed a council for the government of the college. The proposed statutes of Philip and Mary were even more to the point.[4] Only those who proved fit were allowed to participate in the university tests, others were rejected, to re-submit themselves at a later date. As Leader says,[5] few students failed their degree as the University (or colleges) made sure that they did not. The college also had a regular means of assessing the day-to-day progress of its pupils, by holding disputations, which from 1671, by conclusion, required that each man was to be opposed by the three students next in seniority to him. Held on Mondays, Wednesdays and Fridays in term, the disputations or acts were still statutorily a

---

[3] The revised statutes of 1844 were essentially a redrafting of the 1560 statutes, bringing them into line with developments over the three previous centuries. It was not until 1861 that the college statutes were completely reworked, removing much that pertained to the pedagogical role of the college. Before that date, the Master and Seniors adapted the statutes to changing conditions by omitting those parts of each statute that had ceased to be relevant.
[4] 'Nemo ad publica in scholis sophismata generalis sit qui non a praeside, magistro aulae, et quaestoribus idoneus judicetur'. Trinity College Archive Box 34/3. These statutes were prepared in 1554.
[5] D. R. Leader, *A History of the University of Cambridge*, Vol. 1, p. 99.

part of college life in the eighteenth century, but this was not always observed. A conclusion of 22 March 1753 directing the Deans and Head Lecturer to ensure that the acts were kept in the chapel not only indicates that the college felt that they were desirable, but also that they were falling into disuse. If the acts were not being kept, it took away one of the main tools it possessed for maintaining a disciplined and progressive approach to the curriculum by its students.

In parallel with these systems, the college had also had a statutory system of examinations for electing scholars and Fellows to the community. The method was essentially oral, in which each candidate was examined individually by the Master and members of the seniority and in chapel by them acting as a panel, although, at least for the election of Fellows, there appears to have been some written element as on the fourth day of the examination they were sent 'to write their themes'.[6] The credit for introducing competitive written examinations into the college and indeed to the whole of Europe, has long belonged to Richard Bentley, who, for all his arrogance clearly wished to improve the academic life of the college. In 1702, in his second year as Master, Bentley insisted on a written aspect to the system for assessing scholarship candidates. According to his biographer Monk[7] the Master felt that each candidate could be judged at leisure, with greater opportunity for reflection on the merits, or otherwise, of each, but it was still far from the classic written examination of the nineteenth century as there was still a considerable oral element. Monk is not always critical of his subject and rather loose with his sources, and it is now impossible to credit Bentley unquestionably with these sentiments. A more cynical biographer might suggest that the written examination gave Bentley greater control over the whole examination procedure. He was later in his tenure to elevate his son to a Fellowship without troubling the other statutory examiners.

If Bentley's modifications to the scholarship examinations were the result of a desire to increase the academic rigour of the college, the major movements for reform exerted their influence in the second part of the eighteenth century, most notably in the two decades before annual examinations were introduced in Trinity. A major figure in the cause of reform was John Jebb, who tried and tried again to persuade the University authorities to introduce annual examinations for all students and to expand the rather narrow Cambridge curriculum. That Jebb failed in what was something of a crusade for him was as much to do with politics as pedagogy, but the vigorous opinions voiced by both supporters and opponents show that feelings were running extremely high. There is evidence also in Trinity of a movement for reform. In 1786 the Master[8] and Fellows took the dramatic step of admonishing ten of the junior Fellows for making detailed criticisms of the method of examining for Fellowships. The dissenters had gone so far as to suggest that one Senior Fellow in particular

---

[6] See Stray, 'Shift from Oral to Written Examinations'.
[7] J. H. Monk, *The Life of Richard Bentley DD*, Vol. 1 (London, 1833), pp. 159–60.
[8] John Hinchliffe, noted anti-radical.

voted for men that he had not bothered to examine. These charges they laid down not once but twice within a week. The case went to the college visitor. After depositions were taken, the visitor did not wish to pronounce judgement and suggested that he would prefer to see the matter sorted out internally. When this was done the junior Fellows saw measures introduced that ensured that each Fellow responsible for examining the candidates actually did examine them,[9] and they were justified in feeling that they had been completely vindicated. The disrepute into which the examination of candidates for Fellowships had fallen is indicative of the torpor of which the eighteenth-century university is often accused. The stricter methods urged by the band of reforming junior Fellows brought not only greater rigor and discipline to the Fellowship, but was also a step on the road that took it from patronage to meritocracy.

Introduction and early years, 1789–1830

The introduction of the college examinations was one of the first major decisions made in the mastership of Thomas Postlethwaite. Postlethwaite was the Fellows' choice as Master and, it is claimed, immediately set off on a course as unlike that of Bentley as it was possible to be. He had risen through the ranks, and had no wish to quarrel with the men who had until recently been his peers. The result was that much of the college administration was left in the hands of two noted members of the party of reform: Thomas Jones, who had been one of the junior Fellows involved in the case of 1786, and James Lambert, Junior Bursar and supporter of the attempted reforms of John Jebb.[10] If Jones and Lambert were not the architects of the annual college examinations, they were reformers in influential positions who were not likely to hinder their introduction. Contemporary evidence for this event is thin. The only record that we have is the following conclusion of the Master and Seniors of 24 February 1790:

> Agreed by the Master and Seniors that there be a public examination of all the Freshmen who have resided since the last Long Vacation soon after the division of May term. Agreed at the same time that in future there be a public examination of both Freshmen and Junior Sophs[11] at the time above mentioned annually. Agreed also that a sum hereafter to be specified or arranged for the pay of the examiners and the premiums to those who shall appear best upon examination.[12]

As with all Trinity conclusions, this is concise and not particularly revealing as to the reasons behind the introduction of annual examinations. Of course, as the nature of the examination for the BA degree changed in the second half of the

---

[9] This matter stayed in the collegiate memory for many years. In the statutes of 1860 it is specifically stated that only those Seniors who had examined candidates could vote.
[10] M. Milner, *Life of Isaac Milner* (London, 1842), p. 161.
[11] Junior Sophisters, i.e., second-year men. The third years were Senior Sophs.
[12] TCA Conclusions Book 1646–1811, p. 545.

eighteenth century, any means of preparation for this would have to change to remain relevant. As written examinations in mathematics began to take on greater significance in the Senate House, a system of examinations within the college modeled on the University curriculum would have prepared Trinity students for them more effectively than oral assessment in the form of the disputations outlined above. Similar annual examinations had existed in St John's since 1765 and gave a useful example to the Trinity reformers of what might be achieved within that college. That Trinity and St John's competed vigorously for the prize of Senior Wrangler at this time has been noted by Gascoigne and is evident throughout much of the nineteenth century in the excited correspondence of undergraduates. It may have been the case that, in trying to improve the academic excellence of college undergraduates, the reformers looked to Trinity's neighbour and rival. At the same time, teaching ceased to be the sole privilege of the colleges as many students took on private tutors (as Warwick has described above). There was clearly a concern for both the University and the colleges such that the college authorities may have felt moved to ensure that the progress of its students was assessed in the light of this, to check that they were being coached in knowledge of the right sort, both intellectually and politically.

The examinations were the responsibility of the Head Lecturer and four Sub-Lecturers, thus placing these examinations at the heart of pedagogy within the college rather than in the hands of the disciplinary authorities, the Deans. Only freshmen and second years were to be examined. Unlike at St John's, where third-year students were examined from the first, their Trinity peers escaped this test until 1818 when 'at the application of the Head Lecturer and by the recommendation of the Tutors'[13] they were required to be examined at the same time as the first two years. This is not to say that the third years got away scot-free. As we have seen, the Elizabethan statutes made provision that all Trinity men who wished to be admitted 'ad respondendum quaestionem' must first submit to an examination by the Master, Seniors and Head Lecturer to establish that they were fit to do so. It is clear that this requirement did not meet the same fate as the disputations. When the college statutes were revised in 1844 the relevant statute was retained but slightly modified and Whewell, in his evidence to the Royal Commission of 1850,[14] makes it clear that the examination of questionists, as it had come to be called, was still very much a part of Trinity life.

Evidence of the workings of the system in the years immediately after its introduction is limited. We can be confident in suggesting that the subjects of the examinations reflected the familiar Cambridge curriculum of a liberal education: a preponderance of mathematics based on Newton and Euclid and a little moral philosophy and theology. We might also suggest, from what

---

[13] TCA Head Lecturer's Book, 1801–1900.
[14] *Report of Her Majesty's Commissioners Appointed to Inquire into the State, Discipline, Studies and Revenues of the University and Colleges of Cambridge* (London, 1852), p. 415.

went on at St John's and the Senate House, that there were a mixture of written and oral examinations. However, the first detailed evidence of the actual exam week that we have comes from J. M. F. Wright, who records the 1817 examinations that he took as a second year at Trinity in *Alma Mater*.[15] According to Wright, the tests took place in the hall, with viva voce and written examinations being conducted concurrently. The ordeal took four days and each student was required to attempt eight papers that covered a range of subjects within the curriculum. Wright prints what he claims are the papers for both the second years and the Freshmen.[16] In both cases mathematics and its related subjects are to the fore. Classical subjects based on philological discussion of set texts with some prose and poetry composition are also included, although at this time they were not examined at University level. Their inclusion in the Trinity curriculum reflected Jebb's proposals of the 1770s, but Latin and Greek were already strong in Trinity. Knowledge of Latin and Greek was a prerequisite of an educated gentleman, so it may not be so surprising that the college chose to check that its men reached a sufficiently high standard in the subject, or at least in classics as she was taught in Cambridge. However, they were also demanded both by the examinations for scholarships and for Fellowships, which remained independent of the annual examination system, and it should be remembered that it is the college of Bentley and Porson which is credited with saving classics in Cambridge during the onslaught of mathematics during the eighteenth century.

Once the trial was over, Wright was left to wait for his results. In the interim, he tells us something of the marking system. A set number of marks was allotted for each question, with additional marks available at the discretion of the examiners for elegance shown by the examinees. Once all marks were totalled the men were arranged in eight or nine classes which were, as at St John's, listed in alphabetical order as the men of each class were seen as being 'very much on a par'. The class list was pasted on a pillar in hall where it remained, for all to see, until the results of the following year replaced it. Although this enabled a man's peers to see how well or badly he had done and allowed elements such as praise and emulation to act as a spur to effort, it differs notably from the more advanced system of competitive examination where each man is also ranked within his class. In fact, in the early years only the results of the first four classes

---

[15] Wright, *Alma Mater: or Seven Years at the University of Cambridge*, Vol. 1 (Cambridge, 1827), pp. 229–323. An incomplete series of papers is preserved in Trinity College Library from 1816.
[16] According to Wright, the papers for Freshmen were on Hecuba, Livy XXI, mechanics, plane geometry, plane trigonometry and algebra, with viva voce exams in the classical texts. For the second years, subjects were Thucydides, Livy XXI, Newton and conic sections, spherical trigonometry, astronomy, metaphysics and moral philosophy and St Luke's gospel. Vivas were in St Luke and Thucydides. Prose and poetry compositions were included in those set text papers that seemed most relevant. Greek poetry composition would, for example, be examined as part of the Hecuba paper. The progressive nature of the curriculum is seen in the mathematical subjects.

were publicised. The credit for making all classes public knowledge was claimed by George Pryme who felt that, by publishing only the higher classes, the college discouraged those men not so ranked from attempting to improve their position in later years.

The year after Wright sat his examinations saw the introduction of examinations for third-year students. This resulted in the splitting of the subjects previously reserved for the second-year men into two, and the introduction of new subjects that was finalised by Dobree as Head Lecturer in 1820. The result was an increase in the number of examinations devoted to mathematics and related subjects at the expense of classics, which was not examined at all in the second year; only one 'classical subject' appeared in the examination timetable for the third-year men. In order to appear comprehensive, Wright also publishes the examination papers for the third year students of 1820, which includes more advanced material, including a paper on differential and integral calculus. The first paper in differential and integral calculus that survives is from the previous year when it appears to have replaced the paper on fluxions. Many of the supporters of the introduction of continental analytical methods to Cambridge are known to be Trinity men, such as Peacock, Babbage and Whewell, but it perhaps shows just how strong the support in the college was, for such a recent innovation to be incorporated so quickly into the system of annual college examinations. The balance was soon tipped back a little towards the classics, as by the early 1830s each year was examined in classical set books. That this came about is probably the result of two factors, the first being the appointment of Christopher Wordsworth as Master in 1820. Wordsworth was a noted reformer in his early years in the Lodge and a major figure in the introduction both of the Classical Tripos and the Previous Examination. This latter innovation, taken by men in their second year, included examinations in a Greek and a Latin prescribed author. For Trinity preparing its men to sit such an examination, a test of their classical abilities would act as a spur to preparation for the Previous.

The Cambridge curriculum changed more slowly in the first half of the nineteenth century than it was to do in the second. Whewell, who had supported the introduction of analytical mathematics into Cambridge, was able to boast of the Trinity curriculum that 'the system had been repeatedly accommodated to the *progress* of science, but always within the general *spirit* of the statutes. The Mathematical course even now differs little from that described'.[17] All was not, however, set in stone. Although the early books of Euclid were examined year after year, and as we have seen other branches of Mathematics and related subjects were introduced. However, it is not so much the change in curriculum as the way in which the results of the examinations thereon that marks out the Cambridge competitive examination at its peak.

---

[17] Whewell, *On the Principles of an English Education* (Cambridge, 1827), p. 58. My italics.

The mature system before reform, 1831-66

Although its origins are to be found in the eighteenth century, Peter Searby[18] locates the peak of the Cambridge competitive examination system in the period from 1830 to 1870. Essential to this was a means of marking papers in such a way as to allow minute differences between the performance of individuals, revealed in classes ranked in order of merit, which advocates of this system of marking believed encouraged industry through competition. In 1831 we see a change in the records of the Trinity examinations which mimic this system. Before that year each class was listed in surname order and no marks are given. However, from 1831 the classes are listed in order of rank with each man's marks recorded, allowing not only comparison between men in each year but also between men from different years.

In 1833, Thomas Thorp was head lecturer, and particularly thorough in his record of the proceedings of examination week, which gives us a good opportunity to see the examinations in their mature form before the developments of the 1870s. Two examinations were set each day, beginning on Thursday 30 May and ending with a single examination on 3 June. Examinations began at 9.00 and 4.00, taking place in hall, where the participants were served with lunch between sessions.[19] There is still an oral element here: the Freshmen had four vivas, the second-year two and the third-year men one. In the case of the third years, the viva on the Acts of the Apostles was dispatched in a little over two hours, 'by giving a single verse to each man who answered readily, having two books employed at once and stopping a slow man till the rest of that division was finished'. It is perhaps an example of the constancy of the college exams at Trinity that in 1861, although the viva voce had to a great extent fallen into disrepute, Richard Jebb, Henry Jackson[20] and their peers would still have had to undertake the same oral examination in Acts in their third year.

As in Wright's time, mathematics was, unsurprisingly, the predominant subject for those in their second and third year. For the Freshmen, however, classics was the principal subject. One simple practical reason for this development was that this was the dominant subject in the English public school,[21] and thus would be that with which most Trinity entrants would be familiar. There may have been other factors involved, but a major consideration for the earnest Trinity freshman was to allow him to acclimatise while picking up the basics of mathematics and allowing the college to develop an opinion of his general abilities. Not all Trinity men had the same background, however. Alexander Chisholm Gooden was Senior Classic in 1840, but had studied mathematics under Augustus De Morgan at University College London before being

---

[18] Peter Searby, *A History of the University of* Cambridge, Vol. 3 (Cambridge, 1997), p. 601.
[19] C. A. Bristed, *Five Years in an English University* (New York, 1852), p. 95.
[20] Successive Regius Professors of Greek. Jackson proved more successful than Jebb in the college examinations, but Jebb was first to a Fellowship and to the Greek Chair.
[21] See Stray, 'The Shift from Oral to Written Examinations'.

admitted to Trinity. Having clear ability in classics and a good grounding in mathematics, he seems to have been equipped to do well in his first year examinations, and he wrote home complaining that the mathematical curriculum was limited. Although he did reasonably well in the examination, he was embarrassed by his results, and was forced to account to his father for his comparative failure in mathematics, which he blamed on the fact that he was unused to sitting written examinations in that subject.[22] He was, nonetheless, placed in the first class.

Not all examinations carried the same number of marks. For the Freshmen of 1833 a paper on Sophocles' *Philoctetes* was worth 600 marks; Euclid and trigonometry carried 500 and 200 respectively, but filled one examination session. For the Seniors, miscellaneous questions and mathematical problems carried a maximum of 800 marks, but occupied two sessions in the examination timetable while questions on moral philosophy and Butler's *Analogy* were only worth 150 and only occupied half a session each. This marking system differed distinctly from that at St John's, where each paper was marked out of 6, 8, 10, 12 or 14 marks, depending on its importance, while at Trinity, certain individual examinations carried as many as 800 marks. The permissive nature of some of the examinations meant that no-one could achieve full marks. Bristed, writing of the late 1840s, tells us of 'cram' papers which were made to cover as much ground as possible so that everyone could find something to do in them.[23] In his discussion with his tutor 'Travis' (Thomas Taylor) he confesses to having managed to complete fourteen out of twenty-one questions on the Euclid paper.[24]

When the marks were added up, each year was split into eight classes; there were as many as ten in some years. In 1833, T. R. Birks stood head and shoulders above his peers, scoring 2,738 marks out of a possible 3,850, nearly 700 more than the next man. Seven were placed in the first class, the lowest of these achieving only 1,208 marks, and there is a clear distinction between him and the top of the second class who scored 958. The majority of the participants were given pass grades down to an eighth class, but below this in each year there were some men whom it was deemed necessary to re-examine 'on the first day of lectures in the [following] October'. Aegrotats were also required to be examined at this time. It has to be noted that a candidate had to do particularly badly to fall into the last class. While Birks was rated in the high two thousands, seven of his peers failed to score the 63 marks that would have ensured their pass. A few men from the first and second years found themselves in a similar position. Bristed tells us that in his day 50 marks would usually guarantee safety, those failing for a second time being 'asked to try the air of some Smaller College or devote his energies to some other walk of life'.[25]

[22] TCL Papers of Alexander Chisholm Gooden, uncatalogued.
[23] Bristed, *Five Years*, p. 99.
[24] Bristed, *Five Years*, p. 101.
[25] Bristed, *Five Years*, p. 100.

Such was the form of the annual college examination at mid-century. We might ask why such a form of examination developed although it was not a part of the assessment for a degree. It might be argued that within the college system a more humanistic and less scientific means of assessment, such as had existed for many years at St John's, might be more appropriate in nurturing academic ability in young men. We can tell a lot about the purpose of examinations from the way in which they are held and marked. In mid-century the college examinations, with their superabundance of questions and strict ranking of men, seem more a test of examination technique, as it was required in the Tripos, of speed and accuracy. It should be noted that the strict ranking of men within each class encouraged in some a competitive spirit which was to spur them on to greater achievement as they tussled with their peers in subsequent examinations.

However, not all Trinity men were so minded, and not all wished to attempt Honours in the University examination. As the breadth and complexity of knowledge required for the mathematics Tripos increased, the gulf between Honours and pass men did also. The University authorities finally decided in 1859 to sever the examinations for poll men from the Tripos completely by introducing an ordinary examination that could be taken in the ninth term of residence. Trinity acted immediately by instituting an examination for men not wishing to take Honours in the same year. Consisting of examinations in Greek and Latin classics, The Acts of the Apostles, a set period of history and a single paper in mathematics, with the average marks for each paper closer to 70 than 700, this was a markedly different form of test than reading men were required to do. A comparison with the college examinations for Honours men throws into even greater relief the demands on the reading men.

The reformed system, 1866-1900

The spirit of reform arose in Cambridge once again in the second half of the nineteenth century. Pressure from within and without forced Cambridge to re-examine itself minutely and to adjust to the demands of the age. The days of the Cambridge liberal education based around mathematics were numbered. The attacks came from a number of sources. In the sphere of examinations, the Classical Tripos was finally emancipated from mathematics in 1854, while the regulations for the Moral and Natural Sciences Tripos were altered in 1860 so that examinations in these subjects were sufficient to qualify for an Honours degree. Additionally, the method of strictly ranking men according to their results was also brought into question, as the competitive element that this engendered began to be seen as a negative rather than a positive aspect of the system as it was felt to encourage cramming. In 1873 Michael Foster was to complain that

> the order of the marks is doing great mischief to the study of physiology at Cambridge and I continue to believe that were a simple class system,

with alphabetical order in each class, introduced, most beneficial changes would result in the work of the students.[26]

With such changes taking place within the University, and with many of the agents of change being Trinity men, it is not surprising that college teaching underwent a complete remodelling in the period around 1870. Central to this was a group of young Fellows led by the two Henrys, Sidgwick and Jackson and Coutts Trotter. Amongst other reforms within the college, they succeeded in establishing a tutorial fund to strengthen the relationship between the college and its tutors, and were the architects of the supervision system of teaching, which was so much a feature of twentieth-century Cambridge. Their work is admirably described by Winstanley.[27] One reform that he omits is that of the annual college examinations. A system where the majority of students in a given year all took the same examination based for the most part on mathematics and classics was exclusive and no longer viable. However, despite the agitation of Sidgwick and his allies, there was still some conservative opinion in the college which Whewell's successor W. H. Thompson had to balance with the reformers in governing the society with an even hand. In 1869 the Master and Seniors approved the report of a college committee which had sat to consider the improvement of the examinations for second- and third-year students 'according to a general scheme provided by Mr Sidgwick'. Instead of opting for a system of examinations in each Tripos subject, the committee trod a middle path that preserved examinations in many of the subjects of the liberal curriculum while including the opportunity for a little specialisation. It was decided that on each of two mornings of the exam week, special examinations for the second and third years would be set in mathematics, classics, natural sciences, moral sciences, law and history simultaneously, allowing students to choose their speciality. The rest of the week was made up of four examinations in mathematics, four in classics and one Greek Testament paper.

There is some realism in this system. Not only does it nod towards the traditionalists while allowing some specialisation, it also still benefited the majority of Trinity Honours men. Although the new Triposes attracted more and more students throughout the last three decades of the century, mathematics and classics were still held by many to be the most important university tests and still attracted more candidates than the other Triposes. A further reform that took place at this time was the return to listing men alphabetically within each class, so removing what was one of the pillars of the competitive system when it stood at its height. However, there was greater pressure for reform than for reaction and Sidgwick's compromise was to last for only five years. Further changes were decided in 1874. After that year all second- and third-year Honours men other than those taking mathematics and classics were to be classed separately by subject, and the number of examinations in these

---

[26] Natural Sciences Tripos examiners' reports, 1873.
[27] D. A. Winstanley, *Later Victorian Cambridge* (Cambridge, 1947), pp. 236–62.

subjects was increased to four. There is evidence that this increased specialisation stretched the educational resources even of Trinity. In 1876 it was concluded that the Head Lecturer could request the Master and Seniors to appoint an examiner from beyond the membership of the college if it was felt necessary to bring in expertise from elsewhere.

The source of pressure for change not only came from within the newer subjects. Advances in mathematics and a broadening of the study of classics made it difficult for the University examiners to include all the topics that they would have liked in the Tripos examinations. The solution was to divide the examinations into parts: Part I of the Classical Tripos and Parts I and II of the Mathematical Tripos were to include the more general examinations and were deemed sufficient to qualify students for the BA degree. Further examinations (Part II or Part III depending on the Tripos) in more specialised subjects could be taken at a later date. That this had a great effect on the college examinations is explained by the decision to move part I of the Classical Tripos and Parts I and II of the Mathematical Tripos to the May term of a student's third year. Faced with the decision either to move or to abolish the third-year examinations, the college opted for the latter course. Once again, it was first- and second-year men only whose progress was to be tested by college examinations.

Assessment and punishment

The hold that Whewell exercised over the college of which he was Master is indicated above, as is his belief in a liberal education. In one of his defences of this ideal, *On the Principles of English University Education*,[28] he says of the college examinations that they

> approach much more nearly to the character of instruments of direct instruction than the University examinations. They are different each year of the student's progress, and taken in connection, they conduct a pupil through a course of instruction selected with care and judgement.

Interestingly, he goes on to add that they 'are by no means to be carried on as if they were merely preparatory to the examinations required by the University'. In this distinction between university and college examinations, Whewell points up the value of the Trinity examinations as a pedagogical tool. The examinations not only allowed the students to familiarise themselves with examination situations and the type of questions likely to be set by the University authorities. They also allowed the college to set progressively more difficult tests on which it could assess the progress of its students, year by year, through a carefully paced curriculum as they developed towards the BA degree. Ultimately men who did not come up to the mark were, as we have seen, asked to leave the college, but

---

[28] William Whewell, *On the Principles of English University Education* (London and Cambridge, 1848).

these were few. For the many they helped the tutors to see in which areas their pupils had weakness, and, after the poll degree became an option, to decide which examinations they should take. Gooden[29] tells us that he was kept back at for an extra day at the end of the term in order that his tutor could tell his pupils how best they might occupy themselves during the long vacation, and we can assume that in the case of Gooden, his tutor was tolerably pleased with his progress. In some cases the stick was waved en-masse. In 1879, when classics and mathematics were still examined together for Honours men, the examiners in the former subject issued an 'Index Expurgatorius' by which they hoped to bring to the attention of the tutors those first- and second-year students who had performed poorly. The examiners were explicit in their warning. If any of the men listed were engaged to sit or proposed to sit the Classical Tripos, they would stand no chance of passing unless they were 'prepared to work at their very utmost during the remainder of the time'.

How the tutors passed this information in this case on to their pupils and the pupils on to their parents is unrecorded. In extreme cases the tutor would write direct to the parent, as in the case of J. M. Image, tutor at Trinity from 1875 to 1888. He writes to the father of one of his pupils thus:

> Your son's private tutor can only speak of him as thoroughly idle, and in the College examination in Law, which has been held, the examiner informs me that in two papers he obtained scarcely any marks, and the third was shirked altogether. The examiner adds that there is no chance of his being able to pass the Law Tripos for Honours. I cannot for the credit of Trinity permit him to disgrace the College by being ignominiously plucked. I have therefore been compelled to act upon my warning and to remove him from the list of candidates for Honours.[30]

Image has listened to the opinion of his pupil's private tutor, and has given him a final warning, insisting he prove himself in the college examinations. Once the pupil has demonstrated that his private tutor's opinion of him is correct, Image has removed him from the list for Honours *for the credit of Trinity*. This not only recalls the requirement in the Tudor statutes, of students being required to prove themselves worthy in college before being allowed to attempt the university tests, but also shows the pride of the college in the achievements of its students. There is another matter to be noted here, that of the college examination being used as the final test of Image's lazy student. While it gives the student a chance to demonstrate his abilities at the end of the academic year, the college examination also can be regarded as an impartial test, where Image can show no favouritism or otherwise to his pupil. The presumed impartiality of the competitive written examination was one of the reasons that it spread throughout the nineteenth-century English-speaking world. In the college

---

[29] TCL Papers of Alexander Chisholm Gooden, uncatalogued.
[30] Letter book of J. M. Image, TCL, 0.11.19.

situation it allowed the authorities to claim to be dealing fairly with its students, especially in cases where their decision may not have met with the approval of the individual involved or of their family.

Student attitudes

The reaction of the first Trinity men to sit the annual college examination in 1790 is not recorded, and we cannot say how they approached the novel task placed before them. Their successors have left us a better idea of their attitudes with regard to the college examinations, and the way in which they approached them was vital to their effectiveness. For a system of examinations to work as either a pedagogical or a disciplinary tool, it was necessary to persuade students that the tests should be attempted with a certain degree of seriousness. Trinity attempted to encourage industry by a number of additional means, many of which pre-dated the introduction of annual examinations to the college. Scholarships and sizarships were a spur for many, not only because the emoluments therefrom may have been the only means by which a student could maintain himself while at Trinity, but because a scholarship was a necessary preliminary for any man hoping to be elected to a Fellowship. Scholars did have cause to beware the college examinations. This was not because a good performance in these examinations would win a scholarship, but because through a bad experience they might be deprived of this emolument. As we have seen, the college had held examinations to award scholarships from the earliest days. These separate examinations continued throughout the nineteenth century. Once a student had been elected to a scholarship, he was required to reach a sufficiently high performance or, according to statute, the Master and Seniors could deprive him of the benefits that he gained from his award. This was not a particularly common event (often excuses could be found for poor performance), but the existence of annual competitive written examinations in the college gave the governing body a means to test the ability of scholars against other junior members in an impartial manner. In the examination of 1871, A. G. Murray was ranked as unworthy to be classed, though a scholar of the house, and was forced to undergo the forfeiture of his scholarship until he proved himself worthy to regain it. If the purpose of this was to shock Murray into an improvement, it seems to have worked as his scholarship was restored to him the following April after he performed creditably in the Classical Tripos.

Another means of encouragement, though less lucrative, were the college prizes that proliferated from the mid-eighteenth century onwards. Their sponsors hoped that they might encourage endeavour in a certain area of undergraduate study by offering a prize for the student who performed best at the test set for it, whether it was English declamation, a powerful tool in statesmanship, or Latin poetry. Some means of encouragement were related directly to the annual examinations. From the first, prizes were awarded for those who achieved first classes in the annual college examinations, and later prizes were awarded for those who did best in certain examinations: a Greek Testament prize was awarded from 1848. How much the financial aspect of these prizes encouraged diligence in more than a small portion of poorer students is unclear. To those who had to make their own way at the University, an extra ten pounds or a few books here and there would indeed have helped them. But such small prizes could not compete with those offered by the University, where there was real money to be had, and by university and college scholarships and sizarships. Although not forced to support himself, Montagu Butler totalled his yearly income from scholarships and prizes in 1853 as £230.[31] If money was a potential inducement for some students, they were better served by concentrating on those quite separate examinations for scholarships and other emoluments that Trinity and the University provided.

Monk[32] was of the opinion that the introduction of a system of annual college examinations gave general impetus to learning within the college. He praises the annual college examinations for their wonderful effects 'in exciting industry and emulation among the young men and exalting the character of the college'. Some men certainly did take them very seriously, so seriously, in fact, that in combination with the work that they had done throughout the year, they were the cause of a crisis. James Clerk Maxwell, for example, was one to feel the strain. Shortly after working for the college examinations in May, he suffered a collapse that left him debilitated for a month, which his doctor attributed to the work that he had put in for the college tests. However, not all students pushed themselves so hard and the motivation of Trinity students differed from man to man. In the nineteenth century, as before, Cambridge attracted a wide range of students, and Trinity was large enough to accommodate both sons of carpenters to the offspring of the nobility. However, as patronage ceased to be the only route to preferment, the opportunities given by success in examinations produced a class of hard-working students known as reading men, whose approach to study was markedly different from the opposite class of student, the rowing man. Wright compares the 'utmost anxiety . . . on the countenances of the Reading-Men' with the sadness of the 'gay-men and empty-bottles' who are

> compelled for once to sing small and look foolish with their hands in their pockets, whilst their wiser brethren are reaping the rich harvest of fame and emolument, from the labour of the year just ending.[33]

The differing motives of the various classes of student clearly had an effect on their approach to college examinations that were a required element for them all. Some treated them with contempt, others enjoyed their competitive spirit, whereas to the majority they were just another hurdle placed between them and

---

[31] H. M. Butler to George Butler, 10 April 1853, TCL J. R. M. Butler papers M3/1/241.
[32] Monk, *Bentley*, p. 160, n. 22.
[33] Wright, *Alma Mater*, Vol. 1, p. 229.

graduation. James Parker[34] approached the task in hand with cool judgement. Having come up through the Scottish system from Glasgow High School and the College of Glasgow, Parker concentrated on mathematics. Although this subject only constituted two-fifths of the examination marks, he felt that it was wasted effort to attempt to keep up with men who had spent many years studying Latin and Greek. As for cramming, the art of gaining 'that knowledge with which non-reading and stupid men stuff themselves immediately before examinations, merely for the purpose of getting marks'[35] he had no stomach: 'I think that the knowledge which is worth nothing for its own sake is hardly worth acquiring. I have therefore contented myself with reading during the last three terms my mathematical subjects as thoroughly as I could.' He hoped for a second or third.

Parker's method was cool-headed and practical. He had no reason to aim for high marks in the college examinations and his sole intent was to do enough to pass: he had his eyes on a larger prize. He eschews cramming classics for the sake of it but dedicates his time to that subject that would stand him in greater stead when the more important university tests came along. Parker's estimate of his classical abilities was correct – he was placed in the third class in his freshman year of 1822 with at least nineteen men ranked above him. However, in the second and third year, when the subjects of the college examinations resembled more closely those of the Senate House Examination, he was placed in the first class and he eventually graduated seventh Wrangler. It might be noted that in his first year Montagu Butler, who had come up to Trinity with a traditional English public school education from Harrow, concentrated on classics rather than mathematics in order to ensure that he did well in the University scholarships and give himself financial security for his student life.

Writing to Whewell in 1847, Lord Lyttelton, having read Whewell's *Of a Liberal Education in General*, gives a fairly damning account of the college examinations of his day:

> There was a certain fashion, I don't quite know why, of working for a first class at the end of a freshman's year in the college examination: probably because the University Honours were rather remote, and the previous year of College studies were tolerably conducive to these Honours. But after the first year one cannot exaggerate the utter contempt into which the College examinations, and I must add to a great extent the lectures also, fell, in the minds of an ambitious young gentleman: especially to one like me, who was dandled and allowed to do as much as I liked.[36]

Lyttelton was that rare bird at Trinity, a nobleman with academic aspirations who proceeded BA in order to compete for the Chancellor's medal and thus had

---

[34] Sir James Parker, Vice-Chancellor of England 1851.
[35] Copy in papers of R. Robson, TCL Robson E40/2.
[36] TCL Add. Ms a.80/59.

a foot in two camps, the reading men and the noblemen: the one may have despised the examinations because they were pass exams, the other because they were not likely to affect their career. Nevertheless, Lyttelton did get his first in the freshman's year.

Others for whom the examinations meant nothing had a completely different approach. In Lyttelton's day the college examinations may have been treated with contempt, but at least all but a few men got sufficient marks to pass, or at least bothered to attempt the exams at all. Some were not so conscientious. The academic career of another Trinity nobleman, Henry George Francis Moreton (later second Earl of Ducie) was brought to an abrupt end by his rustication by the Master and Seniors for missing the first day of college exams in 1821. It is hard to believe that he did this anything but knowingly; surely he felt that he had spent sufficient time at the University for his purposes. After all, if he had been willing to submit to the Trinity regime, he could have graduated without sitting any university examinations at all as was a nobleman's privilege. One of John Jebb's attempted reforms in the 1770s concerned the abolishment of the privileges of noblemen with regard to examinations. Trinity, at least, had taken this to heart.

The annual Trinity College examinations were the reaction of the late eighteenth century to the essentially medieval practice of assessing the progress of students and preparing them for examinations using oral methods. Once instituted, the examinations were not allowed to fossilise but throughout the nineteenth century were adjusted as progress demanded, following developments in the Senate House and Tripos Examinations. Existing in a college environment, they were a pedagogical tool that took certain facets of the competitive written examination and allied them closely with the teaching process. While encouraging industry, competition and emulation among Trinity men, they allowed their tutors to see how they were progressing, giving ample opportunity for errors to be corrected before they were made in university examinations, and for areas of ignorance to be bolstered. The examinations also protected the image of the college within the University and the wider world. They helped to insure it against accusations of partiality as the perception of written examinations as fair allowed examiner, tutor, student and parent to interact in an impartial environment. They also bolstered Trinity's academic reputation: if the standard required to pass the examinations was not particularly high, they did weed out the intellectually weak. In failing men and then seeing them migrate to another Cambridge college Trinity did give itself a certain air of intellectual superiority. In Bristed's words, men who did not make the grade were recommended to 'try the air of some smaller, less demanding college': Trinity was to be perceived not only as pre-eminent in size but in ability as well.

GILLIAN SUTHERLAND

'Girton for ladies, Newnham for governesses'

My title is a remark made to me in the 1960s by a Fellow of Newnham, a daughter of the house, who had been an undergraduate in the 1930s. Oral tradition is no more to be neglected in a Cambridge college than anywhere else; and this summarizes pithily some major differences of style, status and tactics between the two institutions in their early years. Yet the impact of these differences on styles of teaching and learning was less than might have been expected. Attempts to explain why lead in turn to questions about teaching and learning for men as well as for women in the University in the years after 1870. Such an enquiry underlines the point that gender is never a single or simple dichotomous variable: it interacts in complex fashion with the social, economic and political structures of the society both locally and nationally.

Girton College began at Hitchin in 1869 and moved to its present site at Girton in 1873. Emily Davies, the founder, took the view that women would only be acknowledged to be equal to men if they could be seen to surmount the same hurdles in exactly the same way. Girton therefore expected the majority of its students to take the qualifying entrance examination for a degree course, the Previous or 'Little-Go', including compulsory Greek; then they were to go on to prepare for a Tripos, a degree-level examination. Moreover they were expected to complete the work on the same timetable as the men. Students − or their parents − were thus expected to commit themselves at the outset to three years' worth of fees, payable a year at a time; and from 1873 Girton offered its students sets of rooms, bedroom and sitting room, although not grouped in staircases around a court. Emily Davies was the daughter and sister of Anglican clergymen and the college's association with the Established Church was enshrined in the trust deed, although a chapel was not built until the 1890s.[1]

Newnham, begun in a house in Regent Street in 1871, took an approach which integrated pragmatism and principle. Anne Jemima Clough, who took charge of this house and subsequently became the first Principal, had had no formal schooling of any kind and was well aware that many of her contemporaries and juniors were in a similar position. Yet many of them were also subject

---
[1] See Rita McWilliams Tullberg, *Women at Cambridge* (Cambridge, 1998), p. 33.

to pressures which she too had experienced, to make an economic contribution to their own and/or their family's survival.[2] The Cambridge liberals involved with the enterprise which became Newnham were led by Henry Sidgwick of Trinity, increasingly disenchanted with the existing curriculum, and eager not to inflict it on the newly arriving women. Newnham therefore allowed its students to come for as little as one term, charging (lower) fees on a termly basis. If the students had ambitions to attempt a Tripos course, they could take extra time; and they were encouraged to qualify by taking the new Higher Local examinations instead of the Previous. When Newnham built its first building on its present site in 1875, the student rooms were single bed-sitting rooms. The involvement of several of its founders in the campaign against university tests made it unambiguously a secular foundation.

These distinct approaches attracted slightly different populations. In the first decade or so, up to and including 1880, far more students passed through Newnham than through Girton, 258 compared to 113, ranging in age from sixteen to thirty-seven. Although the patterns of parental occupation, where recorded, did not differ greatly – the vast majority middle-middle or upper-middle class – the Girton parents were of slightly higher social status, a little more secure and affluent. None of the Newnham fathers appeared as a 'landowner'; six Girton fathers were so described. Twelve Newnham fathers to seven Girton fathers were in trade. Dissenting, particularly Unitarian, networks were clearly identifiable among Newnham's students and supporters. Perhaps most tellingly, Newnham appealed for and collected scholarship and bursary funding to support its students from the outset.[3] Girton's first scholarships were created only in the 1890s, from the windfall of the Pfeiffer bequest.[4] Before that Emily Davies had sunk every penny in building.

These differences did not, however, mean that Newnham operated more like a school than Girton. Despite minor differences of social status and the disagreements between the two sets of promoters, the learning experiences of the two populations of women students were very similar, sharing common roots. The question of where school ends and university begins is an altogether more complicated one and can only be tackled subject by subject, raising as many questions about the experiences of the men students as it does about the experiences of the women.

The bedrock of shared experience for the women students was formal

---

[2] See Gillian Sutherland, 'Anne Jemima Clough and Blanche Athena Clough: Creating Educational Institutions for Women', in *Practical Visionaries: Women, Education and Social Progress 1790–1930*, ed. Mary Hilton and Pam Hirsch (Harlow, 2000), pp. 102–3.

[3] See Gillian Sutherland, 'The Social and Political Location of the Movement for the Higher Education of Women in England c. 1840–1880', in *Politics and Social Change in Modern Britain: Essays presented to A. F. Thompson*, ed. P. J. Waller (Hassocks, 1987), pp. 100–1, 103.

[4] B. M. Herbertson, *The Pfeiffer Bequest and the Education of Women: A Centenary Review* (Cambridge, privately printed, 1993), pp. 10–11.

schooling, or more probably the lack of it. Certainty is impossible here. Only about a third of the entries in the Girton and Newnham biographical *Registers* up to 1880 say anything at all about educational experience before Cambridge; and the fragmentary nature of a number of the entries means that absence of information cannot be straightforwardly construed as absence of formal schooling. The previous educational experience of 33 of the 113 Girtonians is recorded: 9 are described as being educated entirely at home or 'privately', 17 as attending a school or schools and 7 as combining home education with some schooling. The previous educational experience of 83 of the 258 Newnhamites is recorded: 28 were educated at home or privately, 48 attended a school or schools and 7 combined both. The numbers recording attendance at a school, particularly among the Newnham entrants, began to rise from 1878 onwards; and the schools named range all the way from anonymous private establishments, through those named after their proprietors, like Mrs Fleming's at Ambleside, the school she took over from Anne Jemima Clough, and Hannah Pipe's celebrated establishment at Laleham, to Cheltenham Ladies' College, the North London Collegiate School and the first of the Girls' Public Day School Company schools.[5]

What variety like this might mean was described rather melodramatically much later by the novelist, Mrs Humphry Ward, nee Mary Arnold:

> As far as intellectual training was concerned my nine years from seven to sixteen were practically wasted. I learnt nothing thoroughly or accurately, and the German, French, and Latin, which I soon discovered after my marriage to be essential to the kind of literary work I wanted to do, had all to be re-learnt before they could be of any real use to me; nor was it ever possible for me ... to get that firm hold on the structure and literary history of any language, ancient or modern, which my brother William, only fifteen months my junior, got from his six years at Rugby and his training there in Latin and Greek.[6]

She had been among the girls of her generation who had had some formal schooling, boarding first at Anne Jemima Clough's school at Eller How in Ambleside, and then at the Rock Terrace School at Shifnal in Shropshire. The recollections of those who taught the lonely and difficult child, prone to epic temper tantrums, suggest that not all the failures were her teachers'.[7] It is worth

---

[5] My calculations from Vol. 1 of the *Newnham College Register 1871–1971*, 3 Vols (Cambridge, privately printed, 1979) and the *Girton College Register 1869–1946* (Cambridge, privately printed, 1948). For Laleham, see Clyde Binfield, *Belmont's Portias: Victorian Nonconformist Education for Girls* (London, Dr Williams' Library, 1981).

[6] *A Writer's Recollections* (London, 1918), p. 96.

[7] John Sutherland, *Mrs Humphry Ward: Eminent Victorian, Pre-eminent Edwardian* (Oxford, 1990), pp. 14–18; Clough – Shore-Smith Papers, British Library Additional MSS 72830 B, fol.76, B. A. Clough's notes of conversations conducted in the Lake District while preparing the *Memoir* of her aunt.

remembering, too, that some boys found the system and classical 'grind' of a high-flying public school sterile and limiting.[8]

However the general point about the variety, unevenness and sheer uncertainty of girls' previous educational experience is a valid one. The Newnham Council recognized this in allowing the early students to pursue a variety of courses at a variety of levels. The Girton stance on the principle of equality precluded any such general flexibility; but the difficulties could not be ignored entirely. It took the first students so much time and effort to master the subjects of the Previous that there was precious little time left for the Tripos itself. In February 1873 the students appealed to Miss Davies and the College Committee to allow them to proceed to a Tripos without having passed the Previous. Seven of their lecturers and various individual members of the Committee supported this appeal; but Miss Davies was adamant.[9] Shortly afterwards Amy Agnes Bulley migrated to Newnham, who did allow her an extra year, at the end of which she was placed in the Second Class of the Moral Science Tripos.[10] Others may have taken evasive action of a less public kind. Despite the policy, 16 of the Girton students in the first decade did not complete a Tripos level course, some falling by the wayside through illness; and a further 23 took only college special examinations, pitched at the level of the Ordinary degree.[11]

Girls' secondary schools and women's colleges grew simultaneously and fed upon each other in late nineteenth-century England. Not all Newnham and Girton students entered paid employment at any point after leaving Cambridge; but of those who did, almost all went into teaching of some kind, often to elite posts in the new girls' boarding, endowed and proprietary schools.[12] And in due course they sent their cherished pupils back to their old colleges. By 1900 the picture had been transformed: the majority of Girton and Newnham students – although still not quite all – had attended a recognisable secondary school. Both colleges expected their students to have met the requirements of the Higher Locals or the Previous before coming into residence; and almost everyone prepared for a Tripos. In 1902 all but six of the 165 students in residence at Newnham were doing so.[13] In the years 1901–3 only 13.9 percent of the

[8] See for example the experience of Molly Hughes' eldest brother, Tom, at Shrewsbury in the 1870s in M. V. Hughes, *A London Child of the 1870s* (first published London, 1934, paperback edn Oxford, 1977), p. 55.
[9] McWilliams Tullberg, *Women at Cambridge*, p. 50.
[10] Newnham College Archives (hereafter NCA), Examiners' Letters 1874–82, J. B. Pearson, Percy Gardner, H. S. Foxwell and W. Stanley Jevons to Marion Kennedy, December 1874. The Girton and Newnham *Registers*, for 1871 and 1873 respectively, appear to be both in error in placing her in the First Class. Until 1882 women candidates were only allowed to sit the examination papers and have their scripts marked and classed by private treaty with an individual examiner. For the concessions represented by the 'Three Graces' of 1881 from the University, see McWilliams Tullberg, *Women at Cambridge*, ch. 5.
[11] My calculations are from the Girton *Register*.
[12] Sutherland, 'Social and Political Location', p. 104, Table 4.3.
[13] Claire Breay, 'Women and the Classical Tripos 1869–1914', in *Classics in Nineteenth- and Twentieth-Century Cambridge: Curriculum, Culture and Community*, ed. Christopher Stray (Cambridge, 1999), p. 56.

Cambridge women students took no final examinations, although over a quarter of the Oxford women students still fell into this category.[14] There was now a pattern of schooling for girls where before there had been none, and on these foundations could be built a more uniform pattern of higher education, one which more closely resembled that offered to young men. In 1902 Henry Sidgwick's brother, Arthur, felt able to resist pressure from the Society of Home Students in Oxford, to allow his daughters to take an extra year over the History course there. 'They are', he wrote:

> just as well able to work as the average man: they live as regular a life, take exercise regularly, (& neither drink nor smoke): they are no doubt more ignorant than the *best* men, but not more than the bulk of the 150 men of any year & I am persuaded that the time-limit is (in the case of normally competent & healthy students) most salutary. To have clearly before them the obligation *to do the work properly in the given time* (as the men all do) is one of the most valuable lessons for them to learn. It strengthens their resolution, forces them to arrange their work, & do it in a business-like way, and acts as a steady force against waste of time, dawdling work, & self-indulgence of various subtler sorts. It gives them self-reliance, and a certain healthy robustness, which girls too often miss.[15]

For the earliest women students, however, the variety and uncertainty of their earlier educational experience ensured that they received teaching which was at first both separate and distinct from that offered to the men. Lectures for ladies, given by male members of the University sympathetic to the cause of women's education, had begun in Cambridge in 1870, ante-dating both Girton's move from Hitchin and the leasing of Newnham's first house.[16] Indeed the house was initially a private venture by Henry Sidgwick, intended simply to accommodate those who lived too far away to come in to the lectures on a daily basis.[17] The management of the lectures was formalised with the creation of an Association for Promoting Higher Education for Women (AHEW) in Cambridge, in 1873, which negotiated with the University for the renting of lecture rooms.[18] The arrival of Girton in Cambridge no doubt contributed to this formalisation. Yet the steady expansion of the two institutions meant that the AHEW had a

---

[14] Janet Howarth, '"In Oxford but not of Oxford": The Women's Colleges', ch.10 of *A History of the University of Oxford VII, Nineteenth Century Oxford, Part 2*, ed. M. G. Brock and M. C. Curthoys (Oxford, 2000), p. 282, Table 10.1. I am indebted to Mrs Howarth for allowing me to consult her text at the page-proof stage and to quote from it.
[15] Quoted *ibid.*, p. 281
[16] *Cambridge University Reporter*, 19 October 1870, p. 23. Lectures were offered in English history, English literature, Latin, French and Harmony, and probably took place in what is now the Pitt Press Building. I am indebted to Phyllis Hetzel, who is writing a history of the Newnham site and buildings, for this and related references and for the discovery of the file of Examiners' Letters 1874–82 in her search for deeds and plans. For Oxford lecture schemes see Howarth, 'In Oxford', pp. 242–4.
[17] *Reporter*, 10 May 1871, p. 344.
[18] NCA, AHEW Minutes, 6 December 1873.

diminishing role and a short life. Weary of renting houses that were always oversubscribed, Henry Sidgwick, Anne Jemima Clough and their supporters leased land from St John's College and in 1874 formed the Newnham Hall Company, in order to build on it. Considerable overlap of membership and the flexibility of the Newnham approach meant that relations between the AHEW and the Company were always close and friendly; and in November 1879 they agreed formally to amalgamate.[19]

Two other powerful pressures made for common experience amongst the women and very strong college bases. The first pressure was the determination of both sets of college authorities to ensure that no breath of scandal should touch the infant enterprises. The second was the exclusion of the women students from the University Library and from some of the laboratories. Concern with propriety meant that from the beginning both colleges kept tight hold of all teaching arrangements, supervision and coaching, as well as lectures. Girton and Newnham students were never allowed into the marketplace to find their own coaches or tutors. As intercollegiate lecturing developed to supplement the University lectures of the professoriate, permission for the women to attend had to be negotiated with each professor and college, or group of colleges; and the women students came with chaperones.[20]

The resource represented by the University Library enabled many men's colleges to neglect their college libraries and sometimes to exclude their undergraduates from them. The women students were in general not allowed to use the University Library, although by 1900 a select few third-year students were allowed to read there. Newnham and Girton therefore set out to provide their own libraries, Newnham beginning in 1882 and Girton following suit in 1884. The laboratory situation was a more complex one. There were both college and University laboratories in this period and some of those in charge were prepared to admit women students. Lectures for ladies in Chemistry in 1872 were offered in St John's College chemistry laboratory.[21] However it was a grace-and-favour situation and always precarious. Already by 1880, therefore, Newnham and Girton had built and fitted out chemistry laboratories in their own grounds. Then between 1881 and 1884 they combined forces to convert an abandoned congregational chapel in Downing Place into the Balfour Biological Laboratory, which the women students used until 1914.[22]

Marginality, anxiety about the proprieties and the inadequacies of previous education would probably have been quite enough on their own to make Girton and Newnham build strong college bases. However, small group or one-to-one

---

[19] *Ibid.*, 26 November 1879.
[20] For lecturing in classics, see Breay, 'Women', p. 58; more generally, see McWilliams Tullberg, *Women*, pp. 56–7, also Ann Phillips, ed., *A Newnham Anthology* (Cambridge, paperback edn, 1988), pp. 9, 12, 51, 59, 75–6.
[21] *Reporter*, 18 October 1871, p. 23, by Mr Main.
[22] Marsha L. Richmond, '"A Lab of One's Own": The Balfour Biological Laboratory for Women at Cambridge University 1884–1914', *Isis*, 88.3 (September 1997), pp. 422–53.

teaching and a strong pastoral support structure were also strategies that their male supporters, led by Sidgwick, Jackson, Peile and Seeley, were urging on their own colleges.[23] The stress in these discussions was on educational benefit. In looking at the recapture of teaching by the colleges in late nineteenth-century Cambridge, it is probably not profitable ultimately to isolate gendered concerns from the broader emphasis. The project for the higher education of women was one aspect of a larger scheme. As Henry Sidgwick put it in 1894, 'the younger University men were in those years from 1860 onwards very much under the influence of Mill. They were ready to help the cause of women's education just as one of the branches of liberal progress and reform.'[24]

Yet although the women's colleges were to be numbered among the progressives of the day as far as teaching structures and methods went, learning outcomes differed from subject to subject. As Claire Breay has shown, neither intensive supervision nor the development of a secondary-school infrastructure had achieved enough by 1914 to give the women the same options in the Classical Tripos as the men had. Systematic Latin teaching from the age of eleven and some Greek later in the new girls' schools was still no match for the sustained exposure to the classical languages provided by English boys' preparatory and public schools. Reporting on the good performance of Margaret Merrifield in the Classical Tripos examinations in 1880, Edward Seymer Thompson, one of the examiners, noted that she had put herself out of the running for a First by not attempting composition in Latin verse.[25] The women's triumphs seldom came in the heavily linguistic Part I, but more often in the archaeological, historical and literary options of Part II.[26] Dr Breay also shows the development of a two-tiered teaching provision in both colleges. The male lecturers, generalled by R. D. Archer-Hind, did the grander stuff; the women resident lecturers, most notably Edith Sharpley at Newnham and Katharine Jex-Blake at Girton, did the basics and plugged the many gaps. Dora Ivens, arriving at Girton in 1910, found Miss Jex-Blake's teaching 'like a class in school. We had to read round and translate every word'. Challenged about this many years later, Miss Jex-Blake told her, 'no man could be trusted to make us do this'.[27]

As this case-study makes plain, the dynamics of teaching and learning in late nineteenth-century Cambridge as a whole cannot be understood without an ample knowledge of the students' previous educational experience. The same point was made in a different way by Stephen Siklos, when he explored the

---

[23] The best discussion of this remains ch. 7, 'The Idea of a College', in Sheldon Rothblatt, *The Revolution of the Dons* (Cambridge, 1981).
[24] Clough – Shore-Smith Papers, British Library Add. MSS 72830C fol. 23, conversation recorded by B. A. Clough.
[25] NCA, Examiners' Letters 1874–82, E. S. Thompson to Marion Kennedy, 24 March 1880.
[26] Breay, 'Women', pp. 62–70. See the problems with Greek experienced by Eva Knatchbull-Hugessen in 1883–6: Margaret Wilson, *A Kent Girl-Graduate* (Tonbridge, privately printed, 1994), pp. 36–41. Note also the continuing reluctance of all but a very few women to attempt Classical Mods and Greats at Oxford – Howarth, 'In Oxford', pp. 281–2.
[27] Breay, 'Women and the Classical Tripos', pp. 57–60, direct quotation from p. 59.

secondary schooling received by Philippa Fawcett, declared to rank above the Senior Wrangler in Part I of the Mathematical Tripos in 1890. Philippa attended one of the new GPDSC schools, Clapham High School; but by fifteen her mathematical ability was already so marked that her parents arranged for her to have extra coaching from G. B. Atkinson of Trinity Hall, her father's college. She also took additional courses at Bedford College and at University College, London, where one of her fellow-students was G. T. Bennett, later to be ranked Senior Wrangler below her. In effect, before she ever set foot in Newnham, she had received the extra teaching and coaching that a male candidate of mathematical promise would have received.[28]

The point about the importance of prior educational experience for all students must also be inverted. A number of subjects were not taught or only beginning to be taught in secondary schools. The women might therefore approach some of these on a more equal footing with the men; and in the process both men and women might receive some very basic instruction. Newnham and Girton were particularly anxious about the provision of laboratory facilities for their students, because they knew these did not exist even in the new girls' secondary schools. But given the dilatoriness of English boys' public schools in responding to the case for science, how many of the men reading for the Natural Sciences Tripos in its early years had done laboratory work before coming to Cambridge?

Mary Paley Marshall remarked of the Moral Sciences Tripos that 'as it required neither Mathematics nor Classics it seemed suited for girls who had done little of either'.[29] Certainly a sizeable number of women opted to take it and some of them did very well indeed. The young Mary Paley's examiners had divided two and two over whether to put her in the First Class or the Second in 1874.[30] When Economics was finally split off into a separate Tripos, women continued to do well. Lynda Grier and Eva Spielmann (later Hubback) were both placed in the First Class in Part II in 1908; and in 1919 Barbara Wootton was the first person of either sex to be awarded a starred First in Part II.[31]

The experience of undergraduates reading History in the early years of that Tripos both underlines the importance of considering schooling and shows how uncertain the definition of a 'higher' education might be. In October 1885 Winnie Seebohm went up to Newnham and her brother Hugh to King's, both

---

[28] Stephen Siklos, *Philippa Fawcett and the Mathematical Tripos* (Cambridge, privately printed, 1990), pp. 21–2.
[29] Mary Paley Marshall, *What I Remember* (Cambridge, 1948), p. 14.
[30] NCA, Examiners' Letters 1874–82, J. B. Pearson, Percy Gardner, H. S. Foxwell and W. Stanley Jevons to Marion Kennedy, December 1874.
[31] For Grier and Spielmann, see the Newnham *Register*; for Wootton, see the Girton *Register* and Barbara Wootton, *In a World I Never Made* (London, 1967), p. 55. For an extended consideration of the performance of men and women students in the Economics Tripos, see Keith Tribe, 'The Cambridge Economics Tripos 1903–55 and the Training of Economists', *The Manchester School*, LXVIII, 1 (2000), pp. 222–48.

to read History. The pattern of Winnie's work seems elementary to us. On 26 October she wrote:

> Constitutional History moves rather like a crab and slowly. But I think Henry II is pretty steadily in focus now, though this week's paper goes right back to Domesday Book and even to Edward Confessor. Hilda will envy me when she hears that I have to write a life of Harold Godwinson – but as it is only a fifth part of the paper, I don't much look forward to writing such a short one as it will have to be.

The next piece of work set she liked better:

> We have a rather nice paper this week, part of which is to show the grievances of the people during Rufus' reign from the Charter of Liberties granted by Henry I. I find the bad Latin of that period much harder to read than Tacitus and that sort – and a dictionary isn't much help! But that kind of work – making out the history for oneself as it were – is much nicer than describing the functions of the Curia Regis etc. from Stubbs. I try to show Miss Gardner the difference by taking pains over the former and writing long answers to them, and for the latter sort of hurriedly patching together sentences from Stubbs.[32]

Tacitus apart, it sounds reminiscent of GCSE. Yet Alice Gardner, who taught Winnie, was no hack. She had been placed in the First Class in the Historical Tripos in 1879. In reporting on her performance in the summer of 1878 in papers in Constitutional History, Political Economy, Political Philosophy and the History of England 1688–1760, Basil Hammond of Trinity noted that her total of marks, 283, was way ahead of the total of 237 secured by the highest-ranking man in the year and only exceeded by the total of 304 marks awarded to her Newnham contemporary, Sarah Marshall. She went on to a distinguished record of publication in Byzantine history.[33]

Hugh Seebohm's letters home have not survived; but the pattern of his work with G. W. Prothero in King's is unlikely to have been very different from Winnie's work with Alice Gardner. Winnie had remarked, 'I *am* so glad Hugh is doing history too, it is so nice comparing lecturers and books.'[34] Peter Slee has demonstrated that in its first ten years the English History paper in the Tripos 'demanded little more than precise knowledge of detail'.[35] Yet while writing summaries of Stubbs, Winnie and Hugh were also in some areas in touch with the latest research. Here is Winnie writing home again:

---

[32] Victoria Glendinning, *A Suppressed Cry: Life and Death of a Quaker Daughter* (London, 1969), pp. 77, 79.
[33] NCA, Examiners' Letters 1874–82, B. E. Hammond 14 June 1878, enclosure in William Cunningham to Marion Kennedy 19 December 1979; Newnham *Register*.
[34] Glendinning, *Suppressed Cry*, p. 73.
[35] Peter Slee, *Learning and a Liberal Education: The Study of Modern History in the Universities of Oxford, Cambridge and Manchester 1800–1914* (Manchester, 1986), p. 75. (Compare Mary Beard's conclusions about ancient history examinations in ch. 5.)

> Yesterday was so wet and cold that I didn't go to Miss Gardner['s lecture], so I had to go to her room in the evening to receive back my papers, commented on. And as I had feared she asked me who was my authority about the land tenure! And I had to say 'my father'; she hasn't read his book and 'would like to look at it sometime'.[36]

Their father was Frederic Seebohm, author of *The English Village Community* (1883), friend of Vinogradoff and Maitland, later recipient of honorary degrees from Cambridge, Oxford and Edinburgh. He was entirely self-taught; and in the obituary Paul Vinogradoff wrote in 1912, he commented that Seebohm's scholarly work had reflected both the strengths and weaknesses of that.[37]

The point here for us is that history in the 1880s was a newly-emerging discipline, one just arriving in the curriculum of universities and schools: conventions, rules and patterns of discourse were still to be established. When Hugh and Winnie began their course, battle was raging among their teachers on the merits of asking Tripos questions more demanding than 'Sketch the career of Godwine and criticize his conduct.'[38] Teaching and learning in a subject newly arrived and rapidly evolving was likely to be a somewhat different experience, for both men and women, from teaching and learning in a subject which had been a staple of formal schooling for boys over generations.

To argue along these lines is not to suggest that some subjects were gendered and others were not, nor that gendering was straightforwardly a function of secondary schooling. A number of the women who took History or Moral Sciences or subsequently Economics did so not simply or even primarily because these Triposes required no prior grounding in Classics and Mathematics; they also thought that these studies might help them to become useful members of society. Like all the History students of the 1870s and 1880s Winnie Seebohm had to prepare to take papers in 'cognate sciences'. She chose Political Economy, with Mary Paley Marshall, who 'looks at Political Economy from a philanthropic woman's point of view and talks to us each separately about the books we might read and the other subjects we are working at'. Winnie's own time at Cambridge was tragically short. In November 1885 her family, anxious about her asthma, insisted on taking her away. Just before she left, she reminded herself of her reasons for coming:

> My first object was to learn history well and thoroughly, that I might be able (should I prove capable later) to write it for the working classes.
> Secondly, I thought after a year or two here I should be better able to judge whether I was likely to be capable of any work of this sort.
> Thirdly, I hoped to learn here self-reliance, judgement and self-confidence.[39]

---

[36] Glendinning, *Suppressed Cry*, p. 73
[37] *Ibid.*, p. 4.
[38] Slee, *Learning and a Liberal Education*, pp. 74–84.
[39] Glendinning, *Suppressed Cry*, pp. 71 and 87. Winnie died at home 18 December 1885.

These were intensely private thoughts. Yet Winnie was not alone among her contemporaries in feeling a sense of social responsibility. There proved to be a continuing tension in Eva Knatchbull-Hugessen's life after Cambridge between family demands and her sense that her education had equipped her, given her a responsibility even, to make a contribution to the wider world.[40] Such views came to be articulated in public. In 1898 Beatrice Lees, History Tutor at Somerville College, Oxford, would commend the Oxford Modern History School to headmistresses and university teachers of women students, as a course producing 'thoughtful, well-educated men and women, with a grasp of method, a power of ready literary expression, a disciplined judgement, and an intelligent interest in modern social problems'.[41]

We will better understand teaching and learning in late nineteenth-century Cambridge and in late nineteenth-century universities more generally if we disaggregate and look at the experience of women and men subject by subject. If we do this, we can explore the importance of prior educational experiences and of the different rhythms and trajectories of newly developing specialisms. We can also consider why students chose the subjects they did, what they hoped to do with them subsequently and what the society around them would allow them to do. It may then be possible to trace the threads of gender in the pattern as a whole.

---

[40] Wilson, *Kent Girl-Graduate*, pp. 51–71. Eva was up between 1883 and 1886.
[41] Quoted in Howarth, 'In Oxford', p. 282.

PAULA GOULD[1]

Models of Learning? The 'logical, philosophical and scientific woman' in Late Nineteenth-Century Cambridge

The arrival of women students at Cambridge University during the last third of the nineteenth century raised many fundamental questions about teaching and learning. As Gillian Sutherland has already explained, two contrasting models for women's higher education evolved in the shape of Girton and Newnham Colleges. The two establishments remained geographically and ideologically distinct: Girton students were housed outside the city boundary, yet expected to follow an identical pattern of study to their male peers; Newnham College grew from within the city centre and initially promoted classes that were specially tailored to suit the needs of its female students.[2] The emergence of the two quite different models should remind us that issues surrounding the right of women to exercise their minds were contested even within the ranks of the educational reformers. Even if one decided that women did have the right to study at Cambridge, there was no consensus on how a University woman would fit in amongst the University men. In an institution with such important, detailed and explicitly male rituals attached to its teaching and learning practices, this was not a trivial point.

There can be little doubt that the actions, demeanour and intellectual achievements of the first women to enter this bastion of male excellence were scrutinised closely, given the concurrent public debates over the nature of intellectual identity and the physical suitability of women for study.[3] Students at

---

[1] This paper draws on material presented in P. A. Gould, 'Femininity and Physical Science in Britain, 1870–1914', unpublished Ph.D. thesis (University of Cambridge, 1998). Correspondence with the author should be addressed 25 Greenway Street, Chester CH4 7JS, UK Email: Paula.Gould@absw.org.uk.

[2] R. McWilliams-Tullberg, *Women at Cambridge: A Men's University – Though of a Mixed Type* (London, 1975), deals with the issue surrounding the formation of Newnham and Girton Colleges and the conflicting ideals of their founders. This theme is also followed in G. Sutherland, 'Emily Davies, the Sidgwicks and the Education of Women in Cambridge', in R. Mason (ed.), *Cambridge Minds* (Cambridge, 1994), pp. 34–7.

[3] These debates are outlined in C. E. Russett, *Sexual Science: The Victorian Construction of Victorian Womanhood* (Cambridge, MA, 1984); J. N. Burstyn, *Victorian Education and the Ideal*

Newnham and Girton were undoubtedly well aware of the widespread interest in their dress, deportment and examination results.[4] But to whom could they look for guidance? Did they strive to follow in the footsteps of a former governess or headmistress? Did they look towards their college principal and teaching staff for inspiration, or did they adopt standards of behaviour exhibited by their male peers?

The significance of appropriate self-fashioning to the female students is indicated by prevailing opinion that questioned the effect of advanced study on women's outward appearance, as well as their intellect. In an editorial published in 1874, just as the two women's colleges were welcoming more would-be scholars, a leading medical journal noted that 'The logical, philosophical and scientific woman commonly departs from the ordinary type of her sex quite as much in her physical as in her mental characteristics.'[5] During subsequent decades, the stream of students passing through the gates of Girton and Newnham Colleges provided ample evidence for interested observers to either confirm or deny these suspicions. However, illustrations of mathematically-minded women and studious female scientists published in satirical magazines and as 'New Woman' fiction, reinforced many of the preconceptions. How relevant were these quasi-fictional representations of intellectual women? The models of learning available to women students in late nineteenth-century Cambridge demand closer investigation. What follows is a brief exploration of the various models that reflected – and perhaps also shaped – the self-identity of the 'logical, philosophical and scientific woman' in late nineteenth-century Cambridge.

Studying like gentlemen whilst behaving like ladies

The contrasting models of education offered at Newnham and Girton Colleges, complementarity versus equality, reflected the complex – and often contradictory – arguments surrounding the effects of advanced work on the female mind and body. Debate over women's capacity for advanced intellectual work was rehearsed vigorously on the pages of periodical reviews, as well as in the medical and scientific journals. Discussion was not confined to a few elite scientists and doctors; it was brought directly into the homes of middle-class families, the very families that would be contemplating the future of their female offspring and watching over their daughters' private study with one eye on the reports of women students at Cambridge.

---

of *Womanhood* (London, 1980); K. J. Rowald, '"The Academic Woman": Minds, Bodies and Education in Britain and Germany, 1860–c.1914', unpublished Ph.D. thesis (University College London, 1996).

[4] Note that although women were allowed to sit university examination papers, their Tripos results were listed separately from the men's and they were not formally awarded degrees until 1948.

[5] *Lancet*, Vol. 1 (30 May 1874), p. 772.

On the one hand, it was argued that intensive mental activity *per se* would prove detrimental to the constitution of women, leading ultimately to their nervous and physical breakdown. This line of argument was taken up by Dr Henry Maudsley, writing in the *Fortnightly Review*. Combining physiology with theories of energy conservation, Maudsley suggested that the subjection of women to 'a system of mental training which has been framed and adapted for men' from puberty onwards, would have unpleasant consequences. 'The energy of a human body being a definite and not inexhaustible quantity, can it bear, without injury, an excessive mental drain as well as the natural physical drain which is so great at this time?' he asked. 'Or will the profit of one be to the detriment of the other?'[6] Intellectual attainment, Maudsley proposed, was a potential threat to the well-being of the more delicate sex.

At the same time, an alternative line of argument focused not on the ability of women to cope with the strain of higher education, but its potential defeminising effect. By exercising the intellect of women along the same lines as men, mental and physical feminine attributes bestowed by nature would be corrupted, it was argued. The assumption that women who sought intellectual fulfilment were masculinising both their bodies and minds was strengthened by the culture of physicality which had developed in boys' public schools, and then continued into university life from the mid-nineteenth century onwards.[7] Discipline of the mind was inextricably associated with discipline of the body, and so athleticism was openly encouraged in schemes of male education. Since intellectual achievement was seen to require a male mind and a male body, the 'fitness' of women for academic work, in every sense of the word, became a critical issue.[8]

At Cambridge, the culture of athleticism fostered on the games field was a key feature in the Mathematics Tripos that, as we have seen, was often perceived as a trial of stamina rather than test of mathematical ingenuity.[9] 'Newtons are born, not made', commented an anonymous author in the *Westminster Review*. 'The object of the Tripos is not to make mathematicians, but to train men (and hereafter women) who are capable of doing anything thoroughly and well.'[10] This ethos was also extended to the University's

---

[6] H. Maudsley, 'Sex in Mind and in Education', *Fortnightly Review*, Vol. 15 (1 April 1874), p. 467. See also E. G. Anderson, 'Sex in Mind and Education: A Reply', *Fortnightly Review*, xv (1 May 1874), pp. 582–94.

[7] J. A. Mangan, *Athleticism and the Victorian and Edwardian Public School: The Emergence and Consolidation of an Educational Ideology* (Cambridge, 1981).

[8] P. Atkinson, 'Fitness, Feminism and Schooling', in S. Delamont and L. Duffin, eds., *The Nineteenth-Century Woman: Her Cultural and Biological Straitjacket* (London, 1978), pp. 92–133. See also the essays by Hargreaves, McCrone, Fletcher and Atkinson in J. A. Mangan and R. J. Parks, eds., *From Fair Sex to Feminism: Sport and the Socialization of Women in the Industrial and Post-Industrial Eras* (London, 1987).

[9] A. Warwick, 'Exercising the Student Body: Mathematics and Athleticism in Victorian Cambridge', in C. Lawrence and S. Shapin, eds., *Science Incarnate: Historical Embodiments of Natural Knowledge* (Chicago, 1997), pp. 288–326.

[10] 'Should University Degrees be Given to Women?', *Westminster Review*, 1 (1881), p. 501.

programme in physical science. From the early 1870s, practical physics classes were made available to undergraduate students in the newly-built Cavendish Laboratory. The building had initially been planned with the intention of teaching heat, light, electricity and magnetism to mathematics students.[11] As the laboratory's programme expanded to cater for graduate researchers and increasing numbers of candidates for the Natural Sciences Tripos, the links between the cultures of physics and physicality were fused. Success in both mathematics and physical science at Cambridge was seen to depend on surviving a rigorous training programme.

The varied reaction of male professors to women mathematics and science students at Cambridge is reasonably well-documented.[12] However, it is also important to note that students at Newnham and Girton were often discouraged from taking classes in trigonometry, the principles of light or electromagnetism by their *female* mentors and peers. Given the legendary toughness of the Mathematical Tripos, and the perception that science subjects were particularly mentally demanding, it is possible that the college principals and the students themselves sought to divert public attention by shying away from behaviour that might invoke yet more speculation and scrutiny. 'Putting aside a few exceptional cases in which a love for Science has been previously acquired, and has so taken possession of a student's mind that she has no hesitation in fixing on her particular line of study,' the *Girton Review* cautioned, 'it might seem somewhat rash to undertake a course of work entailing undoubtedly considerable physical and mental exertion without a sufficient previous knowledge either of the advantages to be derived from the pursuit of Science or of the disadvantages which doubtless to some extent surround the pursuit when it is taken up at Girton.'[13] The suffering of students taking the so-called 'hard' subjects was noted by their peers. 'Those hateful Tripos Exams begin today – and will continue to the end of the term,' Catherine Durning Holt advised her father. 'The mathematical is fearfully hard work; the poor victims are exhausted after their papers.'[14] Writing to her mother at the beginning of her first term at Newnham in 1889, Holt commented that she had been advised by the Principal, Miss Anne Jemima Clough, to 'read either a little History or Literature instead of going in completely for Physics'.[15]

---

[11] The early years of the laboratory are remembered in J. J. Thomson et al., *A History of the Cavendish Laboratory, 1871–1910* (London, 1901); R. Sviedrys, 'The Rise of Physical Science at Victorian Cambridge', *Historical Studies in the Physical Sciences* ii (1970), pp. 127–52; J. G. Crowther, *The Cavendish Laboratory, 1874–1974* (London, 1974).

[12] James Clerk Maxwell's 'rule' for the Cavendish Laboratory that 'all students should be male' is almost legendary. His immediate successors' opinions on women's place at the work bench can be found in P. Gould, 'Women and the Culture of University Physics in Late Nineteenth-Century Cambridge', *British Journal for the History of Science*, xxx (1997), pp. 127–49.

[13] 'The Natural Sciences Tripos', *Girton Review* (December 1882), p. 5.

[14] C. D. Holt, *Letters From Newnham College 1889–1892*, ed. E. O. Cockburn (Cambridge, privately printed), n.d., Cambridgeshire Collection, Cambridge Central Library, p. 41.

[15] Holt, *Letters*, p. 13. Letter of 19 October 1889.

In addition to handing out advice on which subjects to study, Miss Clough took a deep and personal interest in the vitality of her charges.[16] Her concern is not altogether surprising, given the fears of many students about the inability of even 'strong' girls to cope with the strains. After a week of feeling 'rather seedy', Catherine Holt found herself the subject of regular checks by the elderly Principal. 'She actually came all the way up two flights of stairs, twice yesterday to see and console me – pretty good for an old lady of seventy-five isn't it?'[17] In another letter home, Holt noted that most of her contemporaries preferred to get a low place and a more general education, than strive for 'Honours in the Science Tripos'.[18] Troubled by headaches, Holt chose to 'knock off an hour of Chemistry' and took to 'slacking off work' when necessary, rather than changing Tripos.[19] By the end of the first year, she could proudly inform her parents that friends had 'never seen me looking so well, and they think the hard work agrees with me'.[20] Although the ethos of healthy minds and bodies underpinning the study of mathematics and science was a significant and often constraining preoccupation, it is clear that several women students survived the trial.

From the above arguments, it is not difficult to see why the appearance (in both senses of the word) of female students in the traditionally-male environment of Cambridge generated so much interest. It is also apparent that the significance attached to self-presentation was especially relevant to those students who had opted for the Mathematical and Natural Sciences Triposes. At Girton, those women studying scientific or mathematical subjects were encouraged to borrow books from the library of the late Mary Somerville, author of several authoritative scientific works and honorary Fellow of the Royal Astronomical Society. This valuable collection had been presented to the college by Somerville's two daughters following their mother's death. 'The book are enclosed in a very beautifully designed case, which also forms a sort of framework for a cast of Chantrey's bust of Mrs Somerville,' wrote Millicent Garrett Fawcett, the well-known suffragist and campaigner for women's intellectual emancipation. 'The fine and delicate lines of her beautiful face offer to the students of the college a worthy ideal of completed womanhood, in which intellect and emotion balance one another and make a perfect whole.'[21] Whether or not students who used the donated library books modelled themselves on the eminent author of *The Mechanism of the Heavens* is debatable. What is clear, though, is that this 'worthy ideal of completely developed womanhood' was just one of many suggestions put forward for the way in which female mathematicians and scientists at Cambridge could present

[16] For the work of Newnham College's first Principal, see B. A. Clough, *A Memoir of Anne Jemima Clough* (London, 1897).
[17] Holt, *Letters*, p. 21. Letter of 17 November 1889.
[18] Holt, *Letters*, p. 41. Letter of 18 May 1892.
[19] Holt, *Letters*, pp. 15, 17. Letters of 16 and 31 October 1889.
[20] Holt, *Letters*, p. 27. Letter of 29 May 1890.
[21] M. G. Fawcett, *Some Eminent Women of Our Time: Short Biographical Sketches* (London, 1889), p. 43.

themselves. Certainly, the absence of one strong role model left room for rampant speculation. Would women conducting research in the laboratory adopt the ethos of athletic muscularity to fit in with their male colleagues, or would they deliberately reinforce their feminine nature by dressing in an overly decorative style? How would the young students reconcile expected standards of ladylike behaviour with an existing code of manliness?

The contrasting models of self-identity adopted by the 'logical, philosophical and scientific' women at Cambridge can be illustrated with a comparison of two high achievers: Ida Freund and Philippa Fawcett. Ida Freund, who later took up a teaching position at Newnham to fund the continuation of her studies, completed Part II of the Natural Sciences Tripos with a First.[22] On arrival in Britain from Austria, she had been persuaded to enrol in the Natural Sciences Tripos (initially against her wishes) by her uncle.[23] Despite her preliminary objections to the idea, she stayed the course, remaining in Cambridge to carry out her own research. Freund, a student at Girton and then later a staff member at Newnham, had survived the same rigorous programme of education as students in the men's colleges. Yet although her mental capabilities matched up to those expected by male educational standards, her physical appearance suggests that she did not adopt the ethos of physicality that helped to define the 'Science' men. Described by Catherine Holt as 'a jolly stout German, whose clothes are falling in rags off her back', Freund fitted neither the stereotype of the tiny-waisted, fashionable young lady portrayed in magazines of the time, nor the well-honed, athletic male scholar.[24] J. J. Thomson, Professor in Experimental Physics at the Cavendish Laboratory from 1884, noted in a letter to a former student and colleague that: 'Miss Freund is about twice the size she was when you were here to make her run about. If she increases much further we shall have to widen the doors.'[25] A former Cambridge wrangler, Thomson embraced the culture of athleticism with enthusiasm. Ida Freund, on the other hand was reliant on sticks and a wheelchair to help her get around, having lost a leg in a cycling accident in her youth. Her absence from the sports field and apparent disregard for conventional standards of dress doubtless drew attention to her presence as an 'outsider' in the laboratory.

By contrast, Philippa Fawcett succeeded in conforming to both the intellectual and physical standards expected of the Wranglers and 'Science' men, but without attracting the same attention to her outward appearance. In June 1890, Fawcett made the headlines by gaining top marks in Part I of the Mathematical Tripos. Her academic feat, gaining a good 13 per cent (400 marks) more than the recognised Senior Wrangler, is perhaps not surprising given her family history of mathematical excellence and some pre-university coaching from a close family

---

[22] *Girton College Register, 1869–1946* (Cambridge, 1948), p. 21.
[23] Obituary of Ida Freund, *Girton Review* (May 1914), p. 41.
[24] Holt, *Letters*, p. 9. Letter of 12 October 1889.
[25] J. J. Thomson to Richard Threlfall, 7 August 1887, Cambridge University Library, J. J. Thomson Correspondence, Add. MSS 7654, T19.

friend.[26] A keen member of both the fire brigade and hockey team at Newnham, Fawcett fulfilled the athletic ideal promoted among manly intellectuals (Figure 1). However, despite her academic excellence and prowess on the sports field, she chose not to demonstrate her fitness for 'logical, philosophical and scientific' study by adopting a manly self-image. Instead, it seems that she went out of her way to present herself as the epitome of Victorian femininity. 'When Miss Fawcett came to Newnham,' commented Miss Clough, 'she knew that if there were the remotest pretext, even the most innocent, it would be seized upon by all the silly scribblers who try to make out that the women's colleges are peopled by a sort of impossible race of eccentrics.'[27]

Photographs of Fawcett taken in the garden of Newnham College show that she chose to wear bows and frills on her dresses instead of the more

Figure 1 Newnham Hockey Club Team, 1891. Philippa Fawcett is seated on the floor, right hand side. Newham College Archive, published by permission of the Principal and Fellows of Newnham College.

[26] The Fawcett family's tradition in mathematics is described in R. Strachey, *Millicent Garrett Fawcett* (London, 1931), p. 14.
[27] *Pall Mall Budget* (12 June 1890), p. 1.

masculine-looking tailored costumes, complete with jacket and quasi-tie, worn by some of her colleagues (Figure 2). There is little hint on this picture that she often donned a cap, white flannels and dark skirt to chase around a muddy field with the hockey squad.[28] Instead, a process of systematic self-fashioning resulted in the construction of a feminine mathematician, who could compete with the men on their own terms.

Figure 2 Newnham College Teaching Staff, 1896. Philippa Fawcett is seated at the far right. Ida Freund is seated third from the left. Newnham College Archive, published by permission of the Principal and Fellows of Newnham College.

Satire and stereotypes

Many of the suggested models of 'logical, philosophical and scientific' woman at Cambridge were generated outside of the University. Throughout the 1880s and 1890s, the pages of satirical magazines were regularly occupied with debate about the ways in which the new breed of intellectual women would think, dress, and behave. In the first few years after the opening of Newnham and Girton, the pages of *Punch* carried a variety of such stereotypes. There were the 'Sweet Girl Graduates', taking afternoon tea instead of drinking sherry with the male undergraduates and college Fellows, the 'Lady Professor' whose misplaced logic was overlooked by students dazzled by her smile, and 'Miss Hypatia Jones, Spinster of Arts,' who could not enjoy any rational conversation with any man

[28] The hockey costume is described in Holt *Letters*, p. 35. Letter of 9 November 1891.

under forty.[29] *Punch*'s lyricists suggested that the 'Woman of the Future' would 'puzzle men in Algebra with horrible quadratics, Dynamics and the mysteries of higher mathematics', having completed her studies at Newnham and Girton.[30] A few years later, the magazine was celebrating the genuine academic achievements of the women it caricatured, paying tribute to Philippa Fawcett's results in the Mathematics Tripos.[31] In 1894, the mathematical achievements of Miss E. H. Cooke, listed as 'equal to 28' in Cambridge's official class lists, were recognised in verse.[32] Here the compliment was double-edged. Whilst acknowledging that Miss Cooke was the solitary name on the list of Wranglers, *Punch* drew readers' attention to her status as an unmarried woman. An accompanying cartoon entitled 'Girl Graduate: Single Figure' suggested why this might be the case. The illustration depicted an unsmiling, straight-laced scholar, her glasses perched on the end of her beaked nose as she engrossed herself in study. Higher mathematics, *Punch* implied, would not only turn young women's attention away from men, marriage and motherhood, but it would create unattractive spinsters.[33]

Stereotypes of academic womanhood also cropped up time and again in 'New Woman' fiction.[34] Authors Grant Allen, George Bernard Shaw and M. McDonnell Bodkin each published stories in which the central female character had previously studied mathematics at a Cambridge woman's college. Although each author chose to take his heroine on a different set of adventures, the narratives constructed a similar model of post-university womanhood. Vivie, introduced at the very beginning of George Bernard Shaw's play 'Mrs Warren's Profession' (1898) was described as 'an attractive specimen of the sensible, able, highly-educated young middle-class Englishwoman'. Aged twenty-two, she wore a 'plain, business-like dress' that was functional 'but not dowdy'.[35] Similarly Lois Cayley, the story-teller in Grant Allen's serialised fiction 'Miss Cayley's Adventures' (1898), mixed common sense with a pleasing appearance.[36] Dora Myrl, McDonnell Bodkin's 'Lady Detective', provided further reassurance that Cambridge's women students could find their own role model. 'There was certainly nothing of the New Woman, or for that matter the old,

---

[29] C. Rover, *The Punch Book of Women's Rights* (London, 1967), pp. 57–65. Note: the Bachelor of Arts degree covered all Tripos subjects, including Mathematics and Natural Sciences.
[30] *Punch*, 10 May 1884, p. 225.
[31] 'The Ladies' Year', *Punch*, 28 June 1890, p. 309.
[32] 'The Girton Girl B.A.', *Punch*, 23 June 1894, p. 297.
[33] See also *Judy* (10 March 1897), p. 166, which asked whether 'the sweet girl graduate, with her golden hair' would graduate 'as bachelor or spinster or arts?'
[34] My attention was first drawn to this literature by C. Willis, '"All Agog to Teach the Higher Mathematics": The New Woman, University Education and the Suffragettes', paper presented at a one-day meeting on 'The New Woman', 27 March 1998, Birkbeck College, London. The analysis of the material presented in this chapter is my own.
[35] G. B. Shaw, 'Mrs Warren's Profession', reprinted in his *Plays Pleasant and Unpleasant*, i (London, 1898) p. 160.
[36] Grant Allen's stories about Miss Lois Cayley appeared in the *Strand Magazine* throughout 1898.

about the winsome figure that stood at the top of the stone steps', readers were informed.[37] All three male authors were agreed that the study of mathematics had not robbed their female heroines of their feminine looks.

Significantly, the three female characters presented in these stories not only studied the Mathematics Tripos at Cambridge, but also did well in it. Dora Myrl's father 'waited in this world three years beyond his time, so the doctors said', to see her become a Cambridge Wrangler.[38] Vivie, readers were told, tied with the third Wrangler in her year, whilst Lois Cayley claimed simply to have taken 'high mathematical Honours at Cambridge'.[39] Despite the intellectual achievements of each heroine, the stories provided hints that study in itself could prove detrimental to women scholars. For Vivie, taking the Tripos had necessitated absolute devotion to her books to the exclusion of all else. 'It means grind, grind, grind for six to eight hours a day at mathematics and nothing but mathematics', she complained.[40] Lois Cayley worried that mathematics might have impaired the innate feminine characteristics of her trusty sidekick, Elsie. 'Elsie held out her glass. I was annoyed about that', she commented. 'It showed that she had missed the drift of our conversation, and was therefore lacking in feminine intuition.' Elsie's ill-judged action was explained as a consequence of her education at Girton. 'I should be sorry if I had allowed the higher mathematics to kill out in me the most distinctive womanly faculty', Lois continued.[41] Having introduced what were deemed to be appropriate role models, the authors used their carefully-constructed heroines to caution against certain aspects of studying higher mathematics.

On closer reading of these texts, it is clear that there was room for interpretation within the framework of 'sensible, attractive, ambitious young woman'. In fiction, as in real life, the model of academic womanhood was flexible, and the three authors often presented contradictory images. Vivie was described as having a 'hearty grip', so hearty in fact that her handshake left her gentleman visitor with slightly numbed fingers. Fitness provided encouragement that mathematics was not enfeebling a generation of would-be mothers, but brute strength was a sure indication of manliness. Vivie's reasons for taking the mathematical Tripos were also indicative of masculine behaviour. Her choice of subject was not dictated by the need for intellectual fulfilment, but to win a bet:

> Mrs Latham, my tutor at Newnham, told my mother that I could distinguish myself in the Mathematics Tripos if I went for it in earnest. The papers were full just then of Philippa Summers beating the senior wrangler – you remember about it; and nothing would please my mother but that I should do the same thing. I said flatly that it was not

[37] M. McDonnell Bodkin, *Dora Myrl: The Lady Detective* (London, 1900), pp. 1–2.
[38] McDonnell Bodkin, *Dora Myrl*, pp. 5–6.
[39] Shaw, *Plays*, i, p. 163; G. Allen, 'The Adventure of the Inquisitive American', *Strand Magazine*, May 1898, pp. 513–23, at p. 513.
[40] Shaw, *Plays*, i, p. 163.
[41] G. Allen, 'The Adventure of the Pea-Green Patrician', *Strand Magazine*, October 1898, p. 397.

worth my while to face the grind since I was not going in for teaching; but I offered to try for fourth wrangler, or thereabouts, for £50.[42]

Shaw's reference to Philippa Fawcett is thinly veiled. The publicity her personal attainment received in the press, he suggested, had not provided a positive role model for other young women to follow, but directly provoked instances of unfeminine behaviour in other 'Vivies'.

Dora Myrl, on the other hand, was 'a lady *and* a scholar' (my italics) indicating that it was possible to combine both, but that a scholarly life did not necessarily imply ladylike behaviour.[43] So too Lois Cayley prided herself on being a lady, both by breeding and by education. When offered a cheque for twenty guineas as a reward for having saved her employee's diamonds from the clutches of a con-man, she turned it down. 'I glanced at the piece of paper and felt my face glow crimson. "Oh Lady Georgina," I cried, "you misunderstand. You forget that I am a lady".'[44] Her refusal to accept the money reminded readers that whatever the expectations of society, mathematically-minded women had to maintain their self-identity as ladylike intellectuals.

Aside from his construction of the fictional Lois Cayley as a glowing example of an attractive, adventurous and genteel mathematician, in reality, Grant Allen regarded mathematics as a haven for spinsters. 'Out of every hundred women, roughly speaking, ninety-six have husbands provided for them by nature,' he wrote in the *Fortnightly Review*, 'and only four need to go into a nunnery or take to teaching the higher mathematics.' The 'self-supporting spinster', he continued, was not to be regarded as a useful model. 'She is an abnormality not the woman of the future. We ought not to erect into an ideal what is in reality a painful necessity of the present transitional age.'[45] To circumvent the promotion of spinsterhood in his series of stories, his heroine's heart was eventually captured in the last tale by the dashing Harold Tillington.

Grant Allen, George Bernard Shaw and McDonnell Bodkin could only speculate on the experiences of the women they caricatured in their stories. Even when Allen published a short novel about a Girton Girl under a female pseudonym, the perspective of the narrator was undeniably male.[46] I do not want to suggest that the fictional heroines devised by male authors failed to reflect widespread images of academic women. Nor do I want to claim that similar characterisations by female authors were diametrically opposed to the ones already presented. Rather, I would argue that the experiences of women authors — perhaps as former 'Girton Girls' themselves — allowed inclusion of an extra dimension to the already-prevalent stereotypes of the logical, philosophical and scientific Cambridge scholars. Alice Stronach was able to draw on her own

[42] Shaw, *Plays*, i, p. 163.
[43] McDonnell Bodkin, *Dora Myrl*, pp. 5–6.
[44] G. Allen, 'The Adventure of the Supercilious Attaché', *Strand Magazine*, April 1898, p. 424.
[45] G. Allen, 'Plain Words on the Woman Question', *Fortnightly Review* n.s., Vol. 64, 1 October 1889, pp. 448–58.
[46] O. P. Rayner [G. Allen], *The Typewriter Girl* (London, 1897).

time as a student at Newnham College to write *A Newnham Friendship* (1901). Indeed, it would appear that the author herself assumed a key part in the plot as Elspeth, the Scottish fresher who knew that she could only afford to pay her way at college for a short period. Stronach resided at Newnham for the academic year 1887–88, and did not take any Tripos examinations.[47] She later became Assistant Mistress at an elementary school in Mull, writing the book whilst employed there.[48]

Given her own manifest reincarnation as Elspeth, it is likely that the fictitious characters described in *A Newnham Friendship* were drawn partly from life too, and then embellished with retrospective laudatory imagination. Unlike the heroines who assumed centre stage in the first three narratives that I discussed, Stronach's mathematicians were not modelled upon the 'sensible, fit and attractive' mould. Miss Reeves, the college lecturer in mathematics, was described as 'that little person. . . . who looks as if a binomial theorem would knock her to pieces'. Though despite this obvious physical frailty, her mental faculties were far from ailing and Miss Reeves was considered to be 'a tremendous swell at conics'. Pippa, the indisputable fictionalisation of Philippa Fawcett, provided a contrasting model of a mathematician. Solid in both mind and body, Pippa was pointed out in the story as 'that plump and pleasing person with the *pince-nez*'.[49] Contrary to the athletic and bicycle-owning Vivies, Lois Cayleys, and Dora Myrls, Pippa could be seen 'trudging along . . . placid and unconcerned', at a less frenetic pace of life.[50]

As the academic year in *A Newnham Friendship* drew to a close, the students clustered around the Senate House for the reading of their results. 'Everyone was waiting for the reading of the mathematical list,' readers were informed, 'for, true to tradition, Cambridge still believes that there is only one road to glory.'[51] When the results were announced and Pippa, 'That most modest of damsels' was found to have been placed above the senior wrangler, the 'mathematical swell' was shown to be a shrinking violet:

> Pippa's cheeks got hotter as Olive's example was followed by others, and people quite near her began to shake her and vigorously. Quite out of earshot, she stood blankly waiting for an explanation, blinking her short-sighted eyes, and looking uncomfortable under the fire of observation.[52]

This bashfulness was not condemned as a manifestation of social inadequacy, the result of too much mathematical study, but a natural display of an attractive feminine trait. Although Pippa was not portrayed as a physically desirable

---

[47] As Gillian Sutherland explains in her chapter, not all students at Newnham were expected to take Tripos examinations.
[48] *Newnham College Register, 1871–1971*, i, London, 1979, p. 94.
[49] A. Stronach, *A Newnham Friendship* (London, 1901), p. 31.
[50] Stronach, *Newnham Friendship*, p. 198.
[51] Stronach, *Newnham Friendship*, p. 200.
[52] Stronach, *Newnham Friendship*, p. 201.

woman, her character generated instant admiration in all who knew her. The male students 'vied with the women in generous enthusiasm', rushing to congratulate her, for the very reason that 'Pippa was known as one of the most modest, unaffected "fellows" of her year'. Modesty, Stronach suggested, not only marked out feminine mathematicians, but also underpinned an ideal of intellectual womanhood that was admired by both sexes.

For her true dashing heroines, Stronach chose neither mathematicians nor scientists. Carol, the large-as-life central female character, had changed subject, throwing away 'her natural science, her earth worms and sections, and all the rest of it,' to study the Moral Sciences Tripos in the hope of improving her debating logic. Her friends discussed amongst themselves the impracticality of this course of action, commenting that her new subject 'won't be much use to her for teaching, or bread-and-butter lecturing, – you know what I mean, lecturing for pennies'.[53] Carol was assumed to have higher aspirations than her peers, seeking to improve herself as oppose to improving her financial situation. Science students, Stronach implied, should look towards their former teachers as role models, and consider their future as working women, not as educated ladies of leisure.

In writing *A Newnham Friendship*, Alice Stronach produced what seems to have been a very personal and highly autobiographical account. Mrs Annie Edwardes, on the other hand, had not sampled life at either of Cambridge's two women's colleges when she sat down to write *A Girton Girl* (1885), and consequently made sure that the heroine of her trilogy did not enter higher education. Having spent three books (and almost 600 pages) taking coaching in classics and mathematics, Marjorie Bartrand eventually decides to marry he tutor, forsaking her previous ambitions to attend university.[54] Whilst the ending might have seemed predictable, the relationship between the characters was far from straightforward. In *A Girton Girl*, it was the male lead character, Geoffrey Arbuthnot, who was forced to earn his living from teaching mathematics, with his pupil holding the purse strings as an heiress.

The ambiguity of roles was further illustrated in discussions about the appearance of the young female student. At one point in the very first book, Geoffrey is advised by his brother not to expect his pupil to be an English rose. '"All those classico-mathematical girls," observed Gaston, "are the same. Much nose, little hair, freckles, ankles".' The thought quite obviously repelled him. '"Let the subject be changed".'[55] When the mathematics tutor first meets his pupil, then, he is clearly confused by her demeanour:

> So he stood in presence of the heiress; a little country girl with sun-kissed hands innocent of inkstains, a child's fledgling figure, a child's delightful boldness, and not one barleycorn's weight of dignity in her

[53] Stronach, *Newnham Friendship*, p. 49.
[54] A. Edwardes, *A Girton Girl*, iii (London, 1885), p. 298.
[55] Edwardes, *Girton Girl*, Vol. 1, p. 40.

composition. Should he, obeying first impulse, believe in her, and so incur the fate of well-snubbed predecessors? Or should he arm himself against the coquetry, which this very fondness, this assumption of simplicity in dress and speech might mask?[56]

Geoffrey's puzzlement neatly encapsulates the importance of self-presentation to academic women. Expression of character in terms of dress and decorum allowed 'logical, philosophical and scientific' women to follow their ambitions by adopting a socially-acceptable outward appearance.

Following fiction

Stories like *A Newnham Friendship, Dora Myrl: The Lady Detective*, 'Mrs Warren's Profession' and *A Girton Girl* effectively proposed fictional strategies for negotiating the different and often contradictory messages bombarding academic women. There was certainly no single pattern of behaviour and self-presentation for students at Newnham and Girton Colleges to grasp hold of. Rather, the satirical comment and 'New Woman' fiction provided a range of models that embodied the contradictions faced by young women grappling with the expectations of society and the rigors of the Tripos system.

The relevance of this literature to the fashioning of students' self-identity can be seen in the following description of an encounter between a young student at Girton College in the early 1890s and her new mathematics coach:

> In the dusk of the October evening the red light of Miss Welsh's fire made the apartment ruddy and almost dazzled Grace's eyes as she came in through the door. Miss Welsh was in her usual place on the right hand side of the fireplace, and Mr Berry was sitting on a low chair with his back to the door as Grace moved shyly across down the length of the room. Miss Welsh rose slowly, saying: 'Good evening Miss Chisholm, may I introduce Mr Berry?' and taking her by the hand, led her onto the hearthrug. As she was speaking, Grace, in her bashfulness, had the unexpected sight of a young man dressed in a sombre suit of brown. As he got up he seemed all joints, and he held out his hand and took hers with an absence of vigour, which involuntarily repelled the girl. She raised her eyes to his face. He had thrown back his head with an unusual gesture and was addressing the usual greetings to her in a voice that seemed clipped and abrupt.[57]

The account captures the significance of dress, deportment and decorum in an unfamiliar situation. Grace 'moves shyly' and behaves with 'bashfulness' as she greeted the 'young man' in the presence of a chaperon. Mr Berry, who has chosen a 'sombre suit of brown' for the occasion, is obviously ill at ease in the

---

[56] Edwardes, *Girton Girl*, Vol. 1, p. 115.
[57] Quoted in I. Grattan Guiness, 'A Mathematical Union: William Henry and Grace Chisholm Young', *Annals of Science*, 29 (1972), pp. 105–86.

presence of an unmarried woman who he will be expected to tutor, not court. His head is 'thrown back' with an 'unusual gesture' and his greeting to Grace were addressed in a 'clipped and abrupt' manner.

The above narrative is not, as first might be supposed, a piece of romantic fiction. It is a description written at the end of the nineteenth century of the first meeting between Grace Chisholm and the man who had undertaken to prepare her for the rigorous Mathematics Tripos.[58] Both student and mathematics coach were clearly unsure as to what constituted proper behaviour. Like *Punch*'s 'Sweet Girl Graduates' who chose to drink tea as their male contemporaries supped sherry, students at Newnham and Girton studying Mathematics and Natural Sciences in the late nineteenth century, had to find ways of reconciling accepted codes of social etiquette with masculine traditions of academic conduct.

---

[58] The account should be compared with the humorous prose printed in the University's student magazines, which speculated about the nature of intellectual relationships between men and women at Cambridge. See, for instance, 'A Chemical Dream', *Granta*, 14 February 1891, p. 198; 'Science and Sentiment', *Granta*, 8 March 1892, p. 255.

DAVID MCKITTERICK

Where Did Undergraduates Get Their Books?

On returning to his room he found his armchair tenanted by a respectable-looking, commercial traveller kind of man with a portfolio. This individual, in reply to his look of surprise, informed him in the blandest of tones that he had called to solicit his patronage for a work of art that he was now bringing out in numbers – an *Illustrated History of England*. If he would allow him, he would have the honour of showing him a specimen. Whereupon, without further delay, he produced from the portfolio a number of the work in question, dilating with conscious pride upon the superior style in which it was got up; the expediency of Charlie's entering his name at once before all the numbers were ordered, that he might make a certainty of securing a copy; and above all, dwelling upon the satisfaction he should feel in having Mr. Villars' name in his book. He would show him a list of the subscribers; Mr. Villars would doubtless be acquainted with some of them. Ah! that was Mr. Villars' father, was it? (as Charlie pointed to his own father's name in the book), he had no idea that he had been so much honoured already. Finding the respectability of the individual so substantially vouched for, Villars added his name to the list of victims, and became a patron of Smith's new *Illustrated History of England*, in monthly numbers, price half-a-guinea. Amid a profusion of bows and thanks for his kind favour, portfolio and man disappeared, carrying with them the subscription for the five months already published, and Charlie heard no more of his history; that is, no more numbers ever turned up, owing, as the publishers asserted, to financial difficulties, &c., &c. He afterwards found that the insertion of his father's name was nothing but a bare-faced imposition.[1]

Guides to Freshmen are full, in the nineteenth century as they are today, of warnings against unnecessary expenditure in the first few days at Cambridge.[2] The blandishments and temptations of undergraduate societies, joined in a

---

[1] George L. Tottenham, *Charlie Villars at Cambridge*, 2 Vols (London, 1868), 1, pp. 55–6.
[2] See, for example, H. Latham, 'University and College Expenses', in *The Student's Guide to the University of Cambridge*, 3rd edn (Cambridge, 1874), pp. 69–103; similar warnings are contained in 'Martin Legrand' [James Rice], *The Cambridge Freshman; or, Memoirs of Mr. Golightly* (1871 and subsequent editions).

burst of enthusiasm, subscribed to for a lifetime and never followed up, remain the same today. In the nineteenth century there were other dangers: the pressure to buy more furnishings, pans, cutlery, china, etc., than was necessary to equip one's room, only to see it fall into the hands of under-paid bedders and gyps; the warnings about how tradesmen's accounts have an uncomfortable habit of running up with unexpected speed and in poorly documented fashion. One of the more widely-read authors of such advice even cautioned that

> Freemasons' or Odd Fellows' Lodges, as well as all purely convivial societies, should be particularly avoided as causing, at the best, a waste of money and time.[3]

But the travelling salesman who sells spurious subscriptions to publications of dubious worth or use is not a figure frequently to be met. By and large, such people have been evicted from colleges, and can no longer freely invade the privacy of courts and staircases. Even so highly a respected an undergraduate ally as the late eighteenth-century local bookseller 'Maps' Nicholson has been banished from this particular way of pursuing trade. His full-length portrait, now hanging in the University Library (and copied in the widely sold engravings and other reproductions), depicts him striding across Great Court of Trinity College clutching a bundle of rather worn books that almost certainly included lecture notes prepared for those who were more willing to pay for them than to go to the bother of attending and making notes for themselves.[4]

What we would now regard as an invasion of the colleges' privacy was still possible in the 1860s. The novel *Charlie Villars at Cambridge* was the first of four novels by George L. Tottenham, whose membership of Trinity College, heralded on its title-page, was signalled as a recommendation for verisimilitude. Tottenham (1844–1910) had graduated in 1867, just a year before his book was published, and he went on to pursue a legal career in Ireland, the home of his family. How far it is autobiographical, I do not know. It is certainly full of fast men, and of visits to various hunts and other sporting occasions within reach of Cambridge. The topography of the events and the names of the local tradesmen are true enough, and the one lecture that features in it is by none other than Charles Kingsley, Regius Professor of Modern History from 1860 to 1869. There is not much reason to suppose that this particular trick on a fresher was an invention.

Where, however, did more ordinary books come from? How much did they cost? How many were needed? The answers to all these questions of course varied over the century, in the face of changes in attitudes to university education; changes in the tendencies of each generation to look to different

---

[3] Latham, 'Expenses', p. 90.
[4] J. W. Goodison, *Catalogue of Cambridge Portraits. 1. The University Collection* (Cambridge, 1955), p. 44 and pl. xiv. His reputation three-quarters of a century after his death is recorded in Christopher Wordsworth, *Social Life at the English Universities in the Eighteenth Century* (Cambridge, 1874), pp. 378–85.

professions; the introduction of new subjects for study and alterations to the existing mathematical and classical Triposes; the increasing emphasis on the Honours degree as the normal course of study. They varied with the book trade itself; and they varied according to library provision. Rather than rehearse all the changes that took place in these several different areas, all of them directly affecting our undergraduate, I propose instead to look a little at some of the evidence available to us for a better understanding of how books could be obtained.

Macaulay was straightforward, and misleading. He went up to Trinity in 1818. His letters home are full of his reading, usually of the lighter kind; and he has become notorious for his intense dislike of mathematics at the expense of literature. For his Latin declamation prize in 1820 he ordered a set of the works of Samuel Johnson, perhaps from Deighton Bell, the booksellers just a few yards along Trinity Street.[5] Having taken his BA, he set to work to compete for a fellowship. He moved into College from his old digs, and, as he put it, fell on a 'vigorous programme of retrenchment', so as to be able to afford furniture for his new rooms. More to our present purpose, it was apparently (if we are to believe his letters home, an often selective genre) only at this stage – that is, after he had graduated – that he discovered something further that the College had to offer:

> I have found that books may with a little management be got out of the College libraries, and that my Bookseller's bill may be materially reduced without denying myself any work that is necessary for study.[6]

How, we may ask, was it possible for so voracious a reader as Macaulay to have spent three years in Cambridge, and only now to have discovered that books could be borrowed from the college library?[7] In fact, he already knew, and borrowed from, the Library. In June 1820 he took out a group of books on Wales (Pennant, Cox on Monmouthshire, Fenton on Pembrokeshire, Malkin on South Wales) for the long vacation. In August he borrowed Aristophanes. In January 1821 his borrowings included Aristophanes (again) and Dionysius Lardner.

A few years later, Thackeray was more forward, and was borrowing books in his first year. As he reported to his mother, 'they allow you to keep six books out

---

[5] Jonathan R. Topham, 'Two Centuries of Cambridge Publishing and Bookselling: A Brief History of Deighton, Bell and Co., 1778–1998, with a Checklist of the Archive', *Transactions of the Cambridge Bibliographical Society*, 11 (1998), pp. 350–403. Sales ledgers of business with students, c. 1854–71, are now in the Cambridge University Library, Deighton Bell Archives A2/1a, A3/1 and A3/1a. The shop ceased to trade in 2000, shortly after being taken over by Blackwell's as part of the Heffers business.

[6] Macaulay to Selina Mills Macaulay, 16 February 1822: *Letters*, ed. Thomas Pinney, 6 Vols (Cambridge, 1974–81), Vol. 1, p. 170.

[7] A copy of the catalogue prepared of Macaulay's library in 1856 is in Trinity College Library (Macaulay 201); part of his library was sold at Sotheby's, 4–6 March 1863 (a photocopy with names of buyers may also be consulted in the College, Macaulay 202(1)). For the remaining library at Wallington, including many later books, see C. J. Hunt, *Catalogue of the Library at Wallington Hall, Northumberland* (University of Newcastle-upon-Tyne, Library Publications Extra Series 9) (Newcastle upon Tyne, 1968). See also A. N. L. Munby, 'Macaulay's Library', in his *Essays and Papers* (London, 1977), pp. 121–40.

a whole quarter of a year, but they must be returned by the next quarter' (that was written a few days before Lady Day, when his books were therefore due back).

Thackeray did not just use the college library for his set work. Apart from Apuleius, in spring 1829 his choice included Hobhouse on Albania, Grose, Bell's *Anatomy*, Hallam on the middle ages and Strutt's *Antiquities*.[8] By the early summer he was reading Ben Jonson, Beaumont and Fletcher, a miscellaneous volume of seventeenth-century plays, and continuing his medical pursuits with James Drake's early eighteenth-century *Anthropologia Nova; or, a New System of Anatomy* – all signed out, as was required, on the written authority of a Fellow. These loans, recorded in the ledgers kept for the purpose, offer a slightly different view of the Library from that sent home to his family at about this time: 'The books are so outrageously old that there is hardly a book which would be of use to me in the library.'[9] Neither at this date nor for many years later were college libraries thought, or intended, to be provident in their coverage of Tripos subjects. Rather than borrow, Thackeray decided that he must buy Mitford's history of Greece, at the high price of £6 in boards, 'the best & the cheapest copy in Cambridge'.

Thackeray, like many others, used his college library for recreational reading as well as for his daily work. He also belonged to the Union debating society, which possessed a heavily-used library that was well stocked with fiction and other general reading, besides some of the standard works for university examinations. Membership, at half a guinea a term, brought further advantages than simply an active social life and the chance of formal debate.

Borrowing ledgers survive today for several of the colleges. In St John's and in Trinity they date from the late 18th century onwards.[10] At Jesus, they record the reading of the young Coleridge in the 1790s.[11] At Pembroke and at Peterhouse, they reach further back still. For undergraduates, these libraries were for all practical purposes not just the most important, but also virtually the only places where books could be freely read and easily borrowed.

Libraries: college, university, faculty

College libraries were, inevitably, a mixed group. At one extreme were those at Trinity or St John's, long tended and belonging to the two largest colleges: the size of the colleges was also reflected in the numbers of their members who bequeathed their libraries. Both colleges bought books heavily. At the other extreme was Clare College, of which even in 1926, on the six hundredth

---

[8] Trinity College Library, borrowing book, March 1829.
[9] Thackeray to Mrs Carmichael-Smyth, 13–19 April 1829: *Letters and Private Papers*, ed. Gordon N. Ray, 4 Vols (Oxford, 1945–6), Vol. 1, p. 57.
[10] Those for Trinity commence in 1773.
[11] J. C. C. Mays, 'Coleridge's Borrowings from Jesus College Library, 1791–94', *Transactions of the Cambridge Bibliographical Society* 8 (1985), pp. 557–81.

anniversary of its founding, the Fellow in English, Mansfield Forbes, could write

> What then is needed? Surely it is, in every college, an up-to-date and intimately accessible students' library, for easy loan and ready reference . . . In most Cambridge colleges such libraries exist, and are, for we have been investigating, in constant and effective use. Clare lags ignobly, and does not deserve the treasures we can hardly house or care for decently.[12]

His proposal, what he called 'a sort of comminatory appeal', was never taken up: that once the new buildings (i.e. Memorial Court) were completed, there should be a new library constructed in the vacated attic rooms over the Combination Room and old Library. Meanwhile, he described the college library as 'a sort of mental slum' – and this in the grand volumes that commemorated, in the University Press's best style, the achievements of six centuries.

Yet, with no undergraduate library and a student body that was by no means the smallest in Cambridge, Clare had apparently flourished. To those who argue that a college and its members require a library, it presents a conundrum. Although the College was slower than others seriously to consider a new undergraduate library, it was not universally assumed that such was necessary. Mansfield Forbes had his personal answer, and lent his own books heavily to his undergraduates.

The University Library was no substitute.[13] Undergraduates had been banned altogether in 1472. In 1854, new rules permitted them to use the Library for two hours in each day. From 1875, they might use it for the whole of the morning. With the foundation of Girton College in 1869 and Newnham College in 1871, women posed another difficulty altogether. They could not use it as students, but they might apply as adult individuals; and they could only fall into the latter category once they reached the age of twenty-one, when they might apply to the Library Syndicate, supported by two senior members of the University. Girton and Newnham, unable automatically to call even on the University Library, accordingly invested substantially in their libraries: the Yates Thompson library at Newnham, built at the end of the century, was a benefaction from a member of Trinity, while at Girton Lady Stanley gave to found a library there. These libraries offered some of the best facilities in the University; and, at least in Newnham, there was also a separate fiction library for lighter reading.

---

[12] Mansfield D. Forbes, 'The College Library', in Mansfield D. Forbes, ed., *Clare College 1326–1926*, 2 Vols (Cambridge, 1928–30), 2, pp. 303–53, at pp. 352–3; Hugh Carey, *Mansfield Forbes and his Cambridge* (Cambridge, 1984).

[13] The standard histories are J. C. T. Oates, *Cambridge University Library; a History. From the Beginnings to the Copyright Act of Queen Anne* (Cambridge, 1986); and David McKitterick, *Cambridge University Library; a History. The Eighteenth and Nineteenth Centuries* (Cambridge, 1986).

When the Graham Commission reported in 1852,[14] there was no suggestion of higher education for women. The minutes and evidence of the commission make sober reading. At Gonville and Caius College, the Bursar of the day could not even tell the Commissioners how much his college spent on the library, since the structure of the accounts did not permit it. At Peterhouse (undergraduate population 42), junior members were not expected to remain in the library unaccompanied by a fellow. Magdalene, butt of so much criticism at the time as a refuge for gentlemen rather than scholars, was reportedly more advanced than the other colleges: students were provided with keys to the library, to come and go as they wished. As for stock, the picture was equally varied: Pembroke strong on classics and theology, but weak in mathematics; St Catharine's and Queens' working to improve matters; Peterhouse noticeably weak in modern books. 'There is generally', concluded the commissioners, 'a considerable deficiency of modern books for the use of students.' Only at Trinity and St John's, colleges that between them in 1851 contained over 47% of all undergraduates in the University, did the commissioners feel able to comment on the adequacy of the modern collections. The building of new premises for libraries at Pembroke and at Christ's in the last decades of the century was a result of attempts to rectify glaring deficiencies, as well as to meet increasing numbers of students.

While, therefore, we may observe a substantial difference in many college libraries between the middle and the end of the century, some of the old questions remain. How much did a good college library matter? How much were they used? In the absence of books that could be borrowed, where else were books to be had? One writer, in the 1820s, has left a part-fictional and part-real account of the scene in the cloister below the Wren Library at Trinity, just before the short Easter Vacation. Few people went down for this interval, but once Lady Day was past (the quarter-day for the return of all loans) books could be borrowed over the vacation.

> At the hour of ten, on the first day of the opening of Trinity Library, I found the entrance in the Cloisters beset by an ocean of pale countenances undulating to and fro with each succeeding effort to get foremost. Immediately the doors flew open in rushed the torrent, fifty perhaps wanting the same identical book. Such was the eagerness displayed by all, that some tripped up in ascending the lofty stairs, others stumbled over them, caps and gowns flying in most irreverent unacademical confusion . . . Books many wanted I, but being shortlegged and weak-muscled, brought up just in time to meet them on their way out of the Library.[15]

So, according to his story, John Wright, admitted to Trinity in 1813 and an

---

[14] Cambridge University Commission, *Report of Her Majesty's Commissioners Appointed to Inquire into the State, Discipline, Studies and Revenues of the University and Colleges of Cambridge* (1852).
[15] J. M. F. Wright, *Alma mater*, 2 Vols (London, 1827), Vol. 1, p. 183.

accomplished mathematician, had to set to work to obtain the books otherwise in readiness for the coming term. Woodhouse on Trigonometry was bought forthwith for a few shillings; Herodotus, with other books, cost him more than £20.[16] The borrowing register, again, tells a further story. In October 1814 he borrowed Potter on Greek antiquities, two volumes of Herodotus, Nathaniel Hooke's *Roman history* and Blair's lectures on rhetoric – all about three weeks into term. Other books were borrowed of Professor J. H. Monk (fellow of Trinity, Regius Professor of Greek, and then working on his biography of Bentley (1830)) and of some others. On several occasions Wright acknowledged the generosity of Monk in lending him books, and we may suppose that others did likewise to other men.[17]

Lastly, and almost as a footnote, since they make a rather late appearance, are the various faculty libraries. So far as undergraduates were concerned, these were eventually intended in part to make good the needs not met in other ways. But they were a comparatively late development, and do not offer, by themselves, an answer to the conundrum of where undergraduates found their reading at a time when college libraries varied so widely and notoriously, the old circulating libraries had closed presumably for lack of business, and to use the University Library was unusual in an undergraduate. Until the end of the century most teaching was, after all, based on the colleges rather than the University. Prior to the opening of the new Divinity Schoool, and with it a specialist library, in 1879, there were special libraries attached only to the Regius Professorship of Modern History, the Botanical Garden and the University Observatory. By 1890 – that is, within about ten years – libraries had been established either with special funds or by bequest in Moral Sciences, Music, Anatomy, History, Physics and Chemistry. In some sense, the need for such libraries clearly existed, but it remained that some of the largest subjects of all were unsupported in this way: Classics had no library of its own until 1933, when the Mill Lane lecture rooms were opened. In fact, the establishment of these libraries, identified with particular courses of study, depended (with the exception of some specialist collections in the sciences) for the most part not on overall needs in the University, but on the gradual removal of lecturing from colleges to faculties, and on the increased responsibilities assumed by the University itself for undergraduate teaching.

Buying and selling

Not surprisingly, the topography of the book trade was dictated by the population centres of the University. Of the eighteen booksellers and stationers listed in Pigot's directory in 1830, no less than six were in Trinity Street, near to the two largest colleges and to Caius (undergraduate population about eighty).

[16] Wright, *Alma Mater*, Vol. 1, p. 184.
[17] See Warwick's chapter for a developed system of loans in mathematics.

Apart from two stationers, these included Deighton's, which had a quasi-official status, reflected, for example, in the custom of posting up the Vice-Chancellor's notices of university prizes in the shop; William P. Grant; Richard Newby; and Thomas Stevenson. Along with Elijah Johnson, in Sidney Street, they were easily the most important booksellers in Cambridge at this time, and most of them also had small publishing businesses as well. In the case of Deighton, the publishing business was very substantial, and conducted on a national scale. Further to the south, Trumpington Street offered just one: John Hall, opposite the new Pitt Building of the University Press, a man who combined a small printing business with publishing cribs for undergraduates' set texts. With the exception of two small businesses (more stationers than booksellers) in Market Street and in Petty Cury, there were none east of the market, and none, therefore, near to Christ's, Emmanuel or Downing Colleges.

Four of these bookselling businesses also ran circulating libraries. For most of the population of England, such libraries existed for recreational reading, and especially of novels, as a means of countering high prices for new books. In Cambridge, life was different. In the eighteenth century, 'Maps' Nicholson had lent out lecture notes and standard texts from his premises on King's Parade. In the mid-nineteenth century, Thomas Stevenson had a similar business in Trinity Street; but with his death, and the acquisition of his shop by the Macmillan brothers, this side was discontinued. The Post Office Directory for 1869 lists (rather improbably: surely the new Public Library cannot have been so overpowering?) no circulating libraries in Cambridge at all.[18]

By the mid-century, the topography of bookshops had changed a little. Overall, numbers had increased marginally, and there were now four shops in Sidney Street. The centre of the trade remained, as it did for many years subsequently, located in Trinity Street. Elijah Johnson had left Sidney Street and moved to better premises in Trinity Street. It was with Johnson, by now a rather old-fashioned bookseller, set in his ways but enormously knowledgeable about the University and its needs, that the young Daniel Macmillan learned his trade in the mid-1830s. In 1843, with the help of Julius Hare and F. D. Maurice and of further money from another investor, the Macmillan brothers bought the business of T. C. Newby in Trinity Street. Two years later, they sold this and bought Stevenson's old business on the corner opposite the Senate House, and so arrived at what has long been regarded as the best site in the town.[19]

In the 1860s, however, there were major changes. As always in Cambridge, removals of shops and jostlings for business depended not least on rents. Although none of them was a large business, there were now three bookshops

---

[18] Some of their business, for the non-university population, was absorbed into the local book clubs. See Enid Porter, *Victorian Cambridge; Josiah Chater's Diaries, 1844–1884* (London, 1975), pp. 127–8.
[19] Thomas Hughes, *Memoir of Daniel Macmillan* (London, 1882); David McKitterick, *A History of Cambridge University Press. Vol 2. Scholarship and Commerce, 1698–1872* (Cambridge, 1998), pp. 386–401. The premises now house the shop of Cambridge University Press.

in Sidney Street; one in St Andrew's Street; and William P. Grant, formerly of Trinity Street, was now in Hills Road, where there had developed new residential areas between the railway station and the centre of the town. Moreover, with Macmillan's, Deighton's and Rivington's[20] (opposite Trinity College) now in Cambridge, the increased national concern with textbook publishing was becoming obvious: all three firms, with the University Press making its own cautious way in a fast-changing world of secondary and university requirements, were in pursuit of suitable editors among resident graduates for their competing series of standard authors and of educational manuals.

Other names are more familiar today. A gift from the vicar of his parish enabled William Heffer to give up his licence to run a public house in Fitzroy Street, and to open his first bookshop, a modest affair taken over from one Thomas C. Fison, in 1876.[21] Galloway and Porter (at first just Galloway's until Charles Porter joined him as a partner) was founded at the very beginning of the next century, in Sidney Street.

Thanks to the colleges, the centre of the town was relatively prosperous. Other parts were markedly less so. Fitzroy Street, part of the town's rapid growth to the east in the first forty years of the century, was then — as now — more town than gown. At first, William Heffer's main business was in stationery and the modest daily needs of people nearby. One of his earliest triumphs was to persuade local Sunday Schools to buy their many prizes from him, rather than direct from London. In the book trade nationally, the last decades of the nineteenth century were dominated by arguments about 'underselling', that is, about discounts. The trade was bitterly divided. Heffer saw his opportunity when he discovered in the 1890s that many copies of the standard textbooks were not bought in Cambridge at all, but in London, where publishers would give 25% discount for cash. Heffer did his homework, advertised, and attracted a stream of custom to his shop, distant though it was from most of the colleges. When, inevitably, the larger shops in the centre of the town began to do likewise, Heffer took the battle to their own ground. In 1896 he opened his shop in Petty Cury — at first just on the ground floor of one house.

How much were undergraduates expected to spend on books? In 1818, at the end of his first term, Macaulay thought a total of £53 for his tutor's bill 'moderate', notwithstanding mistaken charges of £5 for a shoemaker and £7 for a tailor: if anything was included for books, he did not mention it. Thackeray was willing to pay £6 for Mitford's *Greece*, and was apologetic about it: that would have been extravagant for most people. In the 1850s, undergraduates at Magdalene were advised to allow not more than £10 per term for books — the same as for a cook, and twice what was advisable for the grocer.[22] In 1862, Henry

---

[20] Rivington opened a retail shop in 1862, and it was given up in 1881: Septimus Rivington, *The Publishing Family of Rivington* (London, 1919), pp. 148, 162.
[21] *William Heffer, 1843–1928* (Cambridge, 1952). The firm was sold to Blackwell's in 1999.
[22] Peter Cunich, David Hoyle, Eamon Duffy and Ronald Hyam, *A History of Magdalene College, Cambridge 1428–1988* (Cambridge, 1994), pp. 201–2.

Latham, of Trinity Hall, suggested that a year's bills (26 weeks) for grocer and bookseller might amount to between £10 and £20 in all.[23] When compared with what was to be allowed for other needs, the proportion for books seems high; but in the absence of properly stocked libraries, and in face of the need for set texts, such expenditure was inescapable. Because it was generally cheaper to pay cash (and so receive a discount) than to add it to an account, it is in fact often difficult to judge how much was thought to be generally reasonable.

But the demands were potentially very great indeed, and grew in number over the century even within individual courses of study. Those who pursued the Mathematical Tripos to its conclusion had not only to study geometry, algebra, trigonometry, astronomy, optics, mechanics, acoustics, calculus and equations, but also electricity and magnetism, heat and, by the end of the century, thermodynamics. By the 1880s, the course reached from Euclid and Newton to Maxwell, Rayleigh, Lamb and Cayley, and included some of the principal French and German work in these fields as well.

Clearly undergraduates could not buy everything. Then, as now, the cost of the standard recommended books in law or in medicine was high.[24] To purchase a foundation collection of the books recommended for medicine in the 1870s by G. M. Humphry, Professor of Anatomy, would have cost about £10 – and that just for anatomy, physiology and basic surgery. But then, not all undergraduates spent much on books, even for their professional careers. In 1880, Alexander Frost Douglas, son of a Presbyterian minister in the South Island, New Zealand, came up to St John's College.[25] With a year behind him at Canterbury University College, he settled down to read for the BA and LLB simultaneously. A long way from home, dependent on relatives in Northumberland where he had been born, he kept his accounts punctiliously. The whole of his three years' Cambridge education cost £583 15s. 10d. His book bills were modest. Apart from whatever books were incurred for his first term's bookseller's bill of three guineas, he spent a shilling on Paley, 3s. on Crosse's *Analysis* of Paley (Macmillan,1855), and 10s. for the *Cambridge Review*. The total for everything for this his first term, generally reckoned to be more expensive than most subsequent ones, was £95 12s. 2½d. During the rest of the year, apart from his subscription to the *Eagle* (the college magazine) he spent just 35s. on books, for a second-hand copy of Blackstone's *Commentaries*. The following Michaelmas Term, at the beginning of his second year and now into the serious study of law, he bought just two books: Stephens on criminal law for 13s. 4d., and Campbell on Roman law, for 8s. Passing on to his last two terms of all, we find

---

[23] *Student's Guide* (Cambridge, 1862), p. 64. He revised the lower figure up slightly in the third edition (1874).

[24] E. C. Clark, 'On the Study of Law', *Student's Guide* (1874), pp. 237–70, including (pp. 241–4) a list of books recommended by the Board of Legal Studies; G. M. Humphry, 'Degrees in Medicine and Surgery', *ibid.*, pp. 271–97, including (p. 290) a brief list of the foremost books.

[25] For Douglas's private accounts as an undergraduate, see St John's College MS W2.

just one book (*Verdant Green*, a novel of Oxford undergraduate life, price 5s.) and two periodical subscriptions (the *Cambridge Review* and the *Eagle*): hardly the obvious signs of a reading man. Yet he graduated eighth in his year, was subsequently called to the bar, and practised successfully in London for the rest of his life, specialising in the affairs of the Presbyterian Church.

His accounts, thin as they are for books, record a practice that had been a part of the book trade since the sixteenth century. Preferring to sell the same book, and therefore to take profit on the same investment as often as possible, booksellers sure of their market had long been in the habit of promising a proportion of the retail price on a book's return. Douglas bought his copy of Campbell on Roman law on this principle, the bookseller undertaking to pay 6s. of the 8s. charged should he choose to return it at the beginning of the following term. In other words, Douglas could choose simply to hire it, rather like a book from a circulating library. He did just this, and put the shillings into books on tort, contracts and equity. The bookseller's principle of being content with a small but frequent return (what second-hand bookseller now would give 75% of the price of an ordinary textbook?) was one of the most important features of the undergraduate book-buying economy of the late nineteenth century.[26]

The change over the century was gradual, from a small number of books, supported more or less by special guides and background reading, to a pattern of set texts or established textbooks in particular subjects backed up by an array of specially written supporting literature. J. L. Roget's *A Cambridge Scrapbook* (1859) depicts the so-called 'Freshman's Church' (that is, the Pitt Building of the University Press, distinguished by its ecclesiastical tower) alongside the 'Freshman's Bible', or annual University Calendar. For most of the century, this was published by Deighton Bell. To country clergymen it was no doubt useful in that it gave details of livings and of the ages of those who held them. To the professions it offered a list of those who had passed their examinations. To those in Cambridge itself, it offered (among much else) details of university or college prizes to be won, as well as details of the current syllabus. By 1890, it was preceded by more than eighty pages of advertisements, including the complete list of Deighton Bell and extensive selections from the University Press, the Clarendon Press, Macmillan, Kegan Paul, Blackie, Murray (publishers of William Smith's many popular dictionaries of the Bible, classical antiquity, etc.), Smith Elder (publishers of Leslie Stephen) and others besides. The full-page advertisement for *Hymns Ancient and Modern* was presumably directed at the parish clergy who kept in touch with their old university by its *Calendar*. Much of the advertising was directed generally at the educational market, a market that had, by comparison, hardly existed two or three generations previously: with the special needs of the upper forms of the better schools, or with undergraduates

---

[26] For a light-hearted reflection on selling books after examinations, see 'The Disposal of Books', *Cambridge Review*, 15 June 1893, pp. 403–4.

specifically in mind. In a generation, the price of ordinary new books had come down drastically. The abolition of paper duty in the 1860s, the opportunities to engage in a world-wide market for books printed and published in Britain, and wages that were historically low, all helped to contribute to a world in which the undergraduate, at least for his or her most urgent reading, could expect to buy books on a scale never before possible. It was in this world that a thriving market in second-hand textbooks was characterised by a price structure that distinguished between prices for cash and prices on account, and in which Heffer offered his discounts of 25%.[27]

[27] For help of various kinds, I am grateful to Ian Kidman, Stephen Porter, Jonathan Smith, Chris Stray and the staff of St John's College Library.

JUNE BARROW-GREEN

'The advantage of proceeding from an author of some scientific reputation': Isaac Todhunter and his Mathematics Textbooks

The name of Isaac Todhunter (1820–1884) is familiar to today's mathematicians, if at all, as the author of a large number of nineteenth-century textbooks and a series of scholarly, if rather dry, books on the history of mathematics. A late starter, Todhunter began his career as a schoolmaster before going up to Cambridge. After graduating he remained in Cambridge as a college lecturer and as a mathematical coach for the rest of his life. Todhunter was an able mathematician, but one who elected to use his knowledge as a facilitator rather than as an innovator. Prompted by financial necessity into textbook writing, Todhunter immediately showed an affinity for the task and was remarkably good at it. By setting Todhunter's life against the background of the academic environment within which he worked, and making a detailed examination of his *Euclid* and his *Algebra*, I propose to explore the questions: why was Todhunter so successful, and how did he manage to be so prolific?

The Mathematical Tripos

At the beginning of the nineteenth century the normal route to a Bachelor of Arts degree at Cambridge was through the Senate House Examination, a mathematical examination popularly known as the Tripos.[1] In 1822 the Classical Tripos was established but candidates could only compete in it if they had already obtained an Honours degree in the original Tripos. In 1824, the year the Classical Tripos was offered for the first time, the original examination took on the name of the Mathematical Tripos.[2] The predominance of mathematics was

[1] The Tripos began as an unstructured oral examination that became formalised in about 1710; from 1748 Honours-lists were published and in 1753 the division into wranglers (those in the highest class) and senior optimes was established. A detailed description of the examination as at the beginning of the nineteenth century is contained in the University *Calendar* for 1802.
[2] For a history of the Mathematical Tripos, see J. W. L. Glaisher, 'The Mathematical Tripos', *Proceedings of the London Mathematical Society*, Vol. 18 (1886), pp. 4–38; W. W. Rouse Ball, *A*

preserved until 1851 when the Moral Sciences and Natural Sciences Triposes were introduced. From then on it became possible to obtain an Honours degree in the other Triposes without first obtaining Honours in mathematics, although an elementary part of the Mathematical Tripos remained compulsory.

For students with serious academic intent, known as 'reading' men, the Mathematical Tripos became an increasingly strenuous ordeal. As the century wore on the contest developed more and more into a problem-solving marathon in which speed of pen had ascendancy over original thought. For those in the race to become Senior Wrangler, the enormous number of hours devoted to the study of mathematics and practice at problem solving meant it was both physically and mentally exhausting. But the stakes were high. Leading wranglers were endowed with a status recognised far beyond the boundaries of the University, and success in the Mathematical Tripos meant an assured future in a career of the candidate's choice. But the success had to be paid for, and the financial burden could be considerable. Not only were there the heavy fees that an undergraduate had to pay to the University and to his college,[3] there was also the expense of private tutoring, or 'coaching' as it became known, which was essential for any student nurturing the hope of becoming a wrangler. Although the existence of coaches has been reported as early as the end of the seventeenth century, it was in the nineteenth century that the profession, through the success of William Hopkins and Edward John Routh, a former pupil of Hopkins', reached its zenith.[4] Between them Hopkins and Routh coached 44 Senior Wranglers, and several hundred other wranglers besides. The job of the coach was exclusively to prepare his pupils for the Tripos, and since the coach's reputation, and thus income, depended solely on his pupils' positions in the examination, it was not in a coach's interest for a student to spend time studying outside the Tripos subjects.

During the course of the century the regulations for the Tripos underwent several revisions, with regard both to the length of the examination and to the subjects under test. In 1800 it took place over four consecutive days, with the fourth day devoted to separating out students bracketed together from their performance during the previous three days. Candidates were examined in arithmetic, algebra, fluxions, geometry, trigonometry, mechanics, hydrostatics, optics and astronomy. In 1827, the year in which it was first stipulated that all the papers should be printed, the examination was extended to five days, with further extensions taking place in 1833 and 1839. In 1848 the structure was changed again, the duration being extended to eight days, involving forty-four and a half hours of examination. The provision for testing bracketed students, unofficially discontinued for some time, was officially removed. Only those who

---

History of the Study of Mathematics at Cambridge (Cambridge, 1889); W. W. Rouse Ball, *Cambridge Papers* (London, 1918), pp. 252–316.
[3] Rouse Ball, *Cambridge Papers*, p. 310.
[4] Rouse Ball, *Cambridge Papers*, pp. 307–10.

had acquitted themselves sufficiently well on the first three days (which were assigned to elementary subjects) were admitted to the final five days, and thus to the possibility of obtaining mathematical Honours.

Of the several people responsible for key changes in the content of the Mathematical Tripos during the first half of the century, one of the most influential was William Whewell, who in the early 1820s had introduced continental mechanics into the examination.[5] In the 1830s Whewell's call for the inclusion of more physical subjects into the examination – to balance the increasing number of subjects in pure mathematics, such as analytic geometry, elliptic integrals and Laplace's coefficients, that it had recently come to contain – was successful. The subjects of electricity, magnetism, heat, the wave theory of light, as well as the analytic treatment of the *Principia*, hydrodynamics, planetary theory, capillary theory, and the figure of the earth considered as a heterogeneous body, were all added. Candidates were also expected to be proficient in mechanics, hydrostatics, observational astronomy, and geometrical optics. Not surprisingly it soon became apparent that the enormous number of subjects on which a student could be examined far exceeded what could reasonably be expected. In 1849 several of the recent additions were officially dropped, although in practice some, such as magnetism and electricity on which no mathematical lectures were given, had rarely appeared in the examination. Over the next two decades gradual adjustments were made, until in 1873 a major reform was enacted. By this time it had become clear that certain important branches of mathematics and mathematical physics, such as electricity and magnetism, did not enter at all in the studies of the University precisely because they were not part of the Mathematical Tripos. The reform increased the areas of study, reintroducing much of the subject matter excluded in 1849, and added an extra day to the scheme of the examination. The new regulations had the completely unintended effect of making it possible for candidates to obtain more marks by having a superficial knowledge of all of the subjects than by having a genuine proficiency in a select number of the higher ones. To compensate for this unforeseen consequence, further revisions were made in 1878.

The above sketch, which only scratches the surface of a complex history, gives an indication of the considerable transformation undergone by the Mathematical Tripos during the middle decades of the nineteenth century, the period when Todhunter was most active. The more radical changes were confined to the higher or more advanced parts of the examination, with the lower or more elementary parts remaining relatively unscathed. A detailed knowledge of the structure and likely contents of the examination was of great importance to lecturers and coaches alike and it was essential for them to keep up to date with the revisions. And when these revisions included the addition of new subjects for

---

[5] For a clear discussion of the nineteenth-century reforms to the content of the Mathematical Tripos, and in particular the role played by William Whewell, see H. W. Becher, 'William Whewell and Cambridge Mathematics', *Historical Studies in the Physical Sciences*, 11 (1980), pp. 1–48.

examination, they provided a natural stimulus for the production of new textbooks. Conversely, there were also instances when the change of content was itself stimulated by the publication of new books.[6] Furthermore, the persistent competitiveness of the Mathematical Tripos meant that there was continual demand for good quality textbooks on standard subjects designed with the examination in mind. Nineteenth-century Cambridge was the period and the place for active productivity in the mathematics textbook market and Todhunter, more than anyone else in his generation, took advantage of it.

Isaac Todhunter

Isaac Todhunter was born in Rye, Sussex on 23 November 1820, the son of a Congregationalist minister, George Todhunter. As a child he was rather backward and slow to learn to read.[7] At the age of five his father died leaving the family to enjoy 'the bracing discipline of poverty'.[8] The following year the family moved to Hastings where his mother, who kept a boarding school for girls, gave him and his brothers instruction. He attended the school of Robert Carr for a short time before being moved to a newly-opened school run by J. B. Austin. In 1835 he followed Austin to a school in Peckham where he then became assistant master. In 1841, with Austin on the point of emigrating to Australia, Todhunter left Peckham and began to engage in private tuition. A few months later he took up the position of second (soon to become first) mathematics master at a large school in Wimbledon.

Meanwhile in 1839 he had passed the matriculation exam for London University, winning the mathematics exhibition. While continuing to teach he attended evening classes at University College, where his lecturers included James Joseph Sylvester and Augustus De Morgan. In 1842 he was awarded a BA, winning a scholarship, and in 1844 he was awarded an MA, winning a gold

---

[6] For example, G. B. Airy's *Mathematical Tracts on Physical Astronomy, the Figure of the Earth, Precession and Nutation, and the Calculus of Variations* (Cambridge, 1826), updated and expanded at regular intervals, became essential reading for the Tripos and its contents helped direct the course of the examination, while R. Murphy's *Elementary Principles on the Theories of Electricity, Heat and Molecular Actions, Part 1: On Electricity* (Cambridge, 1833) was produced in response to Whewell's support for the subject. See D. B. Wilson, 'The Educational Matrix: Physics Education at early-Victorian Cambridge, Edinburgh and Glasgow Universities', *Wranglers and Physicists: Studies on Cambridge Physics in the Nineteenth Century*, ed. P. M. Harman (Manchester, 1985), pp. 12–48.

[7] Anon., 'Isaac Todhunter', *The Eagle*, Vol. 13 (1884), pp. 94–7.

[8] J. E. B. Mayor, 'In Memoriam: Isaac Todhunter', *Cambridge Review*, March 5, 12 and 19, 1884. J. E. B. Mayor, who was Professor of Latin and a longstanding friend to Todhunter, was commissioned by the *Cambridge Review* to write Todhunter's biography. Unfortunately, Mayor, who was learned but naive, began by writing so extensively on the life and times of three Dissenting ministers who had educated Todhunter that the editor of the *Review* refused to publish any further instalments. See W. F. Bushell, 'The Cambridge Mathematical Tripos', *The Mathematical Gazette*, Vol. xliv (1960), pp. 172–9. For further information on Mayor, see J. Henderson, 'Juvenal's Mayor. The Professor who Lived on 2d a day', *Cambridge Philological Society*, Supplementary Volume 20 (1998).

medal as the top student. De Morgan proved a decisive influence on Todhunter – it was from him that Todhunter derived 'that interest in the history and bibliography of science, in moral philosophy and logic, which determined the course of his riper studies'[9] – and it was on De Morgan's advice that in 1844 Todhunter, aged 24, went up to Cambridge and became a student at St John's College.[10] Being about six years older than the average student[11] and with more mathematical experience, he was able to spend time studying subjects outside those set for the Tripos,[12] a practice not encouraged. In 1848, having been coached by William Hopkins, he graduated as Senior Wrangler and won the first Smith's prize.[13] In the same year he was also awarded the Burney Prize.[14]

Meanwhile the family fortunes had not improved, but although Todhunter was not financially well off, he lived prudently as an undergraduate and was able to provide his mother with some financial support. Happy in his own company, he did not mind having little money to spend on entertainment, although his reluctance to socialise unfortunately led to the circulation of stories about his lack of generosity.

In 1849 Todhunter became a fellow of his college, and soon afterwards a mathematical lecturer and tutor. He was a successful teacher and it was not long before his lecture notes began to appear in textbook form. The first of these, *A Treatise on the Differential Calculus and the Elements of the Integral Calculus*, was published in 1852 and from then on, and for the next ten years, new textbooks appeared at the rate of approximately one a year. After the publication of *The Elements of Euclid* in 1862 he began to get more involved in the history of mathematics and his production rate slowed. His sixteenth and final textbook, *Natural Philosophy for Beginners*, appeared in 1877. The books

[9] Mayor, *In Memoriam*, 3. For a discussion on De Morgan as an historian of mathematics and science, see A. Rice, 'Augustus De Morgan: Historian of Science', *History of Science*, Vol. 34 (1996), pp. 201–40.
[10] Prior to the 1850s many public schools had little or no provision for the teaching of mathematics and it was not unusual for students to begin their mathematics education at London or one of the Scottish universities. As a result, the level of mathematics necessary to obtain a mathematics degree at one of these universities was not very high, but it was more than ample to provide good preparation for embarking on the Cambridge Tripos course.
[11] C. M. Neale, *The Senior Wranglers of the University of Cambridge*, F. T. Groom & Son (1907), p. 38.
[12] Routh recalls that Todhunter once told him 'how as an undergraduate he read Electricity to fill up his time, though the subject did not enter into the Tripos Examination List.' See E. J. Routh, 'Isaac Todhunter', *Proceedings of the Royal Society*, Vol. 37 (1884), 27–32.
[13] The Smith's Prize competition was established in Cambridge in 1768 by the will of Robert Smith. For a discussion of the competition, see J. E. Barrow-Green, 'A Corrective to the Spirit of too Exclusively Pure Mathematics: Robert Smith (1689–1768) and his Prizes at Cambridge University', *Annals of Science*, lvi (1999), pp. 271–316.
[14] The Burney Prize, which was founded in 1846, is awarded to 'the graduate who should produce the best English Essay on some moral and metaphysical subject, on the Existence, Nature, and Attributes of God, and on the Truth and Evidence of Christian Religion', *The Historical Register of the University of Cambridge*, Cambridge University Press (1917), 320. Todhunter's Burney Prize essay was printed in 1849 under the title 'The doctrine of a divine providence is inseparable from the belief in the existence of an absolutely perfect creator.'

were immediately successful and provided him with a welcome and necessary source of income, as well as enhancing his reputation as a lecturer. Todhunter's first history, *A History of the Progress of the Calculus of Variations during the Nineteenth Century*, was published in 1861.[15] This was followed by *A History of the Theory of Probability* in 1865, the *History of the Mathematical Theories of Attraction* in 1873 and finally, *A History of the Theory of Elasticity*, which was completed and edited by Karl Pearson[16] and published posthumously in two volumes in 1886 and 1893.

While Todhunter was in the process of writing his textbooks and histories he continued a successful college career, although he was not always at one with the authorities. From 1852 he had been a college lecturer under James Atlay (the senior tutor of the college and the tutor responsible for the allocation of the college lecturing) and thereafter had risen to become the senior mathematical lecturer of the college. However when Atlay retired in 1859 Todhunter, instead of finding himself in an improved position, discovered, much to his dismay that, as part of the reform of the college statutes the Master of the college, W. H. Bateson, proposed to appoint him under Stephen Parkinson[17] with a remuneration of less than half of that assigned to Parkinson.[18] Not only did Todhunter stand to lose status by the proposal but also, and pertinently, he stood to lose financially. He was so angered by what he considered to be the 'slur' cast upon him by 'a virtual dismissal from office' that in February 1860 he made a formal statement to the Master and Seniors, citing his grievances and declining the appointment on the given terms.[19] However, since a substantial proportion of Parkinson's remuneration was to be for work associated with the management of the tutorial system, work that Todhunter had refused to undertake,[20] Todhunter does not appear to have had a strong case for complaint, and indeed his statement was initially rebuffed.[21] Nevertheless, whether due to the possibility of losing Todhunter as a teacher in the College or for some other reason, a month later the question was settled in Todhunter's favour. In April 1860 the post of

---

[15] For synopses of Todhunter's histories, see W. Johnson, 'Isaac Todhunter (1820–1884): Textbook Writer, Scholar, Coach and Historian of Science', *International Journal of Mechanical Science*, 38 (1996), pp. 1231–70.

[16] Todhunter's association with Pearson had begun in 1879 when Todhunter was examining for the Smith's Prizes and Pearson was a candidate. Pearson made a particular impression on Todhunter by including in one of his solutions a proof that Todhunter recognised as being better than the accepted one. Later Todhunter referred to Pearson's proof in his manuscript for *A History of the Theory of Elasticity* with the result that Pearson was invited to complete and edit the work.

[17] Stephen Parkinson is probably best known for being the student who in 1845 beat William Thomson (later Lord Kelvin) into second place in the Mathematical Tripos.

[18] Documents relating to Todhunter's 1860 appointment at St John's are held in the St John's College Archives (hereafter SJCA), Drawer 101, Items 107–109; Drawer 104, Items 30–33.

[19] SJCA, Drawer 104, Item 32.

[20] SJCA, Drawer 104, Item 30.

[21] SJCA, Drawer 104, Item 33.

Senior Mathematical Lecturer was created and Todhunter was appointed. And since Todhunter was the only holder of the post – it was discontinued in October 1864 when Todhunter resigned his fellowship – it appears to have been created specifically for him.

In 1863 Todhunter put himself forward as a candidate – although with no real expectation of being successful – for the newly created Sadleirian chair to which Arthur Cayley was eventually elected.[22] By 1864, having established himself as a private coach and having published eleven textbooks as well as his first history, Todhunter decided that he could afford to resign his fellowship in favour of marriage. It was a move that came as a surprise to his colleagues, who had not thought of him as a marrying man.[23] Todhunter's wife, Louisa Anna Maria Davies, was the daughter of Captain (later Admiral) George Davies, RN. The extent of Louisa's interest in mathematics is not documented, but it is reported that Todhunter introduced her to Hamilton's *Quaternions* while on their honeymoon, having previously assured her that she need fear no rivalry from books.[24]

After his marriage Todhunter no longer had an official college position but he continued to lecture and tutor in a private capacity, and more books appeared. He produced little in the way of research papers – the *Royal Society of London Catalogue of Scientific Papers*[25] lists fifteen, mostly short, papers published between 1865 and 1878.[26] The one exception, a substantial memoir on the calculus of variations, was born out of a controversy in the *Philosophical Magazine*, and with it Todhunter won the Adams Prize in 1871.[27] Apart from the textbooks and histories, he also edited the second edition of Boole's *Treatise on Differential Equations* (1865), produced two volumes on the writings and correspondence of William Whewell in 1876, and published a selection of essays on education, mainly mathematical, entitled *The Conflict of Studies* in 1873.

As a textbook author of such ubiquity, Todhunter was ideally qualified to act as a mathematical examiner and he was invited to do so by several institutions. In 1865 he was Senior Moderator for the Mathematical Tripos and the following

---

[22] Prior to the election Todhunter had confided in Boole that he hoped that he (Boole), would be appointed, and that if Boole was unsuccessful then he hoped the position would go to Sylvester, and failing him, Cayley, although he did remark that he thought it obvious that Cayley could not teach or explain anything. Letter from Todhunter to Boole, 23 May 1863. See Desmond MacHale *George Boole. His Life and Work* (Dublin, 1985), pp. 233–4.
There were eight candidates for the chair – Arthur Cayley, Norman Macleod Ferrers, Percival Frost, Thomas Gaskin, James George Mould, Edward John Routh, Isaac Todhunter, John Clough Williams-Ellis – and Cayley was appointed unanimously.
[23] Anon., 'Isaac Todhunter', p. 97.
[24] Mayor, *In Memoriam*, p. 25.
[25] *Royal Society of London Catalogue of Scientific Papers 1800–1900*, 19 Vols, plus 4 index Vols, Cambridge University Press and others (1867–1925).
[26] A list of Todhunter's publications is given at the end of this article.
[27] The Adams Prize was founded in 1848 in recognition of J. C. Adams' discovery of Neptune. A subject is set every two years and the competition is open to anyone who has at any time been admitted to a degree at Cambridge.

year he was Senior Examiner.[28] In 1879 he substituted for James Challis as an examiner for the Smith's Prizes. Outside Cambridge he examined for London University from 1864 to 1869, the Royal Military Academy at Woolwich, the East India Company's military college at Addiscombe,[29] and the Indian Civil Service.[30] The extent to which such institutions relied on his textbooks can be gauged from a letter Todhunter wrote to his wife while examining for the Indian Civil Service in 1878

> There is a library of mathematical books provided by the Civil Service Commissioners for the use of the Examiners. It consists of fourteen volumes, ten of which are by myself. Thus you see I am able to do much of that labour which Matthew Arnold thinks distasteful, namely, that of perusing your own books.[31]

In 1850 he was elected a Fellow of the Royal Astronomical Society and was a member of its Council from 1868 to 1870. In 1862 he was elected a Fellow of the Royal Society, and served on the Council from 1871 to 1873. The citation on his Royal Society election certificate referred to his *History of the Progress of the Calculus of Variations* and concluded with the statement: 'Distinguished for his acquaintance with the science of mathematics and its history. Eminent as a mathematician and for varied erudition.' The list of nominees who supported his election included Sylvester, Cayley, Whewell, Airy and Boole, as well as others from across the mathematical spectrum, and gives an indication of his standing in the mathematical community. In 1866, in the second year of its existence, he was elected a member of the London Mathematical Society.[32] In 1874 he was elected an Honorary Fellow of his college,[33] and in 1883, shortly after the institution of the degree at Cambridge, he was granted an ScD. Outside mathematics, he enjoyed a reputation as a good classical scholar,[34] and had a sound knowledge of several languages, including Hebrew, Arabic, Sanskrit and Persian, as well as French, German, Spanish, Italian and Russian. He was also well read in philosophy and was a prime mover, together with William Whewell, in the founding of the Moral Sciences Tripos for which he was an Examiner from 1863 to 1865.

---

[28] Todhunter was asked on several occasions to examine again for the Tripos but always refused on account of the burden of work and amount of time involved. Several other distinguished mathematicians also examined only once for the same reason. See Routh, *Isaac Todhunter*, p. 28.

[29] Todhunter did not give the dates when he examined for Woolwich and Addiscombe, although it must have been before 1873 as that is the date of the publication in which he mentions it. I. Todhunter, *The Conflict of Studies and Other Essays*, Macmillan (1873), p. 159.

[30] Routh, 'Isaac Todhunter', p. 29.

[31] *Loc. cit.*

[32] Minutes of the London Mathematical Society. J. B. Mullinger, in 'Isaac Todhunter', *The Dictionary of National Biography* (Oxford, 1899), wrongly asserts that Todhunter was elected in 1865, and the error has been repeated in other secondary sources.

[33] According to Routh, this was an honour that Todhunter particularly prized. See Routh, 'Isaac Todhunter', p. 29.

[34] Mullinger, *DNB*, p. 915; Mayor, *In Memoriam*, p. 6.

Todhunter's pupils included Peter Guthrie Tait, Leslie Stephen, John Venn, and the Japanese student Dairoku Kikuchi.[35] Stephen provided an evocative description of his tutor:

> [Todhunter] lived in a perfect atmosphere of mathematics; his books all ranged in the neatest order, and covered with brown uniform paper, were mathematical; his talk, to us at any rate, was one round of mathematics; even his chairs and tables strictly limited to the requirements of his pupils, and the pattern on his carpet, seemed to breathe mathematics. By what mysterious process it was that he accumulated stores of miscellaneous information and knew all about the events of the time (for such I afterwards discovered to be the fact), I have never been able to guess. Probably he imbibed them through the pores of his skin. Still less can I imagine how it came to pass that he published a whole series of excellent educational works. He probably wrote them in momentary interstices of time, between one pupil's entering his sanctum and another leaving it.[36]

Venn, who had settled on Todhunter having already tried William Hopkins and Francis Jameson,[37] paints a not dissimilar picture:

> [Todhunter] was an excellent and learned mathematician, and a very industrious and systematic teacher; but I still feel convinced that my studies, so far as concerns the intellectual and educational profit which is to be made out of mathematics, would have been far more advantageous with a teacher of another stamp. He always had the Tripos prominently in view, and seemed to have no sympathy with those who wished to turn aside to study some detached point which interested them or to speculate about the logical and philosophical problems that arose in the way. I suppose he considered it his duty to prepare us, to the utmost, for our impending examination, for, as I afterwards came to know, he really possessed wide knowledge in other directions, and some speculative taste. . . .[38]

---

[35] Kikuchi studied at University College, London before going up to St John's College, Cambridge in 1873. He returned to Japan in 1877, having graduated as 19th wrangler, and became the first Japanese professor of mathematics at the newly founded University of Tokyo. Influenced by Todhunter, he was keen to promote the type of mathematical education he had received in Cambridge and he used several of Todhunter's textbooks at the University. In particular he directed his efforts towards the teaching of geometry, especially Euclid's *Elements*. Later he himself became the author of several textbooks, mostly on geometry. See A. Horiuchi, 'Sur la recomposition du paysage mathématique japonais au début de l'époque Meiji', *L'Europe mathématique: histoires, mythes, identités*, ed. C. Goldstein, J. Gray, J. Ritter (Paris, 1996), pp. 263–6.
Notes made by Kikuchi while attending Todhunter's classes are in the archives of the University of Tokyo. I am grateful to Chikara Sasaki of Tokyo University for informing me of their existence.

[36] L. Stephen, *Sketches from Cambridge by A Don* (London, 1865), p. 107.

[37] Francis James Jameson (1828–1869), 6th wrangler 1850, Fellow of Caius 1852–1855, Fellow of St Catherine's 1855–1862, Vicar of Coton, Cambridge 1862–1869.

[38] Later Todhunter was responsible for introducing Venn to Boole's *Laws of Thought*, a book that was to have a profound influence upon him. John Venn *Annals* (1854, 1858), Venn

As a tutor Todhunter continued to live a quiet life. J. E. B. Mayor, one of Todhunter's more intimate colleagues and his obituarist, doubted that they had ever been inside each other's rooms.[39] Although Mayor appears to have held Todhunter in high esteem, his thoughts on him are not always clear and it is largely due to his fanciful prose that the more recent literature has treated Todhunter rather unkindly. Using adjectives taken from Mayor's obituary,[40] Noel Annan, in his biography of Leslie Stephen, described Todhunter as 'quaint, crotchety, sour, uncouth, surrounded by cats and canaries',[41] and the description has since taken root.[42] But this opinion is in sharp contrast both to that given by Stephen himself[43] and to that of the historian of St John's College, J. B. Mullinger, who credited Todhunter with a 'gentle kindly disposition' united with 'a high sense of honour . . . and considerable humour'.[44] Added to which Annan's verdict overlooks the positive comments that occur in Mayor's writing.[45] Nevertheless, Todhunter's reclusive disposition did make him a focus for stories. For example, it is told that he once went down to the river to view the May races but never went again, on the grounds that he could visualise in his college room exactly what was happening and considered his presence there unnecessary.[46] And by his own admission he had no ear for music. He 'knew only two tunes: one was God Save the Queen: and the other wasn't. The former he recognised by the people standing up.'[47] Todhunter fell ill in 1880, and died in 1884. He was buried in Mill Road Cemetery, Cambridge.[48] He is commemorated in St John's College by a marble bust now displayed in the college library.

Todhunter's textbooks

Altogether Todhunter published 16 different textbooks.[49] He began in 1852 with *A Treatise on the Differential Calculus and Elements of the Integral Calculus* and ended 25 years later in 1877 with *Natural Philosophy for Beginners* published in two parts. He (and, later, other authors) also provided keys for several of his texts. And

---

papers, Church Missionary Society Archive, Birmingham University. I am grateful to Ellie Clewlow for drawing my attention to these papers.
[39] Mayor, *In Memoriam*, pp. 4–5.
[40] Mayor, *In Memoriam*, p. 25.
[41] N. Annan *Leslie Stephen: His Thought and Character in Relation to his Time*, MacGibbon and Key (London, 1951), p. 26; N. Annan, *Leslie Stephen: The Godless Victorian* (London, 1984), p. 27.
[42] See, for example, E. Miller, *Portrait of a College* (Cambridge), p. 87.
[43] Stephen, *Sketches*, p. 106.
[44] Mullinger, *DNB*, p. 915.
[45] For example, Mayor wrote that 'To his pupils he [Todhunter] was a friend, warm-hearted and very sagacious in encouraging any promise of excellence'. Mayor, *In Memoriam*, p. 5.
[46] Bushell 'The Cambridge Mathematical Tripos', pp. 172–9.
[47] Mayor, *In Memoriam*, p. 26.
[48] Johnson, *Isaac Todhunter*, p. 1268.
[49] A complete list of Todhunter's textbooks is given at the end of this article.

although his histories are not written as textbooks, at least one — the *History of the Calculus of Variations* — was recommended for undergraduate use.[50]

Almost all of Todhunter's textbooks ran into several editions. At the time of his death his *Algebra* (1858) was in its eleventh edition, his *Euclid* (1862) in its thirteenth, and his most popular book, *Algebra for Beginners* (1863), in its fifteenth, having had by that time total print runs of over 100,000, over 250,000 and over 300,000 respectively.[51] After his death the texts continued to be published and some were revised by other authors.[52] Furthermore, Todhunter's success was not confined to Britain. Editions of his books were sold around the globe. As Macfarlane noted, several were published in the United States,[53] although most of these did not appear until near the end of the nineteenth century. Some of the American editions even became the set texts for a particular market, as for example the 1882 New York edition of *Algebra for Beginners* which was the prescribed text for 'public schools' (i.e. publicly funded schools) in Nova Scotia. Editions in English also surfaced in Australia, China[54] and India. The translations were similarly widespread with editions appearing in Italian, Chinese,[55] Japanese[56] and Urdu.

It was not only those in the educational field that appreciated the merits of Todhunter's books, his texts also received glowing notices in professional

---

[50] William Campion 'Mathematical Tripos', *The Student's Guide to the University of Cambridge*, (Cambridge, 1863), p. 97.

[51] The numbers for these and other print runs have been taken from the Prizing Books of Cambridge University Press. Cambridge University Archives, Cambridge University Library CUP 17/1–17/7. Todhunter's publishers were Macmillan & Co and the printers were Cambridge University Press. Todhunter's books were widely advertised by Macmillans — e.g. in 1861 14,000 prospectuses were prepared to promote the publication of his *Theory of Equations*, which was published in 1862 as a sequel to his *Algebra* (Cambridge University Archives, Cambridge University Library, CUP 18/2, 17 and 21 October 1861) — but this and other aspects of the relationship between mathematical authors and their publishers, and the general influence of the book trade on nineteenth-century British mathematics have not been explored in this article although they clearly merit further research.

[52] See, for example, the 1899 edition of Todhunter's *Euclid*, which was revised and enlarged by S. L. Loney.

[53] A. Macfarlane, *Lectures on Ten British Mathematicians of the Nineteenth-Century* (New York, 1916), p. 136.

[54] An English edition of Todhunter's *Plane Coordinate Geometry* was used in High Schools in China. See Hu Mingjie, 'Merging Chinese and Western Mathematics: The Introduction of Algebra and the Calculus in China, 1859–1903', Doctoral Dissertation, Princeton University (1998). I am grateful to Andrea Breard of the Modern Chinese Scientific Terminologies Project, CNRS, Paris, for this information.

[55] Chinese translations were made of some of Todhunter's geometry textbooks but the details of the translations are not yet clear. They are the subject of current research by Andrea Breard (see Footnote 55).

[56] Between 1881 and 1885 at least eight of Todhunter's textbooks and four of his keys were translated into Japanese, probably as a result of the influence of Dairoku Kikuchi (see Footnote 36). It is not clear how much these translations were read or diffused since Japanese authors were also trying to write similar textbooks of their own, and some of the translators, such as Nagasawa Kinnosuke, were particularly active in producing their own original textbooks. I am grateful to Annick Horiuchi of the University of Paris for this information.

journals, as his publishers were keen to point out. Typical is the following review taken from the *Architect's Journal*, which appeared in the publisher's advertisement included in the first edition of Todhunter's *Integral Calculus* (1857):

> One of the most satisfactory evidences of the advancement of education in Cambridge, is the recent improvements of the University Class-Books. The perspicuous language, rigorous investigation, conscientious scrutiny of difficulties; and methodical treatment which characterise Mr Todhunter's works, entitles him to a large share of the honour of that improvement.

Todhunter kept a continual eye on his works, and much of his time was spent correcting and improving successive editions. He also welcomed comments and criticisms from other teachers and mathematicians, for, as he observed in a letter to Thomas Archer Hirst, 'the remarks and corrections of those who are engaged in mathematical teaching are the best aides that can be obtained in revising and improving textbooks'.[57]

Hirst's comments on Todhunter's *Algebra* form, in fact, an interesting example of a clash between traditional British mathematical values, derived in great measure from Euler's *Algebra*, and the new Continental styles which Hirst, one of the most internationally-minded English mathematicians of his generation, will have absorbed during his education in Germany. In 1869 Hirst noted in his journal that he had met Todhunter at the Council of the Royal Astronomical Society and 'mentioned to him an error in his algebra (his proof of the converging of the binomial series does not hold when n is negative and numerically greater than 1)'. He continued 'Todhunter as De Morgan's distinguished pupil ought to be strong in the subject of convergency; yet he has allowed 4 editions of his Algebra to issue with a logically false demonstration of an important theorem.'[58]

One person who did rather more than send Todhunter improvements and corrections was his former student John Sephton, 5th wrangler in 1862. In the mid-1870s Sephton, who was then Headmaster of the Liverpool Institute,[59] helped with the original editing of Todhunter's final two textbooks, *An Elementary Treatise on Laplace's Functions, Lamé's Functions and Bessel's Functions* (1875) and *Natural Philosophy for Beginners* (1877). Todhunter's letters to Sephton give a good indication of his editing style. Details are picked over at length, and

---

[57] Letter from Todhunter to Hirst, 6 April 1861. LMS Papers, University College, London. Todhunter was writing to Hirst to thank him for his 'valuable corrections' to his *Algebra*. As another example, on 25 November 1862 Airy wrote to Todhunter with comments on his *Euclid*. Cambridge University Library, RGO 6/436.

[58] William H. Brock and Roy M. McLeod, *Natural Knowledge in a Scientific Context: The Journals of Thomas Archer Hirst FRS*, Mansell (1980), f. 1842 (dated 12 March 1869). The point at issue was Todhunter's discussion of the binomial theorem for any exponent, which appears in the first edition of Todhunter's *Algebra*, pp. 285–95 and which Todhunter attributes to Euler.

[59] John Sephton (1837–1915) was Headmaster of the Liverpool Institute from 1866 to 1879, and later Reader in Icelandic Studies at University College, Liverpool.

typical amongst the minutiae he discussed were the merits of having woodcuts printed in Paris as opposed to in London.[60] Clarity was an issue to which Todhunter attached great importance.

Todhunter's books, which were used for private study as well as in the classroom, provided for a range of students – from schoolboys to final year undergraduates. Schoolmasters appreciated them and with their recommendations the sales escalated – the total British sales for his *Algebra* exceeded 150,000 copies, those for his *Euclid* exceeded 500,000 copies, while those for his *Algebra for Beginners* reached nearly 600,000 copies.[61] The books also feature prominently in the articles on the Mathematical Tripos contained in the nineteenth-century editions of the *Student's Guide to the University of Cambridge*, from Campion's in 1863 to Besant's in 1893, with twelve of Todhunter's books being included in the latter's list of useful reading. And it was not only in Cambridge that his books were recommended. The Universities in Manchester, Leeds, Liverpool, Edinburgh and Bristol all listed them as course texts well into the twentieth-century. Although Todhunter's books were not the only ones recommended by schools and universities, the scale of Todhunter's enterprise singles him out from the other authors of his time. No one else in Britain in the second half of the nineteenth-century wrote so many mathematics textbooks on such a range of subjects, and no one else achieved such a high volume of sales. What was it about Todhunter's books that made them so successful? And, given his other interests, how did he manage to write so many of them?

Todhunter's views on teaching and on textbooks

When Todhunter went up to Cambridge he not only had had the good fortune to have been taught by De Morgan, renowned as one of the best teachers of the period, but he had also spent several years as a schoolmaster. He was therefore well placed as an undergraduate to notice inadequacies or deficiencies in the teaching and/or the recommended texts. Add to this the fact that after his graduation Todhunter went immediately into university teaching, both as a college lecturer and as a private tutor. Thus, when, in the early 1850s, he emerged as a textbook writer he had already had considerable experience of the three key textbook markets: schools, colleges and private pupils.

Over the years Todhunter developed firm and well-honed views on educational practice and these became widely known through *The Conflict of Studies* (1873), a collection of six essays in which he chronicled his ideas.[62] This publication, which appeared towards the end of his textbook writing career, gives many insights into his pedagogical philosophy. It emerged at a time when

---

[60] Letter from Todhunter to Sephton dated 8 December 1877. SJCA.
[61] Cambridge University Archives, CUP 17/1–17/7.
[62] The six essays are entitled: The Conflict of Studies, Competitive Examinations, Private Study of Mathematics, Academical Reform, Elementary Geometry, and The Mathematical Tripos.

the air was thick with proposals for reform in mathematics education – the Association for the Improvement of Geometrical Teaching (AIGT) had been formed in 1871 and was campaigning strongly against the predominance of Euclid. But Todhunter, although in principle not antipathetic to the AIGT, in practice was unsympathetic to the new ideas and a staunch defender of the status quo. In his essay on 'Elementary Geometry' Todhunter argued for the retention of Euclid in its central position in mathematics courses and in support of its place as the elementary textbook for geometry.[63] His opinions, which were borne out of a long experience of teaching and examining combined with knowledge gleaned from reactions to his books, were not without substance. The robust state of English mathematics, as he saw it, attested to the suitability of Euclid for the purpose for which it was used. In drawing attention to different understandings of the word 'geometry', he emphasised the distinction between the supporters of Euclid, who valued the process of reasoning more highly than the results, and the reformers for whom the facts were more important than the rigour of the method. Although he acknowledged the possibility that a better geometry book than Euclid could exist, he was adamant that the superiority to Euclid had to be established by indisputable evidence and not by

> the author's own estimation, . . .; not by the hasty prediction of some anonymous and irresponsible reviewer; not by the authority of eminent men unless the eminence is founded on mathematical attainments; not even by the verdict of teachers who are not conspicuous for the success of their pupils. The decision must rest with students, teachers, and examiners, of considerable reputation in the range of mathematical sciences.[64]

The debate over Euclid also prompted Todhunter to take issue with Tait, his former student who since 1860 had held the chair of Natural Philosophy at the University of Edinburgh and who had expressed a contrary view in an address to the British Association in 1871.[65] Todhunter did not waste the opportunity to remind 'the justly celebrated professor' that he himself had been trained by exercises in Euclid and that 'twenty years ago his solutions of mathematical problems were rich with the fragrance of Greek geometry'.

In the essay entitled 'The Conflict of Studies', Todhunter gave voice to his scepticism about the educational value of students carrying out experimentation. He wrote:

---

[63] Todhunter's essay was written as a critical response to the arguments articulated by the opponents of Euclid, in particular those expressed in the preface of J. M. Wilson, *Elementary Geometry*, Macmillan (1868). Extracts from De Morgan's review of Wilson's book, together with extracts from Todhunter's essay were reprinted as an appendix in C. Dodgson, *Euclid and His Modern Rivals* (1879). The role of Wilson as a mathematics educator is discussed in A. G. Howson, *A History of Mathematics Education in Britain* (Cambridge, 1982), pp. 123–40.
[64] *The Conflict of Studies*, pp. 171–172.
[65] Todhunter did not name Tait but included a quotation from which he can be identified, *The Conflict of Studies*, p. 143. See P. G. Tait, 'Presidential Address. Section A', *Report of the British Association for the Advancement of Science* (1871), pp. 3–4.

If he [a boy] does not believe the statements of his tutor – probably a clergyman of mature knowledge, recognised ability, and blameless character – his suspicion is irrational, and manifests a want of the power of appreciating evidence, a want fatal to his success in that branch of science which he is supposed to be cultivating.[66]

Several other passages of a similar tenor followed. That Todhunter felt so strongly about excluding experimental science from the Cambridge educational process was due to the inherent difficulties he saw it presenting with regard to examinations. As a subject it simply did not fit in with his ideas about assessment.[67] However he was writing at a time when the idea of using laboratories for the teaching of students was still relatively new, at least in Cambridge. The Cavendish was still under construction and would not be open for another year and Maxwell, only recently appointed, was lecturing in a borrowed room. Nevertheless, Todhunter was swimming against the tide and Tait, who had had his own physical laboratory in Edinburgh since 1868, was so irked by Todhunter's opinion that he publicly protested against it.[68] Such was Todhunter's distaste for the practical that his name became almost a synonym for formalism. William Thomson once retorted, when he had asked what the symbol $\frac{dx}{dt}$ represented and had received the answer that it was the $\lim (\Delta t \to 0)\frac{\Delta x}{\Delta t}$: 'That's what Todhunter would say. Does nobody know that it represents a velocity?'[69]

When it came to the subject of textbooks, Todhunter was on surer ground. His observations were wide-ranging, thought-provoking, and sometimes unexpected:

[66] *The Conflict of Studies*, p. 17. In connection with Todhunter's dismissive attitude towards practical work, Todhunter apparently refused to view Maxwell's experiments on conical refractions on the grounds that having taught conical refractions in physical optics for many years he might find the experience upsetting. W. F. Bushell, 'Cambridge Mathematical Tripos', p. 173. The account of Todhunter's reluctance to view experiments might be thought to have some resonance with the story mentioned earlier in the text concerning Todhunter's reason for not viewing boat races, although balanced against this is the fact that Todhunter was known not to hold great store for those he described as 'watermen'. *The Conflict of Studies*, p. 131. Macfarlane suggests that Todhunter's lack of faith with regard to experiments may have resulted from his own experience of experiments at the hands of Sylvester. Macfarlane, *Lectures*, p. 141.

[67] In *The Conflict of Studies* Todhunter wrote extensively about the pros and cons of examinations in general, and on the Mathematical Tripos in particular. He believed that certain subjects, namely mathematics and classics, were suitable for examination on the grounds that it was not only possible to compare with accuracy the relative performance of students, but also that they were subjects in which their most valuable aspects could be tested. In contrast, as far as history was concerned, while he believed it to be an important and instructive subject, he doubted that it was a satisfactory one for examination since, in his opinion, it only tested the receptivity of the student and not the ability to judge or compare. In the case of the experimental sciences, his experience was that 'nothing is so hopelessly worthless as the products of examinations. Nowhere else is the proportion of what is intelligible and true to what is absurd and false so small.' *The Conflict of Studies*, p. 8.

[68] P. G. Tait, 'Todhunter on Experimental Illustrations', *Nature*, Vol. 9 (26 February 1874), p. 323.

[69] I. B. Hart, *Makers of Science* (London, 1923), pp. 278–9.

> It may seem paradoxical to complain of the merits of textbooks, but yet it may be doubted whether by improving the accuracy and extending the range of our explanatory treatises, we increase the value of mathematics as a discipline.[70]

In Todhunter's view, textbooks could reach such a state of perfection that students would be deterred from thinking and exploring for themselves and the textbook's objective would be destroyed. He commented extensively on the use of textbooks in the private study of mathematics, and did not fight shy of hinting at the benefits of purchasing his own texts:

> Practically the study of illustrative mathematics will usually commence with Algebra. I assume the beginner is fortunate in the textbook which he selects; that he will procure one which has the advantage of proceeding from an author of some scientific reputation. . . . It is obvious that a writer who is himself familiar with mathematical science will be able in writing an elementary book to make provision for the future advantage of his readers, which cannot be supplied by one who himself scarcely proceeded beyond the range of that book.[71]

For Todhunter scrupulous investigation of the text was of paramount importance and he emphasised the necessity for the textbook to be well arranged in separate independent chapters.[72] He also had clear ideas about the order in which the various branches of mathematics should be studied. Algebra should be taken first, followed by plane trigonometry and then plane co-ordinate geometry, while a discussion of the modern methods of abridged notation should be left until the student had made a reasonable acquaintance with the differential and integral calculus, and analytical mechanics.

With regard to examples, Todhunter was almost dismissive about their role in such texts – understanding the text was the prime concern – and he questioned the time and effort spent on the construction of lavish problems for examination purposes. Nevertheless, he did include a considerable number of examples in his own texts. Many of these he devised himself but others were selected others from various college and university examination papers. In the case of examination questions, he was careful to preserve the original wording of the authors so that students could be exposed to a variety of types of questioning. In any case, he considered it presumptuous to change (or rather think to improve) another mathematician's questions.[73] It is evident that Todhunter thought carefully about his audience when writing his books: in both the titles and prefaces he made it clear for whom they were intended. Although mostly aimed at the elementary level, some, such as his *Treatise on Laplace's Functions*, which he

---

[70] *The Conflict of Studies*, p. 27.
[71] *The Conflict of Studies*, p. 67.
[72] *The Conflict of Studies*, p. 68.
[73] *The Conflict of Studies*, p. 79.

wrote as a continuation of his books on the differential and integral calculus, were written for the more advanced student.

Todhunter's *Euclid*

Euclid's *Elements* is one of the most frequently printed books in history – probably second only to the Bible – and during the first 50 years of the nineteenth century more than 200 editions were published in Britain alone.[74] By the mid-nineteenth century, the most popular of these British editions was the school edition of Robert Potts which first appeared in 1846, and of which by 1853 over 56,000 copies had been published.[75] Given that so many editions were available, why in 1862 did Todhunter, with nine textbooks already published and a proven ability to turn his hand to a wide variety of school and undergraduate mathematical topics, produce yet another Euclid rather than attend to some other less well worn subject?

In the first instance, it is significant that Todhunter was De Morgan's student and De Morgan was not only one of the leading supporters of Euclid but also a teacher whom Todhunter greatly admired.[76] Through De Morgan Todhunter had been inculcated with the advantages of Euclid at an early and critical stage in his mathematical career, and De Morgan's influence on him in this connection is evident in Todhunter's essay in *The Conflict of Studies*.[77] Euclid became a subject dear to Todhunter's heart and, given his own interest in teaching, it would have been remarkable if he had not had a very particular view as to how it should be taught. But what Todhunter also recognised was that each of the different editions of Euclid already on the shelves was essentially targeted at a particular group of students. Todhunter, having had experience of using Euclid with different types of students – at school and at university – realised that there was a need for an edition that could be used more flexibly than the editions currently available. In particular he saw that what was missing was a single text that a student could carry through from school to university. Potts had veered towards this idea by producing a shortened version of his Cambridge text that could be used by schools and which, unusually for a book of this type, appeared in editions printed on fine and on common paper, but he had not conceived of a single dual purpose volume.[78] In addition, Todhunter was already experienced at producing books of this sort. Two of his previous books – *Algebra* (1858) and *Plane Trigonometry* (1859) – had been written specifically for the use of both schools and colleges, and each had met with considerable success. He set out to emulate that success with an edition of Euclid that not only would

---

[74] Howson, *History*, p. 131.
[75] Potts' school edition was a shortened version of his university edition, which had been published the previous year. D. McKitterick, *A History of the Cambridge University Press*, Vol. II (Cambridge, 1998), pp. 358–359.
[76] *The Conflict of Studies*, p. 116.
[77] *The Conflict of Studies*, p. 146.
[78] McKitterick, *History*, p. 358.

embrace a wide audience but also (and importantly) would be accessible to beginners. In the preface, Todhunter outlined his strategy:

> It is important to exhibit the work in such a form as will assist them [young students] in overcoming the difficulties which they experience on their first introduction to processes of continuous argument. No method appears more useful as that of breaking up the demonstrations into their constituent parts.

Thus in Todhunter's *Euclid* each distinct assertion in the argument appears on a new line with the necessary references to the preceding principles on which the assertions depend being placed at the ends of the lines. Todhunter had learnt about this method of presentation from De Morgan who, thirty years earlier, had recommended the practice and used it as an exercise for students. The publication of the format was not new with Todhunter – it had first been used in 1726 by Henry Hill (with the formal approval of Edmund Halley),[79] but their versions are very different. In fact the model of presentation most closely followed by Todhunter was that devised by Koenig and Blassiere whose edition of *Euclid* was published in the Hague (in French) in 1762.

As far as the text is concerned, Todhunter's edition is based on that originally published by Robert Simson in 1756. Unlike Hill (and others after him), Simson did not abbreviate the text through the use of symbolic expressions but returned to a full text translation. Simson's edition, however, had the text for a particular demonstration running together, with the references to previous propositions in very small letters in the margin. Todhunter not only began each assertion on a new line but also used paragraphs to break down the longer demonstrations into subordinate parts. Todhunter also took particular care with the overall format of the volume and chose the type and paper to make the design as attractive as possible. He was especially particular over the diagrams, making them unusually large compared with those in contemporary editions – for example, the radius of a typical circle in Todhunter's edition is half as big again as the radius of a typical circle in Potts' edition. In fact, the scale of Todhunter's diagrams is more analogous to that found in Simson. Todhunter also revived the practice which had been adopted by Simson but which seems to have been ignored by others, of, where necessary, repeating the diagrams in order to ensure that they always appear besides the corresponding text. Todhunter's contemporaries admired his diagrams, and Charles Dodgson borrowed Todhunter's electrotypes to use in his own edition of *Euclid* published in 1879.[80]

---

[79] H. Hill, *The six first, together with the eleventh and twelfth books of Euclids elements, demonstrated after a new, plain and easie method* (London, 1726). See J. L. Heilbron, *Geometry Civilised* (Oxford, 1998), p. 75.

[80] C. L. Dodgson, *Euclid Books I, II*, 1879 (Macmillan). Letter from Dodgson to Todhunter dated 20 March 1876 (Todhunter manuscripts (Notes I), St John's College Archives). Dodgson shared with Todhunter a distaste for the modern movement away from Euclid and quoted extensively from *The Conflict of Studies* in his own book in defence of Euclid, *Euclid and his Modern Rivals* (London, 1879).

At the end of the text Todhunter included explanatory notes to help with some of the standard difficulties, and these notes relate exclusively to geometry – there are no developments involving algebra, arithmetic or logic. The non-geometric developments were excluded for the benefit of the less advanced students whom he believed would profit from being able to focus unhindered on geometry. The notes also contain extensive historical references, clearly exposing Todhunter's predilection for the history of the subject and the influence of De Morgan.[81] There is an Appendix of supplementary propositions, after which the text concludes with a collection of exercises. The exercises are divided into two parts: those of an elementary nature and those for examination practice. Todhunter's edition was not the first to include exercises but it appears to be the first to include elementary ones alongside more advanced ones. Many of the questions were taken from Cambridge college and university examination papers, although in contrast to Potts, Todhunter did not identify the precise sources.

Todhunter's *Euclid* was a success on several counts. It was clearly set out, both with regard to text and illustrations, and it contained useful notes and references, together with appropriate collections of exercises. It certainly fulfilled his own desiderata for textbooks as enunciated in the *Conflict of Studies*. And not only did its content appeal to a wide constituency but at 3s. 6d. (equivalent to 17.5p in decimal coinage) it was the cheapest of his books not written exclusively for beginners,[82] and so was financially accessible as well. Furthermore, it was attractive not only to English readers. It was translated into Urdu in 1871, into Japanese in 1883 and a special edition was also prepared for the use of Indian schools (1877). In English it ran into more than twenty editions, the last one appearing as recently as 1932, with a reprint in 1955. Thomas Heath, who wrote the introduction to the 1932 edition, praised Todhunter's Notes for being 'admirably concise and to the point'.[83] It is to Todhunter's credit that Heath left Todhunter's edition almost unaltered. The only changes he made were to include three propositions that Todhunter had chosen to omit and to correct one minor error.

---

[81] Rice, 'Augustus De Morgan'.
[82] The prices for Todhunter's books are listed in *Macmillan's Bibliographic Catalogue 1843–1889*, Macmillan (1891), p. 699. The prices range from 2s. 6d (12.5p) for some of Todhunter's most elementary books, e.g. *Algebra for Beginners*, to 10s. 6d (52.5p) for the more advanced texts such as *Differential Calculus, Integral Calculus* and *Analytical Statics*, and the *Key to the Algebra for the use of Colleges and Schools*. Several, including *Algebra for the use of Colleges and Schools*, were priced at 7s. 6d. (37.5p). His histories were more expensive, e.g., *A History of the Mathematical Theory of Probability* was priced at 18s. (90p) while the two volume *History of the Mathematical Theories of Attraction* was priced at 24s. (£1 20p).
[83] *The Elements of Euclid* (with an introduction by Sir Thomas L Heath) (London, 1932), Vol. 9. This edition formed part of the Everyman Library series.

Todhunter's *Algebra*

Todhunter's *Algebra for the use of Colleges and Schools*, which was first published in 1858, was also immensely popular, running into at least sixteen English editions, with translations in Urdu and Italian published in 1871, and a translation into Japanese published in 1883. Clarity of exposition without loss of accuracy was Todhunter's aim, and he succeeded. However, unlike Euclid's *Elements* where each Book depends explicitly on the contents of a previous Book (or Books), the topics of elementary algebra are mostly self-contained and Todhunter, by making as far as possible each chapter independent, used this feature to advantage. Organising the book in this way made it attractive both to students studying alone – difficulties in one chapter did not preclude advancement to the next – and to teachers who could choose their own route through the material. By taking care over the structure of the book Todhunter effectively ensured the maximum base for his readership.

The *Algebra* contains numerous examples to work through, and despite what Todhunter would later say in the *Conflict of Studies* about examples in general, he included even more in subsequent editions. By the time of the fifth edition of 1870, the book contained more than 2,000 examples, including 300 new miscellaneous ones at the end of the text. Thus although Todhunter may not have believed in the educational necessity of numerous examples, he recognised that they were an essential ingredient if a textbook was to be successful in the examination-ridden undergraduate market. However, although the book was to prove exceptionally popular, when it first came off the press Todhunter had to contend with at least two dissenting voices. The first of these belonged to Archibald Sandeman, Professor of Mathematics and Natural Philosophy at Owen's College, Manchester. On 1 May 1858 Sandeman wrote:

> Let me say freely that I am sorry to find you repeating what I cannot but think the same old confusions and errors

concluding,

> ... your book I think is likely to be popular and think it therefore the more important to draw attention to what in my opinion are serious blemishes. You have the satisfaction however of having the world on your side – since there is no book (so far as I know) lately published which does not contain errors quite as bad or worse.[84]

The errors to which Sandeman referred concerned arithmetical algebra and were founded upon what he considered to be Todhunter's imprecise use of language. For example, he censured Todhunter for not distinguishing between the terms *multiplier* and *multiplicand*. However, Todhunter appears to have been unmoved by Sandeman's comments since he made no attempt to take account

---

[84] Letter from Sandeman to Todhunter. Todhunter manuscripts (Notes I), St John's College Archives.

of them in his second edition. Nevertheless, it is curious that Sandeman's letter was one of very few that Todhunter retained amongst his notes.

The voice of the second dissenter was rather louder. It belonged to Thomas Lund, a clergyman from Alfreton, Derbyshire, author of four elementary mathematics textbooks and editor of the eleventh edition of Wood's *Algebra* (1841).[85] On the 18 June 1858 Lund, in a flysheet entitled *An Exposure of a recent attempt at Book-Making in the University of Cambridge*,[86] published a scathing attack on Todhunter. In it he accused Todhunter, in extremely colourful terms, of plagiarising Wood's *Algebra*. According to Lund, Todhunter was guilty of a plagiarism, 'grosser and more barefaced than any which had been perpetrated in modern times'. It was, he said, a 'glaring act of literary pilfering', adding that while 'Colleges and Schools, doubtless require to be taught algebra, but not less forsooth, honesty and fair-dealing; and I trust we are not come to that pass that colleges and schools will knowingly encourage the sale of stolen goods.' He concluded by listing extracts from the two books side by side, which showed beyond doubt that Todhunter had indeed 'borrowed' from Wood. Both the text and the examples exhibit great similarity. Todhunter had not even bothered to change the numbers or type of objects used in the examples — the numbers of oxen bought and sold remain the same. Todhunter had certainly used Wood and he had made no attempt at disguise.

Less than a month later Todhunter published his reply, also in a flysheet.[87] In the face of such an attack, it is no surprise that Todhunter responded so quickly. However, Todhunter claimed that his reply was prompted more by the fact that the *Cambridge Chronicle* (i.e. the local newspaper) had seen fit to draw attention to the charge — they had included a quotation from Lund's fly-sheet[88] — than by the existence of the fly-sheet itself. In his defence Todhunter reiterated the point, which Lund had himself reluctantly admitted, that the 'legal copyright of Dr Wood's matter' had expired and consequently he had the right to use the material.[89] In other words, Lund's argument was a moral one, not a legal one. And indeed the real nub of Lund's complaint was not that Todhunter had made use of Wood but that Todhunter had made no acknowledgement to Wood. In addition, Todhunter had further aggravated the situation by including on his title page 'right of translation is reserved'. Todhunter cleverly turned the former point to his own favour by declaring that not only did he believe Wood's work to

---

[85] J. Wood, *The Elements of Algebra* (Cambridge, 1795).
[86] T. Lund, *An Exposure of a Recent Attempt at Book-making in the University of Cambridge* (London, 1858). British Library, 8529 ee 25. No copies of the flysheet have so far come to light in Cambridge.
[87] I. Todhunter, *Answer to Mr Lund's Attack on Mr Todhunter*, 15 July 1858. Cambridge University Library, Cam.d.858.2.
[88] *Cambridge Chronicle*, 10 July 1858, p. 4.
[89] According to the Literary Copyright Act of 1842, the copyright in every book published in the life of an author endured for the life of that author and for seven years after his/her death or for forty-two years, if longer, and was the property of the author and his/her assignees. See, Copyright, The Encyclopaedia Britannica, 7, 11th edition (1910–1911).

be so well known that such an acknowledgement was unnecessary but that the real reason he had not included one was out of consideration for Lund. Or, as he put it, because he did not wish to 'appropriate himself, at Mr Lund's expense, the advantage which would arise from the use of such a well known name'. Despite the fact that Todhunter had taken pains to justify his lack of acknowledgement to Wood, he did agree to include one in subsequent editions. The preface to the 2nd edition published two years later in 1860 states clearly which parts of Wood he used, and, perhaps to forestall further complaints, it also included the declaration that 'Dr Wood's Algebra has been so long published that it has become public property'. Added to which he also included a detailed account of the other sources from which the book had been derived. To ameliorate the situation still further, Todhunter also mentioned that he had even had occasion to consult Lund's edition, but that he had taken extreme care to avoid trespassing upon the work! However, the latter comment was excised from later editions, suggesting perhaps that Todhunter wished to expunge as far possible any direct reminder of the affair. From the tone of Todhunter's reply and the revisions to the preface, it is clear that Lund's attack unsettled Todhunter. Nevertheless, given that Todhunter did not hesitate to include acknowledgements in his earlier works, and despite the skill of his defence, there seems no real reason why he should have foregone the practice on this occasion. The dispute was certainly a local event, although to what extent it affected his personal reputation or resonated around Cambridge is not clear. There was no hint of it during the course of Todhunter's employment negotiations with St John's in 1859, but it is of course conceivable that it counted against him. It was not mentioned in any of his obituaries, although Venn, Todhunter's former student, alludes to it later. However, Venn seems to have been aware only of Lund's attack and not Todhunter's defence.[90]

Whether Lund was appeased or not by Todhunter's concessions in the second edition is not known, but doubtless he would have been interested in a story that surfaced several years later in which it was revealed that Todhunter himself had been the victim of copyright malpractice. In 1883 it was reported that a company in Tokyo, The Tokio Bookselling Company, had taken up pirating English and American schoolbooks, and that a number of Todhunter's works, including *Elementary Algebra* and *Euclid*, had fallen prey to their unscrupulous behaviour. According to the report,

> Todhunter's Algebra shows letters upside down, wrong fount letters, letters misplaced, and words improperly spelt, testifying to the slovenly way in which the books have been printed. There is said to be scarcely a page in the book which does not contain one or more errors in orthography, and the mathematical formulae, which always require

---

[90] J. A. Venn, 'Isaac Todhunter', *Alumni Cantabrigienses, 1752–1900*, 6 Vols (Cambridge, 1940–1954).

such care at the publishers' hands, must be in a bad state when ordinary words are so neglected.[91]

As described, the pirated edition would appear to be of limited use; nevertheless, the fact that the Tokio Bookselling Company considered Todhunter's books worth copying illegally provides further evidence of the books' popularity and reputation.[92]

Todhunter's output

Lund's accusation of plagiarism provides, in part, an explanation for how Todhunter achieved his prodigious output. In essence, many of Todhunter's textbooks contained little by way of original content. Not only is there is a limit to the number of topics that can be included in an elementary level mathematics text but also, as Todhunter himself observed, 'Originality however in an elementary work is rarely an advantage'.[93] As Todhunter recognised, what was important, and indeed what determined the success of a textbook, was the way that its content was presented. In his very first textbook, *A Treatise on the Differential Calculus* (1852), Todhunter had openly used existing material. In this instance his objective had been to produce a work of 'utility' and consequently he 'had not hesitated to avail himself of existing elementary works', and he had included a list of those that he had used.

Todhunter therefore did not spend time creating new material when the requirement was for a reworking or representation of old. His talents were expository rather than creative, and, in particular, he understood the importance of writing well and clearly for those just starting in the subject. As Edward Routh, arguably the most successful of the Cambridge coaches, wrote,

> [Todhunter] gives in his books a clear statement of the well-known principles of each subject, arranged in logical order. Each step in the argument is explained at length in clear English. Nothing is assumed but what a reader should know. Every page makes it evident how thoroughly he was keeping in mind that he was writing for beginners.[94]

Todhunter's somewhat utilitarian approach to textbook writing was extremely efficient and naturally encouraged by his publishers, Macmillan & Co. But not everyone had the same attitude towards the recycling of texts. Apart from his *Algebra*, another of Todhunter's books that raised some hackles was his *Treatise on Analytical Statics* (1853). In the preface of this book Todhunter had written:

---

[91] Anon, 'Literary Piracy in Japan', *Nature*, 28 (10 May 1883), p. 43.
[92] It is not clear for whom these pirated editions were intended, i.e., whether they were produced to satisfy a local demand or, as seems more likely, they were produced for export, but it is a question which warrants further research.
[93] I. Todhunter, *Algebra for the Use of Colleges and School*, 2nd edn, pp. vii–viii.
[94] E. J. Routh, 'Isaac Todhunter', *Monthly Notices of the Royal Astronomical Society*, Vol. xlv (1884), pp. 194–9.

> I have made considerable use of Mr Pratt's *Treatise on Mechanical Philosophy* [1836], which was placed at my disposal by the Publishers. Mr Pratt's *Treatise* is now nearly out of print, and the present work may be regarded as a republication, with large additions, of that portion of it which treats of Statics. I am requested by the Publishers to state that it is probable that the remaining portions of Mr Pratt's Treatise will be republished at some future time, with such additions and improvements that may seem useful.

At first glance, it might be thought that Pratt would be pleased that Todhunter had had a sufficiently high opinion of his book to want to use it. However, the preface to Pratt's *Treatise of Attractions* (1860)[95] tells a different story:

> This treatise is in part a reproduction of those parts of my work on Mechanical Philosophy which treated attractions, Laplace's functions, and the figure of the earth. I have frequently regretted having parted with the copyright of that work, as the leading object I had in view in first presenting it to the University has been entirely defeated since the transfer, by the appearance of separate treatises in its place instead of a new edition in one volume. Had I retained the work I should have published a 3rd edition of the whole in its original form, with the improvements which further reading and further thought would have suggested.
> My object in publishing the work was, to comprise in one view and in one volume a complete course of Mechanical Philosophy, leading the student from elementary mechanical principles to the highest branches of the mechanism of the heavens. I conceived that by the uniformity of the system which a single treatise could ensure, students might be assisted in reading higher in these subjects than they had been accustomed to do, without any additional kind of labour. In the present treatise I have become myself an accomplice against my own design as at first conceived, by devoting a separate volume to the republication, with considerable additions and improvements, of one part only of the original work. The disappearance of the Mechanical Philosophy has removed from the student – at any rate for the present, as no other work has appeared at Cambridge to supply the want – one subject of great importance and high interest which that work first introduced into the University – I mean Laplace's coefficients and functions and the calculation of the figure of the earth by means of his remarkable analysis.

It is clear that Todhunter had not deliberately set out to ruin Pratt's design, and in any case Pratt, by disposing of the copyright (for reasons he does not explain, although presumably financial), was essentially the author of his own misfortune. Nevertheless, it is hard not to feel some sympathy for Pratt. In

---

[95] J. H. Pratt, *A Treatise on Attractions, Laplace's Functions, and the Figure of the Earth* (London, 1860).

signing away the copyright it appears not to have occurred to him that large portions of his work could be republished under the name of another author. In any case, there was an eleven-year interval between the publication of the second edition of Pratt's original treatise (which appeared in 1842) and Todhunter's book, time enough for Pratt to produce his promised third edition. The publication of Todhunter's book was clearly an expedient decision on the part of the publisher – although only at the beginning of his career, Todhunter was already showing greater promise as a textbook author than Pratt – and it was a decision that served well. Todhunter's book eventually ran into several editions.

Writing textbooks was clearly rewarding for Todhunter, both financially and otherwise. While the enormous number of books published speaks for itself, *The Conflict of Studies* reveals his concern with educational practice. The work involved in writing and constantly revising the textbooks (as well as in compiling the histories) was substantial and explains why he found little time to engage in strictly mathematical research. Todhunter recognised his skill as an educator and used it to advantage. He was an able teacher who saw deficiencies in existing texts and determined to remedy them. His teaching at school and at university, combined with his private tutoring, gave him the necessary experience to write for a wide-ranging constituency. He was also a more than competent mathematician, as his histories and his Adams prize essay attest. Combine with this fluency with language, an eye for design, and a character obsessed with detail, and the result is the most successful British author of mathematical textbooks of the second half of the nineteenth century.

Todhunter's Publications

Mathematical Papers

1. 'On the Method of Least Squares', *Philosophical Magazine*, Vol. xxx (1865), p. 378; *Transactions of the Cambridge Philosophical Society*, Vol. xi (2) (1869), pp. 219–38.
2. 'Note on a Paper by Balfour Stewart on a Proposition in the Theory of Numbers', *Proceedings of the Royal Society of Edinburgh* (1866), pp. 517–18.
3. 'Property of a Regular Polyhedron', *Messenger of Mathematics*, Vol. iii (1866), pp. 142–4.
4. 'On a Problem in the Calculus of Variations', *Philosophical Magazine*, Vol xxxi (1866), pp. 425–7; xxxii (1866), pp. 199–205; xlii (1871), pp. 440–1.
5. 'On the Method of Demonstrating some Problems in Dynamics', *Proceedings of the Cambridge Philosophical Society*, Vol. ii (1866), pp. 16–18.
6. 'On Jacobi's Theorem Respecting the Relative Equilibrium of a Revolving Ellipsoid of Fluid, and on Ivory's Discussion of the Theorem', *Proceedings of the Royal Society*, Vol. xix (1871), pp. 42–56.

7. 'On Proposition 38 of the Third Book of Newton's *Principia*', *Monthly Notices of the Royal Astronomical Society*, Vol xxxii (1872), pp. 234–6.
8. 'Note Relating to the Attraction of Spheroids', *Proceedings of the Royal Society*, Vol. xx (1872), pp. 507–13.
9. 'On the Arc of the Meridian Measured in South Africa', *Monthly Notices of the Royal Astronomical Society*, Vol. xxxiii (1873), pp. 27–34.
10. 'On the Arc of the Meridian Measured in Lapland', *Transactions of the Cambridge Philosophical Society*, Vol. xii (1) (1873), pp. 1–26.
11. 'On the Equation which Determines the Form of the Strata in Legendre's and Laplace's Theory of the Figure of the Earth', *Transactions of the Cambridge Philosophical Society*, Vol. xii (1) (1873), pp. 301–18.
12. 'Note on the History of Certain Formulae in Spherical Trigonometry', *Philosophical Magazine*, Vol. xlv (1873), pp. 98–100.
13. 'Note on an Erroneous Extension of Jacobi's Theorem', *Proceedings of the Royal Society*, Vol. xxi (1873), pp. 119–21.
14. 'Note on the Value of a Certain Definite Integral', *Proceedings of the Royal Society*, Vol. xxiii (1875), pp. 300–1.
15. 'Note on Legendre's Coefficients', *Proceedings of the Royal Society*, Vol. xxvii (1878), pp. 381–3.

Textbooks and Keys (all published by Macmillan, London)

1852 *Treatise on the Differential Calculus and the Elements of the Integral Calculus*
1853 *A Treatise on Analytical Statics*
1855 *A Treatise on Plane Coordinate Geometry*
1857 *A Treatise on the Integral Calculus and its Applications*
1858 *Algebra for the Use of Colleges and Schools*
1858 *Examples of Analytical Geometry in Three Dimensions*
1859 *Plane Trigonometry for the Use of Colleges and Schools*
1859 *Spherical Trigonometry*
1861 *An Elementary Treatise on the Theory of Equations*
1862 *The Elements of Euclid for the Use of Schools and Colleges*
1863 *Algebra for Beginners*
1866 *Trigonometry for Beginners*
1867 *Mechanics for Beginners*
1868 *Key to Algebra for Beginners*
1869 *Mensuration for Beginners*
1870 *Key to Algebra for the Use of Colleges and Schools*
1875 *An Elementary Treatise on Laplace's Functions, Lam's Functions and Bessel's Functions*
1877 *Natural Philosophy for Beginners* (2 parts)
1878 *Key to Mechanics for Beginners*
1879 *Key to Plane Trigonometry for the Use of Colleges and Schools*
1880 *Key to Exercises in Euclid*

Macmillan's Series of Textbooks for Indian Schools

1876 *An Abridged Mensuration with Numerous Examples for Indian Students*
1876 *Algebra for Indian Students*
1876 *The Elements of Euclid for the Use of Indian Schools*
1876 *Mensuration and Surveying for Beginners, adapted for Indian Schools*

Histories

1861 *A History of the Progress of the Calculus of Variations during the 19th century*, Macmillan
1865 *History of the Mathematical Theory of Probability from the Time of Pascal to that of Laplace*, Macmillan
1873 *History of the Mathematical Theories of Attraction and the Figure of the Earth from the Time of Newton to that of Laplace* (2 Vols), Macmillan
1886 *A History of the Theory of Elasticity and of the Strength of Materials from Galilei to the Present Time* (Karl Pearson, ed.), Cambridge University Press

Other Publications

1849 *The Doctrine of a Divine Providence is Inseparable from the Belief in the Existence of an Absolutely Perfect Creator: An Essay which Obtained the Burney Prize for the Year 1848*, J. Deighton
1865 *George Boole. A Treatise on Differential Equations: Supplementary Volume* (ed. Isaac Todhunter), Macmillan
1871 *Researches in the Calculus of Variations, principally on the Theory of Discontinuous Solutions. An Essay to which the Adams Prize was awarded in the University of Cambridge in 1871*, Macmillan
1873 *The Conflict of Studies, and other essays on subjects connected with Education*, Macmillan
1876 *William Whewell, DD: An Account of his Writings with Selections from his Literary and Scientific Correspondence*, Macmillan

ELISABETH LEEDHAM-GREEN

Afterword

The developments in teaching and in examining in nineteenth-century Cambridge described and discussed in this volume in so many telling ways, to say nothing of the admission of women, are traditionally, and very reasonably, seen as marking the stages by which the caterpillar university of the eighteenth century emerged from a chrysalis woven from strands of clinging Newtonian mathematics, of unchecked amateurism, of bachelorly self-interest and of more, or of less, decorous sloth, as a butterfly, its wings still somewhat crumpled but capable of bringing it, in 'honest idiocy of flight', to the stage where, with a startling leap in evolution, it could soar eagle-like into the empyrean realms of a world-class university. Such a view is both impressionistic and readily demonstrated by anecdote, but notwithstanding the apocalyptic utterances of the more reluctant Heads confronted by the Royal Commission of 1850–2, there was no one morning in which their butler, or a lesser men's gyp, awakened them with the announcement, 'Lovely morning, Sir, new universe', let alone 'new university'.

The statutes of most colleges after the reforms of the 1850s imposed an oath on the admission of Fellows to promote the welfare of the college as a place of 'religion, learning, education and research'. The first element has now been largely dropped, but the prospect of the disappearance of religion would have appalled most inmates of the nineteenth-century university, and this notwithstanding the gradual attrition of religious tests, both before and after the Test Act of 1870. Non-Christians were assumed to be devout followers of their own religion, and even the declared agnostics were assumed to be devout in their agnosticism. These assumptions were probably in many cases false, but the fact remains that, notwithstanding protests at compulsory chapel-attendance, the vast majority of the members of the University were practising members of the Church of England and as such, perhaps, even if unconsciously, the more unwilling to contemplate radical upheavals in an institution which had been so closely associated with the established church for so many centuries. From the 1830s a high church revival was manifested in several colleges, with results still visible today in some of their chapels.[1] Nor were the supporters of the religious

[1] See for example, John Twigg, *A History of Queens' College, Cambridge, 1448–1986* (Woodbridge, and Wolfeboro, New Hampshire, 1987), pp. 721 ff.

status quo impervious to reforming movements in the more whiggish sense: on the one hand there was broad support for the Voluntary Theological Examination introduced by Whewell in 1842, which aimed to ensure that graduates destined for the priesthood were not totally devoid of theological expertise, and on the other, the century witnessed an enthusiastic following of the movements, many of them originating in the previous century, to spread the gospel both overseas and in the poorer quarters of the wildly expanding cities of industrial Britain. The bible societies were strongly supported, universities throughout the empire and beyond were endowed, sometimes copiously, with the products of the University press, and sums were regularly voted by the Regent House for the building or re-building of churches overseas and the support of missions at home and abroad.

Support for protestants overseas had been a feature of the University's charitable endeavours since the seventeenth century, and the cynical might observe that the bible societies had, since the introduction of stereotype enabled the Press to produce bibles far more cheaply than before, provided very lucrative business for it, but the involvement of many members of the University in charitable endeavours in the second half of the eighteenth century and the first half of the nineteenth witnesses to an engagement with the 'real world' which is less easily demonstrable for earlier periods. To cite only one example: the University contributed from the chest 20 guineas annually to Addenbrooke's hospital from 1766 to 1794, while a great number of resident members organised or supported a host of bazaars, concerts, and so on to raise funds. At least until John Bowtell's munificent bequest in 1813, Addenbrooke's was funded almost entirely by corporate or individual donations from the University.[2]

At the same time there was vigorous opposition to subscription on graduation. This movement indeed dates from at least 1766, when Francis Blackburne published his *Confessional, or a full and free inquiry into the right, utility and success of establishing confessions of faith and doctrine in protestant churches*, written some years earlier. Two petitions from undergraduates against subscription followed in 1771, and some two hundred persons signed the Feathers Petition to Parliament the next year. 1772 also saw ten graces proposed by Robert Tyrwhitt for the abolition of subscription for each of the degrees conferred by the University; all were rejected by the non-regent house, those for degrees in divinity by massive majorities, but those for degrees in music by fourteen votes only, and that for the BA by an agonising eight votes only.[3] Faced with the threat of Sir William Meredith bringing a bill before parliament the University introduced a somewhat risible emendation to the subscription oath for BAs who now, rather than subscribing to the thirty-nine articles, were to declare that they were *bona fide*

---

[2] For a detailed account of religion in Cambridge in the late 18th century and the greater part of the 19th, see Peter Searby, *A history of the University of Cambridge, vol. 3, 1750–1870* (Cambridge, 1997), ch. 7 to 10.
[3] For a full account of these excitements see D. A. Winstanley, *Unreformed Cambridge* (Cambridge, 1935), pp. 310 ff.

members of the Church of England. Three years later Edmund Law published his *Considerations on the Propriety of requiring Subscription to Articles of Faith*, which was attacked by Dr Randolph of Oxford and defended by 'A friend of religious liberty', probably William Paley. 1786 witnessed Ely Bates' *Chinese Fragment* and 1787 a further grace against subscription, proposed by Thomas Edwards, which was vetoed in the Caput and provoked in 1789 from the young George Dyer a pamphlet entitled *An inquiry into the nature of subscription to the 39 articles*, published anonymously at St Ives. A second edition appeared in 1792, along with William Frend's *Thoughts on Subscription to religious tests . . . in a letter to the Rev. H. W Coulthurst.*

The arguments against subscription are rehearsed at length in the nineteenth century by an older, and, by all accounts, grubbier, George Dyer both in the 'Dissertations' appended to the first volume of his *Privileges of the University of Cambridge* (London, 1824) and, more fully, in the *Dissertatio generalis, sive epistola literaria viris academicis, praecipue Cantabrigiae commorantibus, humillime oblata*, prefixed to the second volume (pp. i–clxviii). The arguments from conscience he barely troubles to rehearse. He demolishes the forged charters of the University, inveighs against James VI and I as the introducer of subscription, as acting on royal prerogative alone, without the endorsement of parliament; he argues that the Elizabeth statutes, still governing the University, are in many respects obsolete. MAs swearing to serve their 'regency' do not know what that implied, and the syllabus is absurd – had the statutes postdated Descartes, for instance, Cartesian philosophy would be *de rigueur*, which would be even more eccentric than the Aristotelean system still embalmed in the 1570 statutes. He fulminates also against the Caput, constituted as it was such that a single member could prevent any motion from being put to the Regent House; he infers that such a single member, perhaps hoping for promotion from a minister of the crown, was perhaps responsible for the stopping of Thomas Edwards' grace. All this with copious citation of sources as diverse as Erasmus and Blackstone, Cicero and Nemesius, and, more predictably, Locke and Mansfield. The opening of the *Dissertatio generalis* is, however, devoted to eloquent defences of the studies of classics and of mathematics.

Dyer was, of course, a Unitarian, and the acute reader will have observed that most of those named above as warriors in the same army, were, or were to become, of the same persuasion, Bishop Law being a doubtful exception. There is, however, one name not yet mentioned, that of the staunch supporter of Tyrwhitt, John Jebb. He alone, of those who fought for a reformation of the University's statutes, argued passionately for a reform not only of the constitution of the University, including the imposition of religious tests, but also of both the syllabus and the conduct of university examinations. To him we shall return, but for the present I pass over 'education' to consider very briefly the state of 'learning and research' in the early years of the nineteenth century. The two terms were not, and are not, interchangeable, and the notion that one relates to the arts and the other to the sciences, is but superficial, but since this is no place to attempt anything like a comprehensive survey of either learning or research in the period I make bold to use them both together as an umbrella beneath which a number of exemplary figures may be sheltered from the general obloquy of reaction and idleness.

Among classical scholars of the period Porson must take the lead, but with Dobree perhaps not very far behind. E. V. Blomfield (1788–1816), Francis Wrangham (1769–1842), Christopher (1774–1846) and John (1805–1839) Wordsworth and E. H. Barker (1788–1839) are also still memorable for their editorial and textual labours. Oriental studies were significantly advanced by Samuel Lee (1783–1852), W. H. Mill (1792–1853) and D. G. Wait (1789–1850) and they had worthy successors in Cambridge later in the century. Historians who were widely esteemed in Cambridge in the early nineteenth century, not excluding Thomas Babington Macaulay, are not such as to reflect credit on the University from the perspective of the 21st century, but Julius Hare and Connop Thirlwall, the champions of Niebuhr, were not without supporters in their own day. Thirlwall's supposed heterodoxy, however, and that of his supporter F. D. Maurice, could only have provided ammunition for the opposition described by John Wilkes to the introduction of a historical Tripos later in the century. T. K. Arnold (1800–53), Hugh James Rose (1795–1838) and his brother Henry John Rose (1800–73) were well esteemed among theologians but they were easily surpassed by, say, Birks, Nairne and Swainson later in the century.

Among natural scientists the names of Adam Sedgwick in geology and James Stevens Henslow are pre-eminent, not least because of their nurturing of the young Charles Darwin. William Hyde Wollaston (1766–1828) made notable contributions to physiology, chemistry and physics, and amid the galaxy of Cambridge astronomers William Lax (1761–1836), Sir John Herschel (1792–1871), Richard Sheepshanks (1794–1855), James Challis (1803–1882) and above all Sir George Airy (1801–92) had all made their mark before Victoria's reign.

It is a commonplace that until 1822 the only course to honours was the mathematical Tripos, the evolution of which is here expertly described by June Barrow-Green, and that even after the creation of the classical Tripos in that year, another twenty-eight years were to pass before the new Tripos was open to any, except the sons of peers, who had not already achieved high honours in mathematics. There had, however, been classed examinations in law since they were introduced by the Regius Professor, James William Geldart, in 1816. The course in law had, in fact, been founded by his predecessor's predecessor, Samuel Hallifax (1733–90), who published the 'heads' of his lectures as *An analysis of the Roman civil law; in which a comparison is, occasionally, made between the Roman laws and those of England: being the heads of a course of lectures publicly read in the University of Cambridge* in 1774. Hallifax had previously been Professor and the Lord Almoner's Reader in Arabic, although there is no evidence that he had, or ever acquired, any knowledge of that language. On his appointment to the regius chair any legal experience he might have had would have been the result of his having served his college as successively as Praelector, Dean, Tutor,

Steward and Bursar. Nevertheless, his *Analysis*, went through four editions in his life time, and, subjected by his successors to new editions, chiefly comprising the addition of modern instances, was still in use as the standard text up to and including the tenure (1847–54) of (Sir) Henry Maine, no less. The Regius Professors of Law were much discombobulated by their conception that men read for this course, leading to the LLB, for no better reason than that it was perceived as being easier to pass than the course for the BA. This they strenuously denied, while admitting that failure in their course was less conspicuous that failure in the Senate House examination or, later, the Tripos/es. Doubts about the usefulness of the course continued for many years, indeed, up to the time of Maitland, but that takes us beyond the bounds of this volume.

Above all, the mathematical tradition was strong, and Andrew Warwick here describes the flourishing of private teaching from the 1760s, the interaction between such teaching and the formal instruction offered by the University and the colleges, and the progress of the 'analytical revolution', but this brings us to the 'teaching and learning' which is the theme of this volume, and we should perhaps pause to reflect on the 'learning and research' whose existence flourished, as indicated above, in the unreformed university.

The monopoly of mathematics as the only course to an honours degree had been a matter of concern, to some at least, in the University for some years, and proposals for reform had been vigorously proposed by John Jebb in 1772 demanding annual examinations in chronology, history, classics, mathematics, metaphysics, natural and moral philosophy – and international law. Peter Searby has recently given an acccount of his campaign and of the obstacles which blocked it.[4] Apart from mere *vis inertiae*, any extension of the syllabus beyond mathematics and classics would present problems for the smaller colleges, where a mere half a dozen resident fellows could hardly be expected to have the necessary expertise to provide supervision in the 'new' subjects. The same problem was encountered with the introduction of the Moral Sciences and Natural Sciences Triposes in the 1860s. The University did not lack professors, but that the professors should be the sole source of instruction was then, as indeed now, an idea scarcely to be entertained.

In the mid-nineteenth century a scheme was to be introduced whereby men not reading for honours might acquire what in the United States would now be called 'credits' on attending lectures given by certain of the professors – attendance at the lectures was registered, some testing took place, and certificates were issued. The survival of a register of attendance at lectures of the Professor of Botany for the years 1828 to 1891 suggests that this later scheme may have taken its inspiration from the much earlier practice of Henslow. Clearly attendance at Henslow's lectures, from 1828, however assiduous, can have had no direct bearing on anyone's place in the Tripos, or even their

---

[4] Searby, *History*, pp. 163–6.

ranking among the οἱ πολλοί, but the fact that a register was kept has some significance. A high place in the Tripos was not the only road to success. Even within academe an indifferent mathematician, such as Julius Hare, who had demonstrated his excellence in classics, even if disqualified by mathematical incompetence from entering for university prizes, might yet attain a fellowship, and Darwin offers a fine example of the career opportunities that might be presented to those who had shown promise in subjects beyond the formal curriculum. An earlier, and too little known example is provided by Stephen Hales (1677–1761), introduced to natural philosophy by the botanical perambulations of John Ray, and subsequently, outside the academy, a very notable chemist, inventor, physiologist and botanist, known chiefly, but quite insufficiently, for his *Statical Essays* (1727–33).

None of the above suggests, or is intended to suggest, that Cambridge in the eighteenth, and most of the nineteenth, century was a university that could stand comparison with the premier universities of Germany, or indeed of Scotland, except perhaps in a very idiosyncratic form of mathematical prowess comprising a finely cultivated expertise in problem-solving, and, incidentally, in the composition of Greek and Latin verses, in which department only Oxford could bear comparison. It may, however, suggest that as well as 'learning and research' there was also present an element of education. Young men of promise, perhaps only those of exceptional promise, were from time to time drawn out, or were drawn into an intense and life-long engagement with 'academic' subjects, even if most of them pursued their avocations elsewhere. The 'reforms' described in this volume reflect some of the routes by which the University sought to provide a more balanced curriculum and less haphazard courses of instruction, and the many obstacles to that endeavour.

The introduction of the Previous Examination in 1821/2, and the frequent adjustments which it underwent, are at least gestures in the direction of acknowledging the emptiness of the course for the ordinary BA, and the creation of the Moral and Natural Sciences Triposes in the middle of the century signal the first struggles to loosen the stranglehold on the curriculum of mathematics and classics. Meanwhile in Trinity and in St John's, as John Smith and Malcolm Underwood here explain, a system of college examinations, perhaps dating from as early as Dr Bentley's reign, was developed and adapted to take in the new subjects, and intercollegiate lectures fulfilled at least some of the functions which the University was not fully to adopt until 1926.

Certainly it is true that by the end of Victoria's reign the University was transformed. By the end of the century students reading Natural Sciences were numerically rivalled only by those reading classics, but their early years probably confounded the (fairly few) diehard reactionaries little enough. Moral philosophy, in the form of Paley, much decried by the reformers for his utilitarian approach, had long been an element of the syllabus; and the professorships of chemistry, botany and astronomy were of long-standing. Moreover, in the early years of the new Triposes the number of students electing to study for them was very small. It was as easy and natural in the 1870s as in the 1820s to see the University as providing a 'liberal education' for the great majority of its students. The appearance of women on the academic scene was probably more disconcerting to the 'traditional' don than the timid beginnings of new disciplines.

The rise of the Natural Sciences Tripos was given a huge impetus by the foundation of the Cavendish laboratory and chair by the Duke of Devonshire, the Chancellor, in 1870, and by the the extraordinary distinction of the first Cavendish professors. The first, James Clerk Maxwell, could indeed be claimed as a graduate of the University – second wrangler and joint first Smith prizeman. He had, however, previously been a student at Edinburgh, and had made his first communication to the Royal Society of Scotland at the age of fifteen. At Cambridge, moreover, he probably owed more to his coach, Hopkins, than to either Peterhouse, his first college, or Trinity, his second. He was indeed awarded a fellowship at Trinity but left almost immediately to become a professor first at Aberdeen and then at King's College, London. At the time of his appointment to the Cavendish chair he had, at the age of thirty-four, retreated into private life on his father's estate in Scotland. His successor, J. W. Strutt, third Baron Rayleigh, by contrast, was of Cambridge University only: senior wrangler in 1865. Like Maxwell, however, he was lured to the Cavendish chair from the life of a country gentleman, to which occupation he returned in 1884, to be succeeded by J. J. Thomson. These three established the Cavendish laboratory as a place of pilgrimage, and indeed of research, for physicists from far and wide, as witness the appearance of Thomson's successor, Ernest Rutherford, one of the first two students to be awarded the degree of BA by research established two years previously.

The first four Cavendish professors, and their careers, neatly encapsulate the greatest transformation that the University saw in the nineteenth century, perhaps at any time. By the end of Thomson's tenure, engineered to ensure Rutherford's succession, it was no longer an eccentric course of action to choose to spend one's life teaching and researching in Cambridge. Assistants to Professors had been appointed, individually, from 1865 and Demonstrators from 1866 and the posts were regularised in 1892 and 1883 respectively. University Lecturers, apart from a few that were individually endowed, had to wait until 1926. Celibacy was no longer an issue after 1880, though some Heads still endeavoured to enforce it, and its abandonment had been theoretically possible for some twenty years: the first married fellow is recorded in 1861.

BIBLIOGRAPHY

A Member of the Senate, *Letter to a Friend Upon the Proposed Additions to the Academical System of Education* (October, 1848)
Airy, G. B., *Mathematical Tracts on Physical Astronomy, the Figure of the Earth, Precession and Nutation, and the Calculus of Variations* (Cambridge, 1826; 2nd edn 1831)
Airy, W., ed., *Autobiography of Sir George Biddell Airy* (Cambridge, 1896)
Allen, G., 'Plain Words on the Woman Question', *Fortnightly Review*, n.s. xliv (1889), pp. 448–58
Allen, G., 'The Adventure of the Inquisitive American', *Strand Magazine* (May 1898)
Allen, G., 'The Adventure of the Pea-Green Patrician', *Strand Magazine* (Oct. 1898)
Allen, G., 'The Adventure of the Supercilious Attache', *Strand Magazine* (Apr. 1898)
Anderson, E. G., 'Sex in Mind and Education: a reply', *Fortnightly Review* xv (1874), pp. 582–94
Annan, N. G., *Leslie Stephen: His Thought and Character in Relation to His Time* (London, 1951)
Annan, N. G., *Leslie Stephen: The Godless Victorian* (London and New York, 1984)
Anon., 'The Girton Girl, BA', *Punch* (23 June 1894), p. 297
Anon., 'The Ladies' Year', *Punch* (28 June 1890), p. 309
Anon., 'Some Account of Dr Waring the Late Celebrated Mathematician', *The Monthly Magazine; or, British Register* 9 (1810), pp. 46–49
Anon., 'The Mathematical Theory of Electricity and Magnetism', *Philosophical Magazine*, 16 (1908), pp. 830–31
Anon., *Cambridge Problems* (Cambridge, 1810)
Anon., *Gradus ad Cantabrigiam* (London, 1824)
Anon., 'Isaac Todhunter', *The Eagle* xiii (1884), pp. 94–98
Anon., 'Literary Piracy in Japan', *Nature* xxviii (10 May 1883), p. 43
Anon., 'Moral Philosophy at Cambridge', *Westminster Review* xlv (1874), pp. 430–64
Anon., 'The Disposal of Books', *Cambridge Review* (15 June 1893), pp. 403–4
Anon., 'The Natural Sciences Tripos', *Girton Review* (December 1882)
Anon., 'Should University Degrees be Given to Women?', *Westminster Review* liv (1881), pp. 493–505
Anon., *Cambridge Problems* (Cambridge, 1820)
Anon., *Hints to Members of Congregation III* (Oxford, 1849)
Anon., *The Fourth School* (1849), Oxford University Archives G A Oxon c65 (179)
Anon., *William Heffer, 1843–1928* (Cambridge, 1952)
Appleyard, E. S., *Letters from Cambridge* (London, 1828)
Atkinson, P., 'Fitness, Feminism and Schooling', in S. Delamont and L. Duffin, eds, *The Nineteenth Century Woman: Her Cultural and Biological Straitjacket* (London, 1978)
Atkinson, S., 'Struggles of a Poor Student Through Cambridge', *The London Magazine*, April 1825, pp. 491–510
Babbage, C., *Passages from the Life of a Philosopher* (London, 1864)

Baker, T., ed. Mayor, J. E. B., *History of St John's College* (Cambridge 1869)
Ball, W. W. R., *Cambridge Notes* (Cambridge, 1918; 2nd edn 1921)
Ball, W. W. R., 'Edward John Routh', *The Cambridge Review*, 13 June 1907, pp. 480–481
Ball, W. W. R., 'The Cambridge School of Mathematics', *Mathematical Gazette* vi (1912), pp. 311–23
Ball, W. W. R., *A History of the Study of Mathematics at Cambridge* (Cambridge, 1889)
Ball, W. W. R., *Notes on the History of Trinity College Cambridge* (Cambridge, 1899)
Barnes, B. and Shapin, S., eds, *Natural Order: Historical Studies of Scientific Culture* (London, 1979)
Barrow-Green, J., '"A Correction to the Spirit of Too Exclusively Pure Mathematics': Robert Smith (1689–1768) and his Prizes at Cambridge University"', *Annals of Science* 56 (1999) pp. 271–316
Bartholomew, A. T., *A Bibliography of Sir Adolphus William Ward 1837–1924* (Cambridge, 1926)
Beard, M., 'The Invention (and re-invention) of "Group D": an archaeology of the Classical Tripos 1879–1984', in C. A. Stray, ed., *Classics in Nineteenth and Twentieth Century Cambridge*, Proceedings of the Cambridge Philological Society, Supplementary Volume 24 (Cambridge, 1999), pp. 95–134
Becher, H., 'William Whewell and Cambridge Mathematics', *Historical Studies in Physical Sciences* xi (1980), pp. 1–48
Becher, H., 'William Whewell's Odyssey: From Mathematics to Moral Philosphy', in Fisch and Schaffer (1991), pp. 1–29
Becher, H., 'Woodhouse, Babbage, Peacock, and Modern Algebra', *Historia Mathematica*, 7 (1980), pp. 389–400
Becher, H., 'From Mathematics to Moral Philosophy', in M. Fisch and S. Schaffer, eds, *William Whewell: A Composite Portrait* (Oxford, 1991), pp. 1–29
Becher, H., 'Radicals, Whigs and Conservatives: the Middle and Lower Classes in the Analytical Revolution at Cambridge in the Age of Aristocracy', *British Journal for the History of Science* 28 (1995), pp. 405–26
Becher, H., 'The Social Origins and Post-Graduate Careers of Cambridge Intellectual Elite, 1830–1860', *Victorian Studies* 28 (1984), pp. 97–127
Berger, P. and Luckmann, T., *The Social Construction of Reality* (London, 1967)
Bill, E. G. W., *University Reform in Nineteenth Century Oxford: a Study of Henry Halford Vaughan* (Oxford, 1973)
Birks, T. R., 'Natural Science: The Handmaid of Revelation', in *Things that Accompany Salvation* (London and Edinburgh, 1858)
Boase, F., *Modern English Biography* (Truro, 1908)
Bonney, T. G., 'A Septuagenarian's Recollections of St John's', *The Eagle* xxx (1907), p. 299
Breay, C., 'Women and the Classical Tripos 1869–1914', in C. A. Stray, ed., *Classics in Nineteenth and Twentieth Century Cambridge* (Cambridge, 1999), pp. 49–70
Bristed, C. A., *Five Years in an English University* (New York, 1852; 3rd edn 1874)
Broad, C. D., 'The Local Historical Background of Contemporary Cambridge Philosophy', in *British Philosophy in Mid-Century*, ed. C. A. Mace (London, 1957)
Brock, M. G. and Curthoys, M. C., *A History of the University of Oxford*, VII (Oxford, 1997)
Bromwich, T. J. i'A., *An Introduction to the Theory of Infinite Series* (London, 1908)
Brook, W. H. and MacLeod, R. M., *Natural Knowledge in a Scientific Context: The Journals of Thomas Archer Hirst FRS* (1980)
Brooke, C. N. L., *A History of the University of Cambridge, IV, 1870–1990* (Cambridge, 1993)
Brookes, A-L., *Feminist Pedagogy: An Autobiographical Approach* (Halifax, Nova Scotia, 1992)
Burstyn, J. N., *Victorian Education and the Ideal of Womanhood* (London, 1980)

Burt, V., *An Introduction to Social Constructionism* (London, 1995)
Bury, J. P. T., ed., *Romilly's Cambridge Diary 1832–1842* (Cambridge, 1967)
Bury, M. E. and Pickles, J. D., *Romilly's Cambridge Diary 1842–1847* (Cambridge, 1994)
Bushell, W. F., 'The Cambridge Mathematical Tripos', *Mathematical Gazette* xliv (1960), pp. 172–79
Caird, E., Review of John Grote's *A Treatise on the Moral Ideals*, *The Academy* xl (1877), pp. 140–41
Campion, W., 'Mathematical Tripos', in *The Student's Guide to the University of Cambridge* (Cambridge, 1863)
Cannell, D. M., *George Green: a Biographical Memoir* (London, 1993)
Cannon, W. F., 'Scientists and Broad Churchmen: an Early Victorian Intellectual Network', *Journal of British Studies* 4 (1964), reprinted in *Science in Culture: The Early Victorian Period* (New York, 1978)
Cantor, G. N. and Hodge, M. J. S., eds, *Conceptions of Ether* (Cambridge, 1981)
Carey, H., *Mansfield Forbes and his Cambridge* (Cambridge, 1984)
Carr, J., *The First Three Sections of Newton's Principia; with copious notes and illustrations* (London, 1821)
Cartledge, P., Millett, P. and Todd, S., *Nomos: Essays in Athenian Law, Politics and Society* (Cambridge, 1990)
Caswell, E. ('Scriblerus Redivivus'), *Pluck Examination Papers for Candidates at Oxford and Cambridge* (Oxford, 1836)
Chitty, S., *The Beast and the Monk: a Life of Charles Kingsley* (London, 1974)
Clark, J. W. and Hughes, T. M., *Life and Letters of the Rev. Adam Sedgwick* (London, 1890)
Clough, B. A., *A Memoir of Anne Jemima Clough* (London, 1897)
Cockburn, E. O., ed. Holt, C. D., *Letters From Newnham College 1889–1892* (privately printed, n.d.)
Coddington, H., *An Elementary Treatise on Optics* (Cambridge, 1823)
Collini, S., '"Manly Fellows": Fawcett, Stephen, and the Liberal Temper', in Lawrence Goldman, ed., *The Blind Victorian: Henry Fawcett and British Liberalism* (Cambridge, 1989)
Collini, S., Winch, D. and Burrow, J., *That Noble Science of Politics: A Study in Nineteenth-Century Intellectual History* (Cambridge, 1983)
Cooper, C. H., *Annals of Cambridge* (Cambridge, 1908)
Cornford, F. M., *The Cambridge Classical Course; an Essay in Anticipation of Further Reform* (Cambridge, 1903)
Cornish, F. W., ed., *Extracts from the Letters and Journals of William Cory* (Oxford, 1897)
Courtney, W. L., *Constructive Philosophy* (London, 1886)
Courtney, W. L., *Studies in Philosophy, Ancient and Modern* (London, 1882)
Courtney, W. L., *Studies New and Old* (London, 1888)
Courtney, W. L., *The Metaphysics of John Stuart Mill* (London, 1879)
Crook, A. C., *The Foundation to Gilbert Scott* (Cambridge 1980)
Crosland, M. and Smith, C., 'The Transmission of Physics from France to Britain: 1800–1840', *Annals of Science* xxxiii (1976), pp. 1–61
Crotty, M., *The Foundations of Social Research* (London, 1999)
Crowther, J. G., *The Cavendish Laboratory, 1874–1974* (London, 1974)
Cunich, P., Hoyle, D., Duffy, E. and Hyam, R., *A History of Magdalene College, Cambridge, 1428–1988* (Cambridge, 1994)
De Morgan, S. E., *Memoir of Augustus De Morgan* (London, 1882)
De Morgan, A., 'Peacock's Algebra', *Quarterly Journal of Education* ix (1835), pp. 293–311
De Morgan, A., *A Budget of Paradoxes* (London, 1872)
De Morgan, A., 'Ecole Polytechnique', *Quarterly Journal of Education* x (1835), pp. 330–40
De Morgan, A., 'Wood's Algebra', *Quarterly Journal of Education* iii (1832), pp. 276–85

Dealtry, W., *The Principles of Fluxions* (Cambridge, 1810)
Dodgson, C. L., *Euclid and his Modern Rivals* (London, 1879)
Dodgson, C. L., *Euclid Books I and II* (London, 1879)
Drosier, W. H., *Remarks on the New Regulations Recommended by the Syndicate of October 27th 1859 for the Moral and Natural Sciences Examinations* (Cambridge, 1860)
Edgeworth, F. W., *New and Old Methods in Ethics* (Oxford and London, 1877)
Edwardes, A., *A Girton Girl* (London, 1885)
Enros, P. C., 'The Analytical Society (1812–1813): Precursor of the Renewal of Cambridge Mathematics', *Historia Mathematica* 10 (1983), pp. 24–47
Evans, E. J., *The Forging of the Modern State: Early Industrial Britain 1783–1870*, 2nd edn (London and New York, 1996)
Evans, J. H., *The First Three Sections of Newton's Principia* (Cambridge, 1834)
Everett, W., *On the Cam: Lectures on the University of Cambridge in England* (London, 1866)
Farrar, F. W., ed., *Essays on a Liberal Education* (London, 1867)
Fawcett, M. G., *Some Eminent Women of Our Time: Short Biographical Sketches* (London, 1889)
Ferrers, N. M. and Stuart Jackson, J., *Solutions of the Cambridge Senate-House Problems for the Years 1848–51* (Cambridge, 1851)
Fisch, M. and Schaffer, S., eds, *William Whewell: A Composite Portrait* (Oxford, 1991)
Forbes, D., *The Liberal Anglican Idea of History* (Cambridge, 1952)
Forbes, M. D., 'The College Library', in M. D. Forbes, ed., *Clare College 1326–1926* (Cambridge, 1928–30)
Forsyth, A. R., 'Edward John Routh', *Proceedings of the London Mathematical Society* ser. 2 v (5 July, 1907)
Forsyth, A. R., 'James Whitbread Lee Glaisher 1848–1928', *Proceedings of the Royal Society*, cxxvi (1929/30), pp. i–xi
Forsyth, A. R., 'Old Tripos Days At Cambridge', *Mathematical Gazette* xix (1935), pp. 162–79
Foucault, M., *Power/Knowledge: Selected Interviews* (Brighton, 1980)
Francis, H. T., 'John Venn: In Memoriam', *Caian* xxxl (1923), pp. 100–28
Frend, W., *Considerations on the Oathes Required at the Time of Taking Degrees* (London, 1787)
Frost, P., 'On the Potential of the Electricity on Two Charged Spherical Conductors placed at a given Distance', *Quarterly Journal of Pure and Applied Mathematics* xvii (1880)
Galison, P. and Warwick, A. C., eds, *Cultures of Theory*, special issue of *Studies in the History and Philosophy of Modern Physics*, 29B, 3 (1998)
Galton, F., *Hereditary Genius: An Inquiry into its Laws and Consequences* (London, 1869)
Galton, F., *Memories of My Life*, 2nd edn (London, 1908)
Gardner, P., *Autobiographica* (Oxford, 1933)
Garland, M., *Cambridge Before Darwin: The Ideal of a Liberal Education 1800–1860* (Cambridge, 1980)
Gascoigne, J., 'From Bentley to the Victorians: The Rise and Fall of British Newtonian Natural Theology', *Science in Context* ii (1988), pp. 219–56
Gascoigne, J., 'Mathematics and Meritocracy: The Emergence of the Cambridge Mathematical Tripos', *Social Studies of Science* xiv (1984), pp. 547–84
Gascoigne, J., *Cambridge in the Age of the Enlightenment: Science, Religion and Politics from the Restoration to the French Revolution* (Cambridge, 1989)
Gergen, K. J., 'Metaphor and Monophony in the 20th-century psychology of emotions', *History of the Human Sciences* viii.2 (1995), pp. 1–23
Gibbins, J. R., 'John Grote and Modern Cambridge Philosophy', *Philosophy* lxxiii (1998), pp. 453–77

Gibbins, J. R., 'John Grote, Cambridge University and the Development of Victorian Ideas', Doctoral thesis, University of Newcastle upon Tyne (1989)
Gibbins, J. R., 'Liberalism, Nationalism and the English Idealists', *History of European Ideas* xv (1992), pp. 491–97
Girton College Register
Girton Review
Glaisher, J. W. L., 'The Mathematical Tripos', *Proceedings of the London Mathematical Society* xviii (1886), pp. 4–38
Glendinning, V., *A Suppressed Cry. Life and Death of a Quaker Daughter* (London, 1969)
Glover, T. R., *Cambridge Retrospect* (Cambridge, 1943)
Goldman, L., ed., *The Blind Victorian: Henry Fawcett and British Liberalism* (Cambridge, 1989)
Gooch, R. ('Socius'), *Facetiae Cantabrigienses* (London, 1825)
Gooch, R. ('Socius'), *Oxford and Cambridge Nuts to Crack* (London, 1833)
Goodison, J. W., *Catalogue of Cambridge Portraits I: The University Collection* (Cambridge, 1955)
Gould, P., 'Women and the Culture of University Physics in Late Nineteenth-Century Cambridge', *British Journal for the History of Science* xxx (1997), pp. 127–49
Grattan-Guinness, I., 'A Mathematical Union: William Henry Young and Grace Chisholm Young', *Annals of Science* 29 (1972), pp. 105–86
Grattan-Guinness, I., 'University Mathematics at the Turn of the Century: Unpublished Recollections of W. H. Young', *Annals of Science* 28 (1972), pp. 369–84
Grattan-Guinness, I., *Convolutions in French Mathematics, 1800–1840*, 3 vols. (Basel, 1990)
Grattan-Guinness, I., 'Mathematics and Mathematical Physics from Cambridge, 1815–1840: a Survey of the Achievements and of the French Influences', in P. M. Harman, ed., *Wranglers and Physicists: Studies on Cambridge Physics in the Nineteenth Century* (Manchester, 1985), pp. 84–111
Grattan-Guinness, I., *The Development of the Foundations of Analysis from Euler to Riemann* (Cambridge, Massachusetts, 1970)
Gregory, D. F., *Examples in the Process of the Differential and Integral Calculus* (Cambridge, 1841)
Grote, J., 'A Draft Scheme of the Examination in Moral Sciences' (Cambridge, 1860)
Grote, J., 'Remarks on the Proposals of the Syndicate in reference to the Moral Science Tripos' (Cambridge, 1860)
Grote, J., *To the Members of the Senate* (Cambridge, 1860)
Grote, J., *Exploratio Philosophica, Part I* (Cambridge, 1865)
Grote, J., *An Examination of the Utilitarian Philosophy*, ed. J. B. Mayor (Cambridge, 1870)
Grote, J., *A Treatise on the Moral Ideals* (Cambridge, 1876)
Grote, J., *Exploratio Philosophica, Part II*, ed. J. B. Mayor (Cambridge, 1900)
Guicciardini, N., *Reading the Principia: The Debate on Newton's Mathematical Methods for Natural Philosophy from 1687 to 1763* (Cambridge, 1999)
Guicciardini, N., *The Development of the Newtonian Calculus in Britain 1700–1800* (Cambridge, 1989)
Gunning, H., *Reminiscences of Cambridge* (London, 1854)
Hamilton, H. B., *Principles of Analytical Geometry* (Cambridge, 1826)
Hansen, P. H., 'Albert Smith, the Alpine Club, and the Invention of Mountaineering in Mid-Victorian Britain', *Journal of British Studies* 34,3 (July 1995), pp. 300–24
Harrison, H. M., *Voyager in Time and Space: The Life of John Couch Adams, Cambridge Astronomer* (Sussex, 1994)
Hart, I. B., *Makers of Science* (London, 1923)
Harvie, C., *The Lights of Liberalism: University Liberals and the Challenge of Democracy 1860–1886* (London, 1976)

Heilbron, J. L., *Geometry Civilized* (Oxford, 1998)
Henderson, J., *Juvenal's Mayor: The Professor who Lived on 2d a Day. Proceedings of the Cambridge Philological Society*, Supplementary Volume 20 (Cambridge, 1998)
Herbertson, B. M., *The Pfeiffer Bequest and the Education of Women: A Centenary Review* (Cambridge, 1993)
Heyck, T. W., *The Transformation of Intellectual Life in Victorian England* (London, 1982)
Hopkins, W., 'Presidential Address', *British Association Report* (1853), pp. xli–lvii
Hopkins, W., *Remarks on Certain Proposed Regulations Respecting the Studies of the University* (Cambridge, 1841)
Horiuchi, A., 'Sur la recomposition du paysage mathématique Japonais au début de l'epoque Meiji', in G. Goldstein, J. Gray and J. Ritter, eds, *L'Europe Mathématique: Histoires, Mythes, Identités* (Paris, 1996)
Hort, A. F. *Life and Letters of Fenton Anthony John Hort* (London, 1896)
How, F. D., *Six Great Schoolmasters* (London, 1904)
Howard, Sir H., *Finances of St John's College, Cambridge 1511–1926* (Cambridge, 1935)
Howarth, J., '"In Oxford but not of Oxford" the Women's Colleges', in M. G. Brock and M. C. Curthoys, eds, *History of the University of Oxford* VII (Oxford, 2000), pp. 237–307
Howson, A. G., *A History of Mathematical Education in Britain* (Cambridge, 1982)
Hu Mingjie, 'Merging Chinese and Western Mathematics: The Introduction of Algebra and the Calculus in China, 1859–1903', PhD thesis, Princeton University (1998)
Hughes, M. V., *A London Child of the 1870s* (London, 1934)
Hughes, T., *Memoir of Daniel Macmillan* (London, 1882)
Hunt, C. J., 'Catalogue of the Library at Wallington Hall' (Newcastle-upon-Tyne, 1968)
Ingleby, C. M., *Reflections Historical and Critical on The Revival of Philosophy at Cambridge* (Cambridge, 1870)
Jarausch, K. H., *The Transformation of Higher Learning, 1860–1930: Expansion, Diversification, Social Opening, and Professionalisation in England, Germany, Russia and the United States* (Chicago, 1983)
Jeffereys, H., 'Johnian Maths, 1910–14', *Eagle* lx (1964), pp. 154–57
Johnson, W., 'Isaac Todhunter (1820–1884): Textbook Writer, Scholar, Coach and Historian of Science', *International Journal of Mechanical Science* xxxvii (1996), pp. 1231–70
Keynes, J. M., *Essays in Biography* (London, 1933)
Kuhn, T., *The Structure of Scientific Revolutions* (Chicago, 1962)
Lacroix, S. F., *Elementary treatise on the Differential and Integral Calculus*. Translated by George Peacock, John Herschel and Charles Babbage (Cambridge, 1816)
Lagrange, J. L., *Mécanique analytique* (Paris, 1788)
Laplace, P. S., *Traite de mécanique celeste*, 5 vols (Paris, 1798–1827)
Latham, H., 'University and College Expenses', *The Student's Guide to the University of Cambridge*, 3rd edn (Cambridge, 1874)
Leedham-Green, E. S., *A Concise History of the University of Cambridge* (Cambridge, 1996)
Legrand, M. (James Rice), *The Cambridge Freshman or Memoirs of Mr Golightly* (1871)
Luard, H. R., *Suggestions on the Establishment of a Historical Tripos* (Cambridge, 1866)
Lubenow, W. C., *The Cambridge Apostles 1820–1914* (Cambridge, 1998)
Lund, T., *The Exposure of a Recent Attempt at Book-Making in the University of Cambridge* (London, 1858)
Macalister, E. F. B., *Sir Donald Macalister of Tarbert* (London, 1935)
MacFarlane, A., *Lectures on Ten British Mathematicians of the Nineteenth Century* (New York, 1911)
MacHale, D., *George Boole, his Life and Work* (Dublin, 1985)
Mangan, J. A. and Parks, R. J., eds, *From Fair Sex to Feminism: Sport and the Socialization of Women in the Industrial and Post-Industrial Eras* (London, 1987)

Mangan, J. A., *Athleticism in the Victorian and Edwardian Public School: The Emergence and Consolidation of an Educational Ideology* (Cambridge, 1981)
Marshall, M. P., *What I Remember* (Cambridge, 1948)
Maudsley, H., 'Sex in Mind and in Education', *Fortnightly Review* xv (1874), pp. 466-83
Mays, J. C. C. 'Coleridge's Borrowings from Jesus College Library, 1791-94', *Transactions of the Cambridge Bibliographical Society* viii (1985), pp. 557-81
McDonnell Bodkin, M., *Dora Myrl: The Lady Detective* (London, 1900)
McKitterick, D. J., *A History of Cambridge University Press II. Scholarship and Commerce, 1698-1872* (Cambridge, 1998)
McKitterick, D. J., *Cambridge University Library: A History. The Eighteenth and Nineteenth Centuries* (Cambridge 1986)
McWilliams-Tullberg, R., *Women at Cambridge: A Men's University – Though of a Mixed Type* (London, 1975)
Mill, J. S., 'Dr Whewell on Moral Philosophy', in *Mill's Ethical Writings*, ed. J. B. Schneewind (London, 1965)
Mill, J. S., 'Professor Sedgwick's Discourse on the Studies of the University of Cambridge', in *Mill's Ethical Writings*, ed. J. B. Schneewind (London, 1965)
Miller, E., *Portrait of a College* (Cambridge, 1961)
Milner, M., *Life of Isaac Milner* (London, 1842)
Monk, J. H., *The Life of Richard Bentley, D. D.* (London, 1833)
Montgomery, R. J., *Examinations: An Account of their Evolution as Administrative Devices in England* (London, 1965)
Morgan, H. A., 'Rev. Dr. Frost, FRS', *Cambridge Review* xix (1898), p. 405
Morgan, H. A., 1871. *The Mathematical Tripos: An Enquiry into its Influence on a Liberal Education* (London, Oxford and Cambridge, 1871)
Moulton, H., *Life of Lord Moulton* (London, 1923)
Mullinger, J. B., 'Isaac Todhunter', *Dictionary of National Biography*
Mullinger, J. B., *A History of St John's College* (London, 1901)
Munby, A. N. L., 'Macaulay's Library', *Essays and Papers* (London, 1977), pp. 121-40
Murphy, R., *Elementary Principles on the Theory of Electricity, Heat and Molecular Actions, I: On Electricity* (Cambridge, 1833)
Murray, O., 'Ancient History', in M. G. Brock and M. C. Curthoys, eds, *A History of the University of Oxford*, VII (Oxford, 2000)
Neale, C. M., *The Senior Wranglers of the University of Cambridge* (1907)
Nettleship, R. L. 'Memoir', in Nettleship, ed., *Works of Thomas Hill Green, vol. 3: Miscellanies and Memoir* (London, 1888)
Newnham College Register, 1871-1971, 3 vols (Cambridge, 1979)
Oates, J. C. T., *Cambridge University Library: A History. From the Beginnings to the Copyright Act of Queen Anne* (Cambridge, 1986)
O'Boyle, L., 'The Problem of an Excess of Educated Men in Western Europe 1800-1850', *Journal of Modern History* xlii (1970), pp. 471-91
Olesko, K. M., *Physics as a Calling: Discipline and Practice in the Koenigsberg Seminar for Physics* (Ithaca, NJ, 1991)
Owen, D. M., *Cambridge University Archives: A Classified List* (Cambridge, 1988)
Oxford University Hebdomadal Board, *Report and Evidence upon the Recommendations of H. M. Commissioners for Inquiry into the State of the University of Oxford* (Oxford, 1853)
Pall Mall Budget
Panteki, M., 'William Wallace and the introduction of Continental Calculus to Britain: A letter to George Peacock', *Historia Mathematica* 14 (1987), pp. 119-32
Paradis, J. and Postlewait, T., eds, *Victorian Science and Victorian Values: Literary Perspectives* (New York, 1985)

Parry, J., *The Rise and Fall of Liberal Government in Victorian Britain* (New Haven and London, 1993)
Parry, R. StJ., *Henry Jackson O. M.: A Memoir* (Cambridge, 1926)
Pattison, M., *Oxford Essays* (Oxford, 1855)
Paulin, R., 'Julius Hare's German Library in Trinity College Library, Cambridge', *Transactions of the Cambridge Bibliographical Society* ix, 2 (1987), pp. 174–93
Peacock, G., *Examples Illustrative of the Use of the Differential and Integral Calculus* (Cambridge, 1820)
Peacock, G., *Observations on the Statutes of the University of Cambridge* (London and Cambridge, 1841)
Pearson, K., 'Old Tripos Days at Cambridge, As Seen from Another Viewpoint', *Mathematical Gazette* 20 (1936), pp. 27–36
Phillips, A., ed., *A Newnham Anthology* (Cambridge, 1979)
Poisson, S. D., *Traite de mécanique* (Paris, 1811)
Porter, E., *Victorian Cambridge: Josiah Chater's Diaries, 1844–1884* (London, 1975)
Pratt, J. H., *A Treatise on Attractions: Laplace's Functions and the Figure of the Earth* (London, 1860)
Prest, J., ed., *The Illustrated History of Oxford University* (Oxford, 1993)
Preyer, R. O., 'The Romantic Tide Reaches Trinity: Notes on the Transmission and Diffusion of New Approaches to Traditional Studies in Cambridge, 1820–1840', in J. Paradis and T. Postlewait, eds, *Victorian Science and Victorian Values: Literary Perspectives* (New York, 1981), pp. 39–68
Pryme G., *Autobiographical Recollections,* ed. A. Bayne (Cambridge, 1890)
Queckett, W., 'Life at St John's in 1821', *The Eagle* xv (1889), pp. 149–54
Ray, G. N., ed., *Letters and Private Papers of William Makepiece Thackeray* (Oxford, 1945–46)
Rayleigh, Lord, *The Life of Sir J. J. Thomson* (Cambridge, 1942)
Rayner, O. P. [G. Allen], *The Typewriter Girl* (London, 1897)
Reader, W. J., *Professional Men: The Rise of the Professional Class in Nineteenth-Century England* (New York, 1966)
Rice, A., 'Augustus De Morgan: Historian of Science', *History of Science* xxxiv (1996), pp. 201–40
Richards, J., 'Rigor and Clarity: Foundations of Mathematics in France and England 1800–1820', *Science in Context* iv (1991), pp. 297–319
Richmond, M. L., '"A Lab of One's Own": The Balfour Biological Laboratory for Women at Cambridge University 1884–1914', *Isis* lxxxviii (1997), pp. 422–53
Rivington, S., *The Publishing Family of Rivington* (London, 1919)
Roach, J. P. C., 'Liberalism and the Victorian Intelligensia', *Cambridge Historical Journal* xiii (1957), pp. 58–81
Roach, J. P. C., 'Victorian Universities and the National Intelligensia', *Victorian Studies* iii (1959), pp. 131–50
Roach, J. P. C., *A History of the County of Cambridge and the Isle of Ely,* vol. iii (London, 1959)
Roach, J. P. C., *History of Public Examinations in England, 1851–1900* (Cambridge, 1971)
Roby, H. J., *Remarks on College Reform* (Cambridge, 1858)
Rogers, J. E. T., *Education in Oxford* (London, 1861)
Rothblatt, S., 'Failure in Early Nineteenth-Century Oxford and Cambridge', *History of Education* 11 (1982), pp. 1–21
Rothblatt, S., 'The Student Sub-culture and the Examination System in Early 19th Century Oxbridge', in L. Stone, ed., *The University in Society Vol. 2: Europe, Scotland, and the United States from the 16th to the 20th century* (1974), pp. 247–303
Rothblatt, S., *The Revolution of the Dons* (London, 1968)
Rouse, J., *Knowledge and Power: Toward a Political Philosophy of Science* (Ithaca, NJ, 1987)

Routh, E. J., 'Isaac Todhunter', *Monthly Notices of the Royal Astronomical Society* xlv (1884), pp. 194–99
Routh, E. J., 'Isaac Todhunter', *Proceedings of the Royal Society* xxxvii (1884), pp. xxvii–xxxii
Rover, C., *The Punch Book of Women's Rights* (London, 1967)
Rudd, W. J. N., *T. E. Page, Schoolmaster Extraordinary* (Bristol, 1981)
Russett, C. E., *Sexual Science: The Victorian Construction of Victorian Womanhood* (Cambridge, MA, 1984)
Satthianadhan, S., *Four Years in an English University* (Madras, 1890)
Schneewind, J. B., Review of L. D. MacDonald's *John Grote: A Critical Estimation of his Writings*, *Philosophical Quarterly* 18 (1968), pp. 172–73
Schneewind, J. B., *Sidgwick's Ethics and Victorian Moral Philosophy* (Oxford, 1977)
Schultz, B., *Essays on Henry Sidgwick* (Cambridge, 1992)
Searby, P., *History of the University of Cambridge, vol. III, 1750–1870* (Cambridge, 1997)
Sedgwick, A., *A Discourse on the Studies of the University* [1833], ed. E. Ashby and M. Anderson (London, 1969)
Seeley, J. R., *The Student's Guide to the University of Cambridge* (Cambridge, 1863)
Shaw, G. B., 'Mrs Warren's Profession', reprinted in his *Plays Pleasant and Unpleasant*, vol. i (London, 1898)
Shipley, J. A., *'J': A Memoir of John Willis Clark* (London, 1913)
Shotter, J., *Conversational Realities: Constructing Life Through Language* (London, 1993)
Shrosbee, C., *Public Schools and Private Education: The Clarendon Commission 1861–64 and the Public School Acts* (Manchester, 1988)
Sidgwick, A., and Sidgwick, E. M., *Henry Sidgwick: A Memoir* (London, 1906)
Sidgwick, H., 'Philosophy at Cambridge', *Mind* 1 (1876), pp. 235–46
Sidgwick, H., *Philosophy: Its Scope and Relations* (London, 1902)
Sidgwick, H., *The Methods of Ethics*, 7th edn (London, 1907)
Siklos, S., *Philippa Fawcett and the Mathematical Tripos* (Cambridge, 1990)
Slee, P. R. H., *Learning and a Liberal Education: The Study of Modern History in the Universities of Oxford, Cambridge and Manchester 1800–1914* (Manchester, 1986)
Stephen, L., *Sir William Fawcett: A Biography* (London, 1885)
Stephen, L., *Sketches from Cambridge by a Don* (London and Cambridge, 1865)
Stephen, L., *The English Utilitarians*, 3 vols. (London, 1900)
Stobart, J. C., *The Glory that was Greece* (London, 1911)
Stokes, G. G., *Memoirs and Scientific Correspondence of Sir George Stokes*, Vol. 1. (Cambridge, 1907)
Stout, G. F., ed. Stout, A. K., *God and Nature* (Cambridge, 1952)
Stout, G. F., *Mind and Matter: The First Two Volumes Based on the Gifford Lectures Delivered in the University of Edinburgh in 1919 and 1921* (Cambridge, 1931)
Strachey, R., *Millicent Garrett Fawcett* (London, 1931)
Stray, C. A., 'Renegotiating Classics: the Politics of Curricular Reform in Later Victorian Cambridge', *Echos du Monde Classique/Classical Views* xlii, ns 17 (1998), pp. 449–71
Stray, C. A., '"Thucydides or Grote?": Classical Disputes and Disputed Classics in Nineteenth-Century Cambridge', *Transactions of the American Philological Association* cxxvii (1997), pp. 363–71
Stray, C. A., *Classics Transformed: Schools, Universities and Society in England, 1830–1960* (Oxford, 1998)
Stronach, A., *A Newnham Friendship* (London, 1901)
Sutherland, G., 'Anne Jemima Clough and Blanche Athena Clough: Creating Educational Institutions for Women', in M. Hilton and P. Hirsch, eds, *Practical Visionaries: Women, Education and Social Progress 1790–1930* (Harlow, 2000)

Sutherland, G., 'Emily Davies, the Sidgwicks and the Education of Women in Cambridge', in R. Mason, ed., *Cambridge Minds* (Cambridge, 1994), pp. 34–37
Sutherland, G., 'The Social and Political Location of the Movement for the Higher Education of Women in England c. 1840–1880', in P. J. Waller, ed., *Politics and Social Change in Modern Britain: Essays presented to A. F. Thompson* (Hassocks, 1987)
Sutherland, J., *Mrs Humphrey Ward. Eminent Victorian, Pre-Eminent Edwardian* (Oxford, 1990)
Sviedrys, R., 'The Rise of Physical Science at Victorian Cambridge', *Historical Studies in the Physical Sciences* ii (1970), pp. 127–52
Tait, P. G., 'Todhunter on Experimental Illustration', *Nature* ix (26 Feb. 1874)
Tanner J. R., ed., *A Historical Register of the University of Cambridge . . . to 1910* (Cambridge, 1917)
Temple, G., 'Edmund Taylor Whittaker', *Biographical Memoirs of Fellows of the Royal Society* 2 (1956), pp. 299–325
The Cambridge University Calendar for the Year 1904–1905 (Cambridge, 1904)
Thompson, S. P., *The Life of William Thomson*, 2 vols (London, 1910)
Thomson J. J. et al., *A History of the Cavendish Laboratory, 1871–1910* (London, 1910)
Topham, J. R., 'Two Centuries of Cambridge Publishing and Bookselling: a brief history of Deighton Bell & Co., 1778–1998 with a checklist of the archive', *Transactions of the Cambridge Bibliographical Society* xi (1998), pp. 350–403
Tottenham G. L., *Charlie Villars at Cambridge* (London, 1868)
Tribe, K., 'The Cambridge Economics Tripos 1903–1955 and the Training of Economists', *The Manchester School* 68 (2000), pp. 221–48
Tullberg, R. M., *Women at Cambridge* (Cambridge, 1998)
Tyacke, N., ed., *The History of the University of Oxford* IV (Oxford, 1997)
Velody, I. and Williams, R., *The Politics of Constructionism* (London, 1999)
Venn, J. A., *Oxford and Cambridge Matriculations 1544–1906 . . . with a Chart* (Cambridge, 1908)
Venn, J., *The Logic of Chance* (London and Cambridge, 1866)
Venn, J. and J. A., *Alumni Cantabrigienses: A Biographical List of All Known Students, Graduates, and Holders of Office at the University of Cambridge from the Earliest Times to 1900, Part II: 1752–1900*, 6 vols. (Cambridge, 1940–1954)
Venn, J. A., *A Biographical History of Gonville and Caius College* (Cambridge, 1910)
Venn, J. A., *Early Collegiate Life* (Cambridge, 1913)
Vince, S., 1797, 1799, 1808. *A Complete System of Astronomy*, 3 vols (Cambridge, 1797–1808)
Walsh, B. D., *Historical Account of the University of Cambridge* (London, 1837)
Walton, W. et al., *Solutions of Problems and Riders Proposed in the Senate-House Examination for 1864* (Cambridge, 1864)
Walton, W., *The Mathematical and Other Writings of Robert Leslie Ellis* (Cambridge, 1863)
Ward, A. W., *Suggestions Towards the Establishment of a History Tripos* (Cambridge, 1872)
Ward, J., *Essays in Philosophy: With a Memoir by Olwen Ward Campbell*, ed. W. R. Sorley (Cambridge, 1927)
Ward, Mrs H., *A Writer's Recollections* (London, 1918)
Ward, W. R., *Victorian Oxford* (London, 1965)
Warwick, A., 'A Mathematical World on Paper: Written Examinations in Early 19th Century Cambridge', in P. Galison and A. C. Warwick, eds, *Cultures of Theory*, special issue of *Studies in the History and Philosophy of Modern Physics*, 29B, 3 (1998), pp. 295–319
Warwick, A., 'Exercising the Student Body: Mathematics and Athleticism in Victorian Cambridge', in C. Lawrence and S. Shapin, eds, *Science Incarnate: Historical Embodiments of Natural Knowledge* (Chicago, 1997)
Warwick, A., *Masters of Theory* (Chicago, 2001)

Waterman, A. M. C., 'A Cambridge Via Media in Late Georgian Anglicanism', *Journal of Ecclesiastical History* 42.3 (1991), pp. 419–36
Whewell, W., *An Elementary Treatise on Mechanics* (Cambridge, 1819)
Whewell, W., *A Treatise on Dynamics* (Cambridge, 1823)
Whewell, W., *Of a Liberal Education in General; and with Particular Reference to the Leading Studies of the University of Cambridge* (Cambridge, 1845)
Whewell, W., *On the Principles of English University Education* (Cambridge, 1837)
Whewell, W., *Thoughts on the Study of Mathematics as Part of a Liberal Education* (Cambridge, 1835)
Whittaker, E. T., 'Recent Researches on Space, Time and Force', *Monthly Notices of the Royal Astronomical Society* 70 (1910), pp. 363–66
Wilkins, H. M., 'The Oxford University Commission Report', *Blackwood's Edinburgh Magazine* 73 (1853), pp. 216–34
Williams, R., *Culture and Society, 1780–1950* (London, 1958)
Willmott, R. A., 'Cambridge Studies', *Fraser's Magazine* (December, 1845), pp. 663–75
Wilson, A. T. and Wilson, J. S., *James M. Wilson: an Autobiography, 1836–1931* (London, 1932)
Wilson, D. B., 'The Educational Matrix: Physics Education at Early-Victorian Cambridge, Edinburgh and Glasgow Universities', in P. M. Harman, ed., *Wranglers and Physicists: Studies in Cambridge Physics in the Nineteenth Century* (Manchester, 1985), pp. 12–48
Wilson, D. B., 'Experimentalists among the Mathematicians: Physics in the Cambridge Natural Sciences Tripos, 1851–1900', *Historical Studies in Physical Sciences* 12 (1982), pp. 325–71
Wilson, D. B., *Kelvin and Stokes: A Comparative Study in Victorian Physics* (Bristol, 1987)
Wilson, J. M., *Elementary Geometry* (Cambridge, 1868)
Winstanley, D. A., *Early Victorian Cambridge* (Cambridge, 1940)
Winstanley, D. A., *Later Victorian Cambridge* (Cambridge, 1945)
Winstanley, D. A., *Unreformed Cambridge* (Cambridge, 1935)
Wolstenholme, J., *Mathematical Problems* (London, 1867; 2nd edn 1878)
Wood, J., *Principles of Mathematics and Natural Philosophy* (Cambridge, 1790–99)
Wood, J., *The Elements of Algebra* (Cambridge, 1795)
Woodhouse, R., *An Elementary Treatise on Astronomy: Vol. II, Containing Physical Astronomy* (Cambridge, 1818)
Woodhouse, R., *A Treatise on Astronomy, Theoretical and Practical*, 2 vols (Cambridge, 1821, 1823)
Woodhouse, R., *Principles of Analytical Calculation*
Wootton, B., *The World I Never Made* (London, 1967)
Wordsworth, C., *Scholae Academicae: Some Account of the Studies at the English Universities in the Eighteenth Century* (Cambridge, 1877)
Wordsworth, C., *Social Life at the English Universities in the Eighteenth Century* (Cambridge, 1874)
Wright, J. M. F., *Hints and Answers: being a Key to a Collection of Cambridge Mathematical Examination Papers, as Proposed at the Several Colleges* (Cambridge, 1831)
Wright, J. M. F., *A Commentary on Newton's Principia: with a Supplementary Volume* (London, 1828)
Wright, J. M. F., *Alma Mater; or Seven Years at the University of Cambridge*, 2 vols (London, 1827)
Wright, J. M. F., *Self-Examination in Euclid* (Cambridge, 1829)
Wright, J. M. F., *Self-Instructions in Pure Arithmetic* (Cambridge, 1829)
Wright, J. M. F., *Solutions of the Cambridge Problems for 1800–1820* (London, 1825)

Wright, J. M. F., *The Private Tutor and Cambridge Mathematical Repository* (Cambridge, 1830)

Yeo, R., 'Genius, Method and Morality: Images of Newton in Britain, 1760–1860', *Science in Context* ii (1988), pp. 257–84

INDEX

Abdy, John 56
Addenbrooke's Hospital 205
Ad Eundem (dining club) 32–3
Affleck, Lady 72
Airy, George Biddell 20–4, 26, 35, 184, 207
Albert, Prince 51
Allen, Grant 158, 160
Altertumswissenschaft 36
Analytical Society 15–16
Annan, Noel 61, 186
Anonymity in examinations 109
Apostles, Cambridge 39, 66, 78
Archer-Hind, Richard Dacre 145
Aristotle 74–5
Arnold, Thomas 49–50
Arnold, Thomas Kerchever 207
Association for Promoting Higher Education for Women 143–4
Association for the Improvement of Geometrical Teaching 190
Athleticism 152
Atkinson, G. B. 146
Atkinson, Solomon 23–4
Atlay, James 182
Austin, J. B. 180
Austin, John 72

Babbage, Charles 15–16, 20, 23–4
Bacon, Francis 67–8
Bain, Alexander 68, 79–80
Baker, Henry F. 119
Balfour Biological Laboratory 144
Ball, W. W. Rouse 5–6, 9, 11, 26
Barker, Edmund Henry, OTN 207
Barry, Alfred 38
Bashforth, Francis 110–11
Bateson, William H. 99, 182
Becher, H. 15
Bennett, G. T. 146
Benson, Edward William 79

Bentham, Jeremy 68–9, 72, 74
Bentley, Richard 1, 124, 209
Berger, Peter 64
Berkeley, Bishop 74
Bernoulli, Daniel 13
Berry, Mr 163
Besant, W. H. 112
Biot, J.-P. 19
Birks, Thomas Rawlinson 68, 70, 75, 80–1, 86, 130, 207
Blackburne, Francis 205
Blomfield, Edward Valentine 207
Bodkin, M. McDonnell 158, 160
Bonney, T. G. 110, 115
Books 165–76, hiring 175, discounting 173, 176
Booksellers 171–5
Boole, George 184
Botanical gardens 171
Bowtell, John 205
Brass, John 17
Breay, Claire 145
Bristed, Charles Astor 46, 130
Brown, John 16, 18
Brown, W. H. 99
Brunel, Isambard Kingdom 46
Bryce, James 55, 81
Bulley, Amy Agnes 142
Burn, Robert 38, 99–100, 102, 105
Bushe-Fox, Loftus 118
Butler, Bishop 74–7
Butler, Montagu 37, 136

Caird, Edward 85
Cam, River 37
Cambridge Chronicle 197
Cambridge Network 67
Cambridge Public Library 172
Cambridge Review 42
Cambridge style 38; *see also* Oxford style

223

Cannon, Walter (later W. Faye, later Susan Faye) 67
Caput 206
Cavendish Laboratory 114, 153, 191, 210
Cayley, Arthur 183–4
Cayley, Lois 158–60
Celibacy 210
Chairs *see* Knightbridge, Regius, Sadleirian
Challis, James 184, 207
Chantrey, Francis 154
Chapel, compulsory 37
Cheltenham College 38
Cheltenham Ladies' College 141
Chisholm, Grace 164
Cicero 74, 93
Clairaut, A. C. 13
Clare College 168–9
Clarendon Commission (1861–4) 41
Clark, J. W. 52
Clark, W. G. 38, 100, 102
Clarke, Samuel 67, 75
Classical Tripos 24, 31–44, 70, 74, 89–106, 128, 131
Clifford, William K. 79
Clough, Anne Jemima 139, 144, 153–6
Coaches *see* private tutors
Coddington, Henry 24
Colenso, J. W. 80
Coleridge, Samuel Taylor 68, 71, 75, 84, 168
Collini, Stefan 62, 73, 75
Commissions *see* Clarendon Commission, Royal Commissions
Comparative philology 36
Composition, Latin and Greek 35, 145
Compulsory chapel 37
Comte, Auguste 72
Constructionism, introduction to 64–5
Cooke, E. H. 158
Cope, E. M. 101
Cornford, Francis 42
Courtney, Leonard 68, 79–80
Cousin, Victor 69
Cramming *see* tip-fancying
Cunningham, Ebenezer 120

Dairoku, Kikuchi 185
D'Alembert, J. Le R. 13–14, 29
Davies, Emily 139, 142
Davies, John Llewellyn 82
Davies, Louisa 183
Darwin, Charles 67, 207

Declamation 135
Deighton Bell 167, 172–3, 175
De Morgan, Augustus 68, 180–1, 188–9, 193, 195
De Tocqueville, Alexis 72
Dawson, John 10, 12
Devonshire, Duke of 121, 210
Disputations 8
Divinity School 171
d-notation calculus 6, 21, 23, 26, 28
Dobree, Peter Paul 128
Dodgson, Charles 194
Douglas, Alexander Frost 174–5
Drosier, W. H. 53
Dyer, George 206

Edgeworth, Francis Ysidro 83
Edwards, Thomas 206
Elective system 44
Ellis, Robert 76, 78–9
Engineering laboratory 114, 118
Enros, P. C. 15
Euclid 7, 11, 27, 67, 110, 126, 128, 190, 193–6
Euler, L. 13–14, 29, 188
Examinations *see* anonymity; disputations; Higher Local Examinations; Poll Examination; oral examinations; Previous Examination; marks; Mathematical, Classical, Moral Sciences, Natural Sciences and Historical Triposes; Moderators and Examiners; questionists; Senate House Examination; Senior Wrangler; tip-fancying; Voluntary Theological Examination; Wooden Spoon
Evans, Thomas 37

Faculty libraries 171
Faculty of Classics 43
Farrar, Frederic 38
Fawcett, Henry 67–8, 78–80
Fawcett, Millicent Garrett 154
Fawcett, Philippa 146, 155–8, 160–2
Feathers Petition (1772) 205
Ferrier, James Frederick 68–9
Fichte, J. G. 69, 74–7
Fison, Thomas G. 173
Fitness 152
Foster, Michael 131
Field, Thomas 99
Fleming, Mrs 141

Forbes, Mansfield D. 169
Foxwell, Henry 115
Frend, William 10
Freshmen's Church *see* Pitt Building
Freund, Ida 155
Furies 37

Gadamer, Hans 64
Galloway and Porter 173
Gardner, Alice 147
Gardner, Percy 39
General Board of Studies 120
Geldart, James William 207
General Examination *see* Poll Examination
George I 45
Gibson, Edmund 45
Girls' Public Day School Company (later Trust) 141, 146
Girton College 139–64 passim
Gooden, Alexander Chisholm 129, 134
Graces 9
Grant, William P. 172–3
Graves, C. E. 12
Greats *see* Literae Humaniores
Green, Thomas Hill 84, 88
Grier, Lynda 146
Grote, Alexandrina Jessie 79
Grote, George 39, 78
Grote, John 54, 61–88 passim
Grote Society 61–88 passim
Grotius, H. 75
Guillebaud, Claude 119
Guizot, F. P. G. 74
Gunson, William Mandell 99–100, 103–4
Gwatkin, Henry 39, 113
Gwatkin, Richard 15–16, 19–26 passim

Hales, Stephen 208
Hall, John 172
Hallam, Henry 74
Halley, Edmund 194
Hallifax, Samuel 207
Hamilton, H. B. 24
Hamilton, William Rowan 67–8
Hammond, Basil 61, 147
Hare, Julius 36–7, 80, 172, 207–8
Headlam, James 40–1
Headmasters' Conference 40
Heath, Thomas 195
Heffer, William 173
Hegel, G. W. F. 69, 76
Heitland, William 113–14, 120

Imdex 225

Henslow, James Stevens 207–8
Herschel, John 15, 24, 67, 207
Hesiod 37
Higher Local Examinations 140
Hill, Henry 194
Hinchliffe, John 124
Hirst, Thomas Archer 188
Historical Tripos 45–60 passim, 91, 95
History of the University of Cambridge 1
History of the University of Oxford 1
Holt, Catherine Durning 153–5
Hopkins, William 27–8, 178, 181, 185, 210
Hort, Fenton 2, 53, 68, 78
Hume, David 69
Humphry, G. M. 174
Hustler, James 20–1

Image, John Maxwell 134
Index Expurgatorius 134
Industrial Revolution 34
Ingleby, Clement Mansfield 68–70, 78, 80
Intellectual aristocracy 39
Ivens, Dora 145

Jackson, Henry 31–2, 39, 42, 89–106, 129, 132, 145
Jacobi, G. H. 77
James VI and I 206
Jameson, Francis 185
Jebb, John 33, 124, 127, 138, 206, 208
Jebb, Richard 129
Jeffreys, Harold 115–16
Jenkins, H. B. 119
Jex-Blake, Katharine 145
Johnson, Elijah 172
Johnson, Samuel 167
Johnson (later Cory), William 39
Jones, Hypatia, Spinster of Arts 157
Jones, Thomas 125
Journals, scholarly 43; *see also Philological Museum*
Jurisprudence 51, 55

Kant, Immanuel 69, 72, 74–7
Kaye, Charles 35
Kelsall, Charles 34, 37
Kennedy, Benjamin Hall 89, 92–3, 103
Kingsley, Charles 50, 57, 59, 78, 166
Knatchbull-Hugessen, Eva 149
Knightbridge chair of moral philosophy 61–88 passim
Kuhn, Thomas 64

Laboratories, college 111, 115, 144; *see also* Balfour Biological Laboratory, Cavendish Laboratory, Engineering Laboratory
Lacroix, S. F. 14–15, 18–20, 24
Lagrange, J. L. 14, 19, 29
Lambert, James 125
Laplace, P. S. 14, 18–19, 28–9
Larmor, Joseph 113, 116
Latham, Henry 56, 173–4
Law Tripos 55–6, 74
Law, Edmund 206
Lax, William 207
Leader, Damian 123
Lectures 7, 208, intercollegiate 43, 114–16, professorial 8, 108–9, college 107–38
Lee, Samuel 207
Lees, Beatrice 149
Leibniz, G. W. von 13, 23
Liberal Anglicans 72
Liberal education, theory of 45–6
Libraries 165–76 passim
Literae Humaniores 43–4
Liveing, George D. 111–12, 117
Locke, John 12, 74, 110
London Mathematical Society 184
Louis Quatorze 53
Luard, H. R. 55, 57, 68, 80
Lund, Thomas 197–9
Lyttelton, Lord 137–8

Macalister, Donald 116–18
Macaulay, Thomas Babington 167, 173, 207
MacColl, Norman 69
Mackintosh, James 75
Macmillan, Alexander and Daniel 172–3
Magdalene College 170
Main, P. T. 115–16
Maine, Henry 39, 76, 208
Maitland, Frederick William 148
Malthus, Thomas 74
Marks 48, 56, 97–9, 103–4, 127, 129, 131
Marr, John 120
Marriott, Charles 48
Marshall, Alfred 68, 79, 115
Marshall, Mary Paley 146, 148
Marshall, Sarah 147
Mason, P. H. 112
Mathematical Tripos 2, 24, 26, 32, 40, 152–3, 155, 178–9
Mathematics, analytical 5–7, 13, 34–6, mixed 11, 29

Mathematogonia 37
Matthews, G. B. 118
Maudsley, Henry 152
Maurice, Frederick Denison 69–70, 75–7, 79–80, 172, 207
Maxwell, James Clerk 136, 210
Mayor, John Eyton Bickersteth 102, 104–6, 186
Mayor, Joseph 68, 71, 78–88, 111
Meredith, William 205
Merrifield, Margaret 145
Microcosmographia Academica 42–3
Mill, John Stuart 62–3, 68, 71, 74, 80, 87
Mill, W. H. 207
Mill Lane lecture rooms 171
Mitford, William 168
Moderators and examiners 23
Modern History Tripos 60
Monge, G. 18
Monk, James Henry 35, 124, 171
Montesquieu, Baron de 72, 76
Moral Sciences Club 78
Moral Sciences Tripos 2, 51–2, 54, 61–88 passim, 131, 146, 178, 208–9
Moreton, H. G. F. 138
Morley, John 81
Moulton, J. F. 79
Mozley, John Rickards 77, 79, 85
Mullinger, J. B. 186
Murray, A. G. 135
Murray, Gilbert 31
Myrl, Dora 158–60

Nairne, Alexander 207
Napoleon 34–5
Natural Sciences Tripos 2, 32, 51, 131, 155, 208–9
Nettleship, R. Lewis 84
New Woman, the 151, 158, 163
Newby, Richard 172
Newby, T. C. 172
Newnham College 139–64 passim
Newton, Isaac 7, 13–15, 17–18, 26–7, 29, 67, 107, 126, 152
Nicholson, 'Maps' 166
Niebuhr, Barthold 91, 207
Nile, River 37
Noblemen 137–8
North London Collegiate School 141

Oakeshott, Michael 88
Optimes, Junior 37–8

Oral examinations 8, 24, 123–4, 126–7, 129
Ormerod, John 49
Oxford style 44, 209
Oxford, University of 31–3, 35, 48, 85, 108, 149, Literae Humaniores 43–4

Page, Thomas Ethelbert 92–4
Paley, William 12, 74–5, 110–11, 206, 209
Paris 14
Parker, James 137
Parkinson, Stephen 182
Peacock, George 15–16, 18–25, 35
Pearson, J. B. 68, 70, 78, 85, 112
Peel, Talbot 119
Peile, John 145
Pembroke College 170
Pericles 74
Perowne, E. H. 99
Peterhouse 33, 170, 210
Phaedrus 39
Philological Museum 36
Philosophical radicals 63
Pipe, Hannah 141
Pitt Building 175
Plato 67, 74–5
Poisson, S. D. 21
Political Economy 148
Poll Examination 113, 131
Pollock, Frederick 11, 17
Postlethwaite, Thomas 125
Potts, Richard 194–5
Powell, William 1, 33, 109
Pratt, J. H. 200
Previous Examination 109, 111–13, 128, 140, 142, 209
Private tutors 5–31, 109, 144; *see also* pupilising
Prothero, George 61, 147
Pryme, George 10, 17, 128
Publishers' catalogues 175
Pupilising 16–17, 26
Pusey, E. B. 49

Queens' College 170
Quekett, James 108
Questionists 12, 21

Ramsay, Agnata 42
Randolph, Dr 206
Ranke, Leopold von 57
Ray, John 209
Reading men 178

Red Lion Hotel 117–18
Regent House 205–6
Regius chair of modern history 45–60 passim
Reid, James Smith 92
Ricardo, David 74
Rigby, J. 79
Rivers, W. H. R. 120
Rivington's 173
Roby, Henry John 68, 71, 76, 78–9, 111
Rock Terrace School 141
Rogers, Thomas 20
Roget, John Lewis 175
Romilly, Joseph 67
Rose, Henry John 207
Rose, Hugh James 207
Rothblatt, Sheldon 5, 61, 75
Routh, Edward John 48, 178, 199
Royal Commissions 2–3, 43, 107, of 1850 52, 61, 63, 126, 170, 204
Rugby School 34
Ruge, Arnold 80
Russell, Lord John 2
Rutherford, Ernest 210

Sadleirian chair of mathematics 183
Sandeman, Archibald 196
Sandys, J. E. 112, 115–16
Sanskrit 36, 93, chair of, 40
Schaffer, Simon 67
Schelling, F. W. J. von 76–7
Schleiermacher, Friedrich 77
Schneewind, Jerome 85
Scholarships 135
Sedgwick, Adam 49, 61, 67, 207
Seebohm, Frederic 148
Seebohm, Hugh 146, 148
Seebohm, Winifred 146, 148–9
Seeley, John 57–8, 68, 80, 93, 145
Senate House 9, 13, 17
Senate House Examination 8–9, 11–12, 18, 22, 24, 107, 177
Sephton, John 188
Senior Wrangler 2, 32, 178
Set books 39
Sharpley, Edith 145
Shaw, George Bernard 158, 160
Sheepshanks, Richard 207
Shilleto, Richard 37, 39
Shore, Lewis E. 118
Shrewsbury School 34
Sidgwick, Arthur 143

Sidgwick, Eleanor 86
Sidgwick, Henry 55, 57, 61, 67–70, 75, 78–88 passim, 101, 132, 144–5
Sikes, Edward 117–18
Siklos, Stephen 145
Simson, Robert 194
Sizars 34, 135
Slee, Peter 53, 147
Smith, Adam 74
Smyth, William 45
Society of Home Students (Oxford) 143
Socrates 74
Solon 91
Somerset, Ralph Benjamin 78
Somerville, Mary 154
Sorley, William R. 88
Special Board for Classics 41, Moral Sciences 65
Specialisation 31–2, 44, 90, 133
Spencer, Herbert 72
Spielmann, Eva 146
St Catharine's College 170
St John's College 1, 12, 16, 23, 33–4, 37, 107–21, 126–7, 137
Stanley, Lady 169
Stephen, James 51, 53, 78–9
Stephen, Leslie 61, 67, 78–9, 185–6
Stevenson, Thomas 172
Stewart, Dugald 74–5
Stirling, James Hutchinson 68–70, 80
Stobart, J. C. 31
Stout, George Frederick 88
Stronach, Alice 160, 162
Strutt, J. W. 210
Student numbers 27, 36, 50
Student's Guide 54
Summers, Philippa 158–60
Swainson, Charles 207
Sylvester, John Joseph 180, 184
Syndicates 51–2, 57, 59–60, 63

Tait, P. G. 185, 190
Tanner, Joseph 116–19
Tests Acts 3, 204
Textbooks 5–31 passim, 180–203
Thackeray, William Makepeace 167–8, 173
Theory of Ideas 39
Thirlwall, Connop 36–7, 207
Thompson, Edward Seymer 145
Thompson, W. H. 38, 56, 59, 99, 132
Thomson, J. J. 155, 210

Thomson, William 191
Thorp, Thomas 129
Thucydides 39
Tip-fancying 102–3
Todhunter, Isaac 78, 177–203
Tokio Bookselling Company 198–9
Tottenham, George L. 166
Trendelenburg, Adolf 77
Trinity College 1, 12, 16, 20, 36, 122–38
Tripos, the 107
Triposes *see* Examinations
Trotter, Coutts 132
Tyrwhitt, Robert 205–6

Union Society 168
University Library 144, 166, 169, 171
University Observatory 171
University Press 169, 173
Unripe Time, Principle of 43

Vansittart, Augustus 93, 99–102, 106
Venn, John 68, 70, 78, 86, 185, 198
Venn, John Albert 33
Vico, Giambattista 72, 76
Villars, Charlie 165–6
Vince, Samuel 21
Vinogradoff, Paul 148
Voluntary Theological Examination 205

Wace, F. C. 112
Wait, D. G. 207
Waldstein, Charles 40
Walker, Bryan 112
Walsh, Benjamin Dann 50
Waraker, Thomas 56
Ward, Adolphus William 57–8
Ward, James 76, 87
Ward, Mrs Humphry 141
Wedge, Principle of the 43
Webb, Robert 119
Wellington, Duke of 49
Westlake, J. 79
Whewell, William 9, 21, 24, 35, 38, 47, 49, 51, 61–3, 67, 69–70, 73–7, 109, 126, 133, 179, 184
Whitmore, Charles 87
Wilkins, H. M. 48
Williams, Gerard 117
Winstanley, Denys Arthur 36
Wolfe, Arthur 99
Wollaston, William Hyde 207
Women, in the Classical Tripos 42

Wood, James 36, 108, 198
Wooden Spoon 32
Woodhouse, Robert 14, 24
Wootton, Barbara 146
Wordsworth, Christopher (fellow of Peterhouse) 9
Wordsworth, Christopher (master of Trinity) 35–7, 128, 207
Wordsworth, John (fellow of Trinity) 207

Wordsworth, William 36
Wrangham, Francis 207
Wren Library (Trinity) 170
Wright, William Aldis 78
Wright, J. M. F. 16–23, 26–8, 127–8, 136, 170–1
Wynter, Philip 49

Yates Thompson Library (Newnham) 169